# SERVICE AN DOC AMERICAN SOCIETY

MW01130231

### Science, Law and the Evolution
### of Canine Caregivers

*By*

## JOHN J. ENSMINGER, J.D., LL.M

*Foreword by Joan Esnayra, Ph.D.*

CHARLES C THOMAS · PUBLISHER, LTD.
*Springfield · Illinois · U.S.A.*

*Published and Distributed Throughout the World by*

CHARLES C THOMAS • PUBLISHER, LTD.
2600 South First Street
Springfield, Illinois 62794-9265

© 2010 by CHARLES C THOMAS • PUBLISHER, LTD.

ISBN 978-0-398-07931-4 (hard)
ISBN 978-0-398-07932-1 (paper)

Library of Congress Catalog Card Number: 2009053527

*With* THOMAS BOOKS *careful attention is given to all details of manufacturing
and design. It is the Publisher's desire to present books that are satisfactory as to their
physical qualities and artistic possibilities and appropriate for their particular use.*
THOMAS BOOKS *will be true to those laws of quality that assure a good name
and good will.*

*Printed in the United States of America*
*MM-R-3*

**Library of Congress Cataloging in Publication Data**

Ensminger, John J.
    Service and therapy dogs in American society : science, law and the evolu-
tion of canine caregivers / by John J. Ensminger ; foreword by Joan Esnayra.
      p. cm.
    Includes biographical references and index.
    ISBN 978-0-398-07931-4 (hard) ISBN 978-0-398-07932-1 (pbk.)
    1. Service dogs, United States. 2. Dogs, Therapeutic use, United States.
I. Title.

HV1569.6 E57 2010
362.4'048, dc22                                  2009053527

# SERVICE AND THERAPY DOGS
# IN AMERICAN SOCIETY

## ABOUT THE AUTHOR

**John J. Ensminger** is an attorney, writer, and skilled dog advocate. He is a widely known and requested speaker on tax law and financial issues, the U.S.A. Patriot Act, and most recently on the law and science of skilled dogs. He has been the Chair of the Banking & Savings Institutions Committee of the American Bar Association Tax Section, editor in chief of the *Journal of Taxation and Regulation of Financial Institutions,* an adjunct professor, and a legal advocate for mental patients' civil rights. John and his dog Chloe are a therapy dog team and regularly visit hospitals, eldercare facilities, schools, libraries, and a cerebral palsy institute. He reports on legal and scientific issues affecting skilled dogs at doglawreporter.blog spot.com. John lives with his wife Joan in Stone Ridge, New York, and Phoenix, Arizona.

# FOREWORD

Over the last 20 years, there has been a notable expansion in the diversity of service dog types that are being utilized by persons with disabilities. In many cases, persons living with invisible disabilities have adapted the service dog concept to meet their unique needs. Service dogs for persons who experience seizures is one such example, as are psychiatric service dogs (PSDs) for persons living with severe mental illness, and autism service dogs for those living on the autism spectrum. The Psychiatric Service Dog Society has played a significant role in the development of the PSD therapeutic model and is currently engaged in establishing its clinical evidence base.

We recognized as early as 1997 that PSDs would positively impact the lives and functional abilities of tens of thousands of mentally ill individuals, if not millions eventually. Similarly, Patty Dobbs Gross of the North Star Foundation in Connecticut knew when she conceived of autism service dogs in 1997 that there was a great need for the services a dog can provide to a person living on "the spectrum." Acceptance for these newer types of service dogs has been mixed. Seizure-alert dogs have been widely accepted by the disability community, but psychiatric service dogs and autism service dogs were much slower to gain acceptance due to prevailing ignorance, stigma, and society's fear of persons living with brain disorders that have behavioral sequelae. The advent of psychiatric service dogs for military veterans living with post-traumatic stress disorder (PTSD) has greatly facilitated public acceptance for the psych-genre of service dogs. What good American is going to deny a wounded warrior four paws that have the potential to mitigate their PTSD?

With the expansion of new service dog types has come a greater complexity with regard to service animal laws and regulations and the interpretation of these by the courts. John Ensminger's timely book carefully examines these complexities at both the state and federal levels. Concomitantly, the expanded use of therapy dogs in facilities and institutions has brought with it a paradigm shift in society's acceptance and acknowledgement of the canine capacity to contribute in meaningful ways to the lives of ill persons.

The increased use of therapy dogs in new environments and roles challenges society's traditional assumptions about the rights of the dog-loving public relative to those who prefer to live their lives in the absence of dogs. Where do the rights of one group begin to infringe upon those of another? There is a genuine need for scholarly analysis of the impact the changes in uses of dogs are having on social attitudes and therefore on laws and rules at federal and state levels. The analysis provided by John Ensminger's book will be useful to the disabled public, government agencies, private businesses, educational institutions, hospitals, health care providers, housing developments, airlines and other public transportation providers, among others.

With regard to those disabled persons who are partnered with service dogs, there is much information available through the internet that is designed to confuse. For example, a number of physical disability service dog organizations choose to misrepresent federal service animal access laws on their websites, thereby biasing their readership in order to serve a larger political agenda that aspires to exclude other service dog groups from coverage under the law. Such behavior is unethical and intellectually dishonest. Additionally, the internet plays host to numerous websites owned by less-than-reputable dog trainers who provide poorly trained service dogs at a steep price to unsuspecting customers. Some websites sell service dog certifications, ID cards, and service dog jackets indiscriminately so that anyone can take their pet into a restaurant and perhaps claim tax and social service benefits. There is a considerable amount of policing that needs to happen online, yet, we cannot advocate for a higher behavioral or informational standard without first educating the public as to what the laws really are.

This book will level this uneven playing field, and conquer the prevailing digital divide, because the information contained within it is well-researched, factual, and appropriately cited. With a firm grounding in case law and regulatory history, readers will come away with a clearer understanding of the many federal and state laws that bear upon handlers of service and therapy dogs.

## Joan Esnayra

*Dr. Joan Esnayra is the founder of the Psychiatric Service Dog Society (www.psychdog.org) and is an internationally known lecturer, researcher, and author on psychiatric service dog topics. PSDS is located in Arlington, Virginia, and regularly contributes to Congressional and federal agency discussions of prospective statutory and regulatory developments regarding service dogs. PSDS is currently engaged in research projects analyzing the benefits of psychiatric service dogs for veterans of the wars in Iraq and Afghanistan.*

# ACKNOWLEDGMENTS

In an obedience class I took with my labradoodle some years ago, the teacher remarked that Chloe had the right personality to be a therapy dog. I thought she was suggesting that I give up my dog to a sick person and I did not take kindly to the idea. The teacher was Elizabeth Stroter, who had been testing therapy dogs in Ulster County, New York, for Therapy Dogs International, Inc. for many years. She explained that being a therapy dog meant visiting people in various types of facilities, and making them feel better. She said that with Chloe's wide accepting face, big brown eyes, persistent smile, calmness, and obvious love of people and other dogs, she could provide many benefits to children and adults in hospitals and residential care facilities. This book would not have been written had I not followed Liz's advice.

My interest in the law of dogs began when members of the Ulster Dog Training Club in New York State (where we live part of the year) were talking at one meeting about how they drove over two hours to some assignments but could not take the therapy dogs into restaurants on the way or when returning home. Summers in the mid-Hudson Valley can be stifling hot, and winters can be brutally cold. The only solution was to go to a drive-through and eat in the car. I volunteered to look into the legal issues with Frances Breitkopf, then president of the Club. In time this led to a legislative initiative that, as of this writing, is under consideration by various New York legislators. I must also thank Professor David Favre who worked with Fran and me on an article that came from this initial research and was published in the *Journal of Animal Law* of Michigan State University School of Law.

I wish to thank my wife, who took some of the photographs in this book and whose suggestions improved many sections. I should also thank my father, M.E. Ensminger (no longer with us), for instilling in me a love of dogs and appreciation for the science of animals. My father wrote a book, *The Complete Book of Dogs,* that I edited while I was in law school and which I have consulted on a number of matters discussed here. Other people who made suggestions based on various stages of the manuscript include Dr. Joan

Esnayra, Professor Michael Perlin, and Dr. James Lawrence Thomas.

And finally, there is "Chloe," who has brightened the lives of many people, including the patients at the Sunview Skilled Nursing Facility in Youngtown, Arizona, children at the Sahuaro Range Elementary School in Glendale, Arizona, and more children at the Velma Teague Library, also in Glendale. She is now visiting the patients and staff at Benedictine Hospital in Kingston, New York, and the children and adults at United Cerebral Palsy of Ulster County in Lake Katrine, New York.

# CONTENTS

## PART III: CANINE CAREGIVERS, CRIMES, AND PRISONS

## PART IV: CANINE CAREGIVERS AND SOCIAL BENEFITS

# DEFINITIONS

Many definitions can be found of the terms service dog and therapy dog, with variations even between definitions used by professionals, including lawyers, psychologists, social workers, and veterinarians. Related terms, such as assistance or assistive animal, companion animal, emotional support animal, also have inconsistent definitions, and it is often difficult to tell when a term is inclusive or exclusive of other categories. It is appropriate, therefore, to attempt some basic definitions that will apply in this book unless otherwise specified.

## Service Dog

A service dog is a canine service animal that generally serves a single individual with a physical or mental disability. Such a dog works with or performs tasks for this handler. Guide dogs for the blind and visually impaired are a type of service dog in this book, as are hearing or signal dogs for the deaf and hearing impaired. Dogs that help the mobility impaired, say by fetching dropped items or pulling a wheelchair, are another category of service dog, as are seizure-alert and seizure-response dogs.

Not all legal definitions consider that psychiatric service dogs qualify as service animals, but they will be recognized as such here. Dogs in this category may keep people away from a handler who is having a panic attack, or ground someone on the verge of a delusional state in the here and now. Dogs that provide emotional support to a person without a recognized mental disability will, in this book as generally in the law, be distinguished from psychiatric service dogs. Service dogs are increasingly being trained to work with autistic children, keeping them from running away from parents and stopping them from moving into traffic, and to fulfill other functions. Autistic children may also have dogs as pets, but pets for any type of individual will not be called service dogs in this book.

Some state laws use the terms assistance or assistive animal instead of service animal, most commonly where the individual's condition is a physical disability. The term support animal also sometimes means a service animal, but here this term will be restricted to emotional support animals. Dogs providing emotional support may sometimes be called companion animals, but companionship is assumed in human-pet relationships and the terms companion animal and pet will generally not be differentiated here, and neither will be used to describe a service dog.

Although much is made about the level of training required to be a service dog, training can vary considerably depending on the services involved. Seizure-alert dogs may have little or no training, at least initially. Guide dogs and certain other service dogs can require between one year and even two years of training and can cost upwards of $50,000, though charities often pick up most or all of this expense. A rough but somewhat educated guess would place the number of service dogs, of all categories, in the U.S. at between 30,000 and 35,000.

## Therapy Dog

A therapy dog is generally a dog that, with a handler, visits individuals or groups to provide some relief from an institution, such as a hospital, or condition, such as cerebral palsy or Alzheimer's. Therapy dogs may be used one-on-one as part of a treatment program for an individual, which is often called animal-assisted therapy (abbreviated as AAT), but most therapy dogs in the United States today visit facilities to help or at least cheer up the populations of those facilities. These kinds of visitation programs may be called animal-assisted activities (AAA). Therapy dogs licensed by national therapy dog organizations have to pass, with a handler, a test consisting usually of about 20 items, which are assumed to make the dog and the handler a suitable team for visiting schools, hospitals, nursing homes, hospice environments, and many other types of facilities. Professional therapy dogs, sometimes called facility dogs, are animals that live in a facility, such as a nursing home or mental hospital, and interact daily with the residents or patients of the facility. Therapy dogs are generally pets, whose owners or handlers qualify with them in order to work in therapy dog programs. Some specialized search and rescue dogs may also have therapy dog training to aid in comforting individuals until additional help can arrive. Therapy dog work is almost always volunteer work.

Another rough guess, setting qualification requirements rather low to be as inclusive as possible, would place the number of therapy dogs in the United States in early 2010 at around 50,000. Perhaps half of these dogs are making frequent therapy dog visitations.

# ILLUSTRATIONS

# TABLE

# SERVICE AND THERAPY DOGS
# IN AMERICAN SOCIETY

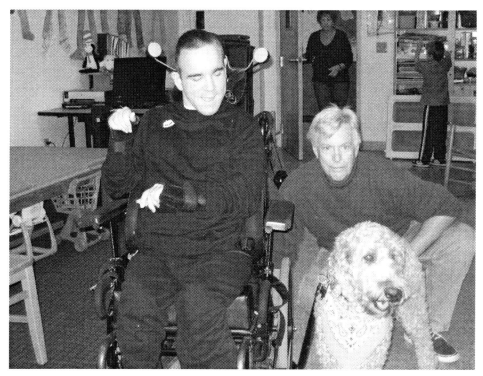

John Ensminger and "Chloe" with a student at the school of United Cerebral Palsy of Ulster County. Photo by Joan Ensminger; permissions obtained by Susan Krogstad-Hill, Educational Director.

# Part I

# CANINES AND CANINE CAREGIVING

# Chapter 1

# CANINE CAREGIVING AND
# SOCIAL RECOGNITION

*A Gulf War veteran with post-traumatic stress disorder is often afraid of going into crowded places but can handle the experience when she has her dog with her. The dog is trained to recognize when she freezes during a panic attack and to sit down behind her, his back pressed against the back of her legs, a defensive posture towards the direction she cannot look. Employees of a warehouse store do not see the dog performing any function and conclude he is a pet. The vest the veteran knitted for her dog reads SERVICE DOG, PLEASE DO NOT PET, but a store employee tells her the vest is clearly not official and she must remove her pet from the store.*

*A blind woman with a guide dog buys a ticket for an hour-long ferry ride. When she learns that there is a VIP lounge that costs $10 more for the journey she asks to upgrade her ticket and tries to give the ticket seller the additional fare. He says he cannot let her into the VIP lounge because a commuting passenger with severe allergies convinced the ferry management some years before to keep the lounge animal-free.*

*A boy with autism is in special needs classes at a regular school. His dog lives and sleeps with him, and is trained to stop him from running into traffic and other dangerous situations. The boy's parents tell the school that the dog can remain at the back of the classroom during the school day but that the boy will feel more secure if he knows the dog is near. The principal says the school is not equipped to deal with the dog, and that since the dog is not functioning as a service dog when it is at the back of the room, the parents must take the dog home during the school day and bring it back when the boy is ready to go home.*

*An elderly couple, both of whom are nearly deaf, move into a no-pets building with their dog, which they have previously informed the management is a hearing dog. They have trained the dog themselves to nudge one of them when the doorbell rings, when the oven timer goes off, when the smoke alarm sounds, or when the computer beeps that they have mail. The dog is not particularly obedient in public areas of the building and has several times relieved herself in the elevator. The couple always clean up after the animal but the building management begins eviction proceedings, saying that the dog is not a certified service animal.*

*A volunteer crisis response team brings both search and rescue and therapy dogs to major disaster locations, often at the invitation of local authorities. To get to one recent disaster, members of the team had to drive over 300 miles. They got into vans at different locations and planned to meet at a particular diner they all knew. The sign on the door of the diner states that only service dogs are allowed. Temperatures are below freezing. Should the handlers be required to leave their dogs in the vans? Fortunately, the owner of the diner knew some of the volunteers and let them bring the dogs inside. When they reached the edge of the city where the disaster occurred, team members parked their vans to make the last leg of the trip on a subway. A guard at the entrance to the subway pointed at a sign saying that guard dogs and police dogs are permitted entry, but no others. One of the team members tells the guard about the request for their services, but has no printout of the email. The guard says he is only doing his job and will not let them on the subway platform with their dogs.*

Such things happen every day. How individuals, businesses, courts, and legislators react to these situations now is very different from how they reacted thirty years ago when only guide dogs, and occasionally hearing dogs, were excluded from no-pet rules. The changes have happened slowly, often with a good deal of pain to those at the center of the landmark disputes, but an overall perspective shows that we, as a society, have come a very long way towards recognizing the gifts that dogs are giving to us and in protecting those who cannot fully function or do their work without these gifts.

The services now performed for us by dogs have been inherent in the human-canine relationship for thousands of years, but most of these functions have only recently been the subjects of formal training, and many uses of dogs are still being studied and developed. The first documented service dogs were guide dogs trained in Germany to help soldiers blinded in the battles of the First World War. The idea of using dogs to guide people may have begun in Roman times, as depicted by a fresco from the ruins of Pompeii of a dog leading a blind man.[1] Occasionally paintings and woodcuts from the middle ages on depicted blind people with dogs that appeared to be guiding them. (See Figure 1 for a 17th century engraving.) Training programs were developed in the United States soon after the German experience was reported, and as the first service dogs, guide dogs remain the most protected dogs in the world.

The functions of guide dogs, and their training, have been adapted to many of the other types of service dogs. Guide dogs have to be big enough to stop the handler from moving forward, and dogs that help the mobility impaired, which include a growing number of veterans and victims of land-mines and improvised explosive devices, are often chosen from the same larger breeds in order to provide stability for individuals who may have to

Figure 1. Blind Man in Engraving, 1639. Courtesy The Seeing Eye Archives.

lean on the animal for support or depend on it to pull a wheelchair.

Dogs are now being trained to help children with autism, not just as companions, but also to keep them from running away from their parents or walking into traffic. With their keen sense of direction, dogs in Israel are being trained as companions to Alzheimer's patients with the skill to lead them home or back to a facility at the command of a handler who has become lost or too agitated to move.

The dog's sense of smell was basic to the earliest functions of domesticated dogs in helping the men of the tribe hunt and in detecting the presence of intruders, either human or animal, in or near the camp. This skill is now being used in search and rescue missions, where human-canine teams are critical to locating people buried in the rubble of collapsed buildings, or in finding bodies. Like hunting dogs flushing game, a search and rescue dog may follow the pointed directions of the handler in crisscrossing an area where the stability of the remaining support is too tenuous for the handler to follow. If the dog finds someone, he barks to bring help, and remains with the victim until help arrives.

Certain cancers can be detected by dogs. Twenty years ago this was anecdotal. Individuals who did not know they had melanoma, or breast cancer, found the dog constantly licking or nudging a place on the handler's body. Subsequent tests found the diseases, and sometimes saved lives. Through a complex training regimen, dogs have been taught to detect lung, breast, and bladder cancers in experimental settings, and there may come a time when doctors visiting remote communities will be able to perform some initial screening with a cancer-sniffing dog.[2]

Some dogs detect and alert to the onset of seizures in their handlers far enough in advance that there is time to take medication to stop the seizure from happening at all. This skill generally arises spontaneously, but if recognized by the handler it can be reinforced and persons with epilepsy now seek to obtain seizure-response dogs with the quite realistic hope that the dog will be able to alert them to an imminent seizure. One study found that 59 percent of dogs trained to respond to seizures also developed the skill to recognize seizures in advance in children to whom they were assigned, though these results were admittedly self-reported by the families of the children.[3] Other scientists doubt that the level of alerting is nearly as high as indicated by studies relying on self-reporting and some have argued that the majority of seizures detected by dogs involve incidents with psychological rather than physiological origins. Still other studies show that seizure-alert dogs reduce the frequency of seizures and allow the handlers to leave home more often, and with more confidence. This issue, and the conflicting perspectives of the medical community, are discussed in detail in a subsequent chapter.

Additional uses for dogs in society have come about as a result of the therapy dog movement, which began in the late 1970s and has grown from several hundred dogs visiting patients in a few communities to a national phenomenon of many organizations, and the involvement of tens of thousands of patients and participants in many different types of facilities. Beginning with anecdotal stories about how various types of patients felt better upon receiving visits from dogs (and sometimes other types of animals), this area has recently begun to be the subject of rigorous scientific studies designed to verify the improvements in health that result as a result of the animals' attentions.

Health benefits of animal visitations are both psychological and physical. Some of the effects that various research teams have documented in the last twenty years include lower blood pressure, fewer heart attacks, more rapid improvement after strokes, higher arterial oxygen saturation in patients receiving chemotherapy, reduced anxiety in hospital and other environments, and less depression. Children have been found to improve their reading and language skills by reading aloud to therapy dogs. This author has spent many hours watching children explain books to dogs when the children were afraid to read if adults came too close. Putting dogs in classrooms has been found to reduce aggressiveness and hyperactivity. One study found that 76 percent of children between the ages of seven and 15, after spending five minutes with an unfamiliar Australian Shepherd, felt the dog knew how they were feeling and 84 percent said they could confide secrets to the dog. As for "being there no matter what," children rate their pets higher than they do their parents, siblings, or friends.[4] Some courts have permitted dogs to lie in the witness box at a child's feet during testimony about abuse the child has suffered at the hands of a man who is sitting only a few feet away and glaring at the child through the testimony.

Therapy dogs are not generally service dogs, in that service dogs work with individual handlers, whose physical or mental condition is affected by what they are trained to do or capable of doing with regard to the condition. The psychological benefits of dogs have also been recognized as useful for individuals with affective disorders, and psychiatric service dogs are now recognized under federal rules and many state codes, provided the dog performs a tangible function, such as creating space for a patient with agoraphobia or reducing the depression of a patient whose condition has reached a certain diagnostic level.

Some situations involving dogs straddle several functions described in this book. Prison programs where prisoners are assigned dogs to train as service dogs have been shown to have benefits both for the prisoners, who develop a skill along with learning the patience to work with an animal that requires a good deal of attention and care, while also producing an animal that will benefit an individual on the outside. These programs have been shown to reduce violence in prisons and are often so popular that prisoners choose to spend their time training dogs rather than leaving the prison for work-release settings.[5]

Laws about dogs were, less than a century ago, largely limited to the dangers that dogs could pose to a community in spreading rabies and killing livestock. With the urbanization of society, leash laws and feces laws became necessary to avoid the less pleasant aspects of living with our best friend. Apartment living requires that dogs not bark through the night and many people with allergies will argue that they should not have to share elevators and hallways with dogs. No-pets policies became popular, though they have always remained controversial in a society divided between dog-lovers and those less enthralled by their neighbors' animals. Society began to favor those who did not want to have to deal with animals over those who claimed they could not live without them.

Service animals required an exception to the no-pets rules that applied to housing and other situations if individuals with disabilities were to be able to participate in society. This meant, at first, guide dogs, but the laws expanded to include, among others, hearing dogs, dogs for the mobility impaired, seizure-alert and seizure-response dogs, and dogs providing psychological benefits to individuals with clinically diagnosed psychological conditions. Inevitably there were people who wanted the benefits of having a service dog without having a condition warranting such an animal's functions. Disputes arose. Sometimes the function of the dog was close to that of a service dog, but the animal was not actually trained for the function. This has been true of hearing dog cases in a number of courts.[6] Dogs may alert a deaf person that someone is at the door, and this alerting may have developed over time as the handler, who initially had some hearing, trained the dog to let him know when the doorbell rang. By most standards this is a hearing dog, but the training is at a less advanced level than that provided by an established service dog school. Similarly, as already noted, seizure alerting appears to be largely untrained, but there are certainly dogs that do it.

Although the most judicially contested aspect of skilled dogs concerns access rules, there are many ways in which they are treated differently from pets. The following list includes legal distinctions of skilled dogs that will be discussed or at least mentioned in subsequent chapters.

1. *Access to public accommodations.* This area can itself be broken into sub-areas such as access to places where food is served or prepared, access to government buildings, etc.
2. *Access to housing.* This again can be subdivided into access to areas where there are zoning restrictions, access to government-supported housing projects, and condominium and neighborhood rules.
3. *Access to transportation facilities.* There are federal rules regarding airliners, cruise lines, and transportation facilities, and state rules regarding these and local transportation services.
4. *Rights to keep animals in workplaces.* Although at the federal level this issue is largely an aspect of the right of access to public accommodations, some states and some federal agencies provide specific rules regarding the rights of employees using service animals.
5. *Access rights of trainers and temporary handlers of trained dogs* (generally a matter of state law).
6. *Traffic precautions.* The blind accompanied by guide dogs, and in some states the deaf and mobility impaired have the right of way at intersections and sometimes a right of way as to other pedestrians.
7. *Crimes involving trained dogs.* There are separate crimes for interference with a person's use of a guide, signal, or service dog. Some states have separate cruelty statutes regarding trained dogs. Other states have laws regarding interference or injury caused to a service dog by someone else's house pet. Some states specify that such interference statutes do not apply if the person with the animal was in the process of committing a crime when the interference occurred (an

uncommon, but not unheard-of event).

8. *Civil and criminal damages for injuring service dogs* (which may include set amounts, as well as veterinary bills for injuries, costs of different accommodations required by the loss of the animal, replacement costs including training costs).

9. *License fees* (often waived for service dogs and sometimes for therapy dogs).

10. *Rights to keep trained dogs in disasters or emergencies,* including the right to keep a service dog with the owner in an ambulance. This became a focus of legislation and regulation after Hurricane Katrina. At least one state also recognizes the right of an assistance animal to receive emergency medical treatment even if its handler cannot afford it.

11. *Quarantine provisions* (less rigorous quarantine provisions for service dogs).

12. *Exemption from state sales tax* (unlike pets, which are subject to sale taxes).

13. *Deductibility of expenses for individuals with disabilities* (though some laws only allow deduction of expenses by individuals with physical handicaps).

14. *Costs of maintaining service dogs taken into consideration in determining eligibility for food stamps, veterans' benefits, and other social services* (generally a matter of state law).

15. *Providing animals and training for school children* (for mobility and safety).

16. *Programs for prisoners and incarcerated youth* to train service animals supported by laws in some states.

17. *Exemption from municipal fines for failure to clean up feces* (particularly as to guide dogs).

18. *Insurance issues* (including insurance coverage for members of therapy dog organizations, and exclusions under homeowners' policies for dangerous breeds made inapplicable to service dogs that belong to such breeds).

In some of these areas there are both federal and state regimes, and the regimes may overlap and even conflict with each other. These conflicts must sometimes be resolved by the courts, but informal adjustment of policies by institutions, such as hospitals, airlines, condominium developments and so forth, often means that the social order is recognizing the increasing values of service dogs and finding ways to adapt rules that superficially might seem to be inflexible.

The reasons for providing exceptions for skilled dogs to the general laws applicable to animals can be reduced to three:

- The functions provided by the dogs.
- The individuals or populations for whom the dogs provide services.
- The level and purpose of the training of the dogs.

For service dogs, the functions are generally provided on an individual basis, though some dogs, such as signal dogs, may alert more than one hearing-impaired individual in a household of a sound requiring the inhabitants to act, e.g., to get out of the house because of a fire alarm. The benefits of service dog status extend to trainers under many state laws, and sometimes even to foster families with whom the animals live before being assigned to the ultimate handler. Therapy dogs, though only legally separated from other animals in limited instances, most often provide services for populations of patients. Police and emergency work dogs benefit law enforcement and fire departments, but also benefit the victims of crimes and fires, and could be said to serve the public at large.

Where the individuals served by the animals have physical disabilities, there is less often a question as to the degree of disability involved to justify separate legal treatment for the handler and animal. Thus, guide dogs may serve the totally blind but also serve those whose vision is impaired. Questions have occasionally arisen as to the degree of deafness necessary for a hearing-impaired person to have the benefit of a signal dog in an apartment where the building has a no-pets policy.[7] With psychiatric disabilities, the condition must reach a clinical level, meaning most commonly that the diagnosis must be of a condition specified in the current version of the *Diagnostic and Statistical Manual*.[8] Neurosis is not such a condition, having been removed in the third edition of the manual in 1980.[9]

As the world of service dogs has become more complex and more functions are discovered for them to perform, it can be expected that there will be more disputes about whether a dog qualifies to live in a pet-free building or fly coach with its handler. Society will have to wrestle with these issues as they develop. There are other questions. What about a search and rescue dog being taken to a disaster site to find survivors? Should it be able to go on a bus with its handler? It is not a service dog, but it is providing a tangible benefit to a class of individuals society recognizes as worth protecting. At least three states provide that search and rescue dogs are to be admitted to public facilities when they are going to and from assignments or in the process of performing their functions.[10] What about a therapy dog that is being taken to the same disaster site to provide comfort to people after they have been rescued? Both types of dogs were present at the disaster site of the World Trade Center on 9/11.[11]

We tend to overlook the complexity of our relationships with dogs when describing what they do for us. It is so familiar. Yet it is that very complexity which explains why our relationship with them continues to create ever more benefits for us. Inevitably the law will have to take account of this complexity if it is to keep pace with the social order of which dogs and men are both a part. Fortunately, most courts and the regulation writers inside of certain federal agencies, particularly the Departments of Justice, Transportation, and Housing and Urban Development, have struggled to determine the rights attendant on the handlers of service dogs by taking into account the research on what the dogs are actually able to do for persons with physical and mental disabilities, and a good deal of nuance has been introduced into the law on this subject in the last five years.

Despite these laudable efforts, the federal agencies have not always given the same weight to the evidence on the services of dogs, and there are inconsistencies between the rules of the various agencies. A woman going to an airport with a dog that provides her with needed emotional support may be able to take the dog into the cabin of an airplane but not into a restaurant in the terminal. Even to get to the airport she may have to use a special car service. The complexities of these rules will be discussed in subsequent chapters.

As already alluded to, some changes have happened without significant legal authority, particularly those involving the admission of skilled dogs to healthcare facilities. The danger of diseases spreading from dogs to man is now known to be less serious than once imagined, and a handler taking a therapy dog into a hospital to cheer the patients is much more likely to bring in a disease than his dog is. Hospitals that once restricted therapy dog visitations to very select rooms in a hospital are now giving the handler and therapy dog access to almost every ward. In some wards, such as emergency and intensive care wards, a therapy dog team may be admitted only at the request of the family (say, for a child injured in an auto accident). This has often happened without announcement or formal change in policy, often because medical administrators have heard from nurses and patients, and the families of patients, that the visitations cheer up the patients more than anything else. A happier patient is a better patient, and today many hospitals actively recruit visitation teams.

Human society is, in many ways, a society to which dogs have adapted. Too often we fail to realize that by taking advantage of their uses, we are also adapting to them. Efforts to put barriers between humans and dogs have not always been wise for either species. Fortunately, legislators, courts, regulators, and society at large, have begun to realize this. The following chapters will attempt to describe how our relationship with trained dogs is changing, and how the law is recognizing these changes. This story is a continuing one. It will never come to an end.

# Chapter 2

# CANINE BEHAVIOR AND THE ADAPTATIONS OF DOMESTICATION

Dogs are descended from gray wolves or, as some would argue, dogs and wolves are descended from a common ancestor that had characteristics retained by both. (See Figure 2 for a recent consensus of the canid family tree.) Various dates have been suggested for separation from the ancestor, but modern genome research suggests it was likely less than 40,000 years ago and perhaps as recent as 14,000 years ago.[12] Though generally regarded as a separate species from wolves, dogs can interbreed with wolves, and even with coyotes and golden jackals, producing fertile offspring. Some scientists regard the dog, denominated *Canis familiaris* in the Linnaean system, as actually a subspecies of the wolf and use a subspecies designation, *Canis lupus familiaris*. This is not the place to resolve this dispute, but it is appropriate to consider how the changes brought about by domestication have made the dog not only a companion, but even a servant to man, a servant that caters to the needs of humans in ways far more diverse than is true of any other domesticated animal.

Juliet Clutton-Brock of The Natural History Museum in London has devoted much of her research life to domestication and has studied the evolution of domesticated species, including dogs and cats. She wrote in 1977 that it "is because the social structure and hunting behavior of the wolf and man are so similar that their association is so closely bonded."[13] She defined domestication as "the exploitation of one group of social animals by another more dominant group which maintains complete mastery over its breeding, organization of territory, and food supply." Domestication has been seen, perhaps even more broadly, as a form of evolutionary change in which a population of animals becomes adapted to man and to the captive environment. As stated by Adam Miklosi, perhaps the leading researcher on the psychology of dogs in our time:

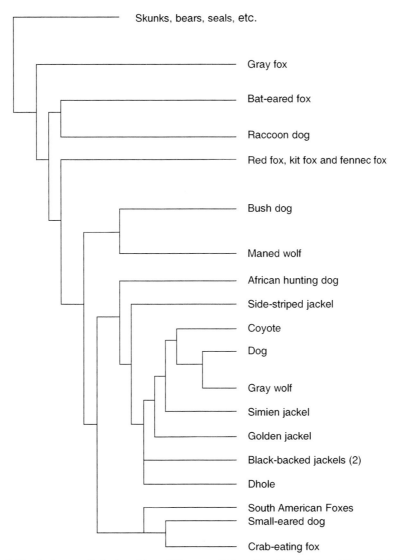

Figure 2. Evolutionary Relationships of Dogs to Other Canids. Adapted from C. Vila, J.E. Maldonado, and R.K. Wayne, Phylogenetic Relationships, Evolution, and Genetic Diversity of the Domestic Dog. *The Journal of Heredity 90*(1) 71 (1990).

Living together or in close contact with members of another species presupposes, for example, novel abilities to form individual social relationships ('attachment'), to adopt a flexible communication system for interspecific communication, to recognize the other species as a source of social information (interspecific social learning) and to have the willingness for cooperation.[14]

Miklosi adds that the behavioral changes in dogs were supported by genetic changes, and thus physical changes. In evolving from wolves, or the common ancestor, dogs became smaller, perhaps because they served human purposes better than larger animals, which were more threatening and less easy to control. The skull shortened and became broader and the jaw shortened, though the teeth did not get smaller as quickly. Brain size reduced, and some parts of the brain developed differently.[15] The distribution of hair pigments altered, with piebalding becoming more common. Among wild canids, differences in size are correlated with differences in gestation time, but in dogs the average gestation time of 60 to 63 days is not correlated with adult size. The growth rate of dogs is slower than wolves during late fetal development and in the period just after birth.[16] Dogs appear to mature at a stage of development more like that of a juvenile wolf than an adult wolf, both in terms of behavior and morphology, a phenomenon called pedomorphosis. Wolves become sexually mature at about two years, but dogs will be sexually mature within six months to a year.

The social behavior of dogs evolved in domestication in such a way as to make them successful in the human social environment. Dogs are more submissive than wolves, and humans would soon have preferred submissive behavior. Dogs explore less than wolves, and remain in smaller areas even if feral. They are more tolerant of crowding.[17] Different breeds of dogs diverge from wolves to different degrees and one study concluded that wolf-like breeds show more distinctly juvenile wolf behavior.

## CHILD OF THE WOLF

Dogs socialize both to other dogs and to humans. People have tried to make wolves into pets but humans can only socialize wolves successfully if cubs are separated from their mothers before eye opening and spend at least 20 hours in close human contact.[18] Socialization of dogs to humans can begin much later and requires much less contact. A study in the early 1980s found that wolf puppies being raised with humans still show a preference for being with other wolves if given the chance, but Malamute pups show a preference for humans.[19] More recent Hungarian research, however, found that the intensely socialized wolf cubs preferred to stay with their caregivers rather than go to other wolves, though the preference was not as strong as with dogs. The dogs in the study, like most domestic dogs, made more vocal distress sounds than the wolves, approached humans more readily, and looked at human faces much more often than did the wolves.[20]

[T]he key difference between dog and wolf behavior is the dogs' ability to look at the human's face. Since looking behavior has an important function in initializing and maintaining communicative interaction in human communication systems, we suppose that by positive feedback processes (both evolutionary and ontogenetically) the readiness of dogs to look at the human face has lead to complex forms of dog-human communication that cannot be achieved in wolves even after extended socialization.[21]

Dogs began wagging their tails at three to five weeks of age and continued this behavior into adulthood. Dogs were less aggressive than the wolves in the study, though other research has found wolves to be no more aggressive than dogs.[22] The Hungarian researchers concluded that during domestication there has been a trend toward an increase in the number and kinds of communicative behaviors of dogs, allowing them to have more complex communicative interactions with humans.

Two evolutionary theoreticians, Wolfgang Schleidt and Michael D. Shalter, ask why man didn't choose to domesticate chimpanzees instead of wolves.[23] They point out that wolves are strong enough to maim or kill us, and it is odd to prefer an animal that is dangerous. Part of the answer, they argue, is that the closest approximation to human morality we can find in nature is that of the gray wolf. "Wolves' ability to cooperate in a variety of situations, not only in well-coordinated drives in the context of attacking prey, carrying items too heavy for any one individual, provisioning not only their own young but also other pack members, baby sitting, etc., is rivaled only by that of human societies."[24]

On the other hand, chimpanzees, despite being our closest evolutionary relatives, are not nearly as sociable as wolves. Indeed, wolves preceded us in forming cooperative communities by millions of years. Schleidt and Shalter argue that the initial contacts between wolves and humans were mutual, and that the subsequent process can be described as a co-evolution. The close cooperation of wolves in hunting is a prime example, where they run as a single group, each aware of where the other pack members are. This behavior may explain why dogs keep track of children in human families, and why guide dogs can pace themselves so well with blind handlers.

Wolves accept greater risks in attacking because, when injured, the needy will be fed by other pack members. Dogs can be ferocious in our defense, perhaps because they know we will care for them if they are injured. Wolves "wolf down" the kill they have made, but when they return to the den they regurgitate large chunks to share with the pups and the babysitter. If they have carried back a leg of prey too large to swallow, it is pulled apart in a tug of war with growling that is actually quite playful. Even before domestication, wolves may have been helpful to humans in hunting herd animals, such as reindeer, by contributing to the breeding of better reindeer. Wolves would have fed on the placentas of calving grounds, the weaklings, sick and aged of the herd, providing a sort of reindeer management. They may have also kept away the big cats, bears, and hyenas. These behaviors may have first bene-fited Neanderthals, though there is no evidence of this so far. Even though wolves are not domesticated, they have been in environments that overlap with ours for a long time and they can learn from watching us. One researcher reported that wolves were able to open the latches of their cages by watching humans perform the act, while dogs in adjacent cages did not learn this.[25]

Dogs, like people, have rank, but enforcement of rank can be "a low-key affair," as it is in the better human societies. Dogs have a preference for large infrequent meals, reflecting the behavior of their ancestors.[26] Dogs also coop-erate with other dogs in hunting, but not so much with each other, as feral dogs tend to scavenge or hunt small prey. Gun dogs, however, cooperate with humans in hunting.

## HOW DID DOMESTICATION OCCUR?

Konrad Lorenz imagined that a wolf puppy, having lost its mother, wan-dering into the human camp whereupon a little girl carried it into her fami-ly's shelter and, to the consternation of her parents, refused to give it up.[27] Although an appealing theory, it is unlikely that this is what happened. The prevailing belief now is that canines domesticated themselves. Raymond and Lorna Coppinger have argued that wolves began scavenging on the edge of human settlements, eating scraps and human feces, and that those wolves that had less of a flight response when humans came near began to get closer and closer to cohabitating with the humans.[28] The animals with the lesser flight response got more food, were healthier and bred more, and their connection to the more spatially distant wolves began to be severed. That connection has never been fully broken, of course, since dogs can still interbreed with wolves (and with coyotes and golden jackals), and some of the more wolf-like breeds in northern environments occasionally still have this contact. (See Figure 3 for one of the oldest pieces of physical evidence of domestication.)

A possible weakness in the Coppinger hypothesis might have been that such a process could have taken so long that it is hard to imagine the break coming about very quickly. The timeframe of domestication, however, was significantly shortened by the work of the great Russian geneticist, Dmitry K. Belyaev.[29] Belyaev argued that the main criterion of domesticated behavior was "the ability of animals to have direct contact with man, not to be afraid of man, to obey him, and to reproduce under the conditions created by him, which constitutes the necessary conditions for the economical use of ani-

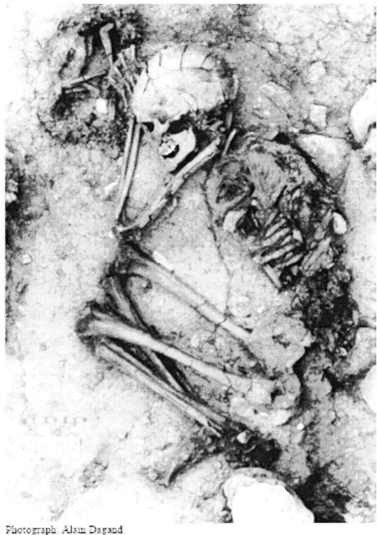

Photograph Alain Dagand

Figure 3. Natufian Human-Canine Burial Excavated in Israel. The human's hand has been placed on the stomach of a dog, probably a pet, as if they will go as companions into eternity. S.J.M. Davis and F.R. Valla. Evidence for Domestication of the Dog 12,000 Years Ago in Natufian of Israel. *Nature 276,* 608–610 (1978). Courtesy of Alain Dagand, archeological photographer.

mals."[30] In the 1950s, Belyaev began a breeding program involving silver foxes, *Vulpes vulpes* in scientific nomenclature, that had been raised for generations in captivity on fur farms in Estonia.

The experiment involved selecting in each generation those foxes that were most tame as breeding stock with the specific purpose of ultimately

Figure 4. Foxes from Belyaev's Farm Fox Experiment. The singe fox demonstrates the piebaldness that became common as the domestication experiment proceeded. As shown in the second photograph, the foxes began to take on many of the behaviors of domesticated dogs. Reprinted from D.K. Belyaev, "Destabilizing Selection as a Factor in Domestication," *The Journal of Heredity, 70,* 301–308, 1979, by permission by Oxford University Press.

obtaining foxes as tame as domestic dogs. At the beginning of the experiment, Belyaev determined that about 30 percent of the foxes were extremely aggressive towards humans, 20 percent were fearful, 40 percent were aggressively fearful, and only 10 percent displayed a quiet exploratory reaction without either fear or aggression. Belyaev found that the foxes formed their defensive behavior in the first two to two and a-half months of life, and determined that the offspring of animals with particular patterns were likely to have the same patterns, meaning that the behavior had a hereditary basis, and that selection for these behavioral traits was possible. He also noted that for females with relatively tame behavior, mating took place earlier in the reproductive season than in females of in the other behavioral categories.

In each generation after the experiment began, selection for further breeding was restricted to 15 percent to 20 percent of the animals. Within a few generations Belyaev had foxes that were quite tame, not as a result of training, but strictly due to breeding selection. In a lecture delivered in 1979, he described his foxes:

> Like dogs, these foxes seek contact with familiar persons, tend to get close to them, and lick their hands and faces. In moments of emotional excitement, they even sound like dogs. There is something moving in the emotions of these foxes, that at the sight of even a strange person, they try actively to attract attention with their whining, wagging of tails, and specific movements.

Belyaev expected that in the process of this artificial domestication he would see changes in non-behavioral traits as well. Charles Darwin had suspected as much. In his treatise, *On the Origin of Species,* Darwin wrote that "not a single domestic animal can be named which has not in some country drooping ears," a feature not found in any wild animal except the elephant. Belyaev's foxes began to display features that were not found in wild foxes but that were quite characteristic of some breeds of dogs, including turned up tails, brown spots around the ears, neck, and shoulder blades, and, as Darwin had suggested, drooping ears. There was also a peculiar piebald spotting, which Belyaev called "star."[31] Several of these aberrations might appear in a single animal, indicating that the connection of the morphological changes to the behavioral changes was not random.

Belyaev's foxes were not trained and spent most of their lives in cages, though they were allowed brief contacts with humans. Tameness was determined by a series of tests beginning at one month of age, when the foxes were offered food from the hand of a human experimenter. At eight months, foxes that fled from the experimenter or bit his hands were considered the poorest in terms of tameness. Those that allowed themselves to be petted but showed no emotionally friendly response to the experimenter were the next level. The tamest category were those that were friendly, wagged their tails, and whined. By the sixth generation, Belyaev had foxes he described as "domesticated elite", animals that were eager to establish human contact, whimpered to attract attention, sniffed and licked experimenters like dogs. They displayed this behavior within a month of birth. By the tenth generation, 18 percent of pups were elite, by the 20th, 35 percent. The foxes in the program were, after 30 to 35 generations between 70 percent and 80 percent elite.

The artificial domestication was accompanied by other behavioral changes besides tameness. Undomesticated fox pups show fear response at six weeks, but domesticated ones show it at nine weeks or later (similar to dogs, which show it at eight to 12 weeks). Wild foxes are seasonal breeders, mating once a year from January to late March as the days get longer. Belyaev's foxes reached sexual maturity about a month earlier and the mating season lengthened, with some breeding well out of season and even twice a year. Belyaev had noted early in his research that "all domestic animals have lost their strict seasonal patterns of reproduction and moulting and tend to reproduce at any time of the year."

As Belyaev had predicted, the foxes do not look the same either. Those in the founding population had erect ears, low slung tails, and silver-black fur except for whiteness on the tip of the tail. The first changes Belyaev and his team recognized were changes in coat colors. Foxes began to lose pigment (become piebald) in areas other than the tip of the tail, and sometimes had a star-shaped pattern on their faces similar to those seen in border collies and certain other breeds.[32] After 15 to 20 generations, some foxes had shorter tails and legs. The skulls of the tame foxes tend to be smaller, with shorter but wider snouts, as happened to dogs in domestication.[33]

As curious as the Russian research is, it was not the first time foxes had been tamed. It was reported in the nineteenth century that South American indigenous people tamed some members of one species of fox, *Dusicyon culpaeus,* having bred it in captivity and used it in hunting.[34]

## ETHOLOGY OF THE DOMESTIC DOG

When I briefly pursued graduate studies in zoology in the late 1960s, ethologists (animal behaviorists with a biological as opposed to a psychological background) largely avoided the study of domesticated animals, finding something unnatural in the behavioral patterns of dogs and cats, as well as horses, cattle, pigs, and sheep. With the animals we eat, man had attempted, and to some degree succeeded, in breeding the brains out of the animals, making it easier to fatten them up and less trouble when it came time to slaughter. With dogs, we had divided and subdivided wolves to make dogs with various types of specializations, such as herding, pointing at and retrieving game, digging for rats, etc. Ethologists generally preferred to study wolves, undomesticated felids, wild boars, and so forth. This perception of a boundary between natural animals and unnatural animals created by domestication and targeted breeding is no longer so firm among scientists, and there is now a large and growing scientific literature that looks at how dogs have adapted to man. The adaptations of dogs to men go a long way to explaining why men have made their own adaptations to dogs, and why their services are becoming so important in modern society. The unique behavior of dogs makes them ideal companions, our best friends, and recently, or perhaps not so recently, our therapists.

## EYE CONTACT

Dogs watch us. They make eye contact. They look at us when they want to go for a walk or be fed, and may bark if sufficiently frustrated by a lack of response.[35] A wolf puppy brought into a house and raised as a domestic dog may make something of a pet, but will seldom make eye contact. The dog's genetics have evolved because of the thousands of years of contact we have had with each other, and a component of that evolution has been behavioral.[36] Dogs obey us better than any other animal, better even than any other domesticated animal, and our expectations are higher. Not only do they watch us, they expect us to watch them. They prefer to deal with a human who is looking at them.[37] This matches our own behavior. We trust someone who looks at us more than someone who avoids eye contact.

Part of the reason for their eye contact with us is that dogs expect us to solve problems. In one experiment to compare the skills of dogs and wolves, the animal being tested had to pull a rope to get a piece of meat. Both wolves and dogs learned to pull the rope and get the piece of meat, and they learned it at the same speed. In a second phase of the experiment, the rope was imperceptibly tied in such a way that when pulling it, the dog or the wolf did not get the meat. Both became frustrated, but the dogs began to look at the human caretaker standing behind them, while the wolves kept pulling the rope. Eventually the wolves gave up and lay down to rest. The dogs looked at the human and performed a variety of solicitation and begging gestures in an effort to enlist the human's help.[38] The researchers concluded that "dogs appear to have an innate readiness to look at human faces, whereas wolves seem to ignore the human gaze." The human gaze may be threatening to wolves and it may be that dogs have evolved in such a way as to lose this reaction.

Dogs obey us better when commands are accompanied with eye contact. If you give a dog a command but look at someone else while giving it, the dog will assume the command is not for her. Dogs do understand that commands do not always have to involve eye contact, however. If you look in a different direction and give a command, the dog is more likely to obey if you are not looking at a person or another dog than if you are looking in precisely the same direction but at another person. She follows your gaze, realizes that you are not issuing the command to anyone who will obey it, and assumes, in many cases, that the command must therefore be for her. These are not intuitive observations, but were among findings of researchers in a carefully controlled study.[39] The researchers also found that given the choice of begging for a piece of a liver sandwich from two people sitting at a dining table, dogs will always prefer to beg from a person who looks at them, not from a person who refuses to look at them.

Dogs are also more likely not to try to figure out how to disobey us if we're watching them. Dogs in a study conducted at the Max Planck Institute for Evolutionary Anthropology in Leipzig, Germany, were given a series of trials in which they were forbidden to take a piece of food with the command "Aus!" ("Leave it").[40] In one set of trials, the experimenter continued to look at the dog throughout. In other trials the person left the room, turned her back, closed her eyes, or engaged in some distracting activity (playing a computer game with a soft audible melody). When the human was looking at the dog, the dog approached the food indirectly (if it did so at all), and ate less food. When the human engaged in the other activities, the dog approached the food more directly and ate more food. The dogs used an indirect approach about 50 percent of the time when the experimenter watched them, but only 20 percent of the time or less when the experimenter was pre-occupied. Dogs are aware of when we're watching them, and vary their responses to us accordingly.

## READING OUR CUES

Dogs follow our hands when we point, and use the cue to find a toy we have thrown. They even follow nods. The ability to follow human vocal or gesture cues to specific locations was probably selected for in herding, hunting, and retrieving dogs. Dogs can interpret gestures as subtle as the handler moving his eyes (with no movement of the head) in the direction of a hidden piece of food on a par or better than chimpanzees and certainly better than monkeys. With dogs, however, the skill comes from thousands of years of mutual adaptation.[41] If food is beyond the reach of a dog, the dog will use eye contact, motion, and barking to indicate what he wants. Cats also use human cues, and almost as well as dogs, but are less able to specify exactly what they are trying to get.[42] Dogs can interpret pointing gestures as well as a child who is one and one-half to two years old.[43] Dogs can also respond to unusual pointing gestures, such as pointing with one's leg.[44] This ability to recognize a variety of gestures helps dogs retrieve items for individuals who have lost limbs or the physical capacity to use limbs.

Another research project found that dogs sometimes follow our gestures to their own detriment. In given a choice between two bowls, they chose the correct bowl if they saw the experimenter put food in it. If the experimenter pointed at the empty bowl after placing food in a different bowl, dogs do not follow the human's gestures blindly but they do not make the correct choice as often as they would without the gesture. They understand that the pointing gesture is communicative, and they sometimes rely on us more than they should.[45]

One English team of scientists found that dogs were nearly as responsive to the trainer when he sat and gave the command as when he stood, and that wearing heavily shaded dark glasses made little difference when the dog could see the rest of the trainer's face. When the trainer's command was tape recorded with high quality equipment and the dog could see the trainer, whose face did not move with the command, this apparently confused the dog and obedience levels declined significantly. If the trainer turned away from the dog, the command to "sit" was not obeyed as well as when the dog could see the trainer, but the command to "come" was obeyed very well. The researchers concluded that both non-verbal cues and sound quality characteristics are important in dogs' ability to respond correctly to commands.[46]

## Knowing What We Want From Knowing What We See

Pointing gives the dog a signal, but do they really know what we're thinking? To some degree it can be demonstrated that they do. If we tell a dog to fetch and there is only one object in the room, the dog will most likely fetch that object. If there are two identical toys and we tell the dog to fetch without looking or pointing at either, we would expect the dog's choice to be random. But what if the dog sees the two toys while the human giving the command can only see one of them? Will the dog realize that the human can only see one of the toys and retrieve that one instead of the one the human cannot see? In other words, will the dog put herself in our shoes and fetch the object in our range of vision over the object hidden from us? This was the question posed by four scientists from Cambridge University and the Max Planck Institute in Leipzig.[47] These scientists wanted to know if dogs could take into account the visual perspective of a human when that differed from their own perspective.

In each trial, the dog was led into a room, about 28 feet by 13 feet. An experimenter sat on a chair equidistant from both toys, but what he could see of the toys depended on whether the arrangement was experimental or one of the controls. The dogs could see both toys in each arrangement, but in the experimental arrangement, the human could only see the toy that was on the other side of the transparent barrier. In the same-side control arrangement, the human could see both toys, just as the dog could. In the back-turned control arrangement, the human could see neither toy because he was looking away from the dog, the barriers, and the toys.

In each trial, the experimenter in the room told the dog to "Bring here" without looking at or pointing to either of the two toys and keeping his eyes fixed on a predetermined spot on the wall. After the dog retrieved a toy, she was rewarded with play and praised, regardless of which toy was fetched. Dogs were randomly selected to perform in one of the three arrangements. The purpose of the research was to determine, in the experimental arrangement, whether the dog would prefer to fetch the toy that the human could see or see with the minimum amount of movement.

All trials were videotaped and scored by someone who did not know the purpose of the experiment. When the human could see only one of two toys, the dogs retrieved the seen toy over 70 percent of the time. When the human's back was turned, the dogs retrieved the toy that would have been visible had the human turned around about 60 percent of the time. When the human was on the same side as the dog and both could see both toys, the dog retrieved the toy beside the transparent barrier slightly more than half the time. The dogs preferred the toy beside the transparent barrier but approached it significantly more often when that was the only toy the human

## Arrangements in Perspective Experiment

**Results**

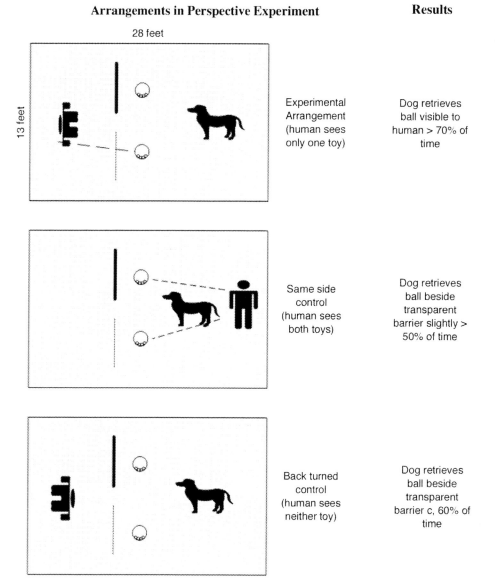

Figure 5. Seeing What We See. Choices made by dogs differed according to their perception of a human's view of a toy. Drawing made from data in Juliane Kaminski, Juliane Brauer, Josep Call, and Michael Tomasello, "Domestic Dogs Are Sensitive to a Human's Perspective." *Behaviour, 146,* 978–998 (2009).

could see. The researchers concluded that the dogs took into account the human's perception when making a choice of which toy to bring the human. That is, they think about what we are able to see. (See Figure 5.) This ability to sense what a human wants is particularly important for individuals who may not be able to gesture towards objects they wish a dog to retrieve.

## READING THEIR CUES

If they read our cues, it seems likely that our sharing of social behavior means that we may be able to read some of their cues as well, and that they may expect this. An experiment (something of the reverse of experiments where humans try to communicate to dogs where food is hidden behind an object) was designed to look at the circumstance when the dog knows where the food is but the human does not.[48]

The tests involved two Vizlas, one Poodle, one Kerry Blue Terrier, one West Highland Terrier, one Hovawart, one Tervueren, and a mixed breed. Owners of the dogs were supplied with three small, identical feeding bowls. The dogs were fed from one of the bowls, or one was used to house a toy while it was not being played with. Three people were necessary for a test: the owner, a familiar person who served as a "hider," and the experimenter. Before the beginning of a test, the three bowls were placed at approximately 1.5 meters or higher somewhere in the room, perhaps on a bookshelf. The dog could not see the contents of the bowls. The experimenter hid a small piece of food behind each bowl to avoid confounding effects of odors. The experimenter then began the videotaping and left the room, leaving the dog and the owner. Then one of the following sequences occurred.

*Sequence A.* "Petting"

1. Dog and owner are in the room; owner reads for one minute, then leaves the room.
2. Hider enters and pets the dog for 30 seconds then leaves the room.
3. Owner enters, sits down and reads for one minute before leaving again.

*Sequence B.* "Dog Alone"

1. Dog and owner are in the room; owner sits and reads for one minute, then leaves the room.
2. Hider enters with food or toy, shows it to the dog and allows the dog to sniff it; hider takes a bowl from the high place and puts the food or

toy in it, placing it back in its original position; hider leaves the room.
3. Dog is alone for one minute. Owner and hider enter the room and the hider gives the contents of the bowl to the dog.

*Sequence C.* "Hiding"

1. Dog and owner are in the room; owner sits and reads for one minute, then leaves the room.
2. Hider enters with food or toy, shows it to the dog and allows the dog to sniff it; hider then takes one bowl, shows it to the dog, puts the food or toy in the bowl, and places it back in its original place; hider leaves the room.
3. Owner enters the room, sits down and reads for one minute; at the end of the session the owner stands up and gives the food or toy to the dog provided the owner finds where it was hidden.

The dog's behavior was noted, including behaviors having nothing to do with trying to get the food, but also vocalizations, sniffing, tail wagging,[49] and direction of gazing (based on head orientation of the dog). The frequency of gazing toward five distinct locations was observed, including gazing at the owner, gazing at the door, gazing into the camera, gazing at the location of the food or toy, and gazing toward an empty bowl. In the "Hiding" sequence, the researchers were particularly concerned with "gaze alternation," consisting of gazing at the owner followed within two second by gazing at the bowl with the food or toy, or vice versa.

The researchers found that in the Hiding sequences, the dogs spent less time standing at the door and increased the amount of time they spent gazing. Sniffing was also more pronounced. The dogs did not vocalize during the "Petting" sessions, though they did in the "Dog Alone" sessions, not at the food bowl but rather at the door, probably from a desire to leave the room. In the Hiding sessions they vocalized (barked or whined) when they were gazing either at the owner or the bowl with the food. Looking at the owner usually began the sequence of gazing, followed by looking at the bowl.

Not surprisingly (at least for any dog lover), every dog owner was able to find the location of the food based on the dog's signaling. This meant that the dogs were able to produce both attention-getting (barking, whining, gazing at the owner) and directional (gazing at the food bowl) signals. The researchers admitted that the experiments do not prove conclusively that the dogs were trying to show something to the owner. For instance, they might have been anticipating the owner's actions without trying to show him anything. Nevertheless, they argued that the most likely explanation is that dogs in this experiment were trying to communicate information to their owners so that the owners would act on the information and give them the food. Dogs are frequently motivated by food and most training systems rely heavily on this fact. The research also shows that dogs have developed a fairly complicated behavioral repertoire in order to communicate with us.

## Convergent Evolution

Some scientists have speculated that the dog's ability to interpret our cues is an aspect of a convergent evolution under which dogs and men have developed similar social and communicative skills. The two species, depending on some of the same food sources and surviving in ever closer proximity, developed analogous behaviors. If two distantly related species share a similar trait, the argument goes, these similar traits may have arisen independently but under similar evolutionary pressures. The convergence of behaviors involved significant cooperative elements in both species and made cooperation between the two species possible. As was observed in one paper on social cognition in dogs: "Domestication may have promoted further social skills in dogs, which allowed the development of complex cooperative social interaction, which might in turn also provide the basis for training dogs to assist blind or mobility-disabled people."[50] In sum, dogs adapted to us during domestication and perhaps we to them. This argument is reinforced by the fact that foxes domesticated under a breeding program selecting for tameness over the last 50 years have also developed interactive skills similar to those of domestic dogs.[51]

Wolves raised identically to dogs in a Hungarian study were able to understand human pointing gestures, but they needed more training for this than dogs did. This may be in part due to the difficulty of establishing gaze-to-gaze contact with wolves, making it more difficult for wolves to attend to a trainer's gestures.[52] Dogs, on the other hand, achieve the ability to interpret gestures at an early age. By five weeks, puppies gaze more towards humans than younger puppies or wolf cubs of the same age. A German team looked at the abilities to follow cues of 64 dogs aged 6 weeks, 8 weeks, 16 weeks, and 24 weeks. Each puppy was tested without its mother or littermates present.[53] Given the early age at which puppies can understand gestures and locate hidden food, the researchers argued that this skill represents a special adaptation present in dogs from an early age and that the skill was derived from a selection process during domestication. That is, dogs inherit the ability to understand human cues as a result of the effects of domestication on canine evolution.[54]

Why do dogs read us so well? Pamela J. Reid of the ASPCA's Animal Behavior Center in Urbana, Illinois, thinks the answer lies in the biological status of the dog as a scavenger, a niche that requires that an animal be acutely aware of other individuals in the social group that are also looking for opportunities to feed.[55] Dogs respond to our gestures towards food sources just as they respond to the other members of a pack that may be on the trail of a food source.

## PLAYING

Dogs play with humans in ways far more complex than is true of any other animal. Play, or something close to it, is often incorporated into training regimens, such as with cancer sniffers and drug detection dogs. In a game of fetch, when the ball is returned to the owner, the human player pauses until he shares eye contact with the dog before throwing the ball again. Dogs wanting to play ball will look at the ball, look at the handler, look back at the ball, and sometimes bark, all to get the handler's attention to initiate the game. There are rules of social distance in our games with dogs. In playing fetch, the dog must bring the object within a retrievable distance of the thrower. The human may use a repetitive set of words each time he throws the ball. "Ready . . . go!" Each party to the game takes turns in being the primary actor.[56]

Dogs often hunt singly, while wolves hunt in pairs or groups. Dogs, such as retrievers, have been selected to hunt with humans, sharing and surrendering prey to people. Thus, if hunting and play involve similar motivations for a dog, it could be expected that dog-human play would involve more sharing, which is what the research has indicated. Play between dogs is something of a competitive sport. Play with humans is partly a way for the dogs to get attention. This and other research suggests that dogs do not become overly submissive if they always lose, or overly aggressive if they always win, when playing with humans.[57] For those concerned that playing games with dogs may teach them to be aggressive, one study found that a dog and his owner often develop a routine of games over time, but the dogs do not generalize the behavior routines of the game to other, functionally different, situations.[58]

When conflicts do arise between dogs that are playing, or as a result of disputes over food or mates, dogs have been found to have effective mechanisms for limiting the strife, at a level equal to that of higher primates.[59] Resolution can involve reconciliation of the two contestants, but can also involve consolation of the loser by third parties not involved in the conflict, or appeasement of the victor, also by a third party. These conflict avoidance skills work well for dogs in dealing with aggressive children and other individuals therapy dogs may encounter when visiting facilities.

## YAWNING

Dogs and humans may share boredom. One group of researchers at the University of London found that yawning may be contagious between dogs and men, at least in their study it appeared that when a dog sees a man yawning, he is very likely to yawn himself.[60] Contagious yawning has, believe it or not, been a subject of extensive research going back as far as 1942, with various theories being advanced for why it occurs.[61] It has been found to be uncommon in children with autism.[62] Researchers tested the difference between dogs watching a stranger yawning, and dogs watching a stranger open his mouth, but not yawning. When the stranger yawned several times, 21 of 29 dogs also yawned at least once. When the stranger opened his mouth without yawning, no dogs yawned. One theory is that contagious yawning indicates some level of empathy, and the London researchers suggest that dogs catching human yawns may be an empathetic response. No doubt many dog owners feel that we may on occasion be boring to our dogs, but perhaps they are reflecting some of our own boredom.[63]

## BARKING

Vocalizations of wolves and coyotes include growling, howling, whining, and barking, but barking tends to be heard more from wolf pups than adults.[64] Wolves bark primarily, but not exclusively, to alert other wolves of something happening, or to claim territory.[65] One study found that howling in wolves served as communication between temporarily separated pack mates (43% of howls), after reunion (18%), before setting out for a hunt (22%), and at a fresh kill (5%). A small number of howls (2%) may be targeted at another pack.[66] Dogs, on the other hand, seem to bark for almost any reason, sometimes for hours on end. Wolves are sometimes repetitive as well, however. During the mating season, male wolves will solo howl for hours with no detectable acoustic reply. It has been suggested that this howling may function as a beacon to attract females from neighboring packs. Feral dogs bark for similar reasons that wolves bark, to rally the pack to head for the local dump site to scavenge, and to warn smaller packs to evacuate the dump site or to try to scare a smaller pack away if its members do not get the message at first. The barking matches seemed to limit the amount of fighting between the packs. Feral dogs did not bark nearly as much as fully domesticated dogs are prone to do.[67]

The frequent barking of dogs may be part of the pedomorphosis of domestication, the tendency of domesticated animals to retain traits of puppies into adulthood.[68] Belyaev, the Russian who artificially domesticated silver foxes, found that the tamed foxes displayed elevated levels of barking, yipping like puppies when greeting humans.[69] This led some researchers to suggest that barking lacked specific communication functions, beyond perhaps being a demand for attention.[70] This may have in part reflected the prejudice against studying domesticated animals on the belief that their behavior has been overly warped by the very process of domestication. An argument could be made, however, that dog barking behavior evolved as our relationship with them evolved, and that dogs began to use barking as a means of increasing their communication skills. One study, for instance, concluded from heart rate analysis that dogs distinguish between warning barks (stranger coming onto property) and complaining barks (dog tethered to tree).[71]

In 2002, Sophia Yin of the University of California at Davis, determined that spectrographic analysis indicated that "bark structure" varied with context, suggesting that barks could be divided into subtypes and might be "a more complex form of communication than given credit."[72] Professor Yin argued that a captive environment may alter an animal's behavior, including its vocal habits. Thus, dogs may vary their communication mechanisms in the domestic context. Those that barked at dangers in the night, for instance, may have been preferred by our human ancestors. This trait is still valued for working dogs that guard livestock. On the other hand, hunting dogs have been selectively bred to be silent so as not to scare game.

Living among humans, according to Professor Yin, may give dogs more opportunities to bark than wolves inhabiting wide, often desolate, spaces. Dogs live in communities where intruders are more common. They hear other dogs barking, and they join in spreading the warning. They need to let their owners know it is time to go for a walk, and they use the sound that wolf puppies use to get the attention of a parent or the pack leader. Owners respond to the communication and validate its use by the dog. Barking is particularly appropriate for guard dogs, and many handlers of service dogs have been thankful for the attention their dogs have brought to them in time of crisis.

In order to find distinctions between barks, Professor Yin recorded barks of six different breeds in three situations: (1) reaction to a doorbell, (2) being locked in a room isolated from the owner, and (3) playing with another dog or the owner. In all, 4,672 barks were analyzed. Disturbance barks (1) were lower in pitch than the other two situations. This is consistent with the hypothesis that birds and mammals use harsh, low-frequency sounds in hostile situations. Bark duration was also longer for disturbance barks, but isolation and play barks were not significantly different in length. Disturbance barks were often repeated so rapidly that they were sometimes fused into "superbarks" of two to four barks. The dogs were barking full force throughout the disturbance barks. Interbark intervals were longer in the isolation situation than in the other two situations. Isolation barks also occurred singly, rather than in clusters. Barks in the isolation and play situations had a larger frequency range.

Researchers in Hungary also began to question the received wisdom that dog barks had no specific communicative function. They, however, put more emphasis on the possibility that dogs were not just barking to communicate with each other, but also to communicate with us. Since dogs have become adept at understanding human communication signals, perhaps we have also adapted to understand them. Scientists have demonstrated that some species will recognize another species' alarm call.[73] The Hungarian researchers therefore asked if humans react to dog barks as communicative signals to the extent of being able to judge the emotional state of the sender or the situation in which the bark was emitted.[74] This research divided human listeners into three groups: (1) Mudi owners, (2) other dog owners, and (3) non-owners. The Mudi is a midsized Hungarian sheep dog with a herding style that involves a lot of barking. The researchers recorded 19 Mudis in six different behavioral situations:

1. *Stranger.* In this situation, an experimenter appeared in the garden of the owner or at the front door in the absence of the owner.
2. *Schutzhund.* A trainer at a training school acted as a "bad guy" and encouraged the dog to bark aggressively and bite a bandage on the trainer's arm.
3. *Going for a walk.* The owner brought the leash to the dog and told the dog, "We are leaving now."
4. *Alone.* The owner tied the leash of the dog to a tree in a park and walked out of sight.
5. *Ball.* The owner held a ball or other favorite toy of the dog about a yard and a half in front of the dog.
6. *Play.* The owner played tug of war, chasing, or wrestling with the dog.

The recordings of the barks were modified by a computer to equate the calls for loudness, using samples that contained at least ten individual barks.

Human listeners were provided with a set of 18 barks, but no two listeners heard exactly the same 18 barks, three different barks from each situation. After hearing each set of three barks the listeners filled out questionnaires. The listeners had to determine the emotional significance of the bark from a choice of five on one questionnaire, and had to guess the situation producing the bark from a list of six possibilities on another questionnaire. The emotional choices were (a) aggressiveness, (b) fearfulness, (c) despair, (d) playfulness, and (e) happiness.

Sound analysis had demonstrated that of the six situations which produced the barks, the *Schutzhund* situation (biting the trainer's arm) had the lowest interbark interval, while *Alone* had the highest, similar to Professor Yin's results. The lower tones were found in the *Stranger* situation. Listeners of all groups correctly gave significantly higher aggressiveness scores to the *Stranger* and *Schutzhund* situations. All listeners also gave the highest scores of fear and despair to barks of dogs in the *Alone* situation. Curiously, Mudi owners and non-owners gave the highest scores of happiness and playfulness to the play situations, but very few owners of other dog breeds got this one right. Even more curiously, on the questionnaire regarding the situations eliciting the barks, Mudi owners were only slightly better at guessing the correct situations than the other two groups, but all were fairly successful. This differed from findings regarding cat meows, where cat owners and lovers scored substantially better than people with limited experience with cats. The researchers concluded that "the acoustic structure of barks provides features that make them recognizable for human listeners."[75] Gestures of dogs are also interpreted in very similar ways by different observers.[76]

## WHY AM I TALKING TO YOU?

We do not just give commands to dogs, though one study found that issuing commands is 61 percent of our verbal communication with dogs. We also want to get their attention, ask them for information, reassure them, describe what we are going to do, and indicate what is happening. People "talk to dogs for many of the same reasons they talk to infants: because they want to influence their behavior, because the communicative recipient (dog or infant) is so responsive to their activities, and because talking to the recipient gives them the feeling of effective communication and control."[77]

People are obviously very repetitive when they talk to dogs. The dog does not talk back, at least in words, so the interaction is not a verbal conversation. Commands are verbal, sometimes accompanied by gestures. Some of those gestures may be intentional, such as the motion to tell a dog to lie down in a competition, but some may be more subtle, and we may not even be aware of the motion we are making that is part of the signal. In play we are highly repetitive with our pets. One study at Eastern Kentucky University videotaped 23 people playing with two dogs, one familiar and one unfamiliar. They found that each person spoke about 208 highly repetitive words per interaction.[78] Eight words accounted for more than 50 percent of the total words used by each person. Sentences consisted of:

- Imperatives
- Attention-getting expressions

- Declaratives about the dog
- Questions.

"Motherese," talking to infants, is also highly repetitive, and human talk to dogs is similar to talk to infants. "You're a good dog. You're a good dog. You are. You are good. You are silly, but good. Yes, you are. You are a silly but good dog." A single statement reformulated and elaborated on, can account for an entire communication.

Talk to infants and domesticated animals, as well as talk between people making love, often shares a speech register with distinct intonation. The researchers found, however, that "talk to dogs had shorter sentences, more repetitions, more imperatives, and fewer questions and declaratives than motherese." Also, people often use ordinary speech when addressing companion animals. The Eastern Kentucky University study focused on talk to dogs during play. The researchers considered that humans might have three objectives in talking during play:

1. To control and get the attention of the dog.
2. To engage in a conversation or have a feeling of effective communication.
3. To plan aloud the activities with the dog.

Also, with something of a variation on the Heisenberg uncertainty principal, the researchers considered that, knowing they were being videotaped, some people might be performing or indirectly talking to the camera.

Short, repetitive sentences to communicate and get the attention of an inattentive listener describe early motherese, but during the child's second year, repeated imperatives begin to predominate. These may be disguised as questions. "Why don't you do xxx?" Control and attention are likely to predominate in talk to dogs during play. Gaining control is, the researchers note, part of the purpose of dog-human play. Imperatives in one study accounted for 57.5 percent of utterances, with 25.5 percent of utterances repeating the dog's name.[79]

People generally believe that their dogs understand some words, such as names of toys and familiar people. As with infants, however, people acknowledge that the animal does not completely understand their speech. As with infants, when a dog does not respond people sometimes speak for the pet, though this is less common than with infants because the pet is likely to answer the verbal question with action.

During play, the human may throw the ball over a fence where the dog cannot get it. "Sorry, you can't get that. I'll have to call up Melinda and see if she's home. Do you think she's home. I hope so." The sentences focus attention on a problem and have a rather introspective tone. There is only the appearance of addressing the statements to the dog.

## DO DOGS LAUGH?

It has been argued that a "breathy pronounced forced exhalation" by dogs, common in play encounters, is a sort of dog laugh used to initiate play.[80] It is described as a panting sound, "hhuh hhuh hhuh."[81] The sound also bears some resemblance to a whisper, and may explain why whispering has been found to help in initiating human-dog play. Other sounds are present in play, including barking, growling, and whining, but only what Simonet calls the dog-laugh is exclusive to play. She found that the sound was made both during solitary play, when the dog is engaging in play activity without a partner, and in social play. Playing a taped dog-laugh had the following effects on dogs in a shelter:

> The young puppies (approximately 4–12 months of age) offered play-bows and dog-laugh vocalizations during the playback. Adult dogs offered responses of orienting and vocalizations of barks and dog-laughs during the playback. Dogs between 1 & 2 years of age oriented toward the sound in silence, usually wagging the tail in a medium pace back and forth at mid height. Dogs over 2 years of age oriented to the sound or the experimenter and assumed the down or sit position.

The researchers recorded stress indications among the dogs at the shelter, specifically looking for a complex of behaviors such as barking, lunging, growling, panting, salivating, pacing, and avoidance (personal observation of shelter dogs). They concluded that the laughing sound reduced stress among the dogs in the shelter.[82]

## DOG LEARNING

Dogs may be genetically predisposed to interact with us, but they also learn from us and learn to control us.

> [B]ehavior directly related to subordinance and dependency is often shaped in dogs from a young age. A puppy that sits by its bowl and whines for food will usually have a greater chance of reinforcement than one who seeks out a source of food on its own, such as from a closet or off a table. Similarly, a dog that gets its leash or goes to the door and barks when it has to relieve itself will likely be praised and be given the opportunity to mark its territo-

ry, in addition to lessening the pressure in its bladder. A dog that urinates in the house, in contrast, is likely to receive punishment in the form of scolding and in having its owner clean away its territorial scent. In this way, dependence and sensitivity to human contingencies are shaped quickly in domestic dogs in human households.[83]

Younger dogs in packs learn from watching the more experienced members of the group.[84] They do not just learn from us when we are trying to teach them. It has been shown that in order to get food they will watch how we get into an enclosed area so that they may get there themselves.[85] (See Figure 6 showing a multiple choice task requiring the dog to infer where an object is hidden.)

Since many service dogs must retrieve items for handlers with physical disabilities, the question arises as to how many names of objects a dog can learn. A Border Collie named Rico had handlers who rewarded him for fetching items from the house. The owners would put three different items in different locations and ask Rico to bring one of them. In this way, he became familiar with an increasing number of items. Upon hearing about this dog, researchers wished to determine more about the Rico's skills. They randomly assigned the 200 items to 20 sets of 10 different items each. While the owner waited with Rico in a separate room, the experimenter arranged a set of items in an experimental room and then joined the owner and the dog. The experimenter told the owner to request that Rico retrieve two randomly chosen items, one after the other, from the experimental room. While Rico searched, he could not see his owner or the experimenter. He retrieved 37 out of 40 items correctly, proving that he indeed knew the names that had been given the items. Having a vocabulary for 200 items makes Rico comparable in this skill to language-trained apes, dolphins, sea lions, and parrots.

What if a dog trained to know a lot of names of items is asked to pick up something that doesn't have a name he knows? Juliane Kaminski and fellow scientists at the Department of Developmental and Comparative Psychology at the Max Planck Institute for Evolutionary Anthropology in Leipzig wanted to know if Rico could infer the object to which a new word referred by a process of exclusion.[86] Thus, they put seven familiar items in the experimental room along with a new object the dog did not know. They did this ten times. In the first trial, the owner always asked Rico to bring a familiar item, but on the second or third trial, he asked him to bring an item using a novel name. Rico got it right 7 out of 10 times, indicating that he was able to link the novel word to the novel item. That is, he knew the familiar items already had names, or that they were not named the word he was given for the unfamiliar item. Four weeks after these tests, the research team presented Rico with a new problem. They placed one of the novel items for the prior tests

Figure 6. Invisible Displacement Task. The dog sees the experimenter hide a toy under an opaque container then slides the device behind one of several boxes, surreptitiously depositing the object beneath the box. The experimenter then shows the dog that the opaque container is now empty. The dog must infer the location of the ball by mentally representing the toy's trajectory. Emma Collier-Baker, Joanne M. Davis, and Thomas Suddendorf, "Do Dogs (*Canis familiaris*) Understand Invisible Displacement?" *Journal of Comparative Psychology* (4)118, 421–433 (2004). Reprinted with permission of lead author.

in a room with four familiar items and four novel items that Rico had not seen before, including in the preceding test. Of these nine items, Rico was first asked to bring a familiar item. On the second or third trial, he was asked to bring the novel item that had been correctly retrieved four weeks earlier (called the target item in the research). He correctly retrieved the target item, recall that he had only seen it once before, in 3 out of 6 sessions. This is a retrieval rate comparable to the performance of three-year-old toddlers. In the sessions where he failed, he always brought one of the new unfamiliar items, never a familiar item. The research team concludes: "These experiments demonstrate that Rico reliably associates arbitrary acoustic patterns (human words) with specific items in his environment. Apparently, Rico's extensive experience with acquiring the names of objects allowed him to establish the rule that things can have names." Thus, he could make a choice by excluding those objects he knew had names, and could store the link between a word and an object in memory.

## ABERRANT BEHAVIOR IN DOGS

Mental and emotional disorders in dogs, including anxiety, attachment disorders, social phobia, obsessive-compulsive disorders, depression, aggression, eating and elimination disorders, etc., have been described, but parallels to treatments of such conditions in humans have only occasionally been the subject of research.[87] (See Figure 7.) Part of the problem of comparing conditions of another species with humans is that with humans, much of the diagnosis involves verbal interaction with a tester or therapist.

Some of the disorders described in dogs have been directly correlated with separation from human caretakers, including excessive barking and

| Condition in Humans (DSM IV, 1994) | Analogous or Homologous Condition in Domestic Dogs |
|---|---|
| Social and attachment anxieties, separation anxiety, generalized anxiety disorder | Canine separation anxiety |
| Obsessive compulsive disorder | Obsessive compulsive disorder |
| Alzheimer's disease | Canine cognitive dysfunction |
| Impulse control disorders | Canine dominance aggression |
| Panic disorder | Panic disorder/noise phobias |
| Social phobia | Social phobia |
| Post-traumatic stress disorder (PTSD) | Canine PTSD associated with abuse, neglect, abandonment |
| Schizophrenia | Endogenous genetic fear, "nervousness," "shyness," withdrawal |

Figure 7. Psychiatric Diagnoses in Humans and Comparable Conditions in Dogs. Adpated from Overall (2000).

destructiveness after the departure of the caretaker, and shadowing and intense greeting on the caretaker's return. These behaviors may occur in 20 percent of home-reared dogs during their first year. The development of drugs and approaches based on genetics may mean that this will be a growth area for laboratory scientists.[88] A study looking at chemical responses indicating nervousness in dogs that had been placed in an unusual environment found that putting a familiar dog in the environment with the dog being tested did not reduce the nervousness of the dog nearly as much as bringing a human caretaker into that same environment.[89] Just as they can be good for our mental health, it appears that we can be good for theirs.

## ANTHROPOMORPHISM

There is a close similarity between how humans interact with infants and how they interact with dogs. Every dog owner in an obedience class is Rover's daddy or Minny's mommy. Thirteen of 16 clients of a large urban veterinary center said there were circumstances in which they would give a scarce drug to the family pet before they would give it to a person outside the family.[90] More than a third of dog owners are closer to their dog than to any human family member.[91] People mourn the loss of a pet as much as they mourn the loss of a family member.[92]

Anthropomorphism has been defined as the "attribution of human mental states (thoughts, feelings, motivations and beliefs) to nonhuman animals." Among characteristics that James Serpell noted as anthropomorphic are feeding animals human food, giving them human names, celebrating their birthdays, dressing them in designer-label fashions, enrolling them in doggie daycare, taking them to specialist doctors, mourning them when they die, and burying them in pet cemeteries with the rituals of a human burial.[93] Indeed, modern humans seem to have difficulty thinking about animals except in anthropomorphic terms. Serpell cites anthropological work which argued that anthropomorphic thinking began in humans about 40,000 years ago, and that it allowed humans to anticipate the behavior of animals better than the Neanderthals had done.[94] Anthropomorphic thinking had survival value because it helped catch prey. It has been argued that without anthropomorphism neither pet keeping nor animal domestication would have been possible. The significance of anthropomorphism is succinctly captured by Dr. Serpell in these words:

> Most pet owners believe that their animals genuinely "love" or "admire" them, "miss" them when they are away, feel "joy" at their return, and "jealousy" when they show affection for a third party. One could, of course,

argue that these people are simply deluding themselves and that the feelings and emotions they impute to their animals are entirely fictitious. Be that as it may. The fact remains that without such beliefs, relationships with pets would be essentially meaningless. Anthropomorphism rules because any other interpretation of the animal's behavior, any suggestion that the pet might be motivated by other than human feelings and desires, instantly would devalue these relationships and place them on a more superficial and less rewarding footing.

Dr. Serpell finds negatives in anthropomorphism. "Docking the tails of pets or surgically removing their claws certainly could be interpreted as anthropomorphic interventions. Humans do not possess tails or claws, and it appears that some of us expect our pets to match our own self-image by doing without these natural animal appendages." Whether dressing dogs in baby clothes and ridiculous costumes particularly bothers them is doubtful, the doctor concedes. There are also negatives in terms of behavior from anthropomorphic selection. Dogs that suffer extreme anxiety on being separated from their owners, chewing up furniture, defecating and urinating on carpets, scratching holes in doors, and so on may have been bred to be so over-dependent as to be destructive and self-destructive.

Anthropomorphism may be another mental process we have in common with dogs. Dogs have been found to treat dog-like robots as social partners if they are covered in fur.[95] This sort of behavior has been called dogomorphism[96] and canine-morphizing.[97]

## BREED LIMITATIONS ON CANINE CAREGIVERS

A discussion of which breeds make the best service dogs usually begins with German Shepherds, which were the first guide dogs in Germany and in the United States. It was not long before other large breeds were used for guide dog work, and by extension, for work with the mobility impaired, which often involves providing the sort of stability for people with balance and movement disabilities. Labrador Retrievers and Golden Retrievers are now often preferred over German Shepherds for such work because of their gentle dispositions. Some hunting breeds, such as retrievers, have been found better at following pointing gestures, and may be better suited for individuals who will make use of a dog's retrieving function.[98]

Hearing or signal dogs are not generally required to be large, though veterans wounded by explosive devices in Iraq and Afghanistan may suffer hearing loss as well as impaired mobility. Aside from such situations, people who are deaf or hearing impaired may often prefer smaller breeds because taking care of smaller dogs is sometimes easier and if alerting involves jumping on a bed or piece of furniture, there is less likely to be damage. Shelter dogs are often trained to be hearing dogs. Seizure-response dogs may be chosen from larger breeds because of the need to keep a person in a seizure from harming himself, but there are smaller dogs that perform this function, as is the case with seizure-alert dogs. Psychiatric service dogs can be of any size, though calmness is an important trait.

Any dog that can pass the test of one of the therapy dog organizations will be appropriate for visiting some type of facility. Large dogs are good for visiting people in wheelchairs but smaller dogs have the advantage that they can be put beside a patient on a bed. A large dog may remain largely invisible to someone who is bedridden unless the dog will stand up beside the bed.

Gentleness is often a desired characteristic in a canine caregiver, and obedience is useful with a dog that may have to make choices when the handler is no longer able to do so. Not all dogs have the same behavioral repertoire, or are capable of the same level of communication, and someone adopting a dog with the intention of using it in one of the canine caregiver categories should consider the traits that are most useful for the function the dog will perform.

Selecting among breeds, or crossbreeds, involves many considerations. Unfortunately, much that has been written concerning behavioral differences between breeds reflects the opinions of the breeding organizations, rather than rigorous scientific analysis. A recent paper looking at the behavioral repertoires of various breeds and comparing those repertoires with the behavioral patterns of wolves has reached the interesting conclusion that dogs that are closer to wolves in appearance, and probably genetically, such as Siberian Huskies, have more of the wolf behavioral repertoire than dogs that are most morphologically different from wolves, such as Cavalier King Charles Spaniels.[99] There is, despite many claims to the contrary, little evidence that any breed is really smarter than another.[100]

It may be that the dog breeding industry, often dominated by show dog breeders, is actually selecting for behavioral traits that make a dog good in the show ring. Kenth Svartberg, a Swedish scientist, studied breed differences using tests of over 13,000 dogs in 31 breeds and concluded that selection in the recent past, particularly for traits sought for show dogs, was changing behaviors of dogs.[101] More disturbingly, no relationship was found between the typical behavior of the breeds tested and the functions of the breeds' origins. He concluded that "domestication of the dog is still in progress."

# Chapter 3

# SERVING INDIVIDUALS
# WITH PHYSICAL DISABILITIES

Dogs that receive special consideration by society do so because of the services they provide and the training they receive. Service animals generally have a one-on-one relationship with a handler, while therapy dogs, as part of a team with their handlers, generally serve populations of individuals with similar needs or in the same location. Dogs involved in police and emergency work could be said to serve police and fire departments, and other governmental agencies, but could just as well be described as servants of society. The protections these animals receive reflect the benefits they give, but also to a degree (such as with compensation-for-injury statutes), reflect the time and cost that goes into their training.

Service dogs are the most protected of trained and skilled dog groups, largely because they share in the protections their handlers receive as a result of having a disability. This discussion will begin with the service dogs that serve the individuals with physical disabilities, since this came first in the development of service dog training.

## DEFINING "SERVICE ANIMAL"

"Service animal" is a term that distinguishes those dogs that serve individuals with physical or mental disabilities, usually on a one-on-one basis, from pets or other types of skilled dogs, such as the various types of police dogs. The term is used so extensively, and though primarily legal, can now be said to be used quite broadly in society. In some state laws, service animals do include police dogs or emergency work dogs, but the term will be used here only for those dogs serving individuals with physical or mental disabilities. Service animals are also to be distinguished from therapy dogs, which may visit individuals with disabilities, most commonly in group settings. Therapy dogs are usually pets that have passed a test qualifying them for a certificate and coverage by a group insurance policy that covers the dogs against damage they may do, usually by biting, to anyone in the facilities they visit.

Most definitions of service animals or service dogs specify that this category of dog includes guide dogs, signal dogs, and service dogs for individuals with other disabilities, such as the mobility impaired or persons with epilepsy. Department of Justice regulations, for instance, define a service animal as a

> guide dog, signal dog, or other animal individually trained to do work or perform tasks for the benefit of an individual with a disability, including, but not limited to, guiding individuals with impaired vision, alerting individuals with impaired hearing to intruders or sounds, providing minimal protection or rescue work, pulling a wheelchair, or fetching dropped items.[102]

The same definitional regulation specifies that a disability "means, with respect to an individual, a physical or mental impairment that substantially limits one or more of the major life activities of such individual." Major life activities are currently defined as functions, such as caring for one's self, performing manual tasks, walking, seeing, hearing, speaking, breathing, learning, and working.[103] Thus, physical exercise at a YMCA gym was held not to be a major life activity.[104] Most of the current activities listed in the above definition of service animal presume a physical limitation, but in September 2009, the Equal Employment Opportunity Commission proposed to expand the definition of major life activities for employment purposes. The proposed definition, adopted as a result of the ADA Amendments Act of 2008,[105] would provide that major life activities include, but are not limited to "caring for oneself, performing manual tasks, seeing, hearing, eating, sleeping, walking, standing, sitting, reaching, lifting, bending, speaking, breathing, learning, reading, concentrating, thinking, communicating, interacting with others, and working."[106] Also "major bodily functions" would be included. Many of the life activities in this proposed definition would apply to psychiatric service dogs.

The Department of Justice proposed in 2008 to revise the definition of service animal in a way that is more explicit and somewhat broadens the category:

> Service animal means any dog or other common domestic animal individually trained to do work or perform tasks for the benefit of an individual with a disability, including, but not limited to, guiding individuals who are blind or have low vision, alerting individuals who are deaf or hard of hearing to the presence of people or sounds, providing minimal protection[107] or

rescue work, pulling a wheelchair, fetching items, assisting an individual during a seizure,[108] retrieving medicine or the telephone, providing physical support and assistance with balance and stability to individuals with mobility disabilities, and assisting individuals, including those with cognitive disabilities, with navigation. The term service animal includes individually trained animals that do work or perform tasks for the benefit of individuals with disabilities, including psychiatric, cognitive, and mental disabilities. . . .[109]

The Department of Transportation has a much simpler definition of service animal, but unfortunately one that would probably not be accepted by other agencies, or even many mental health professionals. In the glossary oF final regulations issued in 2008, the Department defines a service animal as "Any animal that is individually trained or able to provide assistance to a qualified person with a disability; or any animal shown by documentation to be necessary for the emotional wellbeing of a passenger." This has the unfortunate effect of meaning that the pet of a person with a diagnosed mental disability qualifies for cabin space ahead of the pet of a person without such a disability. It is difficult to support this approach from a policy perspective.

The trend in federal and state law has been to recognize that individuals with psychiatric conditions may have service animals, but at least 18 state laws still require that the individual served by the animal must have physical disabilities.[110] The U.S. tax law limits deductibility of service dogs to "a guide dog or other service animal to assist a visually-impaired or hearing-impaired person, or a person with other physical disabilities."[111] Some state statutes are even narrower, referring to "mobility impaired."[112] Most states refer to service animals as serving individuals with disabilities, without limiting the reference to the physical disabilities.

Even with states that define service animals as serving individuals with physical disabilities, or which provide access rights to individuals with physical disabilities accompanied by service animals,[113] it is not clear that state enforcement would be denied an individual with a mental disability using a service animal. Many civil enforcement actions and tort suits refer to both federal and state rules. Some states may not have amended older statutes limiting the definition of service animal to animals that serve individuals with physical disabilities on the assumption that federal coverage is a sufficient protection for individuals having mental health disabilities.[114]

## GUIDE DOGS

Guide or seeing eye dogs have been used by the blind and vision impaired since after the First World War when Dorothy Harrison Eustis, an American living in Switzerland, wrote an article for *The Saturday Evening Post* describing the use of German Shepherds as dog guides for veterans of World War I.[115] Her description of these dogs is still stirring:

> It is little short of marvelous how a raw dog can be taken into the school and in four months be turned out a blind leader, and the miracle is that the dog so perfectly assimilates his instruction. From the very small beginnings of becoming absolutely house-broken, he is taken step by step upward to his life work of leading a blind man, of being that man's eyes and his sword and buckler. He is first let loose to run with all the other dogs and to learn to mind his P's and Q's and not to fight.

The dogs of the Shepherd Dog Club of Germany were initially given obedience training in parks, but it was soon found that to guide handlers in cities, the training had to occur in cities. (See Figure 8, showing training in Lausanne, Switzerland in 1929.)

> From the moment a dog wears the leading harness his schooling is done under actual working conditions. He must go at a fast walk so that the slackening in his gait for an obstacle is instantly felt through the rigid handle of his harness. For curbs he pulls back and stands still so that his master can find the edge with his cane; for steps, approaching traffic and all obstacles barring progress, he sits down; and for trees, letter boxes, scaffoldings, pedestrians, he leans away from his man, who follows the pull and so is led safely around. He learns the direction commands of right, left and forward, and to pick up anything his master drops. He is taught to protect his master from violence and this instinct develops in bounds after he finally wins through to his own blind master. He must be ever watchful and protective, but never aggressive, and it is that quality of perfect balance in instruction that is the success at Potsdam [the city where the first training occurred].

She also noticed the effect the dogs had on their new handlers, which sounds much like the effect of therapy dogs on other populations.

> A comparison of the men completing their course [to learn to work with a guide dog that had been trained at the Shepherd Dog Club] with those just commencing is the proof. The men arrive forlorn, with lined, anxious faces and drooping bodies, thin or over-fat from inertia. In four short weeks they are remade; life takes on a new interest; shoulders lose their droop, backs straighten up and feet forget to shuffle. The thin have won back their appetite through their daily exercising walks and have put on weight and muscle, and the fat ones have trained down. Occasionally, a chuckle is heard which is the opening wedge for a laugh, just as the birds' early morning twitter presages the full song to the sun.

Figure 8. Guide Dog Training in Lausanne, Switzerland, 1929. Ccourtesy The Seeing Eye Archives.

A blind American, Morris Frank, wrote to Ms. Eustis in Switzerland and asked if he also could have his dog, named Buddy, trained to guide him and she agreed. When Frank returned to the United States, he and Buddy got a great deal of newspaper attention. Despite the name, Buddy was a female Shepherd and Frank wrote a book about her, *First Lady of the Seeing Eye.*[116] Eustis and Frank were among the founders of the organization, The Seeing Eye, which has trained about 14,000 guide dogs.[117] It was estimated in 1999 that there were about 9,000 active guide dog teams in the United States, most trained by Guide Dogs for the Blind, Leader Dogs for the Blind, and The Seeing Eye. About 1,600 dogs are trained annually.[118]

Established organizations for the blind in the United States initially resisted the idea of using dogs as guides. Opposition to the idea came from officials of the Red Cross, the American Foundation for the Blind, the New York Lighthouse, the National Society for the Prevention of Blindness, the Philadelphia School for the Blind, and the Perkins School for the Blind, whose director referred to a dog leading a blind man as cur dragging a beggar.[119] This opposition began to crack when Herbert Immelin, director of the New York Lighthouse, applied for a guide dog. Morris Frank obtained permission from Eastern Airlines to take Buddy into the cabin of an aircraft in 1931, and in the same year the Pennsylvania Railroad granted permission for dog guides to accompany blind individuals in coaches. In 1941, the

Postmaster General officially permitted guide dogs to be brought into post offices.

Guide dogs are the most protected assistance dogs in the world,[120] though not all countries are as accepting as the United States.[121] As far as public accommodations are concerned, they are effectively regarded as canes, wheelchairs, or other prosthetic devices. Because of the level of legal protection, and the visibility of the dog's function with a specially designed halter, and other reasons, disputes as to the access of guide dogs are rare, though not unknown. A case in 2007 involved a woman with a guide dog who was denied admission to the VIP lounge of a ferry because the ferry system at the request of a highly allergic regular passenger had designated the lounge as an animal-free area. The ferry changed its policy very quickly after management staff reviewed the relevant law.[122] The Department of Transportation sanctioned an airline for putting a passenger with a guide dog in coach despite the fact she had a first class ticket. The passenger was moved because the person with the seat next to her in first class refused to let the blind women sit next to him. In this situation, the other passenger should have been moved before the passenger with the guide dog.[123]

Disputes rarely center on the degree of blindness of a guide dog user.[124] In *EEOC v. AutoZone, Inc.,*[125] however, an employee needed a guide dog for peripheral vision, but for tasks associated with his work, such as looking at a computer screen, his vision was good. Summary judgment was denied the EEOC because a factual issue existed as to whether the employee was disabled for ADA purposes.

## Excluding Guide Dogs from Public Accommodations

Although guide dogs, as with other service dogs, could be excluded from a place of public accommodation if out of control,[126] this, given the rigorous selection procedures and the level of training guide dogs receive, is almost unheard of. Two exceptions to the general presumption of access for the blind or partially blind accompanied by guide dogs include owner-occupied rentals and zoos. In Wisconsin, a landlord may exclude a tenant with a guide dog from, say, a room in the owner's house, if the owner presents a certificate "signed by a physician which states that the owner or family member is allergic to the type of animal" the potential renter possesses.[127]

**Zoo Exception**. Arizona[128] and California[129] have a specific exception to the guide/service dog access law by which zoos can prohibit trained dogs from coming in direct contact with zoo animals. Direct contact might occur in a petting zoo environment, or on an open-sided train running through a wild animal habitat. The zoo must provide an adequate place to leave the guide or service dog, and must provide a sighted individual to accompany

Figure 9. First Class of The Seeing Eye, Nashville, Tennessee, February 1929. Dr. Howard Buchanan of Illinois with his dog Tartar, and Dr. R.V. Harris of Georgia with Gala. I'm not sure which is which in the photo. The three employees with the students are, from left, Jack Humphrey, geneticist and chief instructor; Adelaide Clifford, instructor; and Willi Ebeling, the first breeder of Seeing Eye dogs. Courtesy The Seeing Eye Archives.

the blind person, if requested.

**Occupying Seats on Public Transportation**. A number of states, while permitting guide and other trained dogs access to public accommodations, specify that such dogs may not occupy seats in buses, trains, or other vehicles of public transportation.[130] As will be discussed in more detail regarding cabin access of service animals, the Department of Transportation does not have a rigid policy about service animals occupying seats on airplanes.

## Training Guide Dogs

Dogs have been lending us their sight for nearly a century (see Figure 9 showing the first class of The Seeing Eye in the United States in 1929, and Figure 11, showing training in New Jersey soon after), but they do not see the same way that we do, and part of their skill is based on scent.[131] They can detect movement better than we do, particularly sudden movement, which makes them an asset in dealing with traffic. They have better lateral vision than we do, seeing things well to the side without turning their heads the way we must to see the same thing. They are what we would call red-green color blind, however, though they can detect colors in the blue and yellow portions of the light spectrum. Dogs sometimes fail to become guide dogs because of their own vision problems. One study found that 53 percent of German Shepherds are myopic, but of German Shepherd guide dogs, only 15 percent were myopic, indicating that the training process effectively weeds out animals with poorer vision.[132]

Leading a blind person has been called the most demanding work human beings have asked of any animal. Researchers looking microseconds of motion in videotapes to determine whether blind people or their guide dogs initiated specific actions, such as going forward, turning left or right, stopping at an intersection, etc., were surprised to find that the interaction between human and dog was very complex, with the dogs initiating some actions more often and the handlers initiating others, but no action being the sole decision of either.[133] The interaction between a service dog and his handler is by no means automatic movement relationship, but rather a kind of inter-species dance.[134]

After being accepted into a training program, a dog generally works with an instructor for at least five months. The dog is taught obedience commands to go forward, halt, move around obstacles but continue going in the original direction. After these skills are mastered in an environment without distractions, the skills are then practiced in situations with traffic and pedestrians. Guide dogs are trained to walk in the center of a sidewalk pavement unless there is an obstacle, not turn corners unless told to do so, stop at curbs and wait for a command to cross a road, or turn left or right, judge height and width so that the owner does not bump his head, and deal with various kinds of traffic situations. Dogs are gradually taught to initiate actions. The distractions become greater and more complex as the training advances, and dogs are taught to add their own intelligence to situations, such as refusing to obey a forward command if they see a car coming into the intersection.[135]

Dogs may sometimes have to simultaneously ignore several commands, such as the handler's command to cross the street, the change in the color of the light, and the clicking and chirping sounds now provided by traffic equipment at many intersections. Once assigned to a blind or visually impaired person, there is an additional training phase in which the new handler learns to work with the dog. This usually takes about a month.[136] Because people live longer than dogs, blind people may go through these programs many times in the course of their lives. Each dog requires the formation of a new working relationship. The transition, and the grief at the loss of a dog, often require counseling.[137]

The risks of releasing a poorly performing dog are so great that many dogs

| | |
|---|---|
| • Suspicious of people, including strangers (raises hackles, gets into flight posture, flees, growls, bites in fear) | 18% |
| • Lacks confidence (nervous when asked to perform tasks, indicated by tucking tail, trembling, salivating, fleeing toward home, overly solicitous to handler) | 16.7% |
| • Distraction (unable or unwilling to focus on guiding, distracted by flying leaves, other animals, children, etc.) | 13.6% |
| • Aggressive or suspicious towards other dogs (barks or growls at dogs) | 12.4% |
| • Overly dominant (not yielding to discipline in training) | 9.0% |
| • Fear of thunder, traffic, noise (with fleeing, trembling, panicking) | 6.2% |
| • Overly protective of its owner (and overly suspicious of those encountered by the owner) | 5.9% |
| • Excitable (has a very difficult time settling down and behaving quietly for extended periods) | 4.6% |
| • Fear of stairs (afraid to approach stairs and once on them rush to get off them) | 3.1% |
| • Emotional urinating | 3.1% |
| • Other (diverse reasons listed by various trainers) | 7.4% |
| • Total | 100% |

Figure 10. Reasons Dogs Fail Guide Dog Training Programs in the First Year (percentages of failing dogs per reason).

are rejected even before entering programs or flunk out during the training.[138] One study surveyed administrators of guide dog programs, asking them to provide the reasons of dog failures over the course of a single year.[139] Of nearly 1,000 dogs that entered programs, about 300 failed for the reasons indicated in Figure 10.

Some dogs failed beyond the one-year parameter. Guide dog trainers tend to restrict their initial selection to certain types of dogs with calm dispositions even as puppies.[140] Without these initial selection biases, the failure rate would be higher. Many of the same reasons cited in the list above also explain dogs failing to become other types of service dogs or to become therapy dogs. Dogs that are rejected from service dog training programs are often put up for adoption by the training schools with the knowledge that despite having failed the program, the dog is already trained at a fairly high level compared to most other dogs available for adoption.

Guide dogs can cost from $15,000 to $50,000.[141]

**Standards for Trainers**. Industry groups, including the International Guide Dog Federation, have begun formalizing training requirements for member organizations, and some universities, including San Francisco State

Figure 11. Training at The Seeing Eye Campus in Whippany, New Jersey, circa 1931. Courtesy The Seeing Eye Archives.

University, offer degrees in guide dog work.[142] California issues licenses for schools that train guide dogs for the blind through its Board of Guide Dogs for the Blind.[143] It may be as greater uniformity comes into guide dog training, more states will set standards or provide licensing requirements for guide dog training facilities.

## Guide Dogs Performing Other Service Dog Functions

One research team reasoned that guide dogs, since they often initiated behavior when their handlers were indecisive, might also be capable of serving simultaneously as seizure-alert dogs, a category discussed in detail below.[144] These researchers worked with a dog whose blind owner had become epileptic. They found that the owner's seizures led to anxiety in the dog. The dog was taught to bark and lick the owner's face and upper arm when it detected a seizure onset, which it began to do three to five minutes before a seizure began. The dog was trained to shepherd its owner to a safe location if they were outside. This dog was a service dog on two counts.

## HEARING DOGS

The first hearing dogs were trained by a dog trainer, Agnes McGrath, starting in 1974. Along with several other trainers, Ms. McGrath formed International Hearing Dog, Inc. in 1979.[145] It was estimated that there were 4,000 hearing dogs in the United States in 2001.[146] The British organization, Hearing Dogs for Deaf People, was formed soon after Dr. Leo Bustad, one of the founders of Delta Society, spoke in 1979 at a veterinary conference in the UK and described dogs being trained to assist deaf people.[147]

Signal dogs alert their handlers to specific sounds, often by nudging an arm or a leg, including a doorbell, alarm clock, someone calling the handler's name, a baby crying, sirens, cars honking, a smoke or security alarm,[148] or a sound made by a computer when an email is received. Hearing dogs may also be trained to find certain objects, take messages to a spouse or companion, and provide protection. There are generally no size restrictions, and smallness may be an advantage since alerting the handler to a sound may best be accomplished by the dog jumping on a bed or the handler's lap in a chair. Hearing dogs are often obtained from shelters.[149] An English study of 51 recipients of hearing dogs from a UK organization, Hearing Dogs for Deaf People, found that after receiving the dogs the recipients had reduced levels of tension, anxiety, and depression.[150] Improved interactions with neighbors and members of their communities have been described by people getting hearing dogs.[151] A very large U.S. survey of 550 hearing dog owners found psychological benefits (relaxation, self-confidence, reduced depression), social benefits (companionship, reduced loneliness, better social life), and practical benefits (greater independence, increased safety, better physical health).[152]

The sound-alerting function is only one of the benefits to deaf people of having hearing dogs. Curiously, a study which compared hearing impaired individuals with dogs and mobility impaired individuals with dogs found that the latter rated the improvement in their lives much higher than those with hearing dogs. The researchers suggested that because hearing impaired individuals are not obviously disabled in many situations, the socializing benefits of the dog may be less important for them.[153]

The biggest complaint owners of hearing dogs make is with other people petting or distracting the dog.[154] Deaf people feel safer after obtaining a hearing dog, but this is also true of all people.[155] One owner of a hearing dog is quoted as saying: "I don't have to wonder if anyone is at the door or be concerned about the phone ringing. I can sleep peacefully at night knowing that if anybody uninvited is around, my dog will let me know it."[156]

Statutory law in most states includes signal dogs, also known as hearing dogs or hearing ear dogs, in the same provisions that apply to guide dogs.

## Training Hearing Dogs

There are at least 50 facilities training hearing dogs. A survey of five of these centers conducted in the early 1990s found that all used rewards, such as treats to encourage alerting responses in dogs, which generally involved running to the sound, running to the user, running back to the sound, and so forth. Most dogs in formal programs are trained to respond to at least four sounds.[157] After the back-and-forth response has been established, the dogs are trained to respond to specific sounds. Training usually occurs in rooms designed to resemble rooms in a typical house or apartment. Once the dog is assigned to a deaf or hearing-impaired handler,[158] a trainer works with the handler for five days to learn how to reinforce the dog's alerting behavior.[159] One center in the survey helped the end-user train her dog in her home environment.

Although many signal dogs receive extensive training, others may not be as well trained or may have been trained by a handler during the period the handler was going deaf. This informal type of training has given rise to disputes as to the qualifications of dogs alleged to be hearing dogs. In a case that went up to a federal appeals court, two profoundly deaf women owned a dog named Pierre. Their landlord evicted the dog, which the tenants claimed alerted them to the ringing of the doorbell and the telephone and the buzzing of the smoke alarm. The dog could also carry notes between the women. On receiving the eviction notice for their dog, the women contacted the Madison Equal Opportunities Commission. After this agency found for the women, the landlord relented. The women later lost their jobs, moved, and sued for the past wrongs in federal court. At trial, the landlord argued that the dog was only minimally trained by a relative of the women. A jury found for the landlord and the women appealed. The federal appellate court determined that the question was whether the landlord had refused "to make reasonable accommodations in rules, policies, practices, or services, when such accommodations may be necessary to afford such person equal opportunity to use and enjoy a dwelling," as is required by federal regulations.[160] The appellate court found little evidence that Pierre was really a service animal, but did not like the district court's instructions to the jury, which had implied that Pierre would have to have formal training to be a service animal. The appellate court said that the jury should have been permitted to decide that Pierre was a service animal by virtue of what he actually did for the women.[161]

A case that arose in Oregon concerned a mother who got a dog for her son, who was deaf, and trained the dog to alert her son to knocks at the door, the sound of the smoke detector, the telephone ringing, and cars coming in the driveway. She notified the housing authority in which they lived about the dog and its functions but the housing authority said she could not keep the dog because it was a pet, pointing out that the tenant had produced no evidence that the dog was certified as an assistance animal and that the dog did not have an orange leash, as required by state law. The federal district court held that federal law did not require any formal training, and that individual training was sufficient if the dog performed functions for an individual with a disability. The court said there "is no requirement as to the amount or type of training a service animal must undergo." The court also said that federal law did not include an orange leash requirement and that federal law preempted state law on this matter.[162]

## SERVICE DOGS FOR THE MOBILITY IMPAIRED

Service dogs may perform functions for the mobility impaired, such as helping with balance, pulling a wheelchair, fetching dropped items for someone who cannot bend over, etc.[163] Guide dogs for the blind can be said to be helping people with a specific kind of mobility impairment, and the large breeds preferred for guide dog work are also commonly used for dogs helping those with sight, but who have other types of mobility impairment. Most legal and regulatory definitions of "service animal," "service dog," "assistance animal," etc., include references to such functions.

Dogs can help people who have fallen get back on their feet by holding a stand position and bracing themselves for part of the weight of the handler. They can also pull someone to his feet using a strap or rope, which is taught as a variation of tug-of-war. For a person who is ambulatory but weak, dogs can learn to brace themselves on command or when they sense that the handler is losing balance.[164] Service dogs for the mobility impaired are sometimes trained in these skills by their handlers.[165]

One well-known assistance dog trainer, Joan Froling,[166] lists the following harness-based tasks that can be taught to dogs:

- Assist moving wheelchair on flat [partner holds onto harness pull-strap] avoiding obstacles
- Work cooperatively with partner to get the wheelchair up a curb cut or mild incline; handler does as much of the work as possible, never asking the dog to attempt an incline unaided
- Haul open heavy door, holding it ajar using six-foot lead attached to back of harness, other end of lead attached to door handle or to a suction cup device on a glass door
- Tow ambulatory partner up inclines [harness with rigid handle or pull-strap may be used]
- Brace on command to prevent ambulatory partner from stumbling

[rigid handle]

- Help ambulatory partner to climb stairs, pulling then bracing on each step [rigid handle or harness with pull-strap may be used to assist partner to mount a step or catch balance]
- Pull partner out of aisle seat on plane, then brace until partner catches balance [harness with a rigid handle and a pull-strap, or pull-strap only]
- Brace, counterbalance, assisting ambulatory partner to walk; the partner pushes down on the rigid handle as if it were a cane, after giving warning command, when needed
- Help ambulatory partner to walk short distance, brace between each step [rigid handle]
- Transport textbooks, business supplies or other items up to 50 lbs in a wagon or collapsible cart, weight limit depends on dog's size, physical fitness, type of cart, kind of terrain
- Backpacking. The customary weight limit is 15% of the dog's total body weight; 10% if a dog performing another task, such as wheelchair pulling in addition to backpacking; total weight includes harness (average 3 to 4 pounds). The load must be evenly distributed to prevent chafing.[167]

Pulling wheelchairs that are designed to be pushed is, in the age of battery-driven machines, not as common a task as it once was. This is fortunate, as some animal rights activists and others have argued that this task requires undue exertion by a dog, more effort than is asked even of a sled dog. Such advocates also suggest that the harnesses used for this task are very uncomfortable for the animal and often cause injury.[168]

Some bracing tasks are done without a harness but some are best accomplished with a harness. Joan Froling lists the following tasks.

- Transfer assistance from wheelchair to bed, toilet, bathtub or van seat; hold Stand Stay position, then Brace on command, enabling partner to keep their balance during transfer
- Assist to walk step-by-step, brace between each step, from wheelchair to nearby seat
- Position self and brace to help partner catch balance after partner rises from a couch or other seats in a home or public setting
- Prevent fall by bracing on command if the partner needs help recovering balance
- Steady partner getting in or out of the bathtub
- Assist partner to turn over in bed; have appropriate backup plan
- Pull up partner with a strap [tug of war style] from floor to feet on command, then brace till partner catches balance.

Retrieval-based tasks, in which dogs use their mouths to perform tasks which a human accomplishes with hands, are also taught to service dogs working with individuals with mobility impairments. Picking up dropped items is often a crucial skill.[169] Dogs can be taught to retrieve a purse, take out medication, and even put it in the master's hand. Dogs can be taught to retrieve items indicated by a laser pointer.

Another way to look at the work that dogs do for the mobility impaired is to describe the activities that service dogs help with. The table on the next page is taken from a survey of 420 recipients of dogs from Canine Companions for Independence.[170] Most of the recipients used the dogs to help with physical disabilities, though some used them as hearing dogs or emotional support dogs. The functions of the dogs were divided into activities of daily living, work and productive activities, play and leisure activities, and miscellaneous activities. The table lists the percentage of respondents who used the dogs for the specified assistance. (See Figure 12 for survey results of percentages of service dog handlers specifying uses of dogs.)

The task mentioned by almost everyone was the retrieval of dropped or unreachable items, which has been described in other studies that will be discussed. The survey findings also indicated that hours of paid human assistance declined for the participants about two hours a week, and the hours of unpaid human assistance, often provided by family members, declined by about six hours a week. When asked what was most difficult about maintaining their dogs, survey respondents said that clipping a dog's nails and bathing it were particularly difficult. Many complained of people approaching and petting the dog while it was working, an issue that has been raised in other studies.

In 1996, two psychologists, Karen Allen and Jim Blascovich, studied the impact of service dogs on the lives of people with severe ambulatory disabilities.[171] They studied 48 wheelchair users who had expressed interest in a service dog and who required substantial personal assistance from family, friends, and paid aides. Disabilities included spinal cord injuries, muscular dystrophy, multiple sclerosis, and traumatic brain injury. Some participants had cognitive impairments in addition to the ambulatory motor impairment, including problems with attention span and memory. Individuals selected for the study either received a dog after one month from being selected, or after 13 months. Data collection occurred every six months over a two-year period. All participants completed questionnaires at each six-month interval. The dogs in the study were raised by foster families and given basic socialization training, then entered into programs in which they learned to provide general assistance. Once paired with a participant in the study, a dog was given individualized special training to expand the dog's commands to meet the needs of the person to whom the dog was assigned. Total training time for the dogs ranged from six to 12 months.

| ACTIVITIES OF DAILY LIVING | |
|---|---|
| Getting around the community | 84.2 |
| Getting around the house | 78.2 |
| Communication | 71.8 |
| Health maintenance | 59.4 |
| Dressing | 48.0 |
| Personal grooming | 44.1 |
| Emergency response | 42.6 |
| Bathing/showering | 19.8 |
| Feeding and eating | 18.3 |
| Toileting | 17.8 |
| Oral hygiene | 17.8 |
| **WORK AND PRODUCTIVE ACTIVITIES** | |
| Shopping | 75.7 |
| Cleaning | 54.5 |
| Engage in work activities more than before the dog | 45.5 |
| Clothing care | 40.1 |
| Assists in performing job | 39.6 |
| Meal preparation and cleanup | 39.1 |
| Household maintenance | 33.2 |
| Assists with school activities | 22.3 |
| Care of others | 21.8 |
| **PLAY OR LEISURE ACTIVITIES** | |
| Allows engaging in leisure activities more than before the dog | 66.8 |
| Participates with you in leisure activities | 63.4 |
| Assists in obtaining leisure equipment | 32.7 |
| **MISCELLANEOUS** | |
| Retrieves dropped items or items out of reach | 99.0 |
| Brings mail/newspaper | 60.9 |
| Turns lights on and off | 56.9 |
| Assists with locating items, people, locations | 46.5 |
| Alerts to noises in the house | 45.5 |

Figure 12. Percentages of Users of Service Dogs Indicating Assistance Function Provided by Dogs. Fairman and Huebner. *Occupational Therapy in Health Care,* 2000.

    The results of the research, summarized in the table on the following page, were dramatic. Psychological scales were used to measure self-esteem, "internal locus of control," psychological well-being, and community integration. Individuals in the experimental group got dogs after one month, and individuals in the control group got dogs after 13 months. As shown on the table, both groups had relatively low self-esteem at the beginning of the experiment (0 months), with the experimental group averaging 13.0 on the Rosenberg Self-Esteem Scale, and the control group averaging 14.1. After just six months, however, the experimental group (members of which had received dogs) averaged 25.8 on this scale while the other group remained at 14.0. After another six months, the group with dogs had 35.3 on the scale, while the control group remained at just 14.3. Then, with the control group also receiving dogs, the same improvement in self-esteem was recorded. This sort of pattern was repeated in the other categories measured by scales. (See Figure 13 for self-esteem and other measures at six-month intervals.)

    The other measures comparing the two groups are just simple numbers. The group with dogs began attending school, while the group without did not until they also got dogs. Thus at one year, 18 individuals who had received dogs were going to school, while none of those who had not were in school. As for the amount of time the individuals had human caregiver assistance, this was an inverse correlation. Individuals receiving dogs needed less in the way of caregiver assistance, either paid or unpaid, than those who had not received dogs. Here again, the control group began catching up once its members got service dogs. The authors calculated that after eight years, an individual would save a total of $60,000 in payments to human caregivers. These savings would, in many cases, not be those of the individuals but to government and charitable agencies providing support to individuals with disabilities. The researchers also noted that there were other positive results for individuals getting dogs. For instance, five participants who were separated or divorced were reconciled with their spouses after they got dogs.

    Admittedly, other studies have produced less dramatic results. One research team compared individuals with service dogs to those without them and found psychosocial benefits for some individuals, but suggested that companion animals might provide many of the same benefits.[176] A masters thesis study of 214 subjects, 99 of whom had service dogs and 115 of whom did not, found that service dog partners were significantly more likely to have incomes below $30,000 than individuals without dogs.[177] They were also more likely to live alone and be unmarried than individuals in the comparison group. The service dog group was over 70 percent women, but the comparison group was about half women. The service dog group had a higher percentage of individuals with progressive disabilities, and were likely to

| Variable | 0 | 6 months | 12 months | 18 months | 24 months |
|---|---|---|---|---|---|
| *Self-esteem*[172]:<br>Experimental | 13.0 | 25.8 | 35.3 | 36.2 | 36.6 |
| Control | 14.1 | 14.0 | 14.3 | 25.3 | 35.3 |
| *Internal locus of control*[173]:<br>Experimental | 64.4 | 135.0 | 179.4 | 187.6 | 189.8 |
| Control | 61.5 | 60.9 | 61.0 | 135.2 | 178.8 |
| *Psychological well-being*[174]:<br>Experimental | 1.6 | 6.2 | 8.0 | 8.1 | 8.8 |
| Control | 1.8 | 1.8 | 1.7 | 6.3 | 8.1 |
| *Community integration*[175]:<br>Experimental | 2.3 | 15.3 | 25.3 | 26.7 | 27.2 |
| Control | 2.2 | 2.3 | 2.3 | 15.7 | 25.3 |
| *School attendance*:<br>Experimental | 0 | 15 | 18 | 15 | 11 |
| Control | 0 | 0 | 0 | 10 | 7 |
| *Part-time employment*:<br>Experimental | 0 | 0 | 14 | 21 | 23 |
| Control | 0 | 0 | 0 | 15 | 17 |
| *Biweekly paid assistance hours*:<br>Experimental | 87.9 | 47.4 | 28.0 | 20.6 | 19.6 |
| Control | 83.5 | 83.5 | 84.2 | 42.1 | 21.3 |
| *Biweekly unpaid assistance hours*:<br>Experimental | 38.4 | 24.5 | 14.8 | 12.8 | 12.0 |
| Control | 39.8 | 39.8 | 39.8 | 22.5 | 13.4 |

Figure 13. Measures of Psychological Scales of Service Dog Recipients at Six-Month Intervals. Adapted from Allen and Blascovich, *Journal of the American Medical Association* (1996), Table 2. (The standard deviation for each variable was given in the original table but is not included here.)

have had the disability longer. This means that individuals with progressive disabilities have to plan ahead. It also suggests that the longer someone lives with a disability, the more likely they will in time obtain a service dog. Given the waiting lists of many organizations for those awaiting service dog placements, this is not surprising.

The masters thesis study concluded that people partnered with service dogs for 14 months to $8^{1}/_{2}$ years scored significantly higher on tests for mobility and physical independence, at least if certain statistical methods were applied. Unlike the Allen and Blascovich study, this research found that service dog users obtained more paid assistance work than the comparison group of individuals with disabilities, but curiously used less unpaid assistance. The difference was not statistically significant, however. In tests for social integration, economic self-sufficiency, and self-esteem, the differences between the groups were not significant. As for loneliness and depression, the service dog group was lower on measures of these factors (i.e., less lonely and less depressed), but this also was not at a level of statistical significance. The researcher noted that the service dog consisted of individuals who had more severe disabilities, so the ultimate finding was that service dogs are very good for many people.

Three researchers in Houston looked at satisfaction issues for recipients of service dogs for the mobility impaired. Tasks that the dogs performed included retrieving items, pulling towels from a rack and placing them in a hamper, carrying a bag, picking items off store shelves, helping pull linens from beds and pulling clean sheets into place, and activating emergency call devices. Retrieving items was the task that had the most positive impact, and was mentioned by 78 percent of the recipients of the service dogs. Many users also mentioned that the dog helped them to stand and walk, and to maintain balance. Dogs were also able to turn lights off and on and open doors. Family members often said that they preferred to have the dog in their vehicles rather than a scooter or other assistive device. The researchers also found that with most individuals receiving dogs a major effect was that they depended less on assistance from other persons after they got the dog.[178] Family members and friends can grow resentful of always being available to provide help. "A dog is not going to keep a record of how many times you ask it to do things for you."[179]

A 1998 study found that as many as 30 percent of individuals paired with service dogs say that getting a service dog was not their own idea, but rather was suggested by doctors, veterinarians, partners, or family members.[180] A questionnaire study of individuals with paraplegia, quadriplegia, cerebral palsy, multiple sclerosis, spina bifida, arthritis, polio, limb amputation, and thalidomide effects, looked at what service dog users valued most among the tasks their dogs performed for them. The tasks they asked about were rated as follows by the dog users:

  • Retrieving and carrying: 84%
  • Opening doors: 40%
  • Companionship: 35%
  • Barking on command: 35%
  • Guarding: 12%

The researchers also asked about the motivation for obtaining a service dog. As to this, responses of users included the following as motivations:

  • Independence: 70%
  • Companionship: 35%
  • Ability to socialize more: 23%

Three-quarters of those questioned said that they had made new friends since getting a service dog, and a third said they had a better social life. One person said: "People see the dog and then they see me. It's a step in the right direction. Without the dog, it's just another guy in a wheelchair. People look at you a bit differently when you have the dog with you."[181] A very high proportion described the dog as a family member and 72 percent said it was one of their most important relationships; 70 percent said the friendship was more important to them than the fact the dog was a working dog. Individuals who said getting the dog was not their own idea were less inclined to call the dog a friend. Almost half, 47 percent, said their health had improved since acquiring the dog, though this was less often a comment of people who got the dog at someone else's suggestion. Such people were also more inclined to emphasize the problems in dealing with the dog. The researchers found the perception of improved health particularly interesting since many of the subjects had degenerative conditions.

Dogs have been paired with children born with cerebral palsy and trained to summon help for the children, as well as helping them to stand and maintain balance.[182] As mentioned regarding hearing dogs, dogs for the mobility impaired function as something of a socialization aid. Children in wheelchairs receive more and friendlier attention from passersby when they are accompanied by service dogs.[183]

## Statutes and Cases on Service Animals
## Helping the Mobility Impaired

Federal and state laws and rules often mention functions that dogs perform for the mobility impaired,[184] "providing physical support and assistance with balance and stability to individuals with mobility disabilities."[185] Missouri defines a "mobility dog" as "a dog that is being or has been specially trained to assist a person with a disability caused by physical impairments."[186] New Hampshire provides that a "mobility impaired person using a service dog shall provide the dog with a leash colored blue and yellow."[187]

A resident of a condominium unit with multiple sclerosis had to fight to keep her dog in a case arising in Pennsylvania. The association had a no-pets policy. Shortly after getting a male puppy, Sampson, the tenant's caregiver arranged for a dog trainer to train Sampson to be a service dog. He was taught to pick up and retrieve objects and to open and shut doors,[188] and to provide the tenant with support when she moved in and out of the wheelchair. The dog also learned to find the caregiver if the tenant needed aid. The case describes an instance:

> Fulciniti awoke during the night, and made her way to the bathroom. While in the bathroom, she fell and cracked her head. She was wedged between the toilet and the wall, and could not move. [The caregiver], who was asleep was unaware of [the tenant's] predicament. Sampson was able to alert [the caregiver] of Fulciniti's accident.

Although trained as a service dog, Sampson was certified and registered by Therapy Dogs International. The association learned of the dog, reminded the tenant of the condominium's no-pets policy, and demanded that she remove Sampson. A psychiatrist sent a letter to the association stating that the tenant needed the dog for "special protection, back-up communication, and physical assistance," and that the tenant's "quality of life should be improved by the dog." A neurologist wrote a letter to the same effect. A federal district court in Pennsylvania found that the condominium association was subject to the Fair Housing Act, that the tenant was disabled under federal law, and that the association should have made a reasonable accommodation to allow her to keep her dog.[189]

A Massachusetts case demonstrates that it may be easier to prove that a cat is a psychiatric service animal than that it helps with multiple sclerosis. In *Nason v. Stone Hill Realty Association,*[190] the tenant had multiple sclerosis and used an electronic wheelchair. She took in her mother's cat when her mother became ill. When she received a letter from the landlord telling her to remove the cat she obtained a letter from her physician stating that there would be serious negative consequences to her health if she was compelled to remove the cat. When the matter was not resolved, the tenant filed a complaint in state court alleging violation of the Fair Housing Act[191] and of state law.[192] To succeed on her claim, the court said that the tenant would need to show that her request for accommodation was both reasonable and necessary, which would require her showing "a clear nexus between MS and the need to maintain the cat."

> The affidavit provided by Dr. Howard L. Weiner, Nason's neurologist, does indicate that removal of the cat would result in "increased symptoms of depression, weakness, spasticity and fatigue." However, the affidavit does not demonstrate that such symptoms are treatable solely by maintaining the cat or whether another more reasonable accommodation is available to address Nason's symptoms. For example, the affidavit fails to illustrate how the presence of the cat, as opposed to some other therapeutic method such as chemical therapy, is essential or necessary to treating her symptoms.

Balancing taking drugs against owning a pet is certainly a novel argument. There is almost no analysis of the law in the case. The argument that drugging the tenant might be preferable to letting her keep a cat is, one must hope, unique to this court. This may be a case of a judge that did not like animals.

## SEIZURE-ALERT DOGS

Some dogs appear to detect physiological changes in the bodies of humans, such as the imminent onset of a seizure, or falling glucose levels. The basis of this skill remains uncertain. The dog may smell a chemical shift in the handler's body or sense a subtle change in the handler's behavior. Surveying prior research in 2003, one team observed:

> Because a dog's primary form of communication is body language and facial expressions, it is plausible that a seizure-alerting dog is cued by the patient's most minute gestures or posturing. However, with reports of dogs being out of sight of their handlers and then suddenly approaching them and alerting, one has to consider the possibility of a scent, auditory cue or some other signal independent of visual cues. It seems possible that any one or combination of these senses play an important part in alerting behavior.[193]

It is also not known what percentage of dogs have this ability since many of the reports so far are isolated accounts of owners and, from a scientific point of view, anecdotal. Some dogs have been found to alert to more than one person, and there is an instance where one dog may have learned to alert for seizures from another dog.[194]

## Training and Seizure Alerting

The Department of Justice's 2008 proposed revision to its service animal rules states, in the definition of "service animal,"[195] that such an animal is "individually trained to do work or perform tasks for the benefit of an individual with a disability, including, but not limited to . . . assisting an individual during a seizure. . . ." The wording is curious as it does not refer to alerting an individual of an oncoming seizure, though the Department of Transportation, in a guide published in 2005, noted that service animals may assist people with disabilities by "[a]lerting persons with epilepsy of imminent seizure onset."[196]

Some states have included seizure-alert dogs among those animals that qualify as service animals.[197] Illinois law provides:

> When . . . a person who is subject to epilepsy or other seizure disorders is accompanied by a dog which serves as a . . . seizure-alert, or seizure-response dog for such person or when a *trainer* of a . . . seizure-alert, or seizure-response dog is accompanied by a . . . seizure-alert, or seizure-response dog or a dog that is being trained to be a . . . seizure-alert, or seizure-response dog, neither the person nor the dog shall be denied the right of entry and use of facilities of any public place of accommodation . . . if such dog is wearing a harness and such person presents credentials for inspection issued by a school for training guide, leader, seizure-alert, or seizure-response dogs.[198]

Thus, Illinois law conceives of trainers of seizure-alert dogs, though the wording might not have to mean that the trainer is teaching the dog to recognize seizures. New Jersey also provides that a service dog includes "a 'seizure dog' trained to alert or otherwise assist persons subject to epilepsy or other seizure disorders."[199] It is likely that most states, even without specific reference in their codes, would recognize seizure-alert dogs as service animals.

Seizure-alert dogs are appropriately classified as service dogs, but it must be noted that there is a problem where statutes refer to service dogs as trained for the functions they perform. The Epilepsy Institute states on its website:

> [T]o date, there is no scientific proof that animals can alert humans to seizures. Even if this ability is confirmed, *it is not known that this apparent ability can be acquired through training* and/or what kind of training is effective. . . . Some reports appear quite viable and warrant scientific research to confirm this ability.[200]

The Epilepsy Institute began one study of the issue, using EEG and video monitoring of people with their dogs, but had to discontinue the study due to limited funding. Some scientists have been skeptical about whether epilepsy seizure alerting almost ever occurs.[201]

In a case report, two researchers at the Jefferson Hospital for Neuroscience in Philadelphia evaluated the detection abilities of seizure-alert dogs in an inpatient epilepsy care unit where patients were undergoing continuous computer-assisted EEG.[202] This is the only research case where alerting prior to seizures was actually the subject of objective observation, as opposed to self-reporting. The report concluded:

> Between March and May of 2004 we monitored two patients who owned "seizure dogs" in the Epilepsy Care Unit at Thomas Jefferson University Hospital in Philadelphia. Both patients were accompanied by their "seizure dogs" during their admission, as the patients felt more secure with the dogs. The dogs' performance in alerting before a seizure was poor for patient 1 [alerting prior to only one of eight recorded seizures] and misleading for patient 2. In our limited but objective experience, the "seizure dogs" were not as effective as previously thought in predicting the seizure activity. At the same time we must be fair and recognize the limitations that the environment of the Epilepsy Care Unit places not only on patients but also on seizure-alert dogs. Similar studies (in epilepsy monitoring units) of larger samples of patients are needed to determine if these trained dogs are responsible for clinical improvement in epilepsy patients.

Other studies, admittedly involving self-reporting, have been more positive concerning the existence of seizure alerting skills. A 2003 study found that of 29 patients that owned pet dogs, nine reported dogs responding to seizures and three reported their dogs were able to alert a seizure onset.[203] This group estimated that the advance warning by their dogs was generally about three minutes before onset. Admitting that their results were too small to be of statistical significance, this group made some interesting observations about the types of seizures that dogs may alert to:

> [A] dog is more likely to alert to a person (1) with complex partial seizures; (2) who experiences migraines; and (3) who most often experiences the following auras: weird feeling in their head they cannot describe, dizziness, nausea, lip smacking/mouth movements, and changes in breathing (usually faster). Our results also suggest that alerting behavior of the dog is not breed, age or gender specific, that the effectiveness of an alerting dog depends greatly upon the human companion to recognize and respond appropriately to the dog's alerting behavior and that dogs can be trained to respond and offer assistance during and/or after the seizure.

The authors argued for more research and mentioned the need for independent verification of prior alerting.

## Dangers for Some Dogs Found in Seizure Alerting

One of the strongest pieces of evidence concerning the seizure alerting capability of many dogs comes from the fact that, for many dogs, sensing an oncoming seizure can be dangerous, even deadly. Although anecdotal, the extent of the reports of negative responses, was particularly persuasive in one English study.[204] Four examples of reactions in dogs to seizures or in advance of seizures included the following behaviors and physiological effects.

- Dog exhibited escape behavior associated with seizures was found to have increased corticosteroid plasma levels, immunosuppression, and impaired neurological function.
- Dog exhibited flight/avoidance behavior when first witnessing a seizure in a young boy and began to show nervous aggression towards similar children.
- Dog was asphyxiated by the lead attempting to escape from owner during a seizure.
- Dog attempted to escape prior to seizures but if unable to escape attacked owner during seizures.[205]

The authors noted that a high proportion of dogs have a negative response to seizures, which may begin before the seizure. They believed that relatively few seizures were necessary for a dog to begin to respond in a negative or inappropriate manner. The Support Dogs group was able to train 20 dogs in how to respond to an oncoming seizure, with dogs able to alert to the oncoming seizure from ten to 45 minutes in advance without adverse consequences to either the dog or the owner.[206] Another English study involving some of the same researchers found evidence that using seizure-alert dogs appeared to reduce the frequency of tonic-clonic seizures.[207] This might indicate that the affected handlers are able to medicate in advance, but could indicate that the confidence in the dog reduces factors that may induce seizures.

## Spontaneous Alerting Ability

A survey of epileptic children in families that owned a dog found that about 40 percent of such dogs showed anticipatory ability, with the anticipatory behavior usually being specific.

- A Sheltie-Spitz cross would forcibly sit on her toddler and not allow her to stand prior to a drop attack.
- An Akita would push her young girl away from the stairs 15 minutes before a convulsion.

- A Golden Retriever could anticipate nocturnal events from sleep by up to 20 minutes.
- A Rottweiler would lick his toddler's feet with absence seizures but forcibly position himself on either side before a drop attack.
- A Great Pyrenees would attach itself to its three-year-old at the exclusion of all else, including eating and drinking, hours before she had a generalized convulsion. The same dog would forcefully lie on the 8-year-old sister 10 minutes before she had a complex partial event with wandering.

The research concluded that quality of life was higher in families where the dog responded to seizures.[208] A program that trained seizure-response dogs working with individuals who had an average of 36 seizures per month and an average medication failure of 4.8 per month, found that 59 percent of the graduated dogs developed alerting behavior spontaneously.[209]

## Alerting to Psychogenic Seizures

One team looked at patients who had acquired seizure-response dogs and who claimed that the dogs were alerting them to the onsets of their seizures. The team determined that the four patients had psychogenic non-epileptic seizures, that is, their seizures were induced by psychological conditions, not by epilepsy.[210] One patient reported that his dog alerted to seizures seven to ten minutes before clinical symptoms developed. The patient had video-EEG monitoring for four days while accompanied by his dog. The alerting consisted of the dog abruptly licking the patient's face. One recorded episode of the licking was followed 30 seconds later by a two-minute seizure, with staring, right arm tonic posturing, and then bilateral, asynchronous arm shaking, followed by crying. The EEG was normal, however, and the patient was diagnosed with a psychiatric conversion disorder.

A second patient was also licked by his dog on the neck, and had two episodes per day during the video-EEG evaluation. The patient's episodes consisted of minute-long periods of right arm shaking and altered awareness with humming sounds and mild confusion, but the EEG was normal. The patient was diagnosed with psychogenic non-epileptic seizures (PNES). The episodes subsequently ceased and the patient was referred to psychological counseling. A third patient had a pet dog that barked repeated during her frequent confusional episodes. There was one episode during video-EEG monitoring in which her awareness was altered but her EEG was normal. Her anti-convulsents were stopped and she had no additional episodes. This team studied but did not report on three more patients, two of which had PNES, but one of which had epilepsy. The researchers conceded that the patient with epilepsy had a dog that alerted prior to her seizures by pacing. They argued that individuals with primarily psychiatric conditions might benefit from the emotional support of seizure-response dogs, but they do not need epileptic seizure dogs.

One area that may deserve investigation concerns the fact that dogs themselves may be subject to epilepsy. A genetic mutation has been identified for a miniature wire-haired dachshund with epilepsy.[211] An interesting if rather esoteric study might involve looking at the behavior of other dogs around a dog before an impending seizure.[212]

## Social Acceptance of Seizure Alerting

Social and legal acceptance of seizure-alert dogs appears to be rather premature and it must be questioned whether any seizure-alert ability can be trained. It may not be accidental therefore, that in June 2008 proposals, the Department of Justice referred only to seizure-response functions, not to seizure-alerting functions. If further studies do not demonstrate that alerting to seizures is really happening in some cases, those dogs (i.e., ones with no seizure-response or other service dog functions) will be more properly classified as pets or emotional support animals whose handlers have seizure conditions.

The Department of Housing and Urban Development squarely faced the issue of service tasks that do not need to be trained in the preamble to recently finalized regulations:

> [T]there are animals that have an innate ability to detect that a person with a seizure disorder is about to have a seizure and can let the individual know ahead of time so that the person can prepare. This ability is *not the result of training,* and a person with a seizure disorder might need such an animal as a reasonable accommodation to his/her disability. Moreover, emotional support animals do not need training to ameliorate the effects of a person's mental and emotional disabilities. Emotional support animals by their very nature, and without training, may relieve depression and anxiety, and/or help reduce stress-induced pain in persons with certain medical conditions affected by stress.[213]

Kansas defines a service dog as one that has been "specially *selected,* trained and tested to perform a variety of tasks for persons with disabilities."[214] Seizure-alert dogs may belong in a category that has been selected, but not necessarily trained, for a specific service function. Even if the initial alerting does not come about as a result of training, those individuals who reinforce seizure alerting by rewarding their dogs for this behavior are undoubtedly engaging in training to continue and enhance the behavior.

## SEIZURE-RESPONSE DOGS

A seizure-response dog is a dog that responds to a seizure by taking some positive action, such as fetching medication from a cupboard, bringing a purse with medication in it, or following an immobile handler's commands to find a bottle containing the medication. Dogs have been trained to bring a mobile or portable phone so that the handler can call for help, and some have been taught to push a device connected to a phone, or a big button on a specially designed phone, so that it will automatically call an emergency number. Devices can be attached to front doors to houses and apartments so that dogs can open the door to admit emergency personnel, either at the direction of the handler or even without the handler's direction in response to the handler's incapacitated state. Dogs can also be taught to open interior doors if specially designed handles are installed.

One organization that trains seizure-response dogs indicates that it takes from 18 to 24 months to teach the dogs before the dogs before they are paired with recipients. Tasks performed by the dogs are initiated by voice commands, such as "Bring the Phone," "Bring the Medicine," etc. Although most seizure-response dogs go to individuals with epilepsy, an official of the organization indicates that requests are increasing from individuals with diabetes who become incapacitated as a result of hypoglycemia attacks.[215] Dogs have also been reported to be able to interrupt tremor episodes or propulsive walking of persons with Parkinson's disease.[216]

Such dogs, given the tasks they are trained to perform, clearly fall within most definitions of service animals.[217]

## HYPOGLYCEMIA-ALERT DOGS

Dogs that detect a sudden drop in a human's insulin level have been called diabetes-alert dogs, diabetic-alert dogs, or hypoglycemia-alert dogs.[218] Researchers in Liverpool, England, described three cases of dogs with this skill.

> *Candy.* A nine-year old mixed breed female dog named Candy was owned by a 66-year-old woman with type 2 diabetes. Candy's owner uses insulin and monitors her blood glucose at least once a day. For two years she experienced increasingly frequent hypoglycemic episodes with excessive sweating, generalized weakness, anxiety, and irritability. She is

generally aware of hypoglycemic symptoms and can usually take quick corrective action, but for a year she began to notice an unusual behavior in Candy. Candy would suddenly jump up, run out of the room, and hide under a chair in the hallway. This would happen before the woman was aware of any hypoglycemic symptoms. Candy would only come out from under the chair after the woman took carbohydrate.

*Susie.* A 47-year-old woman with type 2 diabetes had up to two hypoglycemic episodes each week generally in the afternoon or at night. When they happened at night after a time her seven-year-old mongrel dog, Susie, began to nudge her awake. When they happened in the afternoon the dog began to prevent her from leaving the house until she had taken food to correct her hypoglycemia.

*Natt.* A 34-year-old woman with type 1 diabetes has around two hypoglycemic episodes a week, with sweating and lightheadedness. Her three-year-old golden retriever, Natt, becomes very distressed when she is hypoglycemic and paces up and down and puts his head on her lap. During nocturnal episodes, he barks and scratches the bedroom door, waking her up. He settles down once her hypoglycemia has been corrected.

Over a third of dogs living with diabetic people have been reported to show behavioral changes during the owners' hypoglycemic episodes.[219] Another research team studied three dogs that "were clearly able to sense hypoglycemia accurately under circumstances when the patients themselves were initially unaware of falling glucose levels." This team made a very curious statement in discussing the possible mechanism for the recognition of hypoglycemia.

> The physiological basis is uncertain, but direct contact with the diabetic patient was not required in any of these cases. Possible clues include olfactory changes (possibly related to sweating), muscle tremor, or behavioural alterations such as the patient's failure to respond to her dog in her usual way. We are attracted by the notion of the "sixth sense" with which dogs are commonly credited, but acknowledge that this will need to be substantiated by further research.

The researchers argue that hypoglycemia-alert dogs could be an important aid to patients with poor awareness of symptoms, particularly those prone to nocturnal episodes.[220] An Irish team reported a case of a dog able to detect hypoglycemic attacks in a non-diabetic patient.[221]

## BUILDING ON ANECDOTAL EVIDENCE
## TO NEW TYPES OF SERVICE DOGS

An individual experienced severe migraine headaches about three times a week, with symptoms including nausea, vomiting, and tenderness on the right side. When she had enough warning, she used a nasal spray that sometimes prevented a migraine. When she got a migraine, she sometimes needed assistance to get to a bathroom and take medication, and to bring her ice packs and cold cloths. When her pet Pomeranian, Spicey, was between seven and nine months old, Spicey began to respond to the tenant's migraines by running, jumping, barking, scratching on a door, or pulling the leg of roommates or neighbors to alert them. The person alerted would then assist the tenant. When the tenant received assistance, Spicey stood quietly and watched.[222] A court in Washington State did not accept the animal was a service animal, yet the behavior described is similar to that recorded from some seizure-alert and seizure-response dogs.[223]

Three scientists published a case study of a dog that bumped a woman's elbow with his nose repeatedly when she was at the onset of a hypomanic episode.[224]

# Chapter 4

# SERVICE AND SUPPORT OF PERSONS WITH MENTAL DISABILITIES

S ervice dogs also serve the persons with mental health disabilities.[225] Because an individual's mental disability is often not apparent to other members of society, the individual's need for the dog is much more frequently questioned. Indeed, from society's perspective, the distinction between visible and non-visible disabilities often defines the boundary between when a dog must be accepted as a special category of animal and when it need not be.[226] A person using a guide dog has lost some or all of his sight, as a person using a hearing dog has lost some or all of his hearing, but individuals with physical disabilities, other than mobility impairment, may not to others have an obvious need of an accompanying animal. An individual with a seizure-alert dog, for instance, will not appear, except while having a seizure, to be different from another individual walking a pet (which explains why many individuals with such dogs obtain medical alert vests for them). Many disputes regarding access to public accommodations begin when an individual with a non-visible disability attempts to bring a service dog into a restaurant, theater, or other public location. Although the distinction between visible and non-visible disabilities is not commonly acknowledged in statutory access provisions, there are situations where this will be a significant issue. For instance, rules of the Department of Housing and Urban Development, allow housing providers "to verify the existence of the disability, and the need for the accommodation, *if either is not readily apparent.*"[227]

Although actions the animal has been trained to perform for an individual with mental health disabilities will bolster a claim that a dog is a service dog,[228] service animal status has been accepted where the animal provides assistance that is directly related to a person's mental health-related impairments such as helping a person with a panic disorder or agoraphobia to leave home.[229] Similarly, and following statements of the Department of Justice in the preamble to regulations proposed in 2008, a dog that orients an individual with a dissociative disorder in time and place should be recognized as a service dog.[230]

> Many commenters followed the lead of an umbrella service dog organization in suggesting that "performing tasks" should form the basis of the service animal definition, that "do work" should be eliminated from the definition, and that "physical" should be added to describe tasks. Tasks by their nature are physical, so the Department does not believe that such a change is warranted. In contrast, the phrase "do work" is slightly broader than "perform tasks," and adds meaning to the definition. For example, a psychiatric service dog can help some individuals with dissociative identity disorder to remain grounded in time or place. As one service dog user stated, in some cases "critical forms of assistance can't be construed as physical tasks," noting that the manifestations of "brainbased disabilities," such as psychiatric disorders and autism, are as varied as their physical counterparts. One commenter stated that the current definition works for everyone (i.e., those with physical and mental disabilities) and urged the Department to keep it. The Department has evaluated this issue and believes that the crux of the current definition (individual training to do work or perform tasks) is inclusive of the varied services provided by working animals on behalf of individuals with all types of disabilities and proposes that this portion of the definition remain the same.[231]

Some critics of the concept of psychiatric service dogs say that providing emotional support does not count as a legitimate form of disability-related assistance, but there seems to be no compelling logic for this position. Whatever "emotional support" is, the fact that non-disabled persons feel emotions that may be comforted by a pet has no relevance whatsoever to the use of psychiatric service dogs by persons living with mental health disabilities. Such persons are starting from a place of severe impairment and the assistance provided by the dog restores their ability to function. By way of a metaphor, air conditioning on a hot day is a pleasant modern convenience, but for some people who cannot regulate their core body temperature, it is medically necessary.

There are now close to 10,000 psychiatric service dogs in the United States. Some of the tasks that psychiatric service dogs may be trained to perform are summarized in Figure 14.[232]

| Disorder / Symptoms | Trainable Tasks |
|---|---|
| **Major Depression** | |
| Apathy | Tactile stimulation |
| Hypersomnia | Wake up handler |
| Feelings of isolation | Cuddle and kiss |
| Sadness | Deep pressure stimulation |
| Tearfulness | Lick tears<br>Bring tissues<br>Initiate play |
| Insomnia<br>Suicidal ideation | Stay with and focus on handler |
| Psychomotor retardation | Walk on a leash |
| Memory loss | Remind to take medication<br>Help to find keys or telephone |
| Disorganization | Assist with daily routines in the home |
| **Bipolar** (manic phase) | |
| Thoughts racing<br>Distractibility | Tactile stimulation |
| Hyper focus<br>Irritability<br>Hyper-locomotion<br>Olfactory cue? | Alert to incipient manic episode |
| Aggressive driving | Alert to aggressive driving |
| Insomnia | Alert to insomnia |
| Memory loss | Remind to take medication<br>Help to find keys or telephone |
| Disorganization | Assist with daily routines in the home |
| **Panic** | |
| Derealization<br>Depersonalization | Tactile stimulation |
| Olfactory cue? | Alert to incipient anxiety or panic attack |
| Fear<br>Fight or Flight response | Lead handler to a safe place |

*continued on next page*

| Disorder / Symptoms | Trainable Tasks |
|---|---|
| **Panic** *continued* | |
| Pounding heart<br>Trembling<br>Nausea<br>Sweating | Staying with and focusing on handler |
| Dizziness | Brace or lean against the handler |
| Chills | Lay across handler's body |
| Memory loss | Remind to take medication<br>Help to find keys or telephone |
| **Anxiety** | |
| Restlessness<br>Distractibility | Tactile stimulation |
| Sleep disturbance | Staying with and focusing on handler |
| Anxiety | Assist handler to leave situation |
| Muscle tension | Walk on leash |
| Memory loss | Remind to take medication |
| **Agoraphobia** | |
| Anxiety<br>Fear of what could happen | Tactile stimulation |
| Anxiety<br>Fear of being vulnerable | Staying with and focusing on handler |
| Fear of leaving home | Assist handler to leave the house |
| **Social Phobia** | |
| Anxiety | Tactile stimulation |
| Nervousness around others | Facilitate social interactions |
| Distress | Staying with and focusing on handler |
| Feeling overwhelmed | Assist handler in leaving a social situation |
| **Post Traumatic Stress** | |
| Distractibility<br>Anxiety<br>Intrusive imagery<br>Dissociation<br>Flashbacks | Tactile stimulation |

*continued on next page*

| Disorder / Symptoms | Trainable Tasks |
|---|---|
| **Post-Traumatic Stress** *continued* | |
| Hallucinations | Hallucination discernment |
| Feelings of isolation | Cuddle and kiss |
| Hypervigilance | Alert to presence of other people |
| Fear<br>Startle response | Environmental assessment |
| Fear<br>Anxiety | Turn on lights and safety check a room |
| Rumination<br>Avoidance behaviors | Staying with and focusing on handler |
| Nightmares | Interrupt by waking up handler<br>Turn on lights for calming and reorienting<br>Turn off lights for resuming sleep |
| Feelings of being threatened | Create safe personal space |
| **Obsessive Compulsive** | |
| Distractibility<br>Intrusive thoughts or images<br>Anxiety | Tactile stimulation |
| Repetitive or compulsive behavior | Interrupt |
| Memory loss | Remind to take medication<br>Help to find keys or telephone |
| **Dissociative Identity** | |
| Distress<br>Flashbacks | Tactile stimulation |
| Startle response | Assess threat |
| Olfactory or behavioral cue? | Alert to incipient dissociative episode |
| Dissociation<br>Self-mutilation | Interrupt |
| Hallucinations | Hallucination discernment |
| Nightmares | Wake up handler |
| Forgotten personal identity | Carry handler identification documents |
| Anxiety | Staying with and focusing on handler |
| Dissociative fugue | Help handler to cross streets safely |

*continued on next page*

| Disorder / Symptoms | Trainable Tasks |
|---|---|
| Schizophrenia | |
| Flat affect | Tactile stimulation |
| Hallucinations | Hallucination discernment |
| Catatonic behavior Disorganized speech or behavior Psychosis Delusions | Staying with and focusing on handler |
| Forgotten personal identity | Carry handler identification documents |
| Confusion or disorientation | Take handler home |
| Social withdrawal | Facilitate social interactions |
| Feeling overwhelmed | Buffer handler in crowded situations |
| Memory loss | Remind to take medication Help to find keys or telephone |

Figure 14. Psychiatric Disorders, Symptoms, and Trainable Tasks for Service Dogs. A non-exclusive list developed by Drs. Joan Esnayra and Craig Love in collaboration with the psychiatric service dog community of handlers, 2009.

## SERVICE ANIMALS DEALING WITH PANIC, ANXIETY, AND POST-TRAUMATIC STRESS DISORDER

People suffering from panic attacks, persistent anxiety, and post-traumatic stress disorder are often made very anxious when someone gets too close to them, or when they cannot escape the press of a crowd. Dogs can be taught to make room for such people by circling them, standing behind them, and bracing for the possible impact that might be caused when someone steps into them.[233] As with other non-visible conditions, individuals claiming service dog status for dogs that protect them in these ways may find themselves disputing with businesses for their need to have the dog accompany them.

Courts have recognized dogs helping people to live normal lives, leave their houses, go into places where crowds might frighten them, and so forth, are valid types of service animals. A homeowners association in California was chastised by a court for attempting to remove a dog from a residence because it violated a no-pets policy.

> If Auburn Woods needed additional information about the Elebiaris' medical condition or their need to keep Pooky, it was obligated to request it. It could not simply sit back and deny a request for reasonable accommodation

because it did not think sufficient information had been presented or because it did not think the Elebiaris had spoken the "magic words" required to claim the protections of FEHA [The California Fair Employment and Housing Act].[234]

In *Crossroads Apartments Associates v. LeBoo,* a federally assisted apartment complex sought to evict a tenant because of his possession of a cat in violation of his lease.[235] The tenant had been diagnosed as having panic disorder with agoraphobia, mixed personality disorder, and chronic anxiety, with a history of episodic alcohol abuse. The court held that to prove that the landlord violated the Rehabilitation and Fair Housing Amendments Acts, the tenant had to prove:

1. He was handicapped. This was not in dispute.
2. He otherwise qualified for the tenancy. There was no dispute as the tenant met all other criteria for tenancy in the building.
3. Because of his disability, it is necessary for him to keep the pet in order to use and enjoy the apartment.
4. Reasonable accommodations can be made to allow him to keep the pet.

As to the third criterion, the court said that the tenant had to demonstrate he had an emotional and psychological dependence on the cat, requiring him to keep it in his apartment. He submitted affidavits of his treating psychiatrist, his clinical social worker, and a certified pet-assisted therapist, all describing his mental illness, the course of his treatment, and that he received therapeutic benefits from the cat. The landlord, however, submitted an affidavit of a psychiatrist who had seen the tenant twice, who concluded that there was "no significant clinical evidence that the cat is necessary or required for LeBoo [the tenant] to be able to fully use and enjoy his apartment." Because of this disagreement between the experts, there was a triable issue of fact.[236] Although this book is focused on dogs, *LeBoo* indicates that a cat, serving as an emotional support animal rather than as a service animal, may have sufficient significance in the life of a mentally ill tenant to require an exception to a building's no-pets policy.[237]

Stores have also been taken to task for attempting to keep out psychiatric service animals that help handlers with post-traumatic stress disorder.[238]

## DOGS AND AUTISM

Dogs have been trained to keep autistic children close to their parents and to prevent children from running into traffic. In a double leash and belt system widely used in parts of Canada (see Figure 15), the autistic child is attached to the dog by a leash fastened to the child's belt or halter. The parent, holding a separate leash attached to the dog, gives the dog commands to go forward (in a straight line), turn left or right, or stop. On reaching a curb, the dog will brace itself to slow the child down and stop him from going off the sidewalk.[239] Golden and Labrador Retrievers are preferred because of their stable personalities, physical size, and tractability. Dogs are trained for a year or more to learn this two-leash arrangement and are placed with families when they reach 18 to 24 months of age.

A Canadian research group studied the integration of service dogs into ten families with an autistic child.[240] They noted that propensities, such as bolting, irritability, or meltdowns, often prevent families from traveling or even engaging in everyday activities such as shopping.

> The primary function of a service dog in the context of autism is child safety. The dog must be able to resist a child's attempt to bolt. The child is attached to the dog via a leash and belt system, and the dog responds to commands from the parent (handler) to proceed or stop. If the child tries to bolt or move dangerously (e.g., walking off the sidewalk), the dog will resist by using its weight to brace against the child, slowing or stopping movement, which gives the parent walking behind the child time to intervene.

Walking beside the dog also allows a child to regulate his or her pace, so that taking a walk became more pleasant for the whole family. The attention the family received from people in public was much more positive.

A dog also provides a second set of eyes even around the home. Most of the families in the study preferred to have the service dog sleep on the child's bed or in the child's room. One parent said:

> Definitely [the dog]'s there as the bed buddy, you know, and to alert us of issues though the night rather than us lie there with one eye open, both ears . . . and I can get a sounder sleep and that's helped out immeasurably. I remember the first time we brought the dog home, it was the first time in nine years our son slept through the night.

Safety was not the only advantage of a service dog, however, as the dog provides stimulus and play for the child.

> Parents reported a wide variety of physical tasks that were facilitated by the dog's participation. One child learned how to take the lid off a dog food container, pour the food into the dog's bowl, place the bowl on the floor, and look at the parent to give the dog a command to eat the food. A number of children learned how to pick up and throw a ball for their dog. Motor func-

tion improvements were gained by the parents sitting with the child and helping him/her learn how to pet the dog. Many of the children struggled to control their movements to pet the dog, and by using the dog as a therapeutic tool the parents were able to teach the children to pet or caress the dogs gently. Children learned to throw a ball and manipulate grooming tools.

Some families found that an effect of the service dog was to allow for the possibility of vacations.

> One family visited Disney World because the presence of the dog meant their daughter could cope with the long car ride to Florida, and was able to take in the new environment without being overwhelmed. Other families reported that ferryboat rides, airplane flights, weekends spent at a cottage (cabin), and hotel stays were all more manageable with the assistance of the service dog. For many of these parents, sending their child to day camps or overnight camps with the dog was the first step in giving themselves some respite from the constant demands of care for their child.

The Canadian team found that no parent reported a decline in the autistic child's behavior as a result of having a service dog.

Autism Service Dogs of America (ASDA), a non-profit organization that provides trained dogs to children with autism, argues that a dog helps a child with socialization, and should accompany the child at all times when the child leaves home, including going to school. ASDA says that the presence of the dog calms the child and reduces outbursts.[241] ASDA describes two phases of training a service dog for an autistic child:

> The first phase of training, requires the primary caregiver ( the individual who will handle the dog when the child is tethered to the dog) to travel to ASDA headquarters in Oregon, spend 7 days in daily training, and 6 evenings alone with the service dog establishing a relationship, a positive bond with the service dog. The dog then returns with the primary caregiver to its new home where the dog will spend 2 weeks making the adjustment to his/her new home and becoming a family member. Both dog and family need 2 weeks to get to know each other. No in-pack training, work or tethering is done during this time. The second phase begins after the two-week adjustment period. At that time the trainer arrives and begins the tethering process, learns the family's and child's routine, and visits the environments of the child (park, school, stores, etc.), assisting and guiding the primary caregiver (dog handler) and child navigate these environments. This phase is important because the specific needs of the child and family are assessed, and the service the dog will provide is fine-tuned to meet the specific needs of the child and family.

Figure 15. Two-leash System for Autism Service Dogs. Permission National Service Dogs, Cambridge, Ontario.

Wilderwood Service Dogs, a service dog training organization, lists autistic symptoms and specific reactions dogs can be trained to have to the symptoms:

- *Impulsive running.* The dog retrieves the child to a parent.
- *PICA (impulsive eating of non-food items such as dirt, chalk, coffee grounds, cleaning chemicals, feces, soap, etc.).* The dog interrupts the behavior.
- *Self-stimulation (slapping the face, etc.)* and self harming. The dog interrupts the behavior.
- *Mood swings.* The dog crawls onto the child's lap and calms him.
- *Night awakenings.* The dog barks to alert the parents.
- *Refusal to speak.* The dog maintains eye contact when child tries to

speak and responds to verbal commands; other people may engage with the child by paying attention to the dog.[242]

More tasks could undoubtedly be demonstrated for dogs working with autistic children. Service dogs assigned to autistic children may sometimes become sufficiently stressed that they become a danger to the child or to other children. This issue is discussed below in the section on ethical issues of service dog work.

## ALZHEIMER'S SERVICE DOGS

In Israel, a social worker and a dog trainer worked with a Shorthair Border Collie named Polly to train her as a guide dog for Yehuda, a 62-year-old man with Alzheimer's. Polly walks everywhere with Yehuda. If Yehuda forgets where he is, all he has to do is say "Home" and Polly will take him home. The Israeli team notes that Alzheimer's guide dogs do not need to walk as close to their handlers as guide dogs for the blind must do, but they do have to have a good sense of direction.[243]

Therapy dogs have also been introduced into populations of Alzheimer's patients to good effect, as will be discussed in the chapter below on therapy dogs.[244] Individuals who have long since forgotten the names of loved ones are, according to anecdotal reports, often able to remember the name of a favorite dog.

## DEGREES OF MENTAL ILLNESS AND
## SERVICE DOG CATEGORIZATION

The Department of Housing and Urban Development specifies that to require a landlord to make a reasonable accommodation for an animal in a no-pets building, the individual should have a condition recognized by mental health professionals as a diagnosis under the latest version of the *Diagnostic and Statistical Manual.* The other federal agencies have not been as specific, in part because of the privacy issues that provide something of a barrier to inquiries about an individual's disability. As previously discussed, the Department of Justice defines a disability as a physical or mental impairment that substantially limits one or more of the major life activities. Whether this kind of language actually helps businesses determine the access rights of an individual may be doubted. This issue will be discussed in the chapter below on federal legislation and major issues considered by regulatory agencies.

## DISTINGUISHING PSYCHIATRIC SERVICE
## FROM EMOTIONAL SUPPORT

Three federal agencies have, in rulemaking after 2007 spent considerable space in the *Federal Register* dealing with the question of what rights attach to individuals who own or use animals to help them with mental disabilities. The agencies are the Department of Justice, which provides general public accommodation access rules, the Department of Housing, which has three sets or rules applicable to various types of housing situations, and the Department of Transportation, which provides rules regarding air carrier and cruise line access. In addition, some states have looked at this issue, while others have not.

While none of the federal agencies argue that a dog that helps an autistic child by alerting his parents to a dangerous situation would not meet access standards for service animals, there is more confusion concerning a dog whose function is to have an effect on a mental condition by alleviating the condition or a symptom of that condition. This would include, for instance, a dog that keeps a dissociated individual grounded in the here and now. Such dogs are sometimes called emotional support animals, but because emotional support may involve comforting individuals without diagnosed psychiatric conditions, the better term is psychiatric service animal. This distinction has been correctly made by the Department of Justice, which does not grant any access to an animal whose sole function is emotional support, yet acknowledges that a dog whose presence calms an individual with a psychiatric condition is "doing work" of a sort that can justify its categorization as a service animal. The Departments of Housing and Transportation have been open to distinguishing emotional support animals from pets as far as access to transportation and public housing is concerned, but have been less clear about distinguishing psychiatric service animals from emotional support animals.

## ETHICAL ISSUES OF SERVICE DOG WORK

A study of guide dog users and their dogs looked at whether the fact that guide dogs form bonds with one set of individuals before they are assigned to a blind person (usually a foster family,[245] then a training facility) disturbed the dog's ability to form a bond with a human. Guide dogs have a rather unusual upbringing, "chopped-up lives," as one critic noted.[246] A protocol introduced by some guide dog training facilities involves bringing future guide dogs to the facility for veterinary testing and overnight visits even before dogs start the programs, which is designed to habituate the dogs to unfamiliar people and the facility's routines. The study found that despite these aspects of their upbringing, guide dogs form intense bonds with their blind owners.[247] Some organizations that lease service dogs to users require that the dogs be periodically inspected by a veterinarian for signs of stress, abuse, or neglect.[248] Ideally, foster families should live in an environment similar to the location the ultimate user lives, and perhaps should even receive visits from that user.

It must also be acknowledged that guide dogs pay a price for living so close to a single individual. The most challenging aspect of owning a service dog is usually caring for it.[249] Nevertheless, as a professor at the Hebrew University in Jerusalem has noted, dogs seem "able to transfer their social needs onto humans, and some of the prolonged training can arguably be an advantage, providing important (and pleasurable) mental stimulation to these dogs."[250] Also, becoming a service dog may save some dogs' lives. In North Carolina, dogs impounded that are not redeemed are to be donated to a non-profit agency engaged in training service dogs, on the agency's request.[251]

Dogs assigned to autistic children may encounter stress as a result of frequent or constant contact with the child. They may be kept in a school during the day without sufficient breaks to relieve themselves. A child that wakes frequently or is often unsettled may prevent the dog from getting enough sleep.

> Children with autism often exhibit "meltdowns" or aggressive behavior. This behavior was often directed at the dog because it was the closest target for the child's anger. Some of the more aggressive children would hit or thrash out at the dog, startling the dog and causing the dog to move away from the source of physical abuse. Fortunately, the dogs developed a learned sense of when to move in to distract or comfort the child and when to move away to avoid the child's anger.[252]

I, as a lawyer, was contacted concerning a teacher at a school which allowed an autistic boy to bring a service dog to classes. The dog seemed well adjusted at first, but became progressively more nervous over time. The child dragged the dog around but did not pet or otherwise interact with it. The parents were described as having unrealistic expectations regarding the effect the dog would have on their child, but seemed unwilling to provide any safety net for the dog. Schools allowing dogs to accompany children with disabilities such as autism should insist on the ability to have direct contact with the organization that supplied the service dog and to request an evaluation of the situation by such an organization. Other children could be put at risk if the dog becomes sufficiently stressed.

Both in service dog training and in training other skilled dogs, concerns have been raised about whether some regulation of trainers is appropriate. Guide dog training schools in California must be approved, but most other trainers only need a business license. As one commenter noted:

> Trainers are not required to have any health assessment skills, and they are not bound by a code of ethics. . . . There is no organized, validated educational system available for a person to learn to train service dogs; trainers either teach themselves or apprentice with someone else. . . . The medical community should . . . more closely examine the current unregulated service dog supply system and demand that valid mechanisms for quality control, practitioner expertise, and professional ethics be initiated to protect the consumer. The training and provision of service dogs is not just a dog training issue, it is a health care issue.

These remarks, made by Susan Duncan of the National Service Dog Center in Renton, Washington, were written in 1996.[253] Regulation of the industry is easily imagined at the state level, and the best solution may ultimately be to draft a uniform code that could be adopted by states as is true of other uniform laws.

# Chapter 5

# THERAPY DOGS AND THE
# THERAPY DOG MOVEMENT

A girl confined to an adolescent psychiatric ward writes in her journal:

*Graham, you are my best friend and I hope to keep it that way. I would like to be a normal 16 year old. What I was trying to tell you was I wish I had a family that I can call my own, having a mother and father that loves me and doesn't abuse me. I would like it if I got to go on a date with a guy that loves me and really cares about me. What I really wanted was a family that didn't sexually abuse me, physically abuse me, and verbally abuse me. I didn't want to be raised in foster homes, group homes, shelters, and then a drug shelter. I just wanted to be the one that got cared for and when I needed something very important they would be there to get it for me. So, do you understand where I'm coming from?*

The conversation the girl imagines is not with a friend, nor with a psychologist or a nurse, but with a two-year-old cocker spaniel named Graham. Graham's interactions with residents of the ward were the subject of a handler's thesis submitted to the University of Florida by a nurse, Norine Bardill.[254]

One of the first psychologists to study the uses of dogs in psychotherapy began his research in the 1960s when a boy arrived early for an appointment and the psychologist did not have time to take his dog into another room, as had been his practice. The boy, uncommunicative for many sessions, began telling the dog his problems. The psychologist, Boris Levinson, wrote several papers and a book about his experiences, and became one of the founders of what, in psychology and other medical literature, has come to be called animal-assisted therapy.[255]

Dogs have been found to reduce anxiety among children and adolescents about being in therapy, improve rapport between a patient and a therapist, provide comfort, allow children to nurture, and serve as models of relationships with other people and animals.[256] Although they are not judgmental or critical the way people may be of other people, they do react to us, and a child or adolescent that plays roughly with a dog may find that the dog tries to leave him. Children want the dog's attention, and they alter the tones of their voices, their gestures, and the games they play in order to keep the dog from going away. The child teaches himself to play nicely in order to receive the reward of the dog's attention, rather than just obeying a command of a parent or teacher the child may resent.[257]

Two major therapy dog organizations were formed in the 1970s. Therapy Dogs International, Inc. was formed in 1976 by Elaine Smith. The first visit occurred the same year with five handlers and six dogs, all but one of which was a German Shepherd.[258] Delta Foundation was formed in 1977 in Portland, Oregon, with Dr. Leo K. Bustad as its first president. I grew up in Pullman, Washington, a few houses away from where Dr. Bustad lived. Dr. Bustad, who became dean of the veterinary school at Washington State, was a frequent guest in our house, particularly at parties my parents gave for the foreign students who could not go home during holidays when there were no classes. In 1981, the organization's name was changed to Delta Society. Dr. Bustad wrote many of the seminal articles on animal-assisted therapy[259] and also founded the People-Pet Partnership at Washington State University.[260]

Therapy dogs are usually privately owned pets that have received behavioral training to provide comfort to individuals in institutional settings, including hospital, nursing and retirement homes, mental institutions, schools, facilities for autistic and abused children, halfway houses for prisoners, and other environments that are not places such as visiting individuals who have been through stressful situations such as natural disasters. The benefits of therapy dogs have been found to be universal and probably derive in part from the physical contact with another being.

It is not the scientific background, however, which explains the phenomenal growth of therapy dog teams in the United States. Many people have taken their dogs to obedience classes with the intention of taking one of the certification tests for therapy dog status without ever knowing anything about the scientific support for what they are doing. They may have read an article in a local paper. Pictures of therapy dogs can be very cute, even too cute. Many people taking the tests know someone else who has taken it before them. It seems like such a good idea and they intuitively feel that their dog will make other people feel better. They are not always correct in these hunches.

There are at least 30,000 therapy dogs registered with the three major therapy dog organizations, Delta Society, Therapy Dogs International, and Therapy Dogs, Inc. There are probably 20,000 more registered with local or regional organizations. There arc also a great many dogs that visit facilities of one sort or another despite the fact the dog has never taken a test or registered with a therapy dog organization. Informal relationships like these are, however, giving way to a preference by institutions to accept only dogs certified by established organizations. This concern arises for only one reason, insurance. The major organizations carry insurance to cover up to $1 million or $2 million per incident.[261]

There is a hunger for therapy dogs. When I began to look in Phoenix for places to take Chloe, I met a couple that was volunteering at a read-to-a-dog program at a library in Glendale. The couple was moving to San Diego and said the library was desperate to find a replacement for them. They were right. The library was extremely happy to find a replacement. Soon there was a poster of me with Chloe in the lobby of the library. "Come read to Chloe." The poster brought questions. It brought business. The same was true of the Sahuaro Ranch Elementary School in Glendale, Arizona. Chloe was only the second therapy dog to visit, and we began going every other week. The school is looking for more therapy dogs. There are more pictures of Chloe in the yearbook than there are of any teacher.

It is gratifying to take your dog on a walk with the red therapy dog bandana (supplied by Therapy Dogs International), or wearing her vest (supplied by Hospice of the Valley). People, at least dog people, notice.

"Is that a therapy dog?"

"Yes, she is."

"What's her name? Can I pet her?"

"Yes. That's what she's for."

"Do you take her to a hospital?"

My wife tells me I "puff up and beam" during these conversations. Of course. Who wouldn't?

That is why it is a movement. There are so many people doing it for so many reasons, but there is also a good deal of science behind it.

## TERMINOLOGY OF ANIMAL THERAPY

Depending on the environment and the approach or intervention used, a number of terms and descriptions have been applied to therapy work with animals. Terms sometimes used include:

- Pet therapy
- Pet psychotherapy
- Pet-facilitated therapy
- Pet-facilitated psychotherapy

- Four-footed therapy
- Animal-assisted therapy
- Animal-facilitated counseling
- Pet-mediated therapy
- Pet-oriented psychotherapy
- Companion-animal therapy
- Co-therapy with an animal.[262]

The most general term in this taxonomy is probably animal-assisted intervention, which means that some benefit is sought from the presence of an animal in a situation.[263] One group of authors at a conference on animal behavior and welfare divided animal-assisted interventions into three subgroups:

1. Animal-assisted therapy (AAT)
2. Animal-assisted activities (AAA)
3. Animal-assisted education (AAE).

They further divided AAA into passive situations, e.g., with residential animals, and active programs, where animals are brought to institutions and individuals for the benefits of a visit.

A person giving AAT is a psychologist, psychiatrist, or other professional trained in delivering a therapeutic modality where animals can be incorporated into a treatment plan. Most of the therapy dog movement, however, fits into the active AAA category. In AAA situations, professionals may be present, but the animal is interacting directly with the individual or population, often with only a handler present. The handler will have generally been certified to work with a therapy animal, most often a dog but sometimes a horse or other animal, but may have little knowledge of human psychology. Arguably the term "therapy dog" claims rather too much. Two leading figures in the field of animals and therapy have argued that "the term *animal-assisted therapy* continues to be applied to an array of programs that would not qualify as therapy in any scientific or medical sense of the word."[264] Although therapy dogs are probably not often providing therapy, it must also be admitted that things can be, in common parlance, therapeutic without being formal therapies. In any case, the term therapy dog has entered the culture at a level where it is likely to remain in use.

Although there have been rigorous scientific studies concerning the beneficial effects of animals in traditional therapeutic situations as well as from visitation programs, there is something of a prejudice against this research. One author has called this resistance a "furry ceiling," noting that the more established psychology journals still shy away from the topic.[265] It has also been noted that there are particular difficulties in conducting research on animal-assisted interventions, including costs for:

1. Housing, food, management, vaccinations, and other veterinary care.
2. Training the animals for their assignments and maintenance expenses.
3. Suitable locations, particularly if larger animals, such as horses, are involved.
4. Additional personnel, such as trainers and handlers
5. Expensive insurance policies, particularly where insurance companies see risks that are probably not very significant.[266]

Funding may be more difficult to obtain because of the same "furry ceiling" attitudes that make it difficult to get research published in the more prestigious scientific periodicals.

Therapy dogs are of every breed and every type of mixed breed. Although some facilities may discourage owners of therapy pit bulls or Rottweilers, even these breeds are well represented among dogs visiting facilities. Individuals obtaining dogs with the purpose of making them into therapy dogs might consider that some dogs have more of a teddy bear quality than others, but personal preferences should not be ignored either. Therapy dogs encounter people who are not "dog people" and the dog must not react aggressively towards people who run at them and reach over them in ways that experienced dog handlers would never do. Thus, breeds that react to human aggression with strong avoidance or aggressive responses must be trained to avoid such behaviors. One study that looked at the responsiveness of different breeds to aggressive approaches by humans found that certain breeds are more likely to respond with aggression than others.[267]

## POPULATIONS WHERE THE BENEFITS OF DOG VISITATIONS HAVE BEEN DEMONSTRATED

Various theories have been advanced for why dogs are therapeutic. Many of these ideas are rather philosophical, speaking of the collective unconscious, the need to keep contact with our animal roots, etc. No one really knows. Petting animals made 74 percent of nursing home patients feel better.[268] Therapy dogs have been found to have beneficial effects on a number of populations (see Figure 16).[269] Although the studies discussed in this section sometimes involved one of the variants of animal therapy, there is less research here than is needed. Consequently, some studies reviewed are based on interactions between people and their pets. It might be objected

Figure 16. Therapy Dog with School Children. Courtesy, parents and teachers of United Cerebral Palsy of Ulster County. Photo by Frances Breitkopf; permissions obtained by Susan Krogstad-Hill, Educational Director.

that these studies have limited validity to periodic visitations involving therapy animals, and this limitation must be accepted as a weakness in drawing conclusions from the research.

## PAIN MANAGEMENT

Adults and children in a Midwest regional hospital were asked to describe their reactions to animal-assisted therapy in which they were visited by a dog, which would usually get on a patient's bed.[270] Relaxation was a frequent theme: *"Shortly into the visit it was clear to me that this was more than a social visit. I saw [my son] slowly start to relax and calm down. His breathing became deeper and his face and body relaxed."* Pain reduction was commonly noted. A parent wrote concerning a therapy dog's visit:

The [handler] asked him, do you feel any pain? The dog's neck started to twitch, my son said "some in my neck." [The dog] moved his front leg. My son said it hurt some in his shoulder too. Then [the handler] took the dog off the bed. [The dog] seemed to be tired and weak. The man laid him on the floor and massaged the dog and rubbed him down. My son's pain was gone. I have never seen anything like this before.

A teenager described how a dog's visits made him feel:

I was injured in a snowboarding accident. I ruptured my spleen and lacerated the bottom third of my kidney. I met [the dog] for the first time on Friday, the day after my surgery, when I was hurting a lot. [The dog] took away all of the pain. The next visit I started to bond with [the dog]. She got into me quicker. She started to take away the pain faster. I felt a draining feeling when she was lying there, like she was draining away all the pain. My stomach unclenched and my whole body cooled down. When she wasn't there I could think about her and the pain would go away. Each time she started taking the pain away faster. The last visit she got into me in ten seconds. I think that [the dog] is better than Tylenol® with codeine because she takes the pain away better and works faster.

Relatives and friends of patients who receive visits from therapy dogs often notice the effect the dogs have: *"I see a change in him when [the dog] comes to visit. His nausea lessened, he relaxed and his attitude changed for the better. The two of them seem to be quite comfortable with each other."*

[My son's] spirits were deflated, he was angry with the news he had just received and he was tired of being poked with needles. He was instantly comforted by [the dog] when she laid by him in bed. The smile on his face was such a welcome sight.

[The dog] lay on [my son's] arm to get comfortable and close. [The handler] told [my son] to close his eyes and think about [the dog] and leave everything else go. Take a deep breath. [The dog] was breathing the same time as my son. [My son] immediately became relaxed and said his left leg was feeling warm from his foot up to his knee. Then after he and [the dog] laid together for about 5 more minutes, he said his whole body felt relaxed and warm.

Descriptions of the breathing of the patient and the dog beginning to coincide were fairly common, as were descriptions of the dog giving the patient more energy.

## EFFECTS ON THE IMMUNE SYSTEM

Higher levels of Immunoglobulin A have been correlated with less frequent illness and less susceptibility to upper respiratory infection. One study found increases in Immunoglobulin A from petting dogs for 18 minutes. A control group of individuals, who did not pet a dog but were comfortably seated to induce relaxation, did not register an increase in Immunoglobulin A. The research team also discovered that petting a stuffed animal had the same chemical effect, but the researchers acknowledged that the subjects may have found the situation humorous, which may have affected the results.[271]

## CHILDREN WITH HEART PROBLEMS

For children who are severely ill and cut off from their everyday lives, a visit from a dog has been called a liaison with hope.[272] Pet visits were found to relieve stress for children in a pediatric cardiology unit in The Hospital for Sick Children in Toronto.[273] A research team at the hospital noted that human love and comfort must be earned but pets offer a source of comfort that can be scheduled in almost any quantity.

> The animal accepts without condition, loving without care or consideration, regardless of illness, deformity, or disability, offering security in that love and giving both child and parent a sense of empowerment in a sometimes overwhelming environment. For children, pet visitation is also thought to reduce separation anxiety and offer a pleasant diversion from anxiety-provoking treatments. Interaction with the animal helps reinforce the child's sense of self-concept in the face of the adult therapist, who is perceived as an authority figure.

The researchers described a visiting dog as a receptacle for the projection of feelings of fear, pain, and anxiety. "The pet becomes a pillar of support and a source of strength, psychological sustenance, and optimism." There were several dogs involved and the researchers believed that the presence of two dogs was useful in giving the child a pet to interact with while his parents interacted with another dog. One patient said of a dog that "he has a love me look that makes you feel needed."[274]

## BLOOD PRESSURE AND HYPERTENSION

Blood pressure of 38 children from 9 to 15 years old was measured while they rested silently, as well as when they read aloud either to a researcher with a dog or to a researcher without a dog. Average mean arterial, systolic, and diastolic blood pressures were lower for children reading when the dog was present.[275] A study of 5,741 people in Australia found that pet owners had significantly lower systolic blood pressure, but not diastolic blood pressure, and significantly lower plasma triglyceride levels and plasma cholesterol levels compared to people who did not own pets.[276]

One study looked at the blood pressure of stockbrokers who were taking lisinopril, an ACE inhibitor.[277] Although lisinopril lowers resting blood pressure, it does not diminish blood pressure or heart rate responses during stressful tasks. Stockbrokers who owned pets, however, had lowered blood pressure in response to stressful tasks. The researchers concluded that "the presence of pets provided the kind of social support that is critical to buffering physiological responses to stress."[278]

## HEART ATTACKS

In one of the first quantitative studies of the effects of pets, it was found that pet owners were more likely to be alive one year after discharge from a coronary care unit than non-owners. Only 5.7 percent of 53 pet owners died in that period, while 28.2 percent of 39 patients who did not own pets died. Since the researchers considered that walking the dogs might explain this increased survival rate, they also looked at owners of pets other than dogs and found their survival rate was also higher. Being married or living with others, on the other hand, were not significant predictors of survival.[279]

## STROKE VICTIMS

A study of stroke victims, all men who had lost speaking ability from left-hemisphere strokes, found that traditional speech-language therapy and animal-assisted therapy were equally effective, but that patients who received animal-assisted therapy were more motivated, enjoyed the therapy sessions more, and found the sessions less stressful compared with traditional therapy sessions.[280]

## CANCER

Researchers in Carrara, Italy, compared two groups of patients receiving chemotherapy, one group receiving visitations by therapy dogs and one group that did not. It may not have been surprising that the patients receiving therapy dog visitations were less depressed during chemotherapy, but it was also found that this group demonstrated higher arterial oxygen saturation.[281]

## ANXIETY

Dogs are very effective at reducing anxiety. Just how effective was demonstrated by a study of 230 hospitalized psychiatric patients who were given either a single animal-assisted therapy session or a single regularly scheduled therapeutic recreation session.[282] Statistically significant reductions in anxiety were found after the animal-assisted therapy (AAT) session in patients with psychotic disorders, mood disorders, and other disorders, though statistically significant reductions in anxiety were found only with patients suffering from mood disorders after the recreational session. This means that AAT is more effective for a broader range of patients than certain other well-established therapies used in institutional settings. In the group sessions involving the therapy dog in this study, the dog's handler was present and the sessions lasted about half an hour. The handler talked about the dog, which moved freely about the room. The recreational sessions, against which the AAT sessions were compared, involved about the same number of people and involved discussions and presentations. The anxiety levels of patients were determined by a short report that each patient filled out.

Therapy dogs have been used to relax patients the day preceding surgery. A woman about to undergo a coronary artery bypass graft was visited by two therapy dogs the night before the surgery. She later said that she survived surgery because of the visit. "Visiting with the therapy dogs the night before surgery reminded me that I needed to get better to get home to take care of my own animals."[283] Another study found that children awaiting dental procedures were measurably less anxious when there was a dog present before the arrival of the dentist.[284] Children undergoing physical examinations have been found to have lower behavioral measures of distress if a therapy dog was present.[285]

People do not need to be in mental hospitals or facing surgery to have anxiety reduced by a dog. Three researchers looked at 120 couples, half of which had a single pet, a cat or a dog, and half of which did not. None took cardiovascular medications and all had normal blood pressure less than 140/90. Each non-pet owning participant was asked to identify a same-sex close friend who could participate in the experiment. Couples were recruited through radio announcements and each participant received $25 for participation. A room in the house of each couple was used for the testing procedures, usually a den, living or family room, or library.[286]

Heart rate and blood pressure were recorded once a minute throughout the experiment. After a baseline was established with the participant resting for ten minutes, participants listened to tape-recorded instructions about how to perform a task. In one test, the participant was told to subtract three from a four-digit number (1,000 or greater) sequentially for five minutes. Thus, the participant was to say: "1,000, 997, 994, 991, 988. . . ." The other task involved putting a hand in ice water. After each task, there was a 15-minute rest period. The potential source of support, pet, spouse, or friend, was in the room from the beginning of the experimenter's visit. The experimenter remained behind and out of sight of the participant when the task was being performed. The dog or cat could roam the room freely. The spouse and/or friend sat on a sofa approximately three feet away from the participant and at a 90 degree angle. The participants, spouses, and friends were told that the experiment was about "social support and reactions to stress" and that they could be supportive. Women had higher heart rates than men during the math task, and the presence of a spouse was more likely to *increase* heart rate and blood pressure reactions among all participants. However, pet owners had lower heart rate and blood pressure readings than non-pet owners during the math task. Pet owners also returned to normal readings more quickly than non-pet owners. Pet owners had significantly lower blood pressure during the ice water task. Here also the presence of a spouse raised blood pressure and heart rate, but the presence of a dog or cat significantly reduced this effect. The researchers concluded that pets buffer reactions to acute stress and diminish perceptions of stress. One result that was not explained was that pet owners were faster than non-owners at the mental arithmetic.

It seems that spouses can be bad for your heart but pets are good for it.

## Patients Awaiting Electroconvulsive Therapy (ECT)

Patients awaiting electroconvulsive therapy treatments were, on some days, giving a 15-minute visit with a therapy dog, and on other days 15 minutes with magazines. Tests indicated that the sessions with the dog significantly reduced fear, though the effect on anxiety was not as clear. There was no measurable effect on depression.[287]

## EDUCATIONAL ENVIRONMENTS

It has been argued that children improve their non-verbal communication abilities when interacting with dogs, and learn to send clearer messages to the dogs and to other children, while also understanding better the messages given by others. This reduces the risks of misinterpreting the meanings of others, and reduces the tendency to react aggressively. There is, in other words, a connection between empathy with animals and empathy with people.[288]

Studies conducted in Austria found that putting dogs in classrooms of elementary school children reduced aggressiveness and hyperactivity.[289] It has been demonstrated that interaction with dogs reduces both direct aggression, bullying, and "relational" aggression, spreading mean rumors or purposeful-ly excluding a child from a group.[290] The social benefits of having dogs in the classroom were greatest if the dogs were actually involved in classroom activ-ities, as opposed to just being at the back of the class and available for inter-action during breaks. The dogs were involved in classroom activities in var-ious ways. For instance, the children might be asked to draw a card which would show an activity to be undertaken, such as petting a dog, throwing a ball to it, brushing it, walking around it, etc. This finding could be significant for classrooms where autistic children are allowed to bring their dogs into a classroom.

Not all dogs are right for being with children. It is best to use animals that have an energy level similar to that of the children they will be with. Similarly, not all children should be with animals. Aside from children that are allergic to animals, children that are aggressive have been seen to try to harm visiting dogs. This can make the dog shy away from children for months or longer. Unfortunately, teachers do not want to deprive any children of the experience of being with a dog, but the dog handler has to be concerned about the dog as well, and not all children are raised to respect animals.

## Children with Attention Deficit/Hyperactivity Disorder

Research published in 2009 concerned students at a special school whose purpose was to facilitate the transition of students back to a classroom in a regular school.[291] Of the 30 students in the school, 22 had parental consent to participate in a program involving a therapy dog, though the final study only looked at statistics involving 17 children. All but one of the children had attention-deficit/hyperactivity disorder, and one was diagnosed with opposi-tional defiant disorder (ODD). Several of those with ADHD also had ODD and one had mental retardation. Most of the children lived in a household with a dog.

Children were tested for 15 minutes on each of two test days. Systolic blood pressure (SBP), diastolic blood pressure (DBP), and heart rate (HR) were measured at the end of each five-minute period during the 15 minute sessions. The dog was placed on a child's lap for the first five minutes but the child was not told how to interact with the dog, a 13 pound, four-year-old blonde female Shi-Tzu.

The researchers found that DBP significantly increased while children held the dog and SBP significantly increased during the interval that fol-lowed holding the dog. HR, on the other hand, decreased both when the children held the dog and following that. The researchers interpreted the increase in blood pressure as a response to a positive stimulus. They noted that their results seemed to differ from those of the study of children during

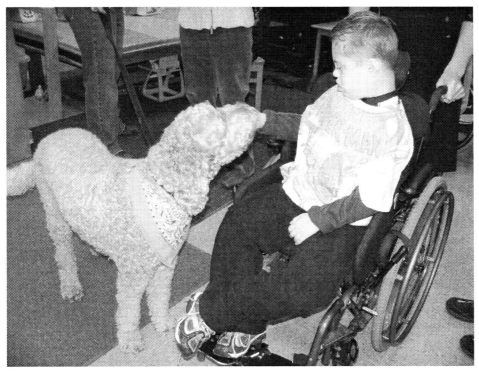

Figure 17. Therapy Dog Visiting a Child at the School of United Cerebral Palsy of Ulster County. Photo by Frances Breitkopf; permissions obtained by Susan Krogstad-Hill, Educational Director.

a physical examination.[292] They pointed out that in this study, the children were not encountering the dog in a stressful situation. Also, the children with ADHD could have been reacting somewhat differently. This is an area deserving of further study.

Therapy dogs often visit special schools and special needs classes (see Figure 17).

## VICTIMS OF SEXUAL ASSAULT AND ABUSE

Sexual assault and rape are often followed by post-traumatic stress disorder ("PTSD"), with three principal symptoms:

1. Re-experiencing the traumatic event in nightmares and flashbacks.
2. Persistent avoidance of trauma-related stimuli (including memories and feelings) and a numbing of general responsiveness.
3. Increased physiological arousal.

While many woman overcome these symptoms, a high proportion do not show much improvement and many refuse to seek help. A team of therapists at Widener University in Wilmington, Delaware, designed a treatment program specifically to incorporate therapy dogs into treating these patients.[293] These researchers noted that when a patient interacts with or cares for an animal, the patients sees herself as capable and nurturing, and that survivors of sexual assaults should be encouraged to care for animals outside of therapy sessions. Victims of sexual assault often fear to travel, lose their sense of independence and become less likely to meet new people and maintain friendships. Walking dogs can get them out of the house and increase their sense of security.

Adults who were sexually abused as children have sometimes reported that the only supportive entity in their childhood was a pet.[294] Having had an animal they were close to may also portend less anger and better adaptation for survivors as adults.[295]

## Testimony Dogs

A piece posted as a video on CNN described a dog named Dory that helps children to testify. The piece showed the dog with a girl who had been abused by her grandfather. The girl's mother had not known about this until she read the girl's diary and told the police. The girl was afraid to testify but was comforted by the dog lying at her feet while she was in the witness box. A judge noted that people are allowed to have service dogs in the witness box.[296] The dog was more of a therapy dog, given that it went from one child witness to another. Programs providing therapy dog support for children during testimony have been adopted by courts in a number of states,[297] including California, Colorado, Florida, Idaho, Maryland, Michigan, Mississippi,[298] Texas, and Washington.[299]

A group that advocates the use of therapy dogs in courtroom settings has posted a sample brief for arguing that a dog should be able to accompany a child witness on the stand. The case law cited in the brief relates to stuffed animals and dolls accompanying children while testifying. The analogy is a fairly good one as some research has indicated that petting a dog and petting a stuffed animal can produce similar physiological effects.[300] The organization recommends avoiding use of the term "therapy dog" in the courtroom context.

> Avoid using the term "therapy dog" because the use of this term may create grounds for a mistrial or raise an issue on appeal. . . . A defense attorney could argue that the use of the term "therapy dog" by the judge or the prosecutor implies to the jury that the witness is in fact a victim in need of ther-

apy and could be construed as a comment on the evidence. It is up to the jury to decide if the witness was victimized by the defendant.

The group points out that the presence of the dog can also help defense counsel elicit testimony from a child on cross-examination, which may work for the defendant.[301]

A recent review of the law applicable to comfort objects used by minors while testifying argues that "sound reasons exist for allowing the use of service dogs in court, but only in cases where the witness can demonstrate a truly compelling need for the emotional support and only where the proper balancing of defendants' rights is performed."[302] In this analysis, Marianne Dellinger notes that opponents to the use of testimony dogs may argue that the association of the witness with a cute dog may send a message to the trier of fact of the child's innocence and need for protection. Dellinger analogizes the use of a service dog to testimony of a child holding a doll, which has been approved in judicial opinions.[303] As for defendants' rights, Dellinger notes that lawyers or judges could ask jurors about their willingness to disregard the presence of a service dog during testimony of a witness, and a jury instruction could indicate that the presence of the dog should not be considered by the jury in considering the testimony of a witness. The dog and the witness might be required to enter the witness box without the jury present so that the jury would not even see the dog. There might even have to be proof that a witness would be unable to testify without the presence of the service dog.

It has also been suggested that the presence of therapy dogs could help mediate disputes outside of the courtroom.[304]

## ALZHEIMER'S PATIENTS

Dogs are used in animal-assisted interactions and therapy situations with Alzheimer's patients. Despite losing the use of language, non-verbal communication has been found to be similar to that of individuals without dementia. Patients remain responsive to touch, facial expression, voice, tone, and posture. Social skills may be maintained even when there is significant loss of cognition. Patients can still have fun, laugh, and play. Activities are often best if kept simple and limited to 20 or 30 minutes. Two researchers at a nursing home in Cincinnati, Ohio, conducted pet therapy sessions at a unit with 18 patients.[305] The researchers found that the pet therapy sessions provided some physical exercise as the patients walked the dogs up and down the hallway on a leash, and even chair-bound patients leaned forward to brush, stroke, and feed a dog. The patients hugged, stroked, smiled at, and talked to the dogs. The researchers found the sessions also increased patient-to-patient and patient-to-staff interactions. The nursing staff said the patients were calmer during and shortly after the sessions.

## BENEFITS FOR THE ELDERLY

Visits from therapy animals have shown great benefits for the elderly. Animal therapy visitations are most common for individuals in institutional settings though individual visitations to private homes are sometimes included in programs of various service organizations. The importance of animals to individuals living alone is demonstrated by the fact that fewer than 5 percent of elderly people live in institutional settings, and less than half the aged population will ever live in a nursing home. A study by Lynette Hart on topics of conversation for older dog owners and non-dog owners found that the dog owners often spoke of the present and the future, whereas older non-dog-owners spoke mostly about the past.[306] Even obtaining a pet is an act of optimism on the part of many older people, an expectation or hope that they will live for the life of the animal.

A study of 938 Medicare enrollees who were followed for one year showed significantly fewer doctor contacts by those who owned pets compared to those who did not. Owners of dogs seemed to be buffered from the impact of stressful life events more than owners of other pets or individuals who had no pets.[307] A strong attachment to a pet has been statistically correlated with less depression.[308] In another study, senior citizens in an institutional setting walked further, and therefore got more exercise, walking with a dog than walking without one.[309] Occupational therapists working with the elderly have noted that using grooming tools on a dog may encourage an individual to pay more attention to his own personal care.

Elders in skilled nursing facilities who had refused therapy before were found coming to sessions when they knew animals were going to be present.[310] The residents also demonstrated increased range of motion and higher tolerance for physical activity despite pain. Being around the therapy animals brought out memories of personal pets the residents had once owned or known. The environment became more home-like. Observers said that when the animals nudged the hands of a resident for one more pat it gave the resident a sense of being needed. "Caring for a small animal that requires holding, stroking, talking to, and feeding may symbolize the mother or parent role for many residents of long-term care facilities." Smiles were common when the residents were around the animals, and they usually asked when the animals would return. Dogs also encourage interactions with therapists by providing an external focus for conversation.

One study noted that although pet visitations produced an increase in social behaviors of nursing home residents, the effects were to a degree limited and those behaviors declined four weeks after the test.[311] The researchers introduced a pet-facilitated therapy program into a nursing home, where 18 males and 35 females participated, all averaging just over 75 years of age. Nurses administered a test designed to assess social interactions of the residents on four dates: (1) the first day of the study (pretest), (2) the fifth week of the study (midpoint), the tenth week (post-test), and a month after the final week (follow-up). The visiting animals were four cats, two small dogs, and one rabbit, which were generally brought in once a week for ten weeks, two hours per visit. Participants were assembled in day rooms and encouraged to handle and pet the animals. Student volunteers talked to the residents about their own, mostly former, pets. The sociability of the residents, as determined on the numerical scale of the testing procedure, was averaged as follows:

| Test | Mean Score |
|---|---|
| Pre-Test | 39.14 |
| Midpoint | 48.77 |
| Post-Test | 53.57 |
| Follow-up | 47.37 |

This means that the sociability of the residents, measured at times other than during the visitations, increased during the test, reaching a high point in the tenth week, but declining after the visitations stopped. Still, the decline did not bring the residents back to the starting point.

Male and female residents had markedly different patterns, with the midpoint scores of males significantly higher than females. Males did not improve after that, while females tended to improve all the way to the end. Both fell off after the test, but males declined more in sociability.

| Test | Males | Females |
|---|---|---|
| Pre-Test | 32.90 | 41.64 |
| Midpoint | 52.90 | 47.24 |
| Post-Test | 52.90 | 53.84 |
| Follow-up | 43.10 | 49.08 |

Table 1. Numerical Scale of the Testing Procedure.

These results also demonstrate what staff at nursing homes already know, that males interact less than females in general. The researchers also noted: "Eleven residents had to be dressed by others prior to the start of the study; only three had to be dressed by others at the time of the post test. Unfortunately, this number increased to seven at the follow-up." The researchers argue that the results demonstrate the desirability of a resident companion animal, a category that receives legal recognition in the state of Kansas as a professional therapy dog. This study, conducted in 1993, was possible because the institution had a cooperative administration and staff, but the researchers noted that experience and the literature indicate that most institutions are not at all amenable to the introduction of animals of "any type." It may be doubted whether this statement would now be valid.

Therapy dogs have been taken into hospice environments (where most, but not all residents are elderly).[312] Themes in the accounts of residents of the visits included "brightening my day," "bringing up memories," "getting my mind off things," and "making the family feel better." Those using animal-assisted therapy have also noted that having a dog around seems to make time move at a pleasant pace.

## MENTAL HOSPITALS

In the 1970s, Samuel Corson, a professor of psychiatry and biophysics at Ohio State University and his colleagues began using pets in psychotherapy with hospitalized mental patients, most of whom had failed to respond to traditional therapies.[313] Five patients were studied in depth, with videotapes made of the patient-pet interactions to provide a form of feedback therapy, and all showed marked improvement, as did other patients in the program who were not studied so intensively. Corson believed that the attachment of humans to dogs might result from two qualities of dogs, "their ability to offer love and tactile reassurance without criticism and their maintenance of a sort of perpetual infantile innocent dependence that may stimulate our natural tendency to offer support and protection." Corson thought that many patients could accept the love of a dog before they could accept love from, or give love to, another human. Caring for a dog also induced a sense of responsibility in patients, leading to ego strengthening and a feeling of self-respect. He considered that pet therapy was a kind of reality therapy.

> [I]nteraction with a dog sooner or later tends to impress on the patient that there are limits within which the patient must behave in relation to the animal. If the patient begins to abuse the dog, the dog will react either by growling and showing obvious signs of displeasure or by trying to get away.

In either case, the patient obtains a valuable lesson in reality testing. He also learns that love and devotion require a give and take arrangement.

Corson argued that pet-facilitated psychotherapy (PFP) was not a substitute for other therapies, but "an adjunct to facilitate the resocialization process." He hoped that using dogs in mental hospitals would decrease the dosage and/or duration of psychotropic drugs.

The dogs were kept in a kennel adjacent to the hospital and could sometimes be heard. This led to complaints from some staff members, but some adolescent patients that had previously been uncommunicative broke their silence to ask if they could play with the dogs. The patient chose the dog he or she wanted to interact with. Corson said that a "good deal of insight into the patient's feelings may be obtained by ascertaining what type of dog a patient chooses and by the reasons given for the particular choice."

Soon after being assigned their dogs, some patients began to walk and even run with them, and some went to the dog kennels to groom their dogs. Patients began to interact more often and at a better level with other patients and with the staff of the hospital. Although patients were not allowed to take dogs home, Corson considered that this might be a useful idea to implement. The dogs, instead of being seeing eye dogs, could be called, Corson said, "feeling heart dogs."

The hospital's dogs came primarily from five breeds: Wirehair Fox Terriers, Border Collies, Beagles, Labrador Retrievers, and a German Shepherd/Husky hybrid. A Collie named Wallace was described as pathologically withdrawn, yet was selected by one patient because, in the patient's words, "I felt that this dog needed me." Corson published a number of case studies, but one will have to do to indicate the sort of improvement he regularly encountered:

*Marsha.* Patient Marsha was a 23-year-old licensed practical nurse who was brought to the hospital disoriented, shouting "'destroy the world," and making sounds like "puss," "scat," and "meow." The diagnosis was catatonic schizophrenia, excited type. She was treated with fluphenazine and 25 electroshock therapy sessions, without improvement. Rather, she became withdrawn, frozen, and almost mute. Therefore, it was decided to add PFP to her treatment program. At first there was no improvement in Marsha's behavior on the unit. She remained withdrawn, and the only signs of communication were when she was with the dog. When the dog was taken away, she would get off her chair and go after it. She began to walk the dog a little and began to have less difficulty in stroking the dog. She was given a written Schedule of the hours when the dog would come to visit her; she began to look forward to the visits and to talk about the dog with the other patients. Six days after the introduction of the dog, Marsha suddenly showed marked improvement, and shortly thereafter she was discharged.

## Disasters

Dogs have been used to calm people after natural disasters and the terrorist attacks of 9/11.[314] Dogs are now included in incident response programs, where they help establish rapport with victims, help normalize the experience, act as calming agents, and serve as catalysts for physical movement.

## Drug Dogs

Narcotics detection dogs are used in hospitals for the criminally insane, but also in other mental hospitals, particularly where street drugs are found to interfere with the treatment of patients. The creation of a drug-free environment in a hospital has been described as a clinical necessity.[315]

## COMPARING THERAPY AND SERVICE DOG TRAINING

Therapy dogs are generally trained to the level of service dogs, but they are much more highly trained than most house pets. Basic training requirements of service and therapy dogs, as well as the requirements of the American Kennel Club for becoming a "canine good citizen," are indicated in Figure 18. Although the particular testing program for service dogs used here (Assistance Dogs International) requires a minimum of three tasks specific to the individual served, the other testing requirements are substantially the same as those for the other two categories. Service dogs are often trained in dozens up to a hundred commands.[316]

## STRESS OF ASSIGNMENTS ON THERAPY DOGS

Just as with people, dogs can become physically ill from stress. Handlers of therapy dogs frequently describe dogs being exhausted by visits to certain facilities.[319] A doctor at the University of Illinois at Urbana Champaign School of Veterinary Medicine kept records on a dog named Cody. Cody's experience must be a warning to any therapy dog handler who is entering an environment where staff members are not prepared to consider the needs of the dog.

| | **Service Dogs**[317] (Assistance Dogs International) | **Therapy Dogs** (Therapy Dogs International) | **Canine Good Citizen** |
|---|---|---|---|
| Basic Obedience | 90% of time | | |
| Sit | Required | Required (CGC) | Required |
| Sit-stay | Required | Required (CGC) | Required |
| Lie down | Required | Required (CGC) | Required |
| Heel | Required (staying near handler) | Required (walking on a loose lead, heeling next to handler) | Test 3[318] (walking on loose lead, heeling next to handler) |
| Come | Required | Required | Test 7 (come when called) |
| Urinate and defecate on command | Required | Cannot during test or working | |
| Calm demeanor in public | Requied (does not annoy member of the general public, disrupt normal course of business, vocalize unnecessarily) | Required: Test 1 (acceptance of friendly stranger); Test 2 (sitting politely for petting); Test 4 (walking through a crowd) | Required (walking on loose lead; no jumping) |
| Reaction to distractions | "able to perform tasks in public" | Loud sound, jogger running; walk by items being dropped, thrown, people yelling | Test 9 (reaction to distraction) |
| Leave-it command | Required | Required | |
| Reaction to medical equipment | Not specifically mentioned but would be required if individual served used specific medical equipment | Dog must be tested around and not negatively reactive to common medical equipment (wheelchair, crutches, cane, walker, etc.) | |

*continued on next page*

| | **Service Dogs**[317] (Assistance Dogs International) | **Therapy Dogs** (Therapy Dogs International) | **Canine Good Citizen** |
|---|---|---|---|
| Reaction to strangers | Required (no aggression towards people or other animals | Required: Test 11 (say hello); tolerant of being held very tightly (sometimes done by mental patients, Alzheimer's patients), yelled at, poked, etc. | Test 1 (accpeting a friendly stranger); Test 2 (sitting politely for petting); Test 4 (walking through a crowd); Test 8 (reaction to another dog) |
| Supervised separation | | 3 minutes | Test 10 (supervised separation) |
| Appearance and grooming | Required to be neat | Required | Required: Test 3 |
| Specific tasks | 3 tasks to mitigate the client's disability | N/A | N/A |
| Identification | Laminated ID card | Laminated photo ID | Certificate |
| Gear | Cape, harness, backpack, or other similar piece of equipment or clothing with a logo | Anything that helps (and does not impede) dog being handled, held, stroked, hugged, etc. | N/A |

Figure 18. Testing Criteria for Service Dogs, Therapy Dogs, and the AKC Canine Good Citizen Designation.

Just as not every animal is a suitable partner for an animal-assisted therapy program, so too, not every child is an appropriate candidate for this type of intervention. The child with allergies or those prone to seizures due to high levels of excitement must be excluded. Additionally, children who exhibit aggression toward animals must likewise be excluded for the safety of both the animal and the child. Before an animal is allowed to enter a facility, staff should be prepared to maintain distance between the animal and aggressive children. During this program staff members did not receive instruction regarding this issue, which often resulted in the animal being deluged by children, some of whom deliberately tried to injure him. These incidents

were unsettling to him, causing him to react with tentativeness for periods
of time thereafter.

After eight weeks of therapy sessions, Cody experienced some physiological
changes, including excessive panting and frequent urination. The dog was
found to be suffering from both ear and urinary tract infections. After these
were successfully treated, the dog still appeared lethargic and depressed.
Further tests found that Cody had Cushing's Syndrome, also known as
canine hyperadrenocorticism, a hormonal disorder involving elevated blood
cortisol concentrations. This is often the result of chronic stress, and a possible if not likely source of stress in this case came from the therapy sessions.[320]
As a personal observation, I have experienced situations in classrooms
where students descended on Chloe, my therapy dog, while the teacher used
the dog's visit as an opportunity to disengage from the class and grade papers
in a different part of the room. It is advisable for therapy dog teams visiting
schools to explain to teachers and other staff in the rooms that a dog should
only be expected to interact with one or two students at a time. The handler
has to remain close because some students will not pet the dog in a calm
manner. One autistic boy in a class I visited insisted on poking the dog,
rather than petting it, and I had to move Chloe away from the boy. One dis-
advantage with the rapid growth of the therapy dog phenomenon is that
many people feel that a visit from a therapy dog will be good for a class, or
a ward, or any other group setting, but they do not know that responsibilities
lie with the administrators of the facility, not just with the handler of the dog.

## TRAVEL REQUIREMENTS OF THERAPY DOGS

The Department of Transportation, in 1996, considered that therapy dogs
might accompany a handler to a location where the animal would interact
with a population. The handler had no rights with regard to the animal
beyond those provided to pet owners.

Sometimes, an animal that is trained to work with people with disabilities
may travel by air but not be accompanied by an individual with a disability for whom the animal performs service animal functions. For example, a
non-disabled handler may transport a "therapy dog" to a location, such as a
rehabilitation center, where it will perform services for individuals with
physical or mental disabilities.

The Department's Air Carrier Access Act regulation intended to assist passengers with disabilities by ensuring that they can travel with the service animals that perform functions for them. When a service animal is not accom-

panying a passenger with a disability, the rule's rationale for permitting the animal to travel in the cabin does not apply. While the animal may be traveling to a location where it will perform valuable services to other people, it would be subject to the airline's general policies with respect to the carriage of animals.[321]

Given situations, such as requests of specially trained therapy dogs to go to disaster sites, this issue should be reconsidered. The author has drafted legislation presently under consideration in New York providing limited travel accommodation for therapy dogs on assignments.

## STATE LAWS ON THERAPY DOGS

Therapy dogs are only referred to in the statutes of a few states, although such dogs have been around for more than 20 years. Kansas defines a professional therapy dog as:

> a dog which is selected, trained and tested to provide specific physical or therapeutic functions, under the direction and control of a qualified handler who works with the dog as a team, and as a part of the handler's occupation or profession. Such dogs, with their handlers, perform such functions in institutional settings, community-based group settings, or when providing services to specific persons who have disabilities.[322]

The final sentence of the provision would exclude most certified therapy dogs, however, by stating that a professional therapy dog "does not include dogs, certified or not, which are used by volunteers for pet visitation therapy."

In Kansas, a "qualified handler of a professional therapy dog" may bring such a dog on public transportation, into motels, hotels, and other temporary lodging places, and into businesses and establishments to which the public is invited, "including establishments which serve or sell food." Because the definition of professional therapy dog presumes that the animal lives in an institutional setting, no rental accommodations are mentioned.

> If a question arises as to whether a dog handler is qualified, or whether the dog accompanying the handler is qualified as a professional therapy dog, to enter in or upon the places [of public accommodation], and amendments thereto, an employee or person responsible for such places may request, and the qualified handler shall produce, an identification card or letter, provided by the training facility, school or trainer who trained the dog. Such card or letter shall contain the following information: (1) The legal name of

the qualified dog handler; (2) the name, address and telephone number of the facility, school or trainer who trained the dog; (3) information documenting that the dog is trained to provide therapeutic supports; and (4) a picture or digital photographic likeness of the qualified handler and the dog. If a card is used, the picture or digital photographic likeness shall be on the card. If a letter is used, the picture or digital photographic likeness shall either be printed as a part of the letter or be affixed to the letter.[323]

It is a misdemeanor in Kansas to represent oneself as having the right to be accompanied by an assistance dog or professional therapy dog into places of public accommodation.[324]

In New York, a therapy dog "any dog that is trained to aid the emotional and physical health of patients in hospitals, nursing homes, retirement homes and other settings and is actually used for such purpose, or any dog owned by a recognized training center located within the state during the period such dog is being trained or bred for such purpose."[325]

A therapy animal, is defined for purposes of the Oregon criminal interference statutes, is an animal that has been professionally trained for, and is actively used for, therapy purposes."[326]

Access to public accommodations should be legislatively permitted when therapy dogs are being taken to and from appointments, similar to the limited access provisions in a few states regarding search and rescue dogs.[327] Such access provisions should not apply to therapy dogs in training, however, since such animals are primarily pets and are not generally permitted to go on any assignments prior to certification.

# Chapter 6

# THE CANCER SNIFFERS

Trained detection dogs have long been used to find drugs and explosives, as well as termites,[328] tortoises,[329] tree snakes,[330] gypsy moths,[331] screwworms,[332] and bed bugs.[333] A very active area of research involves the ability of dogs to alert to cancers. When the scientific community began to investigate reports of patients who claimed their dogs knew about their diseases before they or their doctors did, some very interesting and newsworthy research was produced.

## FROM ANECDOTE TO SCIENTIFIC TOOL

In 1989, the British medical journal, *Lancet,* published a letter from two doctors who wrote about a woman who sought medical help because her dog showed inordinate interest in a skin lesion that turned out to be melanoma.[334] Another woman's Dachshund began to have the odd habit of sniffing and poking at her left breast while she watched television. After a month of this annoying behavior, she pushed the dog aside and discovered a lump in the breast. She was found to have ductal carcinoma.[335] Following more anecdotal claims about extraordinary claims, the hypothesis became a research area. Tumors produce volatile organic compounds that are released into the air through breath and sweat and the predominant theory is these compounds can be detected by dogs because of their high olfactory acuity.

In 2008, a team of Polish scientists reported that variations in olfactory receptor genes "might affect the olfactory ability of service dogs in different fields of specific substance detection."[336] Twin dogs with a specific genetic variant were found to significantly differ in the detection skills from dogs with other variants. It might, therefore, soon be possible to predict, both for cancer sniffers and other detection dogs, whether a puppy is a good candidate for such work.

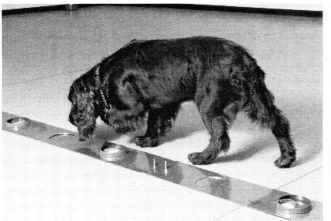

Figure 19. Cancer Dog Sniffing Row of Samples and Alerting to Sample. Courtesy Carolyn Willis, 2009).

## DETECTING BLADDER CANCER

An English team approached an organization, Hearing Dogs for Deaf People,[337] and asked them to train dogs for a project to see if the dogs could detect bladder cancer.[338] Bladder cancer was chosen because these tumors release distinct organic compounds into urine.

Urine was obtained from 36 patients with bladder cancer, 27 of the samples of which were used in training. A total of 108 control participants were otherwise diseased or healthy. Seven Petri dishes were prepared for each test, only one of which had urine from a bladder cancer patient. The dogs were trained to lie down next to a sample that smelled of cancer. If the dogs chose the samples randomly, they would be right about 14 percent of the time (1/7th of 100% = 14.28%). They did better than this random level, alerting to the correct urine on 22 of 54 occasions, a success rate of 41 percent. The dogs trained on wet urine specimens were right slightly more often, about 50 percent of the time. One participant whose urine was "chosen" by all of the dogs, despite being a control, was later found to have kidney cancer. This research was promising, but hardly argued that dogs should be hired for cancer-detection work. (See Figure 19a and b showing a dog sniffing cancer samples, and then alerting to one.)

## DETECTING LUNG AND BREAST CANCER

A group of American and Polish scientists looked at the ability of dogs to detect lung and breast cancers, but this group developed a highly sophisticated training program for the dogs, one very similar to the regimens used to train bomb sniffers. These researchers recruited 55 patients with lung cancer and 31 patients with breast cancer (one was a man). They also found 83 volunteers with no cancer history to serve as controls. Five dogs, from seven to 18 months were selected: three Labrador Retrievers and two Portuguese Water Dogs. The dogs were taken from a group of 13, having been identified as more eager than the others to sniff objects and respond to commands. The dogs could not always detect patients in remission, but for one individual who was thought to be in remission, the dogs sat before her breath and the cancer was later found to be active. Dogs detected lung cancer with 99 percent consistency with biopsy-confirmed diagnoses, and breast cancer with 88 percent consistency.[339] This was substantially better than prior research and it is worth looking at the training regimen used for the dogs, which followed the model for drug and bomb detection dogs.

## Training Cancer Sniffers

The dogs trained to detect lung and breast cancers went through a series of training stages to develop this skill. Dogs were not moved from one stage to the next unless they had made 30 correct decisions without a mistake. The dogs began by distinguishing a tube with a cancer breath sample and food from blank tubes. In the first stage they were taught to SIT before the correct sample, then received food and praise in the second stage. In the third stage they received food and praise, but there was no food in the tube with the cancer breath sample. They were reprimanded if they chose the wrong sample. In the fourth phase, each tube had a breath sample, but only one had a cancer breath sample. In the final phase, it was possible that all five breath samples were cancer-free samples, so that alerting to any of them would be a fail. Neither the handler or the experimenter knew if there was a cancer sample. The dog received no reward at this stage for a correct alert. (Training stages are presented graphically in Figure 20.)

Training took two to three weeks. Various precautions were taken to make sure that one dog could not leave any indications for the next. The stations were in a line each about a yard from the others and the location of the cancer sample was always randomly chosen. The correct response was indicated by the dog sitting or lying in front of the sample station containing the cancer breath. A dog was graduated when it could correctly distinguish, for at least 30 consecutive trials, the cancer patient's breath sample from among those of four controls in a line-up of five samples.

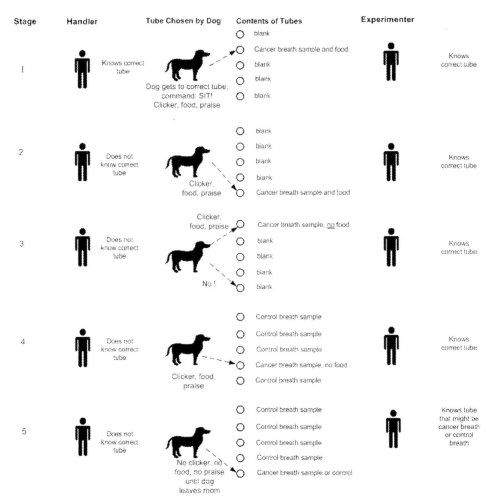

Figure 20. Training Stages for Cancer Sniffing Dogs. As described by McCulloch et al., *Integrative Cancer Therapies* (March, 2006).

# Part II

# LIVING AND GOING PLACES WITH CANINE CAREGIVERS

# Chapter 7

# ANTI-DISCRIMINATION LEGISLATION
# AND REGULATORY IMPLEMENTATION

The laws and government rules concerning dogs with medical and psychological functions have been in flux because the science and social acceptance of these dogs have been undergoing dramatic development in the last twenty years. Before 1990, most legal recognition of canine caregivers was restricted to guide dogs and occasionally hearing dogs. As other uses began to appear, and to receive scientific support as well as social and political recognition, references in the laws began to generalize to refer to service or assistance dogs, and often service or assistance animals since dogs were no longer the only species recognized as capable of assisting people physically or psychologically. Nuance was required to deal with conditions that were not visible, or not visible much of the time, such as with epileptic seizures or panic attacks, meaning that the functions of the animals were also not usually seen in public. This also meant that verification procedures had to be established so that a restaurant, airline, or landlord could verify a claim about the animal accompanying a potential customer or tenant, but the rights of the business had to be balanced against the privacy rights of the service dog user. The chapters of this Part will describe the laws and rules as they have come to define the limits on where service dogs can be taken.

It must be noted that social acceptance has, in recent years, often outpaced legal requirements. Much of the healthcare system, for instance, has found the presence of service and therapy dogs so valuable for the mood and perhaps the health of clients and patients that there is now often more openness to these animals than any set of laws would require. The same may be said of businesses in general. Where once most businesses were quick to eject a skilled dog without a good reason for being in a store, many dog owners, myself included, often safely assume that except for restaurants and theaters, a dog will be welcome, at least an obedient dog. A social change is occurring and the law may be irrelevant to access issues when the owner of a business is a dog lover or has enough customers with dogs that he must pretend to be.

References to service animals are rare at the federal legislative level, but the regulations that have been issued, in particular by the Departments of Justice, Transportation, and Housing and Urban Development are grounded principally in the Americans with Disabilities Act, the Rehabilitation Act, the Fair Housing Act, the Air Carrier Access Act, and in various amending acts that have been passed by Congress and signed into law. Many of the regulations issued by the federal agencies refer to provisions in Acts beyond those under which they were implemented, so a brief summary of these Acts and the provisions frequently referenced in the rules will prove useful. The Pets Evacuation and Transportation Act of 2006[340] will be discussed in the chapter dealing with keeping animals with masters in disasters and emergencies.

## AIR CARRIER ACCESS ACT

An air carrier may not discriminate against "an otherwise qualified individual" because the individual has "a physical or mental impairment that substantially limits one or more major life activities," "has a record of such an impairment," or "is regarded as having such an impairment."[341] The Act covers domestic and foreign carriers, though as discussed below, other laws may affect rules in international travel.

## AMERICANS WITH DISABILITIES ACT

The Americans with Disabilities Act of 1990 applies to public accommodations.[342] Under 42 U.S.C. Chapter 126, Subchapter III, Public Accommodations and Services Operated by Private Entities, discrimination on the basis of disability is prohibited, and individuals with disabilities are entitled to "the full and equal enjoyment of the goods, services, facilities, privileges, advantages, or accommodations of any place of public accommodation by any person who owns, leases (or leases to), or operates a place of public accommodation."[343] A public accommodation is described broadly, and the definition is repeated in regulations discussed below.[344] Discrimination includes

> . . . a failure to make reasonable modifications in policies, practices, or procedures, when such modifications are necessary to afford such goods, services, facilities, privileges, advantages, or accommodations to individuals

with disabilities, unless the entity can demonstrate that making such modifications would fundamentally alter the nature of such goods, services, facilities, privileges, advantages, or accommodations.[345]

Discrimination is also prohibited as to private entities that operate a fixed route system. A fixed route system is a "system for providing transportation of individuals (other than by aircraft) on which a vehicle is operated along a prescribed route according to a fixed schedule."

Private clubs and religious organizations are exempted from Subchapter III.[346] Enforcement is assigned to the Attorney General.[347]

## FAIR HOUSING ACT

The Fair Housing Act was Title VIII of the Civil Rights Act of 1968,[348] and was significantly amended by the Fair Housing Amendments Act of 1988, which expanded the FHA to include persons with disabilities among those protected from housing discrimination.[349] This Act, as does the ADA, has a religious organization and private club exemption.[350] Separate provisions deal with discrimination in the sale or rental of housing,[351] residential real-estate related transactions,[352] and in providing brokerage services.[353] As with the ADA, discrimination includes . . . a refusal to make reasonable accommodations in rules, policies, practices, or services, when such accommodations may be necessary to afford such person equal opportunity to use and enjoy a dwelling.[354] This is the most commonly referenced provision in the Act in housing discrimination cases involving service and support animals. The FHA is administered by the Department of Housing and Urban Development, though the U.S. Attorney General or private persons may enforce the FHA. Relief for private plaintiffs may include monetary damages.

## REHABILITATION ACT OF 1973

The Rehabilitation Act of 1973[355] has been revised many times. Although specific regulations have not been promulgated under the Act regarding service or support animals, it is frequently cited by courts and federal agencies for its requirements regarding federally subsidized programs. Under 29 U.S.C. 794, Nondiscrimination under Federal Grants and Programs:

> No otherwise qualified individual with a disability in the United States . . .
> shall, solely by reason of her or his disability, be excluded from the partici-

pation in, be denied the benefits of, or be subjected to discrimination under any program or activity receiving Federal financial assistance or under any program or activity conducted by any Executive agency or by the United States Postal Service.[356]

A program or activity includes "a college, university, or other postsecondary institution, or a public system of higher education," or a "system of vocational education,[357] or other school system." It also includes a private business "principally engaged in providing education, health care, housing, social services, or parks and recreation."[358]

The standards used to determine if the provision has been violated are those in certain sections of the Americans with Disabilities Act.[359]

## GENERAL ISSUES CONSIDERED BY FEDERAL AGENCIES

There has been a general trend, most noticeably in the regulatory releases of the Department of Housing and Urban Development and the Department of Transportation, to acknowledge that tenants and passengers should often be accommodated in their requests to be accompanied by animals that are not as specifically trained as guide dogs and most other service animals, and that these requests come from legitimate needs for emotional support. Even here, however, there is an acknowledgement that the health and comfort of the tenant must be balanced against the inconvenience to other tenants and the costs to the housing facility.

There is also an increasing acknowledgment that, even where the standard for admission of an animal is its qualification as a service animal, such animals may not always have to be trained, at least beyond a basic obedience level. There is, for instance, increasing evidence that seizure-alert dogs are often *not* trained to react to oncoming seizures (though their skill in recognizing seizures may be encouraged by a training regimen). This may also be true of hypoglycemia-alert dogs (a new category), or severe migraine alert dogs (a skill documented several times). Many states specify that service animals must be trained yet also include seizure-alerting as a type of service that qualifies a dog as a service animal.[360] Federal and state legislators and courts have begun to recognize that the number of tasks that dogs can perform is increasing, and that the level and type of training needed to make dogs useful to individuals with disabilities varies depending on the service provided. The boundary between pets and service animals is no longer as simple as it once seemed.[361]

Courts that have faced inconsistencies between federal and state law regarding the rights of the disabled with respect to service and emotional support animals have favored the federal laws.[362] State laws cannot be ignored, however. A number of states, for instance, put trainers of service animals on a par with the individuals who will ultimately use the animals once they have been trained. Thus, many states have statutes that provide a trainer of guide dogs can take such a dog into a restaurant. Some states give such blanket equality in this respect that it is clear that a trainer would have a right to housing at the same level as the ultimate user of the animal. This is almost never the subject of litigation, however, as trainers work with a number of dogs, not all of which are being trained as service animals, and most would not particularly want to live in a building which was not friendly to animals.

Among the issues that have been considered by all the agencies in issuing rules on service, support, and assistance animals are:

1. *Whether certain species should be excluded,* such as the exclusion of farm animals in the 2008 proposals of the Department of Justice.
2. *Whether training should be required, and whether training should be formal.* The agencies generally agree that a service animal can be trained by the individual for whom it provides services. Some organizations in the assistance dog industry have lobbied for rules that would require some degree of formal training, but instances of dogs being trained by handlers with disabilities, just as many pets are trained by their owners, have made regulators leery of acceding to such pressures. Many dogs performing hearing dog functions begin to be trained as their handlers go deaf, without the involvement of a professional trainer. Even informal training is, under more recent rules, generally not required, which is at least partly a recognition of the fact that seizure alerting seems to arise spontaneously in many dogs.
3. *What services animals (usually dogs) can perform for the individuals with mental health disabilities.* Recent regulatory releases generally spend more time discussing this issue than was true before 2000, and the federal agencies, other than the IRS and some outdated but still valid regulations of other agencies, have accepted that service animals can serve the individuals with mental health disabilities. Many state laws still restrict service animal status to animals that serve individuals with physical disabilities, and some states restrict service animal status to animals that serve the mobility impaired.
4. *Whether emotional support is enough to distinguish an animal from a pet.* On this issue, the agencies diverge, though their differences make sense in the context of the rules each provides. Restaurants have argued that they should not be expected to admit an animal providing only emotional support but they are required to admit psychiatric service ani-

mals, which have training and perform functions. Airplanes on the other hand are required to admit emotional support animals only under specified conditions. Apartment buildings should also be open to allowing individuals with mental disabilities to have animals that provide emotional support, given that the presence of the animal is less likely to be disturbing than it would be to other patrons in a restaurant. Where they are allowed, however, emotional support animals can be expected to be good citizens.

5. *Whether an emotional support animal is a type of service animal.* The Department of Justice considers a psychiatric service animal as a type of service animal, with the same access rights as other service animals, though perhaps with stiffer verification requirements. The Department of Transportation regards emotional support animals as a type of service animal, but allows airlines to require advance notice and separate verification procedures that do not apply to other service animals. There is a good deal of confusion concerning the distinction between emotional support and psychiatric service, which confusion can also be found in state law.[363]

6. *How qualification for access should be verified.* The Department of Justice largely limits inquiry to the functions the service dog performs. The Department of Transportation advises airline employees to use common sense, restricting requests of written documentation to psychiatric service and emotional support animals. The Department of Housing and Urban Development has moved from a certification to a verification procedure.

The perspectives of the agencies regarding animals whose handlers live with mental health disabilities will be discussed in detail in the next section. The positions of the agencies are summarized in Figure 21. Detailed positions of the agencies will be discussed in subsequent chapters.

## ACCESS FOR ANIMALS SERVING PERSONS WITH MENTAL DISABILITIES

Training animals specifically to assist persons living with mental disabilities is comparatively recent in the history of service animals and has since 2000 received considerable attention from the federal agencies, and by some states. As with any new area of the law, however, solutions differ based on the perspectives of the agencies and the input they have received from individuals using such animals and the organizations that represent them.

| Animal/ Issue | Department of Justice | Department of Transportation (regulations applying after May 13, 2009) | Department of Housing and Urban Development (general housing requiements) | Department of Housing and Urban Development: Public Housing and Projects for Elderly, Persons with Disabilities | Internal Revenue Service |
|---|---|---|---|---|---|
| Guide dog | Covered | Covered (absent safety regulation problem) | Covered | Covered | Deductible by regulation |
| Hearing (signal) dog | Covered | Covered (absent safety regulation) | Covered | Covered | Deductible by Revenue Ruling |
| Service dog for individuals with physical disabilities | Covered | Covered (absent safety regulation) | Covered | Covered | Deductible according to IRS Publication |
| Service dog for individuals with mental health disabilities (psychiatric service dog) | Covered (does not include transvestism, pedophilia, etc.) | Access permitted where passenger has diagnosed mental or emotional disorder (under DSM-IV) and recent documentation from licensed mental health professional; behavior must be appropriate in public setting | Covered under case law; HUD's website provides example of severe depression | Covered | Apparently not deductible (absent service for physical disability) |

*continued on next page*

| Animal/ Issue | Department of Justice | Department of Transportation (regulations applying after May 13, 2009) | Department of Housing and Urban Development (general housing requiements) | Department of Housing and Urban Development: Public Housing and Projects for Elderly, Persons with Disabilities | Internal Revenue Service |
|---|---|---|---|---|---|
| Emotional support animal | Not covered | Access permitted where passenger has diagnosed mental or emotional disorder (under DSM-IV) and recent documentation from licensed mental health professional; animal must be trained to behave in public setting | Covered under case law and probably by agency discussion of regulations regarding elderly and disabled | Disability-related function includes "providing emotional support to persons with disabilities who have a disability-related need for such support" | Not deductible |
| Unusual animals (snakes, etc.) | Not excluded under existing rules but might be excluded if 2008 proposed rules are finalized | Not excluded, but carrier can make "judgment call" concerning threat to health or safety of others | Cases refer to animals other than dogs; zoning issues sometimes conflict with general openness of regulations (e.g., pot-bellied pigs) | No specific exclusion | Guide horse should be deductible |

*continued on next page*

| Animal/ Issue | Department of Justice | Department of Transportation (regulations applying after May 13, 2009) | Department of Housing and Urban Development (general housing requiements) | Department of Housing and Urban Development: Public Housing and Projects for Elderly, Persons with Disabilities | Internal Revenue Service |
|---|---|---|---|---|---|
| Training requirement | "Individually trained to do work or perform tasks"; proprosed rules state a task is not required | "Individually trained or able to provide assistance" | HUD recognizes training not required for certain functions, such as seizure alerting | Animals necessary as reasonable accommodation do not necessarily have to have specialized training | None specified (though animals that qualify for deduction would generally be trained, with possible exception of seizure-alert dogs) |
| Verification | Questions about disability precluded; but inquiry can include whether the animal is required because of a disability and what work or tasks the animal has been trained to perform | Must accept identification cards, written documenta-tion, prescence of harnesses, tags, and "credible verbal assurances"; certification not required | Landlords authorized to verify that an animal qualifies as a reasonable accommoda-tion; tenant must be able to demon-strate rela-tionship between disability and the assistance the animal provides | Must be nexus between requested accommoda-tion and disability and a relationship between the disability and the assistance provided by the animal | No guidance specified for field agents |

Figure 21. Recognition by Federal Agencies of Service and Emotional Support Animal Qualifications and Owner Requirements.

Because this area is in flux and likely to remain so for some time, it is appropriate to look at this issue more closely.

## Department of Justice Perspectives

In proposing revisions to service animal regulations in June 2008, the Department of Justice noted that there was considerable confusion as to whether persons with mental health disabilities can have animals qualifying as service animals.

> The Department believes that psychiatric service animals that are trained to do work or perform a task (e.g., reminding its owner to take medicine) for individuals whose disability is covered by the ADA [Americans with Disabilities Act] are protected by the Department's present regulatory approach.

> Psychiatric service animals can be trained to perform a variety of tasks that assist individuals with disabilities to detect the onset of psychiatric episodes and ameliorate their effects. Tasks performed by psychiatric service animals may include reminding the handler to take medicine; providing safety checks, or room searches, or turning on lights for persons with Post-Traumatic Stress Disorder; interrupting self-mutilation by persons with dissociative identity disorders; and keeping disoriented individuals from danger.[364]

In recognition of these types of animals, the Department included the following sentence in its proposed definition of service animal: "The term *service animal* includes individually trained animals that do work or perform tasks for the benefit of individuals with disabilities, including psychiatric, cognitive, and mental disabilities."[365] The agency noted that "a psychiatric service dog can help some individuals with dissociative identity disorder to remain grounded in time or place." This is "work" without a specific "task." Thus, doing work or performing tasks can be satisfied by one or the other of these elements. The Department cited a commenter on the rules as follows: "A psychiatric service dog can help some individuals with dissociative identity disorder to remain grounded in time or place. As one service dog user stated, in some cases critical forms of assistance can't be construed as physical tasks, noting that the manifestations of brainbased disabilities, such as psychiatric disorders and autism, are as varied as their physical counterparts."[366]

Although an individual with a mental disability can have a service animal, the animal must do more, in proposed rules issued by the Department of Justice, than provide emotional comfort and support to qualify as a service animal. "Animals whose sole function is to provide emotional support, comfort, therapy, companionship, therapeutic benefits, or to promote emotional well-being are not service animals."[367] The Department, in the proposals, acknowledges that there are situations in which an animal providing emotional comfort and support should be covered by access provisions, but seems to regard this as largely a perspective appropriate for transportation, employment environments, and housing: "[T]here are situations . . . , particularly in the context of residential settings and employment,[368] where there may be compelling reasons to permit the use of animals whose presence provides emotional support to a person with a disability. Accordingly, other federal agency regulations governing those situations may appropriately provide for increased access for animals other than service animals."[369] The Department of Justice emphasizes that an animal that provides comfort and support may be used by an individual whose impairments "do not rise to the level of a disability."[370] Such an animal would be, for these purposes, no different from a pet. Whether such a perspective would be held by the Department of Justice after the Americans with Disabilities Amendments Act of 2008 must be questioned.[371]

## Department of Transportation Perspectives on Air Carrier Responsibilities

The Department of Transportation (DOT),[372] in introducing final rules on air carrier responsibilities, summarized comments on the issue of emotional support animals as follows:

> Unlike other service animals, emotional support animals are often not trained to perform a specific active function, such as pathfinding, picking up objects, carrying things, providing additional stability, responding to sounds, etc. This has led some service animal advocacy groups to question their status as service animals and has led to concerns by carriers that permitting emotional support animals to travel in the cabin would open the door to abuse by passengers wanting to travel with their pets.[373]

The agency does distinguish between psychiatric service and emotional support animals, noting that an emotional support animal "need not have specific training" for a function, though it must behave appropriately in public. Psychiatric service animals, on the other hand, "may be trained by their owners, sometimes with the assistance of a professional trainer, to perform tasks such as fetching medications, reminding the user to take medications, helping people with balance problems caused by medications or an underlying condition, bringing a phone to the user in an emergency or activating a specially equipped emergency phone, or acting as a buffer against other people crowding too close."

Despite making this distinction in the preamble to its final rules, the agency defines a service animal as any "animal that is individually trained or able to provide assistance to a qualified person with a disability; or any animal shown by documentation to be necessary for the emotional wellbeing of a passenger." This accepts emotional support animals, at least those owned by individuals with diagnosed psychiatric conditions, as a type of service animal.[374] The Department notes that both psychiatric service and emotional support animals may "be a source of abuse by persons attempting to circumvent carrier rules concerning transportation of pets."[375] Indeed, the potential for abuse is, from the Department's perspective, a reason for treating the two types of animals the same way.[376] The agency's final rules limit access of both types of animals to handlers with a diagnosed mental or emotional disorder, and carriers may insist on "recent documentation from a licensed mental health professional to support the passenger's desire to travel with such an animal."

The final rule fleshes out the documentation requirement:

> If a passenger seeks to travel with an animal that is used as an emotional support or psychiatric service animal, you are not required to accept the animal for transportation in the cabin unless the passenger provides you current documentation (i.e., no older than one year from the date of the passenger's scheduled initial flight) on the letterhead of a licensed mental health professional (e.g., psychiatrist, psychologist, licensed clinical social worker, including a medical doctor specifically treating the passenger's mental or emotional disability[377]) stating [four items].

The four items that the mental health professional's letter must state are:

1. The passenger has a mental or emotional disability recognized in the *Diagnostic and Statistical Manual of Mental Disorders*–Fourth Edition (*DSM IV*). This does not include being neurotic, a category that was not included after *DSM II*.
2. The passenger needs the emotional support or psychiatric service animal as an accommodation for air travel and/or for activity at the passenger's destination.
3. The individual providing the assessment is a licensed mental health professional, and the passenger is under his or her professional care.
4. The date and type of the mental health professional's license and the state or other jurisdiction in which it was issued.[378]

Even with such documentation, carriers may require advance notice of 48 hours of a passenger's wish to travel with an emotional support animal. "Of course, like any service animal with a passenger that wishes to bring into the cabin, an emotional support animal must be trained to behave properly in a public setting."

The Department of Transportation notes that businesses in airport terminals, such as restaurants and stores, are not covered by the rules applicable to airlines, but rather to those imposed by the Department of Justice, and that Department of Justice rules (described above) may deny access to an animal that the airlines might have to accept. Therefore, an individual with an emotional support animal might arrive at an airport and not be able to take an animal into a restaurant, despite being able to later take the animal onto a airplane. The DOT is reduced to counseling on this issue:

> [A] concession could, without violating DOJ rules, deny entry to a properly documented emotional support animal that an airline, under the ACAA [Air Carrier Access Act], would have to accept. On the other hand, nothing in the DOJ rules would prevent a concession from accepting a properly documented emotional support animal. We urge all parties at airports to be aware that their services and facilities are intended to serve all passengers. Airlines, airport operators, and concessionaires should work together to ensure that all persons who are able to use the airport to access the air transportation system are able equally to use all services and facilities provided to the general public.[379]

It is rare to find this kind of wishful thinking in federal regulations.

The Department of Transportation recently issued regulations concerning flights to the United Kingdom, noting that UK carriers have more restrictive pet policies than U.S. carriers.[380] UK law generally provides that only guide and assistance dogs may accompany owners in the passenger cabin on a flight.[381] Therefore, passengers flying internationally may not be able to take advantage of the Department's more liberal domestic policies on flights to England. Passengers should contact airlines in advance of flights regarding service animals in any case since some flights will limit the number of animals that can be brought onto a plane. It is not uncommon for passengers anxious to travel with animals to pay for an extra seat.

## Federal Housing Rules

In October 2008, the Department of Housing and Urban Development amended regulations governing requirements for pet ownership in HUD-assisted public housing and multifamily housing projects for the elderly and persons with disabilities.[382] HUD generally lumps a number of functions together.

> Certain animals provide assistance or perform tasks for the benefit of a person with a disability. Such animals, often referred to as "assistance animals," "service animals," "support animals," or "therapy animals," provide disability-related functions including, but not limited to, guiding visually impaired individuals, alerting hearing-impaired persons to sounds and noises, providing protection or rescue assistance, pulling a wheelchair, seeking and retrieving items, alerting individuals to impending seizures, and providing emotional support to persons who have a disability-related need for such support.[383]

The HUD regulations do not use the term "psychiatric service animal." A person requesting an exception to a no-pets policy for an assistance animal

> . . . must demonstrate a disability-related need for the animal, such as service, or assistance, performing tasks for the benefit of a person with a disability, or providing emotional support that alleviates one or more identified symptoms or effects of a person's disability. Examples of disability-related functions, include, but are not limited to, guiding individuals who are blind or have low vision, alerting individuals who are deaf or hard of hearing to sounds, providing rescue assistance, pulling a wheelchair, fetching items, alerting persons to impending seizures, or providing emotional support to persons with disabilities who have a disability-related need for such support.

Thus, no task is associated with providing emotional support, but it is acknowledged to be a disability-related function. No training is required.

> [E]motional support animals do not need training to ameliorate the effects of a person's mental and emotional disabilities. Emotional support animals by their very nature, and without training, may relieve depression and anxiety, and/or help reduce stress-induced pain in persons with certain medical conditions affected by stress.

To commenters who objected that HUD was creating different standards than those issued by the Department of Justice under the Americans with Disabilities Act, HUD noted:

> There is a valid distinction between the functions animals provide to persons with disabilities in the public arena, i.e., performing tasks enabling individuals to use public services and public accommodations, as compared to how an assistance animal might be used in the home. For example, emotional support animals provide very private functions for persons with men-

tal and emotional disabilities. Specifically, emotional support animals by their very nature, and without training, may relieve depression and anxiety, and help reduce stress-induced pain in persons with certain medical conditions affected by stress. Conversely, persons with disabilities who use emotional support animals may not need to take them into public spaces covered by the ADA.

It could be argued that HUD's perspective on this issue should have more general application than just to housing.

## State Laws on Service Animals for Persons with Mental Disabilities

Many states confine the legal protections of individuals with service animals to those who have physical disabilities or are mobility impaired. Individuals with mental health disabilities have more often been successful in obtaining permission to retain animals that provide emotional support in housing accommodations than elsewhere, presumably in large part because other individuals are less likely to be bothered by what a neighbor does behind the door of his apartment.[384]

In Utah, broad provisions regarding emotional support and psychiatric therapy animals were repealed in 2009.[385] Psychiatric service dogs have occasionally been the subject of litigation. One case from the state of Washington concerned a dog that would put herself between her handler and other people, thereby lessening the owner's anxiety attack.[386] There was some question as to whether the dog had been trained to engage in this "circling" behavior, and the appellate court remanded the case for trial on the issue of the animal's qualifications as a service animal.

## Need for Uniformity on Psychiatric Service Animals

Psychiatric service dogs are often highly trained and skilled animals and it is unfortunate that their users are not provided with uniform access rules. The needs of their users are often every bit as pressing as the needs of individuals with physical disabilities, and the law should recognize this in its treatment of the animals that serve them. The proposed approach of the Department of Justice on this issue should be followed by the other federal agencies and the states. On the other hand, emotional support animals are appropriately recognized as pets in most situations, and do not need the same level of protection.

# Chapter 8

## TAKING DOGS INTO RESTAURANTS, HOTELS, AND MOST OTHER PUBLIC PLACES

*A former member of the armed services brings her dog to a warehouse store. It is a 12-week-old puppy and she provides store employees a letter from a psychologist describing her disabilities arising in part from her military service. The dog is admitted without issue. Two months later she returns. This time the dog is wearing a home-made vest with the words "Service Dog in Training." Store employees allow the woman to go through the checkout line, but approach her near the exit and tell her that the dog's vest is "not regulation." This encounter with the staff is embarrassing and the veteran thinks that acquaintances who were passing by probably thought that she was being stopped for shoplifting.[387] After this visit, a store lawyer sends her a letter asking how the dog had been trained and what tasks it performs. The dog was able to alert her to panic attacks. This type of alerting often involves sitting in front of the master or circling her to keep people away until she can calm down.*

The Department of Justice has rules in place, but is considering others, and both will be discussed.[388] A service animal is defined in rules issued by the Department of Justice as a

> . . . guide dog, signal dog, or other animal[389] individually trained to do work or perform tasks for the benefit of an individual with a disability, including, but not limited to, guiding individuals with impaired vision, alerting individuals with impaired hearing to intruders or sounds, providing minimal protection or rescue work, pulling a wheelchair, or fetching dropped items.[390]

Costco employees doubted that an animal accompanying a woman into a warehouse store was actually a service animal in the fact situation outlined in the opening paragraph of this chapter. In *DiLorenzo v. Costco,*[391] the woman, a veteran, brought a pug named Dilo, into Costco's Bellingham warehouse, informing an employee at the entrance that the dog was in the process of being trained to be a service animal. She was taken to a podium and given a copy of the store's service animal policy, where she produced a letter from her psychologist. The letter described her disabilities and attested her suitability for a service animal. On a second visit, the dog was wearing a vest that read "service dog in training." A store manager asked her what tasks the dog performed, to which the owner replied that Dilo alerted her to "spells." The manager and another employee later on the same visit objected that the dog's vest, which was at least partially home-made, was not "regulation." The plaintiff found the manager's tone to be inappropriate, loud, embarrassing, humiliating, and degrading. She was informed that companion animals were not allowed in the warehouse and that in the future the dog should remain in her car. She sued, arguing that Costco had failed to comply with its obligations as a public accommodation under the Americans with Disabilities Act.

The federal district court did not fault the initial inquiry of the Costco employees, noting that the first time the plaintiff brought her dog into the store the dog was a 12-week-old puppy. The court was also bothered by the fact that DiLorenzo's husband had brought the dog in without her on one occasion, at which time he claimed that the dog was a "comfort animal" for him. Although service animals need not always be with the master for whom they provide service, only the person with disabilities in the relationship can claim access rights for a service dog (the husband was not a trainer). The court also mentioned that DiLorenzo sometimes carried the dog, which was probably of significance because one of the dog's functions was protection. There is no rule against carrying service dogs, however, though this may have reinforced Costco's suspicions. DiLorenzo apparently made little attempt to explain what services the dog performed for her. The court said that if she had, Costco might have had no reason to preclude her from bringing the dog into the store. As is sometimes true, the dog owner might have been able to avoid the problem had she been somewhat better prepared, but then the same could be said of the Costco employees. After finding that no facts could sustain other aspects of the dog owner's claim, the court granted summary judgment to Costco.[392] The employees were justified in their inquiries.

Courts have recognized good faith efforts of store chains to train staff on the significance of service animals.[393]

## RESPONSIBILITIES OF BUSINESSES

Federal rules provide that a public accommodation must modify policies, practices, or procedures to permit the use of a service animal by an individual with a disability.[394] Public accommodation "means a private entity that owns, leases (or leases to), or operates a place of public accommodation." A place of public accommodation is a facility, operated by a private entity, whose operations affect commerce and fall within at least one of the following categories:

1. An inn, hotel, motel, or other place of lodging, except for an establishment located within a building that contains not more than five rooms for rent or hire and that is actually occupied by the proprietor of the establishment as the residence of the proprietor.
2. A restaurant, bar, or other establishment serving food or drink.
3. A motion picture house, theater, concert hall, stadium, or other place of exhibition or entertainment.
4. An auditorium, convention center, lecture hall, or other place of public gathering.
5. A bakery, grocery store, clothing store, hardware store, shopping center, or other sales or rental establishment.
6. A laundromat, dry-cleaner, bank, barber shop, beauty shop, travel service, shoe repair service, funeral parlor, gas station, office of an accountant or lawyer, pharmacy, insurance office, professional office of a health care provider, hospital, or other service establishment.
7. A terminal, depot, or other station used for specified public transportation.
8. A museum, library, gallery, or other place of public display or collection.
9. A park, zoo, amusement park, or other place of recreation.
10. A nursery, elementary, secondary, undergraduate, or postgraduate private school, or other place of education.
11. A day care center, senior citizen center, homeless shelter, food bank, adoption agency, or other social service center establishment.
12. A gymnasium, health spa, bowling alley, golf course, or other place of exercise or recreation.[395]

Notice that a terminal or station used in public transportation is included among public accommodations, but the transportation vehicle itself is not. Transportation services will be discussed in a following chapter. A disability is defined as ". . . with respect to an individual, a physical or mental impairment that substantially limits one or more of the major life activities of such individual; a record of such an impairment; or being regarded as having such an impairment." In this definition, a *physical or mental impairment* means:

1. Any physiological disorder or condition, cosmetic disfigurement, or anatomical loss affecting one or more of the following body systems: neurological; musculoskeletal; special sense organs; respiratory, including speech organs; cardiovascular; reproductive; digestive; genitourinary; hemic and lymphatic; skin; and endocrine.
2. Any mental or psychological disorder such as mental retardation, organic brain syndrome, emotional or mental illness, and specific learning disabilities.
3. The phrase physical or mental impairment includes, but is not limited to, such contagious and non-contagious diseases and conditions as orthopedic, visual, speech, and hearing impairments, cerebral palsy, epilepsy, muscular dystrophy, multiple sclerosis, cancer, heart disease, diabetes, mental retardation, emotional illness, specific learning disabilities, HIV disease (whether symptomatic or asymptomatic), tuberculosis, drug addiction, and alcoholism.
4. The phrase *physical* or *mental impairment* does not include homosexuality or bisexuality.

*Major life activities* are functions such as caring for one's self, performing manual tasks, walking, seeing, hearing, speaking, breathing, learning, and working. A *record of such an impairment* means a history of, or has been misclassified as having, a mental or physical impairment that substantially limits one or more major life activities. Someone *is regarded as having an impairment* if one of the following is true of an individual:

1. Has a physical or mental impairment that does not substantially limit major life activities but that is treated by a private entity as constituting such a limitation.
2. Has a physical or mental impairment that substantially limits major life activities only as a result of the attitudes of others toward such impairment.
3. Has none of the impairments defined in paragraph (1) of this definition but is treated by a private entity as having such an impairment.

A *disability* does not include transvestism, transsexualism, pedophilia, exhibitionism, voyeurism, gender identity disorders not resulting from physical impairments, other sexual behavior disorders, compulsive gambling, kleptomania, pyromania, or psychoactive substance use disorders resulting from current illegal use of drugs.[396]

The requirement on allowing access to public accommodations does not mean that such facilities have any responsibility to supervise or care for a service animal.[397] Nor must a public accommodation make modifications if these would "fundamentally alter the nature of the goods, services, facilities, privileges, or accommodations."[398] A concert hall invoked this fundamental alteration argument in *Lentini v. California Center for the Arts, Escondido*[399] to exclude the dog of a quadriplegic woman. Lentini had a Shih Tsu/Poodle mix named Jazz. Although the facility had a policy of admitting service animals, the dog had barked or yipped when people approached Lentini at several concerts. The manager of the facility also believed that only guide dogs were service animals, but the barking, which apparently occurred because the dog was protecting its handler from people who came too close, was the precipitating cause of the exclusion. A federal district court noted that people often made similar loud sounds at the concerts but were not being excluded and awarded damages of $7,000 against the facility, $5,000 against the manager, and $1,000 against an employee. The Ninth Circuit affirmed, noting that the concert hall could remove disruptive service animals, but that it had to ascertain the reason for the disruption first. The reason here was not good enough.

## Landlords Not Usually Liable for Tenant's Business

When the business that discriminates against an individual with a service animal is a commercial tenant in a building, the tenant's discriminatory behavior does not make the landlord liable, unless the tenant is enforcing a policy of the landlord.[400]

## LODGING

The first item on the list of places of public accommodation includes a "place of lodging." Residential hotels, or single room occupancy hotels (SROs), will generally be considered places of lodging. This kind of public accommodation is to be distinguished from rental buildings, but there are complexities here:

> [I]n a large hotel that has a separate residential apartment wing, the residential wing would not be covered by the ADA because of the nature of the occupancy of that part of the facility. This residential wing would, however, be covered by the Fair Housing Act. The separate non-residential accommodations in the rest of the hotel would be a place of lodging, and thus a public accommodation subject to the requirements of this final rule. If a hotel allows both residential and short-term stays, but does not allocate

space for these different uses in separate, discrete units, *both the ADA and the Fair Housing Act may apply to the facility.*

Where SROs provide social services through federal or state grant programs, they are considered "social service center establishments" a different type of public accommodation. In this situation, the length of stay of the occupants does not matter. Also covered in this category are homeless shelters, shelters for people seeking refuge from domestic violence, nursing homes, and residential care facilities. There are exceptions to exceptions:

> [A] homeless shelter that is intended and used only for long-term residential stays and that does not provide social services to its residents would not be covered as a place of public accommodation. However, if this facility permitted short-term stays or provided social services to its residents, it would be covered under the ADA either as a "place of lodging" or as a "social service center establishment," or as both.

A private home is not a place of public accommodation, but if the home includes a doctor's or dentist's office, that area would be open to the public and would be considered a place of public accommodation. A house where the owner lives and rents out not more than five of his rooms is not covered by ADA requirements.

## DEPARTMENT OF JUSTICE CONSIDERS NEW ISSUES AND PERSPECTIVES

In a document released in June 2008, the Department of Justice said that it "continues to receive a large number of complaints from individuals with service animals."[401]

> [S]ome individuals with impairments, who would not be covered as individuals with disabilities, are claiming that their animals are legitimate service animals, whether fraudulently or sincerely (albeit mistakenly), to gain access to hotels, restaurants, and other places of public accommodation. Another trend is the use of wild, exotic, or unusual species, many of which are untrained, as service animals.[402]

The Department thus proposed a significant, some would say radical, revision to the definition of service animal, which would exclude "wild animals (including non-human primates born in captivity), reptiles, rabbits, farm animals (including any breed of horse, miniature horse, pony, pig, or goat), ferrets, amphibians, and rodents." The Department of Justice finds support for excluding monkeys in a position statement of the American Veterinary Medical Association, which stated "The AVMA does not support the use of non-human primates as assistance animals because of animal welfare concerns, the potential for serious injury and zoonotic [animal to human disease transmission] risks."[403] This proposed narrowing of acceptable service animal species seemingly to dogs and cats was apparently to allay concerns of restaurants, grocery stores, and performing arts venues. These proposals were issued at the end of the Bush administration, but it is not clear that officials in the Obama administration will be so quick to dismiss the idea of guide horses and other less common service animals.

The 2008 proposals, as discussed in the preceding chapter, indicate that the Department of Justice is quite open to psychological functions for service animals, which it acknowledges can "do work or perform tasks for the benefit of individuals with disabilities, including psychiatric, cognitive, and mental disabilities."

## Department of Justice Declines to Set
## Training Standards for Service Animals

In 2008, the Department stated that it had rejected suggestions that it establish training standards for service animals in order to differentiate them from untrained pets, noting that in many cases, owners have done their own training. It may also be that the Department is reluctant to effectively endorse the dog training industry.

> Because of the variety of individual training that a service animal can receive, from formal licensing at an academy to individual training on how to respond to the onset of medical conditions, such as seizures, the Department is not inclined to establish a standard that all service animals must meet. While the Department does not plan to change the current policy of no formal training or certification requirements, some of the behavioral standards that it has proposed actually relate to suitability for public access, such as being housebroken and under the control of its handler.[404]

## Hospital Access

The 2008 proposals also discuss hospital access, but as will be described in detail in a subsequent chapter, many hospitals have been very open regarding service and therapy animals. The Department of Justice notes that hospitals have unique issues.

> As required by the [Americans with Disabilities Act], a healthcare facility must permit a person with a disability to be accompanied by his or her serv-

ice animal in all areas of the facility in which that person would otherwise be allowed, with some exceptions. Zoonotic diseases can be transmitted to humans through trauma (bites, scratches, direct contact, arthropod vectors, or aerosols). Although there is no evidence that most service animals pose a significant risk of transmitting infectious agents to humans, animals can serve as a reservoir for a significant number of diseases that could potentially be transmitted to humans in the healthcare setting. A service animal may accompany its owner to such areas as admissions and discharge offices, the emergency room, inpatient and outpatient rooms, examining and diagnostic rooms, clinics, rehabilitation therapy areas, the cafeteria and vending areas, the pharmacy, rest rooms, and all other areas of the facility where visitors are permitted, except those listed below.

. . . Based on [Center for Disease Control and Prevention Guidance], it is generally appropriate to exclude a service animal from areas that require a protected environment, including operating rooms, holding and recovery areas, labor and delivery suites, newborn intensive care nurseries, and sterile processing departments.[405]

The federal district court of Kansas granted summary judgment to a hospital which excluded service animals from non-public areas of the hospital, which included the emergency services department.[406]

A personal note may be appropriate here. I take my therapy dog into a hospital in Kingston, New York. I am not permitted to go into the intensive care units, but can even go into an emergency ward if this is requested by a family, particularly for a child.

# Chapter 9

# TRAVELING WITH SERVICE
# AND SUPPORT DOGS

*A local ferry service that takes passengers from Long Beach, California, to Catalina Island has a VIP lounge. To go in the lounge during the crossing costs $10 more than a general admission ticket. A regular passenger is dangerously allergic to animals and several years before requested that some part of the ferry be designated animal-free. The only part of the ferry that could allow sufficient isolation for the passenger was the lounge and the ferry company designated it as animal-free. A blind woman came to the ticket office and asks to buy a ticket to the lounge. She is accompanied by her guide dog. The ticket sellers are aware of the policy, but check with their supervisor.*

What should the ferry line do for the woman with the guide dog? Before this question can be answered, we must discuss the different requirements for different types of transportations, including airplanes, cruise ships, and transportation systems such as bus and ferry lines.[407]

## AIRPLANE ACCESS

The Air Carrier Access Act of 1986 prohibits discrimination against "an otherwise qualified individual" on three grounds:

1. The individual has a physical or mental impairment that substantially limits one or more major life activities.
2. The individual has a record of such an impairment.
3. The individual is regarded as having such an impairment.[408]

As with other federal agencies, rules regarding service animals are provided by regulation, not by statute. The only statutory references in Title 49 to ani-

142

mals concern loss, injury, or death of an animal during air transport. The final rules issued in May 2008 became effective May 2009, and apply to both domestic and foreign carriers.[409] In a glossary to the final regulations issued in 2008, a service animal is "Any animal that is individually trained or able to provide assistance to a qualified person with a disability; or any animal shown by documentation to be necessary for the emotional wellbeing of a passenger." This definition is purposefully broad and includes emotional support animals. As discussed in the chapter regarding general regulatory issues of the federal agencies, the final air carrier access rules limit access of emotional support animals to individuals with a diagnosed mental or emotional disorder, and carriers may insist on "recent documentation from a licensed mental health professional to support the passenger's desire to travel with such an animal."

## Advance Notice Requirement

Airlines can require a passenger with a mental health disability to provide up to 48 hours' advance notice and check in one hour before check-in time for the general public to receive various services, including transportation of psychiatric service or emotional support animals in the cabin.[410] This can present a problem if an individual with such an animal must fly in an emergency or for a death in the family. The requirement extends to all service animals if the flight is to last eight or more hours.[411]

## Training as an Indication of Service Animal Status

In the guide accompany the 2008 regulations, the Department notes that, in deciding whether an animal is a service animal:

> In most situations the key is training. Generally, a service animal is individually trained to perform functions to assist the passenger who is a qualified individual with a disability. In a few extremely limited situations, an animal such as a seizure alert animal may be capable of performing functions to assist a qualified person with a disability without individualized training. Also, an animal used for emotional support need not have specific training for that function. Similar to an animal that has been individually trained, the definition of a service animal includes: An animal that has been shown to have the innate ability to assist a person with a disability; or an emotional support animal.

Thus, two types of service animals are recognized as possibly having little or no training: seizure-alert dogs and emotional support animals.

## Determining Whether an Animal is a Service Animal or a Pet

The Department provides five steps that airline personnel can go through to determine whether an animal qualifies for service animal status. (See text box.)

## Qualified Individuals with Disabilities

Airlines can ask how an animal assists a person with a disability, but personnel are advised to avoid asking "What is your disability?" The Department calls this question "intrusive and inconsistent with the intent of the ACAA." The airline can ask the passenger whether he has documentation to verify the medical necessity for traveling with the animal. Documentation can only be required if the passenger's verbal assurances are not credible and the airline cannot in good faith determine whether the animal is a service animal. Documentation can also be required if the animal is to be used as an emotional support or psychiatric service animal.

## Two or More Service Animals

The Department acknowledges that a passenger may have more than one service animal. In such cases, a passenger may be permitted to purchase a second seat, or may virtually have to in order for the cabin to satisfy safety regulations.

If carriage in the cargo compartment is unavoidable, the airline is to notify the destination station to return the service animal(s) to the passenger at the gate as soon as possible, or to assist the passenger as necessary to retrieve them in the appropriate location.

## Service Animals in Training and Service Animals Not Traveling with Primary Handlers

The Department of Transportation states that service animals in training are not pets, but they do not partake of the access rights of other service animals "because 'in training' indicates that they do not yet meet the legal definition of service animal." The Department notes that airline policies on service animals in training vary, and states that some airlines "permit qualified trainers to bring service animals in training aboard an aircraft for training purposes."[412] Thus, trainers wishing to travel with animals they are training to be service animals would have to verify a particular airline's policy and satisfy the airline of their qualifications as trainers.

## Five Steps for Determining Status of an Animal as a Service Animal or a Pet.

1. *Obtain credible verbal assurances:* Ask the passenger: "Is this your pet?" If the passenger responds that the animal is a service animal and not a pet, but uncertainty remains about the animal, appropriate follow-up questions would include:

   ➤ *"What tasks or functions does your animal perform for you?"* or

   ➤ *"What has it been trained to do for you?"* or

   ➤ *"Would you describe how the animal performs this task (or function) for you?"*

- As noted earlier, functions include, but are not limited to:

   A. Helping blind or visually impaired people to safely negotiate their surroundings;

   B. Alerting deaf and hard-of-hearing persons to sounds;

   C. Helping people with mobility impairments to open and close doors, retrieve objects, transfer from one seat to another, maintain balance; or

   D. Alert or respond to a disability-related need or emergency (e.g., seizure, extreme social anxiety or panic attack).

- Note that to be a service animal that can properly travel in the cabin, the animal need not necessarily perform a function for the passenger during the flight. For example, some dogs are trained to help pull a passenger's wheelchair or carry items that the passenger cannot readily carry while using his or her wheelchair. It would not be appropriate to deny transportation in the cabin to such a dog.

- If a passenger cannot provide credible assurances that an animal has been individually trained or is able to perform some task or function to assist the passenger with his or her disability, the animal might not be a service animal. In this case, the airline personnel may require documentation.

- There may be cases in which a passenger with a disability has personally trained an animal to perform a specific function (e.g., seizure alert). Such an animal may not have been trained through a formal training program (e.g., a "school" for service animals). If the passenger can provide a reasonable explanation of how the animal was trained or how it performs the function for which it is being used, this can constitute a "credible verbal assurance" that the animal has been trained to perform a function for the passenger.

*continued on next page*

2. *Look for physical indicators on the animal:* Some service animals wear harnesses, vests, capes or backpacks. Markings on these items or on the animal's tags may identify it as a service animal. It should be noted, however, that the absence of such equipment does not necessarily mean the animal is not a service animal. Similarly, the presence of a harness or vest on a pet for which the passenger cannot provide such credible verbal assurance may not be sufficient evidence that the animal is, in fact, a legitimate service animal.

3. *Request documentation for service animals other than emotional support or psychiatric service animals:* The law allows airline personnel to ask for documentation as a means of verifying that the animal is a service animal, but DOT's rules tell carriers not to require documentation as a condition for permitting an individual to travel with his or her service animal in the cabin unless a passenger's verbal assurance is not credible. In that case, the airline may require documentation as a condition for allowing the animal to travel in the cabin. This should be an infrequent situation. The purpose of documentation is to substantiate the passenger's disability-related need for the animal's accompaniment, which the airline may require as a condition to permit the animal to travel in the cabin. Examples of documentation include a letter from a licensed professional treating the passenger's condition (e.g., physician, mental health professional, vocational case manager, etc.)

4. *Require documentation for emotional support and psychiatric service animals:* With respect to an animal used for emotional support (which need not have specific training for that function but must be trained to behave appropriately in a public setting), airline personnel may require current documentation (i.e., not more than one year old) on letterhead from a licensed mental health professional stating (1) that the passenger has a mental health-related disability listed in the *Diagnostic and Statistical Manual of Mental Disorders (DSM IV);* (2) that having the animal accompany the passenger is necessary to the passenger's mental health or treatment; (3) that the individual providing the assessment of the passenger is a licensed mental health professional and the passenger is under his or her professional care; and (4) the date and type of the mental health professional's license and the state or other jurisdiction in which it was issued. Airline personnel may require this documentation as a condition of permitting the animal to accompany the passenger in the cabin. The purpose of this

*continued on next page*

provision is to prevent abuse by passengers that do not have a medical need for an emotional support animal and to ensure that passengers who have a legitimate need for emotional support animals are permitted to travel with their service animals on the aircraft. Airlines are not permitted to require the documentation to specify the type of mental health disability, e.g., panic attacks. There is a separate category of service animals generally known as "psychiatric service animals." These animals may be trained by their owners, sometimes with the assistance of a professional trainer, to perform tasks such as fetching medications, reminding the user to take medications, helping people with balance problems caused by medications or an underlying condition, bringing a phone to the user in an emergency or activating a specially equipped emergency phone, or acting as a buffer against other people crowding too close. As with emotional support animals, it is possible for this category of animals to be a source of abuse by persons attempting to circumvent carrier rules concerning transportation of pets. Consequently, it is appropriate for airlines to apply the same advance notice and documentation requirements to psychiatric service animals as they do to emotional support animals.

5. *Observe behavior of animals:* Service animals are trained to behave properly in public settings. For example, a properly trained guide dog will remain at its owner's feet. It does not run freely around an aircraft or an airport gate area, bark or growl repeatedly at other persons on the aircraft, bite or jump on people, or urinate or defecate in the cabin or gate area. An animal that engages in such disruptive behavior shows that it has not been successfully trained to function as a service animal in public settings. Therefore, airlines are not required to treat it as a service animal, even if the animal performs an assistive function for a passenger with a disability or is necessary for a passenger's emotional well-being.

(Taken from *Guidance Concerning Service Animals,* 73 Fed. Reg. 27657, May 13, 2008.)

The Department allows airlines to set policies on passengers traveling with service animals that do not serve them, such as where a friend is bringing a trained service animal to its new handler.

## Location of the Service Animal during Flight

A service animal must be permitted to accompany a passenger with a disability "at any seat in which the passenger sits, unless the animal obstructs an aisle or other area that must remain unobstructed to facilitate an emergency evacuation."[413] A bulkhead seat will generally be optimal.[414] The Department notes that service animals generally sit on the floor and "it is unlikely that a service animal would ever actually occupy a separate seat."[415] If the animal cannot be accommodated at the seat location assigned to the passenger, the airline "must offer the passenger the opportunity to move the animal to another seat location, if present on the aircraft, where the animal can be accommodated."[416]

> The only situation in which the rule contemplates that a service animal would not be permitted to accompany its user at his or her seat is where the animal blocks a space that, per FAA [Federal Aviation Administration] or applicable foreign government safety regulations, must remain unobstructed (e.g., an aisle, access to an emergency exit) AND the passenger and animal cannot be moved to another location where such a blockage does not occur. In such a situation, the carrier should first talk with other passengers to find a seat location where the service animal and its user can be agreeably accommodated (e.g., by finding a passenger who is willing to share foot space with the animal). The fact that a service animal may need to use a reasonable portion of an adjacent seat's foot space, that does not deny another passenger effective use of the space for his or her feet, is not, however, an adequate reason for the carrier to refuse to permit the animal to accompany its user at his or her seat. Only if no other alternative is available should the carrier discuss less desirable options concerning the transportation of the service animal with the passenger traveling with the animal, such as traveling on a later flight with more room or carrying the animal in the cargo compartment.[417]

The 2008 rules state that an airline must provide a bulkhead seat or a seat other than a bulkhead seat at the request of the individual traveling with a service animal.[418]

If a service animal has to fly in a cargo compartment, the carrier cannot charge the passenger for transporting the animal in this manner, even though other passengers pay for flying their pets in cargo.

## No First Class Seating Obligation

The Department of Transportation rejected comments that airlines should be required to move individuals with service animals into first class or to reconfigure cabins to provide more room for passengers with service animals. These suggestions were rejected as too costly.

## Discomfort of Other Passengers

Although some people have religious or cultural objections to sitting near animals, the Department has stated that it "has long been a principle . . . that it is improper for a transportation provider to deny or restrict service to a passenger with a disability because doing so may offend or annoy other persons. . . ." Thus, the discomfort of those with allergies or religious objections "must yield to the non-discrimination mandate of the ACAA," though "carriers should do their best to accommodate other passengers' concerns by steps like seating passengers with service animals and passengers who are uncomfortable with service animals away from one another." "Forcing the passenger with the service animal to move to another seat to make another passenger more comfortable, let alone denying transportation in the cabin to the service animal or its user, is not an option."

In a news release of September 28, 1999, the Department of Transportation announced the settlement of a case against America West with assessment of a penalty of $1,000. A blind passenger with a guide dog was not permitted to sit in her assigned seat in the first-class cabin because the passenger sitting next to her refused to sit next to a dog and would not allow her to take her seat. The passenger was eventually seated in coach with her dog. In its consent order, the enforcement office said that under the department's rules travelers with disabilities have the right to bring their service animals on board aircraft and that the service animal must be accommodated close to the owner. If another passenger objects to the animal, the carrier must advise that passenger of the rights of the traveler with the disability and, if necessary, find another seat for the objecting passenger *or remove that person from the aircraft.*[419]

If a passenger were extremely allergic, with reactions rising to the level of a disability, the Department concedes that there are cases where a service animal might be bumped off the flight.

> Since one disability does not trump another, the carrier should consider a disability-neutral means of determining which passenger would have to be rebooked (e.g., which passenger made the earlier reservation). We empha-

size that we expect any such situation to be extremely rare, and that carriers should not rebook a passenger absent strong evidence that the mere presence of an animal in the cabin, even in a location distant from the allergic passenger, would produce an allergic reaction rising to the level of a disability.

In such a case, the airline should ask the person with the serious allergies for medical documentation.

## Unusual Service Animals

The Department of Transportation believes that stories of unusual service animals cause more concern than is probably justified, given the infrequency with which airlines have actually had to deal with such issues. "Because they make for colorful stories, accounts of unusual service animals have received publicity wholly disproportionate to their frequency or importance. Some (e.g., tales of service snakes, which grow larger with each retelling) have become the stuff of urban legends." The agency was willing to allow carriers to always exclude some animals, such as rodents and reptiles.

> For others (e.g., miniature horses, pot-bellied pigs, monkeys), a U.S. carrier could make a judgment call about whether any factors (e.g., size and weight of the animal, any direct threat to the health and safety of others, significant disruption of cabin service) would preclude carrying the animal. Absent such factors, the carrier would have to allow the animal to accompany its owner on the flight.

The DOT rules do not require foreign carriers to carry animals other than dogs.

## Denial of Service

Service animals can be denied entry to the cabin if they pose a direct threat to the health or safety of others or if they would disrupt cabin service. A direct threat could include growling, snarling, lunging at, or attempting to bite other persons. Reasonable limitation of foot space is not a reason to deny a service animal carriage in the cabin. If an airline declines to accept an animal as a service animal, it must explain the reason for their decision to the passenger and document it in writing. A copy of the explanation must be provided to the passenger either at the airport, or within *10 calendar days* of the incident.[420]

## Care of Service Animals

Passengers are solely responsible for caring for their service animals during flight. No charge may be imposed by an airline for passage of a service animal, but passengers can be charged for damage done by the animal, including cleaning a seat that an animal defecated on.

## Relief Areas in Terminals

U.S. airports, under the final rules, will have "to provide, in cooperation with the airport operator, animal relief areas for service animals that accompany passengers who are departing, arriving, or connecting at the facility."[421] On request, a carrier operating at a U.S. airport must escort a passenger to a service animal relief area.[422]

## Liability Waivers Prohibited

The DOT prohibits carriers from requiring passengers to sign waivers or releases of liability for the loss, injury, or death of a service animal: "You must not require passengers with a disability to sign waivers of liability for damage to or loss of wheelchairs or other assistive devices, or for the loss of, death of, or injury to service animals."[423]

## Foreign Carriers and Overseas Flights

Foreign carriers may be more restrictive regarding service animals than the requirements of the Air Carrier Access Act and its regulations. Some only allow dogs, some only dogs certified by recognized training schools or associations. Some do not allow any animals in the cabin or restrict service animals to certain locations. The Department's policy is stated as follows:

> It would be inconsistent with the ACAA to permit a foreign carrier, for example, to deny passage to a U.S. resident's service animal because the animal had not been certified by an organization that the foreign carrier recognized. When flying to or from the United States, foreign carriers are subject to requirements of U.S. non-discrimination law, though carriers may avail themselves of the conflict of laws waiver and equivalent alternative provisions of this Part. We acknowledge that some foreign carriers may be unused to making the kinds of judgment calls concerning the credibility of a passenger's verbal assurances that the Department's service animal guidance describes, and which U.S. carriers have made for over 17 years. However, the comments do not provide any persuasive evidence that foreign carriers are incapable of doing so or that making such judgment calls will in any important way interfere with the operation of their flights.[424]

The DOT precludes foreign carriers, absent a conflict of laws waiver, from imposing certification or documentation requirements for dogs beyond those permitted U.S. carriers. Thus, if an airline flies to a country that prohibits a hearing dog from entering the country, the airline could apply for a conflict of laws waiver to be relieved of carrying a hearing dog to that country. If the airline flies to another country that does allow guide hearing dogs, the airline would have take hearing dogs on such flights.

The DOT noted that some "equivalent alternative provisions" are acceptable but, if a foreign carrier's policies are more restrictive, "modifying carrier policies to accommodate U.S. civil rights requirements is something foreign carriers must accept as part of their obligation to comply with U.S. law when flying to and from the U.S."

**Transport of Service Animals on Flights to the UK.** In a "Notice of Guidance Concerning the Carriage of Service Animals in Air Transportation from the United States to the United Kingdom,"[425] the Department of Transportation (DOT) addressed the differences between UK and U.S. laws regarding the transport of service animals. The guidance also provided procedures for carriers wishing to comply with both countries' sets of rules. In April 2004, UK laws were changed to allow certain animals in the aircraft passenger cabin. This followed EU Regulation (EC) 998/2003,[426] establishing health requirements for animals traveling into the EU. On July 5, 2006, The Council of the European Union adopted a community regulation concerning the rights of persons with disabilities and persons with reduced mobility when traveling by air.[427]

UK law generally provides that only guide and assistance dogs may accompany owners in the passenger cabin on a flight.[428]

> The FODCOM [UK guidance] defines guide and assistance dogs as dogs trained by an individual or organization accepted by and affiliated with the International Guide Dog Federation to provide assistance to a person with a disability and requires formal identification indicating such training. Dogs not meeting the above criteria for guide or assistance dogs, as well as cats and ferrets, are considered pets and are not recognized as service animals in the U.K., even if trained to perform a function to assist a person with his or her disability. FODCOM 3/2005, which is mandatory for U.K. carriers and guidance for non-U.K. carriers, states that PETS-compliant animals other than guide and assistance dogs should be carried in the cargo hold.

Because of the UK restrictions:

> U.S. and non-U.K. foreign carriers that permit only service dogs and serv-

ice cats to accompany their owners in the passenger cabin (or in the cargo hold when safety requires) on flights from the U.S. into the U.K. will be considered in compliance with the ACAA and Part 382. U.K. carriers that permit only guide and assistance dogs in the passenger cabin (or in the cargo hold when safety requires), and transport other PETS-compliant service animals in the cargo hold on flights from the U.S. into the U.K. will also be considered in compliance with the ACAA. Due to the quarantine restrictions for other animal species and their subsequent unavailability to their owners for six months following entry to the U.K., carriers that accept only PETS-compliant animals on flights from the U.S. into the U.K. will be considered in compliance with the ACAA and Part 382.[429]

## Foreign Quarantine Rules

Some foreign countries have quarantine rules that severely delay and effectively prevent the entrance of service animals into the country. Airlines traveling to such countries should, according to the DOT, apply for a conflict of laws waiver to be relieved of carrying a service animal to such a country. Airlines should, however, take steps to comply with foreign regulations regarding transport of service animals into a country, such as the UK's Pet Travel Scheme. The UK's Department for Environment, Food and Rural Affairs, specifies requirements for bringing a pet into the UK without putting it into quarantine. The Scheme requires a blood test six months before admission of the pet (including service animals) into the UK. Pets must be fitted with a microchip, vaccinated for rabies, carry an EU pet passport (generally issued by a veterinarian) or an official veterinary certificate for countries not issuing pet passports, treated against certain parasites, and meet certain documentation requirements.[430]

## Relief During Long Flights

An issue that becomes compelling, at least for a dog, is the length of an overseas flight, during which the animal must eat, drink, and most importantly, urinate and defecate. As to flights of eight hours or more, there is a regulation stating: "If a flight segment is scheduled to take eight hours or more, the carrier may require documentation that the service animal will not need to relieve itself or can do so in a way that will not create a health or sanitation issue on the flight."[431] This is one of the few instances in the federal rules where documentation may be required. Given the fact that in recent years many flights that are not supposed to be so long are, in fact, turning out to be much longer, this can be expected to be a continuing problem. It is also difficult to imagine many veterinarians issuing letters about the elimination needs of animals, even animals they treat. It is to be hoped that this does not itself become a basis of precluding animals from passenger cabins.

## PASSENGER VESSELS

In November 2007, the Department of Transportation proposed rules on accessibility standards of passenger vessels for individuals with disabilities. The Department wanted industry opinion as to whether passenger vessel operators should be required to permit passengers with disabilities to travel with service animals.[432] The International Council of Cruise Lines (ICCL) had raised a number of specific issues regarding U.S. law. The Department noted that even if a country would not allow an animal to enter, this would not preclude a line from allowing an animal on board since it would not have to leave the ship when it docked. Passengers with service animals would have to be informed about those ports where an animal would have to stay on board. Ships would not be required to stock or sell animal food, and passengers would have to bring enough food on board in case the ship did not carry any. The Department sought industry comment on whether refrigeration services would have to be provided where passengers could store animal food.[433] The Department of Transportation would apply the same proofs of service animal status to ships as are used in air travel: "You must accept the following as evidence that an animal is a service animal: identification cards, other written documentation, presence of harnesses, tags, and/or the credible verbal assurances of a passenger with a disability using the animal."[434] The Department sought input from the cruise industry about requirements for animal relief areas.

## TRANSPORTATION SERVICES

Entities, both public and private, providing transportation services are covered by the Rehabilitation Act of 1973 and may be subject to regulations under the Americans with Disabilities Act.[435] Under the rules regarding transportation services,[436] a service provider, such as a bus[437] or train line,[438] or a taxi company,[439] must permit service animals to accompany individuals with disabilities in vehicles and facilities. A service animal is defined in exactly the same words as are used by the Department of Justice, that is:

> Service animal means any guide dog, signal dog, or other animal individually trained to work or perform tasks for an individual with a disability, including, but not limited to, guiding individuals with impaired vision, alerting individuals with impaired hearing to intruders or sounds, providing minimal protection or rescue work, pulling a wheelchair, or fetching dropped items.[440]

As discussed in a previous chapter, the Department of Justice proposed to significantly revise the definition of a service animal to exclude farm animals and exotic types of animals. Because of the language in the regulatory releases of the Department of Transportation concerning airline cabin access, it seems unlikely that the Department of Transportation would agree with such a change. In an appendix to the DOT regulations concerning their construction and interpretation, the agency specifically insists that monkeys be allowed on transportation services if they are trained service animals.

> Service animals shall always be permitted to accompany their users in any private or public transportation vehicle or facility. One of the most common misunderstandings about service animals is that they are limited to being guide dogs for persons with visual impairments. Dogs are trained to assist people with a wide variety of disabilities, including individuals with hearing and mobility impairments. Other animals (e.g., monkeys) are sometimes used as service animals as well. In any of these situations, the entity must permit the service animal to accompany the user.[441]

Extra charges may not be sought from individuals with service animals. A $20 ride for another passenger is a $20 ride for a person with a service animal, even if the animal has to take up the space of a passenger. (See Figure 22 for a service dog on public transportation.)

The fact situation outlined in the first paragraph of this chapter is taken from *Lockett v. Catalina Channel Express, Inc.,*[442] where a blind passenger sued a ferry operator for refusing to allow her in the ferry's lounge area. In response to earlier requests by a regular passenger, the line had a policy excluding animals from the Commodore Lounge, a separate and more expensive section of the ferry (a ticket to the lounge cost $10 more than a regular ticket). Tricia Lockett was legally blind and used a guide dog to assist her. In 2002, Lockett requested a ticket in the Commodore Lounge but Catalina refused to sell the ticket. Two weeks later, Catalina changed its policy, and two months later Lockett filed suite against Catalina for a violation of the Americans with Disabilities Act. The district court held that the ferry could keep the plaintiff from the lounge.

The Ninth Circuit affirmed, but emphasized that it was doing so on the narrow ground that the line, "when suddenly faced with a possible threat to the health and safety of its passengers, made a one-time reasonable judgment to deny admission to the lounge while it investigated the competing interests." The district court had granted summary judgment by accepting that the line had provided Lockett with an accommodation that was different or separate and that this was necessary to provide another passenger who was high-

Figure 22. Veronica Morris riding with Ollivander on the Bay Area Rapid Transit System. Permission of Veronica Morris; thanks to Joan Esnayra.

ly allergic to animals with a separate accommodation.[443] The district court also held that the refusal to permit Lockett into the Commodore Lounge was permissible under the Department of Justice regulations.[444]

The Ninth Circuit said that line had not offered Lockett a separate arrangement or facility, but rather relegated her to the general passenger area, which was certainly not equivalent to the Commodore Lounge. In any case, this was a question for the jury and should not have been resolved on summary judgment. Nevertheless, the circuit court acknowledged that, under Department of Justice regulations,[445] the employees of Catalina could reasonably wonder whether the presence of the dog could have posed a significant risk to the health or safety of others. The court did not consider regulations issued by the Department of Transportation.

## STATE TRANSPORTATION STATUTES AND RULES

More than half the states specify public transportation or common carriers in their definition of public accommodation, and some specify a range of types of carriers. Others use broad enough definitions ("any place to which the public is invited") to be presumed to include means of transportation. Many specify that there is to be no extra charge for a service animal.[446] Some of the provisions (e.g., Kentucky) mention that a dog is not to occupy a seat on a public conveyance.

# Chapter 10

# SERVICE AND SUPPORT
# DOGS AS TENANTS

Almost 30 percent of relinquishments of companion animals to shelters occur because of "housing issues." One study concluded that about half of rental housing is pet-friendly to some degree, but only 9 percent of rental buildings have no limitations on animal size or type.[447] Only 11 percent of housing allows large dogs. Around 82 percent of tenants reported having trouble finding a rental unit that would take their pets, and 100 percent of tenants with more than one dog had trouble. An effective deterrent for some people will be a pet deposit, and 75 percent of pet-friendly housing requires one, with an average cost being between 40 percent and 85 percent of a month's rent. Pet-friendly housing generally charged more in any case. Tenants with pets move less often than those without them, obviously reflecting the fact that finding a new place to live is a bigger problem for pet owners. The study found that damage by tenants with pets was only marginally higher than damage by tenants without pets, considerably at variance with the opinion of many landlords. There is, in short, a very strong benefit for a tenant to have a service dog that can, in most cases, not be excluded from an apartment, and for which a separate deposit may not be charged.

Determining the rights of a tenant, or the purchaser of a house, in the face of a no-pets policy requires a determination of what law applies to the specific situation.[448] There are four federal regulatory regimes (though two of them are now virtually identical), as well as separate state statutory systems, some of the latter of which are specific to housing and real estate and some of which are mixed in with more general public accommodation access rules. A number of courts have faced issues of tenants claiming to have special animals that they argue should be excepted from no-pets policies and these courts have interpreted statutory and regulatory regimes in various ways, sometimes quite clearly and convincingly, sometimes by mixing laws more frequently applied to public accommodations such as restaurants with laws specific to landlords and tenants. Many of the leading cases were decided before the current regulatory regimes were implemented, as well as before publication of much of the scientific evidence about the benefits of animals to humans, and it is not clear to what extent these decisions would, or should, influence courts facing similar issues today.

Some governmental agencies that supply housing to employees and others, such as the Department of the Interior, have policy pronouncements regarding service animals.[449]

## REGULATORY REGIMES ON HOUSING

Three sets of regulations have been issued regarding housing and pets or service animals by the Department of Housing and Urban Development, covering respectively (1) a person with disabilities in almost any dwelling unit,[450] (2) persons in projects for the elderly or persons with disabilities under federally administered and subsidized housing programs,[451] and (3) persons with disabilities in public housing.[452] Both the second and third sets of regulations implement legislation designed to recognize the importance of animals in the lives of the elderly, disabled, and individuals living in subsidized housing.[453]

The Department of Justice pursues investigations against potentially discriminatory housing situations, and employs "fair housing testers," individuals who pose as renters to gather information about possible housing discrimination. Discrimination awards for discrimination against owners and managing agents have been substantial.[454]

The Office of Public and Indian Housing of the Department of Housing and Urban Development issued accessibility guidance under which recipients of federal housing funds must "allow a tenant with a disability to have an assistive animal if the animal is needed as a reasonable accommodation."[455]

A prior chapter discussed regulations issued by the Department of Justice that apply to places of public accommodation, which include inns, hotels, and other places of lodging, including single room occupancy hotels where renters may rent for a short term. In addition, state laws commonly (but not always) provide specifically for housing and rental accommodation access for individuals with disabilities using service animals.

## REASONABLE ACCOMMODATION REQUIREMENT

The first of the three HUD regulations implements the Fair Housing Amendments Act of 1988.[456] Discrimination in the sale or rental of a dwelling to any buyer or renter because of a disability is unlawful,[457] and for this purpose discrimination includes a "refusal to make reasonable accommodations in rules, policies, practices, or services, when such accommodations may be necessary to afford such person equal opportunity to use and enjoy a dwelling."[458] The statute does not apply to a single-family house sold or rented by the owner who owns fewer than three single-family houses, but if he owns more, it is covered. This exception also does not apply if the owner, in selling or renting the house, uses a real estate broker, agent, or salesman.[459] The rule also does not apply to "rooms or units in dwellings containing living quarters occupied or intended to be occupied by no more than four families living independently of each other, if the owner actually maintains and occupies one of such living quarters as his residence."[460] A regulatory example of the "reasonable accommodations" requirement states that refusing to permit an applicant in an apartment with a guide dog because of a no-pets policy would be a violation.[461] That the reasonable accommodation principle is broader than guide dogs is indicated by a joint statement issued by the Departments of Justice and Housing and Urban Development, which in giving an example of a nexus between a requested accommodation and an individual's disability, provides the following example:

> A housing provider has a "no pets" policy. A tenant who is deaf requests that the provider allow him to keep a dog in his unit as a reasonable accommodation. The tenant explains that the dog is an assistance animal that will alert him to several sounds, including knocks at the door, sounding of the smoke detector, the telephone ringing, and cars coming into the driveway. The housing provider must make an exception to its "no pets" policy to accommodate this tenant.[462]

An example on HUD's website stretches this even further:

### Situation
John has been diagnosed with severe depression and is disabled as defined by the Fair Housing Act. His doctor prescribes John a dog to help alleviate some of his symptoms. John asks his landlord if he can have a dog as a reasonable accommodation for his disability. His landlord says yes, but tells John he'll need to pay a $250 pet deposit and must provide proof that the animal is trained.

***Question:*** Did John's landlord correctly handle John's request under the Fair Housing Act? What if John wanted a cat or a ferret instead?

***Answer:*** No, John's landlord did not handle his request correctly. The landlord cannot charge John a pet deposit for his animal because it is not a pet, but rather a service/companion animal required for disability. Further, the landlord cannot ask for proof that the animal is trained. Lastly, service/companion animals do not have to be just dogs; they can also be other animals, such as cats or ferrets.[463]

The dog "alleviates" some of John's symptoms (presumably additional evidence could support this), but does not appear to do so in a manner consistent with the dog being a service animal. Obviously this is true of a cat or a ferret. Thus, the website question and answer (which is presented as an example of the application of the Fair Housing laws to real life situations), suggest that emotional support animals satisfy general Fair Housing Act requirements.

## COURTS AND HOUSING ISSUES

Regulators can posit a single issue and provide a straightforward solution. An individual has a guide dog but a landlord refuses to rent to him because of a no-pets policy. No other facts are provided. The landlord is wrong, and liable for his error. Courts do not have the luxury of such simple situations. The man may not be completely blind and may sometimes leave the house with dark glasses and a cane he does not seem to need. His dog may not wear a harness when the man uses it. The dog may be snap at strangers.[464] The man can produce a letter from a doctor in another state saying that he should use a guide dog, but attempts to locate the doctor are unsuccessful. Yet a social worker is willing to testify that she arranged for the man to attend a day program for the blind. Confusing sets of facts may be presented to a jury, which may reach a verdict that even the judge does not understand. If the judge's instructions to the jury were taken from a case that bears only a superficial similarity to the matter at hand, and if the result is appealed, the higher court may have to speculate at what the jury actually decided. A fair number of service dog cases are remanded for further proceedings.

Problems often arise with restrictive condominiums, cooperatives, and homeowners associations.[465] Condominiums often see themselves as above such laws, and perhaps they are in some states. I lived for many years in a cooperative apartment building in Brooklyn Heights. A neighboring building had an applicant for an apartment that was blind and used a guide dog.

The cooperative board was inclined to reject the blind woman's application, despite the fact she was willing to pay more than any other purchaser for the apartment. Many tenants thought the building would go from a no-pets building to a pets-allowed building. A lawyer on the coop's board assured the other members that this would not happen. The board still wanted to reject the application, but the lawyer said he would resign from the board if they did, and that he would not join the board in opposing any lawsuit the woman might bring against the building. Common sense at length prevailed, though the lawyer told me that some residents never spoke to him after this incident.[466]

## Tenant May Be Compelled to Allow
## Independent Evaluation of Dog's Functions

Courts have on occasion favored housing authorities. A West Virginia case, *In Re Kenna Homes Cooperative Corporation,* concerned a couple residing in a cooperative housing project that claimed their dog qualified as a service animal.[467] The housing project originally permitted pets, but in 1996 the stockholders voted to phase out animals. As a result, tenants could not replace dogs and other pets that died, though an exception was made for seeing-eye, hearing-aide, and dogs trained and certified for a particular disability. A stockholder had to obtain a certificate or authorization request from a licensed physician specializing in the field of the specified disability. Two tenants, the Jessups, purchased two dogs and presented a physician's statement that "it is a medical necessity for [the Jessups] with their present health ailments to be able to keep their pets to suppress both the physical and mental need for companionship as well as the confinement due to the various illnesses." Mr. Jessup had been diagnosed with Stills Disease, high blood pressure, and depression. Mrs. Jessup had elevated liver enzymes, palpitations, super-ventricular tachycardia, and diabetes. The board rejected the request of the Jessups to keep the two dogs and the tenants brought an action under the federal Fair Housing Act. The trial court found for the board, noting:

> None of the [Jessups'] physician statements correlate dogs, generally, or the Jessups' two dogs, specifically, to the claimed disabilities. Nor has there been any link by expert affidavit or other offering that these two dogs are a necessary reasonable accommodation. The "necessity" for these dogs as indicated by the physicians is not related to any specific disability and is not related to the Jessups' ability to stay or live at Kenna Homes. In other words, even if one accepts the physician's statements as true, the Jessups can live and function at Kenna Homes without their dogs.

The Jessups appealed. The court reviewed statutes under the federal Fair Housing Act, West Virginia fair housing statutes (which the court noted follow the federal statutes very closely, if not verbatim), and some relevant cases. The court also cited state rules on human rights.[468] Although the court found that a dog might not have to be professionally trained, it must be "individually trained,"[469] since "a dog cannot acquire discernable skills as a service dog without some type of training." Further, "federal case law holds that an animal does not have to have professional credentials in order to be a service animal under the FFHA. This is because there appear to be no uniform standards or credentialing criteria applied to all service animals or animal trainers." There is no federal or West Virginia certification process. The court found, however, that under the Federal Fair Housing Act and the West Virginia Fair Housing Act,[470] a landlord may require a tenant seeking to keep a service animal:

> to demonstrate that he or she made a bona fide effort to locate a certifying authority and, if such authority is located, to subject the service animal to the specialized training necessary for such certification. If the tenant fails to locate a certifying authority, it is reasonable for the landlord or person similarly situated to attempt to locate a certifying authority and, if one is located, to require certification of the service animal. If neither the tenant nor the landlord or person similarly situated can locate a certifying authority after reasonable attempts to do so, it is reasonable for the landlord or person similarly situated to require that a recognized training facility or person certify that the service animal has that degree of training and temperament which would enable the service animal to ameliorate the effects of its owners disability and to live in its owner's household without disturbing the peace of mind of a person of ordinary sensibilities regarding animals.

The court placed an evidentiary burden on the tenants:

> [T]he burden is on the person claiming the need for a service animal as a reasonable accommodation to show that his or her animal is properly trained. In light of this, it is not unreasonable to require proof of proper training in the form of a written assertion by the dog's trainer that the dog has been trained to perform specific tasks.

Thus, even though there was no certification requirement, the court imposed a training requirement and effectively a testing requirement, at least for a dog not trained by a recognized training facility.

> In order to show that the disabled person needs the assistance of a service animal to ameliorate the effects of his or her specific disability, it is reason-

able to require the opinion of a physician who is knowledgeable about the subject's disability and the manner is which a service dog can ameliorate the effects of the disability. . . .

[W]here a tenant suffers from a disability which is not apparent to a person untrained in medical matters, it is reasonable for a landlord or person similarly situated to require a second concurring opinion from a qualified physician selected by the landlord or person similarly situated to substantiate the tenant's need for a service animal.[471]

The court then noted that even a trained service dog can be a nuisance, and could be excluded on those grounds. The court also argued that palliative care and ordinary comfort were not sufficient to justify a request for a service animal under the Fair Housing Act. The court affirmed the lower court's decision that the housing project could require the Jessups to get additional verification of the skills of their dogs and their need to have them. This case might have gone the other way had the tenants' physician more carefully correlated the functions of the dog with the disabilities of the master. If the dog were a psychiatric service dog, this should have passed muster. The case may say more about how the tenants' lawyer prepared for trial than anything else, or it may indicate that the court was one that sought to raise the barriers rather than lowering them.

## Ignoring Rules Gets Some Tenants and Dogs in Trouble

Tenants are sometimes their own worst enemies in disputes with landlords over animals.[472] In *Prindable v. Association of Apartment Owners of 2987 Kalakaua*,[473] a tenant argued that his dog helped him cope with stress, poor sleep patterns, and the trauma from an assault. A behaviorist wrote a letter to the effect that the tenant's condition would be exacerbated by being separated from his dog, Einstein. The behaviorist recommended continued animal-assisted therapy. While the matter was under consideration by the court, the tenant was told to keep the dog out of common areas of the condominium development. Tenant's attorney, however, acknowledged that Einstein had not been individually trained and had no abilities beyond those possessed by dogs in general.

Plaintiffs' counsel suggested canines (as a species) possess the ability to give unconditional love, which simply makes people feel better. Although this may well be true, counsel's reasoning permits no identifiable stopping point: every person with a handicap or illness that caused or brought about feelings of depression, anxiety or low self-esteem would be entitled to the dog of their choice, without regard to individual training or ability. And if certain people liked cats, fish, reptiles or birds better than dogs, there would be no logical reason to deny an accommodation for these animals. The test would devolve from "individually trained to do work or perform tasks" to "of some comfort."

The court concluded that "if Einstein is not a proper service animal (as opposed to a pet), an exemption . . . is not necessary to afford [the tenant] an equal opportunity to use and enjoy the dwelling." The court found that "there is no evidence that would lead a reasonable jury to conclude that Einstein is an individually trained service animal and, therefore, nothing to show that an accommodation for Einstein may be necessary to afford [the tenant] an equal opportunity to use and enjoy the dwelling."

The case is intensely fact specific and paints a picture of a troublesome and litigious tenant who disputed the condominium's attempt to preclude him from bringing his dog into all the common areas, and taking it through those areas even when going elsewhere. The case apparently means that to obtain a reasonable accommodation for a dog living in an apartment in a no-pets residence in Hawaii, a tenant would have to have a trained service animal. The result may be correct because of the facts, but the conclusions are broader than necessary.

A case that relied on *Prindable* occurred in Iowa, where a woman faced eviction because she had not applied to the housing authority governing the building where she lived to have her pet allowed. Despite providing letters from several doctors and the Iowa Division of Persons with Disabilities, the housing authority proceeded with the eviction and was upheld by a state court in granting the authority's motion for summary judgment. On appeal, the appellate court noted that there were genuine issues of material fact and the case should not have been decided on summary judgment. There was evidence that the woman's dog, a Doberman Pinscher named Sam, preceded the plaintiff into rooms because, as a result of post-traumatic stress disorder, she feared that "someone will be lurking there." The dog could also switch on lights in darkened rooms and was trained to bring the plaintiff her cell phone. The appellate court remanded for further proceedings.[474]

## Accommodating Some Dogs but Not Others

A question that arises occasionally concerns whether a building that allows pets can apply restrictions applicable to pets to a service animal. This should not be permitted in most cases. A 20-pound limit on dogs, for instance, would preclude most or all guide dogs as well as most dogs for the mobility impaired. In *Oras v. Housing Authority of the City of Bayonne*,[475] a New Jersey appellate court considered the case of a 48-year-old paraplegic that sued a public housing authority that would not permit him to keep a dog he claimed assisted him with daily activities. The authority permitted dogs to senior citizens and persons with disabilities, but limited dogs to weighing no more than 20 pounds. The tenant had a dog named Peaches that the tenant's sister had trained to retrieve the tenant's keys from the floor and would pull him back from the supermarket when his arms were full of groceries and he could not operate his manual wheelchair. The authority attempted to enforce the weight limit. The tenant provided letters from two doctors stating it was medically necessary for him to keep Peaches. The tenant argued that to remove the dog from his apartment would be analogous to removing a seeing eye dog from a blind person. The appellate court found that the housing authority was obligated to accommodate the tenant's disability "to the extent necessary to provide the disabled person with an opportunity to use and occupy the dwelling unit equal to a non-disabled person."[476] The court reinstated the tenant's punitive damages claim and remanded to the trial court for further proceedings.

Unfortunately, not all courts have reasoned so well on this issue. In *Zatopa v. Lowe*,[477] a tenant, who had AIDS and long-term clinical depression,[478] obtained a letter from his doctor explaining that he needed an emotional support animal. The landlord claimed not to have received the letter until after the tenant had obtained a pit bull mix from the Pinole, California dog pound. A veterinarian wrote an evaluation saying that the dog would not be a problem. The landlord demanded that the dog be removed, but said that if he was legally compelled to permit the tenant to have "a service dog of some sort," it should be one of a safe and gentle breed, but not a pit bull. By the time this action was taken, the tenant had formed a strong bond with the animal.

The district court said that a reasonable accommodation need not be on the tenant's terms only, and noted the problems associated with pit bulls.

> The objection to pit bulls is plainly supported by a reasonable basis. Pit bulls have killed more humans in the past eleven years than any other breed (save Rottweilers). Once a landlord has a reasonable basis for excluding a certain type of dog presenting a heightened risk, the law does not impose on the landlord any case-by-case duty to assess the psychological proclivities of any specific individual dog affected by the exclusion.

Further:

> The landlords do not argue that Tenant Lowe is not entitled to a service dog, only that they are not required to allow this particular service dog.

The landlord argued that it could put restrictions on the service dog, e.g., a breed restriction, perhaps a weight limit, etc. The court agreed, since in the same discussion it states that it "is unwilling to create a right of a tenant to maintain a pit bull in an apartment house." Further, the landlord's offer of a dog belonging to a safe and gentle breed "constitutes a reasonable accommodation under both federal and state law." Although testimony about the gentle nature of the specific dog was presented, testimony about the number of pit bull attacks was persuasive to the court and the fact that pit bulls have powerful jaws and if they do attack can do more harm than most other breeds.

At its worst, the case may stand for the proposition that in the balancing test that must be applied to determine what is a reasonable accommodation, a court may consider the general reputation of a breed of dog as being an imposition on landlords of sufficient weight to override a tenant's need for continued emotional support from a dog. This is a poorly reasoned case.[479] An animal that is or becomes dangerous need not be tolerated, but a particular dog should not be rejected just because it belongs to a breed that the public has labeled as aggressive or violent. The case is similar to *Nason v. Stone Hill Realty Association,* where a Massachusetts court suggested that a tenant could use chemical therapy and a reasonable accommodation to a cat need not be made.[480] It is possible that the court in *Zatopa,* which took place in the Bay Area, was influenced by the killing of a woman outside her San Francisco apartment in January 2001 by two Presa Canarios, which are sometimes used in dog fighting. The case received national attention and the owners of the dogs were convicted of second degree murder for the attacks and sentenced to prison.[481]

It is worth noting that modern DNA testing may lead to a new issue regarding pit bulls. Some dogs may look like pit bulls, but DNA results may establish that the appearance is superficial. A *Wall Street Journal* article contained a picture of a dog with a strong resemblance to a pit bull, but DNA testing revealed that the dog probably had Italian Greyhound, Boston Terrier, and a number of other breeds, pit bull types not among them.[482] It is not difficult to imagine that suits involving prejudices against breeds will soon come to involve DNA testing.

## PUBLIC HOUSING AND HOUSING FOR THE ELDERLY AND PERSONS WITH DISABILITIES

In October 2008, the Department of Housing and Urban Development amended regulations governing requirements for animal ownership in HUD-assisted public housing and multifamily housing projects for the elderly and persons with disabilities.[483] In the release, HUD conformed the language of its regulations regarding animal ownership for public housing for the elderly and disabled with other public housing requirements.[484] There were, prior to this, minor differences between the exceptions to no-pets rules in public housing for the elderly and disabled and the rules for other public housing.

Under HUD's 2008 regulations, project owners and public housing agencies may not apply or enforce policies (such as no-pet policies) against animals "that are necessary as a reasonable accommodation to assist, support, or provide service to persons with disabilities."[480] The new rule applies to animals that reside in projects for the elderly or persons with disabilities, as well as to animals that visit the projects. Animals that visit the projects to provide support could include therapy dogs and their handlers involved in visitation programs.

## Verification Replaces Certification

Prior to the amendment to Part 5, a tenant had to certify that he or a member of his family was a person with a disability, the animal had been trained to assist persons with that specific disability, and the animal actually assisted with that disability. This requirement was eliminated. Now, public housing agencies,

> are *authorized to verify that the animal qualifies as a reasonable accommodation* under section 504 of the Rehabilitation Act of 1973 (29 U.S.C. 794[486]) (Section 504) and the Fair Housing Act (Title VIII of the Civil Rights Act of 1968, as amended (42 U.S.C. 3601-3631)). An animal qualifies as a reasonable accommodation if: (1) An individual has a disability, as defined in the Fair Housing Act or Section 504, (2) the animal is needed to assist with the disability, and (3) the individual who requests the reasonable accommodation demonstrates that there is a relationship between the disability and the assistance that the animal provides.[487]

## Nexus Requirement

HUD requires a relationship between the disability and the accommodation sought before that accommodation will be labeled reasonable.

> To show that a requested accommodation may be necessary, there must be an identifiable relationship, or nexus, between the requested accommodation and the person's disability. Thus, in the case of assistance/service animals, an individual with a disability must demonstrate a nexus between his or her disability and the function the service animal provides. The

Department's position has been that animals necessary as a reasonable accommodation do not necessarily need to have specialized training. *Some animals perform tasks that require training, and others provide assistance that does not require training.*

This position is also described by HUD in its Public Housing Occupancy Guidebook and its Multifamily Occupancy Handbook.[188]

The animal does not need to be a trained service animal, or even be a service animal, as long as the tenant needs the accommodation. This does not mean that any animal providing some benefit to a tenant must always be accepted. The mental health professional must connect the tenant's possession of the animal with an alleviation of at least one symptom of the disability. This requires more than a mere statement that a dog or cat makes a tenant feel good. Alleviating depression (if depression is a symptom of the mental condition, or the condition itself) is a function of an emotional support animal, and should satisfy the requirement.

Landlords and housing authorities may verify the existence of the disability and the need for the accommodation if either is not readily apparent. Thus, someone seeking a reasonable accommodation for an emotional support animal may be required by the landlord to provide documentation from a physician, psychiatrist, social worker, or other mental health professional that the animal provides support that alleviates at least one of the identified symptoms or effects of the existing disability.[189]

A landlord need not accept a dog with a history of dangerous behavior.[190] Nor would an animal have to be tolerated if it defecated or urinated in public spaces other than those designated as dog walks, was frequently sick in public places, etc. Just because a tenant has a need for an animal does not mean that he or she must not care for it.[191]

## Disability-Related Functions, Including Emotional Support

As discussed above in the chapter on general issues by federal agencies, HUD has been willing to accept emotional support as a reason for requiring a reasonable accommodation:

Examples of disability-related functions, include, but are not limited to, guiding individuals who are blind or have low vision, alerting individuals who are deaf or hard-of-hearing to sounds, providing rescue assistance, pulling a wheelchair, fetching items, alerting persons to impending seizures, or providing emotional support to persons with disabilities who have a disability-related need for such support.[192]

## Training Not Required for Some Skills

HUD recognizes that seizure-alert dogs may have an untrained skill:

> [T]there are animals that have an innate ability to detect that a person with a seizure disorder is about to have a seizure and can let the individual know ahead of time so that the person can prepare. This ability is not the result of training, and a person with a seizure disorder might need such an animal as a reasonable accommodation to his/her disability. Moreover, emotional support animals do not need training to ameliorate the effects of a person's mental and emotional disabilities. Emotional support animals by their very nature, and without training, may relieve depression and anxiety, and/or help reduce stress-induced pain in persons with certain medical conditions affected by stress.

The correlation of seizure-alert animals (which under Department of Justice and most other federal pronouncements are service animals), with emotional support animals is unfortunate, as these two categories are best distinguished.

## RULES REGARDING SHORT-TERM LODGING

As discussed in the chapter on public accommodations, the Department of Justice defines a service animal as a:

> guide dog, signal dog, or other animal individually trained to do work or perform tasks for the benefit of an individual with a disability, including, but not limited to, guiding individuals with impaired vision, alerting individuals with impaired hearing to intruders or sounds, providing minimal protection or rescue work, pulling a wheelchair, or fetching dropped items.[493]

This is a much narrower definition than that used in the HUD rules in that it requires that the animal be trained and "do work or perform tasks." This excludes emotional support animals and may exclude seizure-alert dogs that have not been trained to perform other functions. (However, many seizure-alert dogs are trained for other functions. One study found that 59 percent of dogs trained as seizure-response dogs spontaneously developed seizure-alert capabilities once placed with families. Seizure-response dogs are trained to bring medication and help to the owner during a seizure.[494])

Service animals, under Department of Justice rules,[495] are to be admitted to places of public accommodation, which include an "inn, hotel, motel, or other place of lodging, except for an establishment located within a building that contains not more than five rooms for rent or hire and that is actually occupied by the proprietor of the establishment as the residence of the proprietor." Appendix B to 28 CFR Part 36 (originally the preamble to the 1991 regulatory issuance) distinguishes places of lodging from a residence:

> [I]n a large hotel that has a separate residential apartment wing, the residential wing would not be covered by the ADA [28 CFR Part 36] because of the nature of the occupancy of that part of the facility. This residential wing would, however, be covered by the Fair Housing Act [for our purposes, 24 CFR 100.204]. The separate non-residential accommodations in the rest of the hotel would be a place of lodging, and thus a public accommodation subject to the requirements of this final rule. If a hotel allows both residential and short-term stays, but does not allocate space for these different uses in separate, discrete units, both the ADA and the Fair Housing Act may apply to the facility.

Extensive revisions to 28 CFR Part 36 were proposed by the Department of Justice in 2008 which, among other things, would alter the definition of "place of lodging" to include time-shares, condominium hotels, mixed-use, and corporate hotel facilities.[496] The preamble to the proposal discusses places of lodging in detail, but as of this writing there are no indications when, or even if, the proposal will be finalized. Despite the limited application of 28 CFR Part 36 in the context of rental housing, this part of the Code is sometimes relied upon by courts analyzing more permanent housing situations.[497]

The Department of Justice in the 2008 proposal made its position clear that animals "whose sole function is to provide emotional support, comfort, therapy, companionship, therapeutic benefits, or promote emotional well-being are not service animals." Curiously, however, the Department conceded that this viewpoint may not be appropriate in the housing context:

> The Department recognizes, however, that there are situations . . . particularly in the context of residential settings and employment, where there may be compelling reasons to permit the use of animals whose presence provides emotional support to a person with a disability. Accordingly, other federal agency regulations governing those situations may appropriately provide for increased access for animals other than service animals. (73 Fed. Reg. 34516)

This perspective may not be the current view of the Department of Justice, given the changes to the Americans with Disabilities Amendments Act of 2008.

## STATE LAWS ON HOUSING ACCOMMODATIONS

Although most states have largely ceded regulation of the rights of individuals with disabilities using service animals to the federal agencies, there are a number of reasons why it is important to verify state law. Criminal interference statutes regarding denial of access to individuals with disabilities using service animals may be more easily enforced than federal crimes based on such discrimination. Since many states define service animals as animals serving only the individuals with physical disabilities, or in a few cases the "mobility impaired," federal law may be the only enforcement possible as to persons with mental health disabilities. However, some states have statutes protecting only the rights of certain categories of individuals with disabilities or certain dogs with regard to housing accommodations. Tennessee, for instance, has detailed rules regarding the blind and guide dogs that do not apply to other service animals.

A number of states include trainers under the protections that persons with disabilities have as to access to housing accommodations (e.g., Utah), while others specifically exclude housing from the exceptions for no-pets rules as to service dog trainers (e.g., Texas). Unfortunately, many states provide that trainers of service dogs are entitled to bring dogs they are training into public facilities but it is not clear whether public facilities are broad enough to include housing accommodations. I assume that facility will generally be interpreted narrowly enough so as to exclude housing. Efforts to call officials in some states provided no enlightenment as many states have never really had to resolve disputes concerning the housing rights of trainers since trainers are often going to be training dogs other than service dogs and will be sure to live in apartment buildings where dogs are permitted.

# Chapter 11

# TAKING SERVICE AND
# SUPPORT DOGS TO WORK

*An accident early in life left a woman almost unable to move one side of her body. She owned a strong Australian Shepherd that helped her stand and move. Her employer, a state agency, was happy to let her bring the dog to work and keep it with her during the day. The building she worked in, however, had very slippery floors in the lobby and the dog often slipped. She got booties for the dog but the dog still slipped. The woman asked her boss to get the building to put down carpeting as the situation was dangerous both for her and for the dog. Although there was no outright refusal, nothing ever seemed to get done. Was there a failure to make a reasonable accommodation? Were money damages appropriate for the woman?*

Employment litigation regarding service animals has not been common, which probably indicates the success of policies which encourage employers to hire and reasonably accommodate individuals with disabilities.[498] The general anti-discrimination rules of the Department of Justice are often mirrored in state codes. Nevertheless, issues do arise, and there may be continuing conflict over emotional support animals in the workplace, an issue on which recent regulations and proposals have shown considerable flexibility.

## FEDERAL EMPLOYMENT ISSUES

In passing the Americans with Disabilities Act, Congress noted that "discrimination against individuals with disabilities persists in such critical areas as employment," etc. The Act was intended to "provide a clear and comprehensive national mandate for the elimination of discrimination against individuals with disabilities."[499] Discrimination, under the Act, includes:

(A) not making reasonable accommodations to the known physical or mental limitations of an otherwise qualified individual with a disability who is an applicant or employee, unless such covered entity can demonstrate that the accommodation would impose an undue hardship on the operation of the business of such covered entity; or

(B) denying employment opportunities to a job applicant or employee who is an otherwise qualified individual with a disability, if such denial is based on the need of such covered entity to make reasonable accommodation to the physical or mental impairments of the employee or applicant.[500]

Reasonable accommodation is defined to include:

job restructuring, part-time or modified work schedules, reassignment to a vacant position, acquisition or modification of equipment or devices, appropriate adjustment or modifications of examinations, training materials or policies, the provision of qualified readers or interpreters, and other similar accommodations for individuals with disabilities.[501]

The statutory concept of reasonable accommodation underlies the regulatory elaboration, which provides that "a public accommodation shall modify policies, practices, or procedures to permit the use of a service animal by an individual with a disability."[502]

The "reasonable accommodation" concept is also found in Department of Labor regulations,[503] where an explanatory appendix adds that "it would be a reasonable accommodation for an employer to permit an individual who is blind to use a guide dog at work, even though the employer would not be required to provide a guide dog for the employee."[504] The Equal Employment Opportunity Commission, which enforces Title I of the Americans with Disabilities Act, provides that an employee with a disability may need leave for training of a service animal.[505] Title I covers non-federal employers with 15 or more employees. The Department of Labor has not further elaborated on this reasonable accommodation requirement for the workplace, making it unclear if the concept includes emotional support animals as it does with the Department of Housing and Urban Development.[506]

Even the U.S. Postal Service has failed to make a reasonable accommodation, unfortunately in a decision without a published opinion of the Eleventh Circuit in 2002.[507]

## Emotional Support Animals in the Workplace

Although the Department of Justice has been conservative in its interpretation of what a service animal can be, in the preamble to its recent proposed revisions to its public accommodation access rules, the agency concedes that emotional support animals may be appropriately admitted to employment environments, though not to other public accommodations.

> [T]here are situations . . . , particularly in the context of residential settings and employment,[508] where there may be compelling reasons to permit the use of animals whose presence provides emotional support to a person with a disability. Accordingly, other federal agency regulations governing those situations may appropriately provide for increased access for animals other than service animals.[509]

## An Employment Case

In *McDonald v. Department of Environmental Quality,*[510] the situation outlined in the opening paragraph of this chapter, the Supreme Court of Montana considered the case of Janelle McDonald, a former employee of the Montana Department of Environmental Quality (DEQ), which McDonald sued for unlawful discrimination. A hearing officer of the Montana Department of Labor and Industry found for McDonald, a decision affirmed by the Montana Human Rights Commission in 2006.[511] DEQ then filed for judicial review in the First Judicial District Court, Lewis and Clark County, which reversed the decision of the Human Rights Commission. The Montana Supreme Court reversed the lower court and remanded for further proceedings.

McDonald had been certified in July 2002 as a person with a disability by the Montana Department of Public Health and Human Services. McDonald had two permanent disabilities, a physical injury to her left leg caused by a fracture early in life, which hindered her ability to navigate stairs, walk on certain surfaces, particularly hard surfaces like concrete floors, and to walk long distances. The second disability was diagnosed as chronic depression and dissociative identity disorder.

> During bouts of depression, she experiences poor concentration, poor memory, and a sense of isolation. She withdraws from social interaction and, on occasion, misses work. During dissociative episodes, McDonald becomes inattentive and unable to complete tasks. She also loses track of time and her surroundings, and she may have no memory afterward of interactions and events which took place during a dissociative period. Dissociative episodes come on suddenly and without warning, can last a few minutes or several hours, and may occur a few times a week or several times a day.

For assistance in overcoming the limitations caused by the disabilities, McDonald used a trained Australian Shepherd named Bess. She acquired Bess in 1999 from CARES Inc., a non-profit organization that trains and provides service animals for persons with disabilities. Bess provided bracing support, which McDonald could use in going up and down stairs, and assisted McDonald to stand up if she fell. She also provided tactile stimulation during dissociative episodes, bumping or nudging McDonald until she calmed down and came back into reality. The dog also prevented McDonald from oversleeping and kept her active.

McDonald began working for DEQ as a fiscal officer in August 2002. She informed DEQ that she needed Bess to carry out her job duties, and DEQ advised its employees that McDonald would be bringing a service dog to work. The room where McDonald worked was carpeted but the hallways were tiled with linoleum. Bess had been trained to walk on buffed tiled floors and slippery surfaces, but the dog had difficulty with the floors in the building and repeatedly slipped. CARES recommended that McDonald practice walking with Bess on tile floors and McDonald came to the building on weekends for practice, as well as going to Wal-Mart and Kmart for practice, but Bess continued to have trouble with DEQ's floors. McDonald tried dog booties, trimmed Bess's toenails and the fur between her toes, and consulted a veterinarian who concluded that the dog did not have arthritis. In the end, McDonald requested that DEQ provide non-skid floor coverings, such as runners or carpeting on the ground-floor hallways of the building. The request was made verbally at first and eventually in writing, but no change was made to the floors. DEQ notified the General Services Division of the issue but nothing changed. In September 2003, Bess fell with both legs splayed out, hit her chin on the floor, and needed assistance getting up. The state ADA coordinator determined that DEQ had made a reasonable accommodation in allowing McDonald to bring her dog to work, and that DEQ did not have to go further an modify its hallways. General Services delivered three mats to DEQ in November 2003, but these only covered a small portion of the floors that McDonald and Bess had to walk on, and Bess continued to suffer slips and falls. Another serious fall occurred in January 2004 and a veterinarian found that Bess had cervical disk disease as a result of this fall. After that Bess could not perform her bracing function and walked with a pronounced limp. Still nothing was done, and after another serious fall, McDonald began to leave Bess at home. McDonald left DEQ in August 2004 for another job. McDonald retired Bess because she did not want to risk more injuries to the dog. As a result she had a higher frequency of absences at her new job.

McDonald filed a complaint with the Department of Labor and Industry in January 2005, alleging unlawful discrimination in violation of the Montana Human Rights Act and the ADA. The examiner held that the placement of non-skid floor coverings was necessary for McDonald to do her job. DEQ also argued that the accommodation requested by McDonald was not for herself but for the dog. The Examiner responded to this as follows:

"[T]his is analogous to arguing that failing to build an affordable wheelchair ramp for an otherwise qualified paraplegic who must use a wheelchair to access her job is not discrimination because there is no obligation to accommodate the wheelchair." The Examiner determined that McDonald was due $10,000 for her emotional distress. Since she had to replace the dog, which the Examiner determined to have a market value of $18,000. Travel and veterinary expenses of $1,500 were added to this.

DEQ appealed to the Human Rights Commission, which affirmed the Department of Labor and Industry. DEQ then petitioned to the District Court, which reversed. The District Court concluded that DEQ had made a reasonable accommodation by allowing McDonald to bring Bess to work. On appeal, the Montana Supreme Court concluded that McDonald needed an accommodation and modifying the floor surface was not beyond the scope of an employer's duties. Montana disability law was patterned largely on ADA principles.[512] An employer has a duty to provide a reasonable accommodation to a person with a physical or mental disability if, with such an accommodation, the person could perform the job's essential function. DEQ's position was, however, that the agency engaged in voluntary efforts to assist McDonald but that it did not owe her an accommodation concerning the hallways as a matter of law. The Montana Supreme Court said that DEQ was interpreting its obligations too narrowly.

> Requiring an employer to provide a non-skid floor surface so that an employee may use her service animal to move freely about the building is analogous to requiring an employer to provide a ramp or widen a door so that an employee may use his wheelchair to travel from one part of the building to another. When an employer does the latter (e.g., widens a door), it is an accommodation to the employee using the wheelchair, not to the wheelchair itself. Likewise here, installation of runners or carpeting would have been an accommodation to McDonald, not Bess.

DEQ also argued that McDonald was essentially asking that it accommodate a poorly performing assistive device because Bess was "professionally trained to work on all types of surfaces and was not performing as trained." DEQ argued that this was the same as requesting accommodations for a wheelchair that was not functional. Although Bess might be having problems with the floors, the court said that this did not relieve DEQ of its duty to make reasonable accommodations to McDonald's physical and mental disabilities. The requested accommodation was reasonable, would not have imposed an undue hardship on DEQ, and would not have endangered the health or safety of any person. Therefore, the accommodation should have been made.

## STATE EMPLOYMENT STATUTES
## AND ADMINISTRATIVE CODES

In Colorado, an employer must make reasonable accommodation to make a workplace accessible for an employee accompanied by an assistance dog trained for the employee.[513] "The mere presence of an assistance dog in a place of public accommodation shall not be grounds for any violation of a sanitary standard, rule, or regulation. . . ."[514] Waiving a no-pet requirement so that an employee can use a service animal is, under Maryland regulations, a reasonable accommodation.[515] In New Jersey, it is an unlawful employment practice "to deny an otherwise qualified person with a disability the opportunity to obtain or maintain employment, or to advance in position in his job, solely because such person is a person with a disability or because such person is accompanied by a service or guide dog."[516] Some states have provisions protecting rights to employment of individuals with disabilities that do not specifically mention service dogs, but the provisions may be located in or adjacent to a statute devoted to service dog access issues.[517] The Wisconsin state code protects employees who use service animals.[518]

In the state of Washington it is unfair to refuse to hire someone with a service animal, or to let someone go because he or she gets such an animal.[519] Labor unions cannot refuse to make someone a member because of his or her use of a service animal, or to expel someone from membership for this reason.[520] Employment agencies cannot discriminate against someone with a service animal in referring such a person to possible jobs.[521] The state administrative code provides that it is not an unfair practice to show preference to a person because of a disability.[522]

Georgia provides that service animals may be used by a employee in areas of a food establishment so long as no health or safety hazard results from the animal's presence.[523] Indiana provides that food employees may handle their service animals when at work but must wash their hands before handling food.[524] Rhode Island specifies that employees involved in food preparation may care for their service animals.[525]

As noted above regarding EEOC requirements, some states have provisions regarding use of leave by an employee to acquire or train a service animal. Full-time Connecticut state employees and employees of "quasi-public agencies" are to be able to use accumulated sick leave, not to exceed 15 days

> to participate in training conducted by a guide dog organization or assistance dog organization, provided such organization is a member of a professional association of guide dog or assistance dog schools, to prepare the employee to handle a guide dog or assistance dog for the employee's own use. The appointing authority may require up to seven days' advance notice

of an employee's intention to use such leave and may require the employee to provide reasonable documentation that such leave is being taken for the purpose permitted under this section.[526]

New York has a similar provision allowing the use of 26 days of sick leave and other credits.[527] A New York state employee who sought in federal court to receive paid leave without using such credits was denied this relief on a motion for summary judgment, finding that the right to use sick leave was a sufficient reasonable accommodation on the state's part.[528]

# Chapter 12

# TAKING SERVICE AND SUPPORT
# DOGS INTO SCHOOLS

*A boy with spinal muscular dystrophy was given a service dog that could open and close doors for him, retrieve the telephone for him, and turn lights off and on. He did not particularly need these services while he was at school, but the agency that provided the dog for him recommended that the dog stay with him all the time. The school noted that the boy had a motorized chair and that he did not need the dog while at school. School officials recommended that the boy go to a different school. The parents got tired of arguing and put their son in another school, but did not pursue administrative remedies available to them in the school district. Did they have a claim in discrimination?*

Dogs can be found in schools for a number of reasons. Children with autism are sometimes accompanied by service dogs nearly everywhere, including schools, though sometimes the dogs remain in the back of the room. Dogs that enter schools to look for drugs are not necessarily perceived negatively by the students. One canine team created cards to give to the students, who often want to interact with the dog. The police handler was reported to have given out more than 15,000 cards to children.[529] Courts that have considered the issue of the legality of random dog sniffs at schools have not reached a consensus on the boundaries that are appropriate.[530]

Under the Rehabilitation Act, no "otherwise qualified individual with a disability" may be denied participation in a program or activity, which includes:

- a college, university, or other postsecondary institution, or a public system of higher education; or
- a local educational agency, system of vocational education, or other school system.

General access laws do not always specify that service animals may be brought into educational institutions, though some do.

In *Gaudiello v. Delaware County Intermediate Unit,* outlined in the opening paragraph of this chapter, a 13-year-old child suffering from spinal muscular atrophy and confined to a wheelchair obtained a support/service dog from Independence Dogs.[531] When the child's parents decided to get their son a service dog, they wrote the following in a letter to his school:

> In a few weeks Michael will be taking part in a three-week course in training a dog to help him with his daily everyday activities, the dog will help him be more independent and build self-pride. Instead of Michael waiting for someone to turn on and off a light, get him the telephone, opening and closing doors, not being able to be left in the house alone for a little while, go to the store by himself like most children his age is doing the dog will be trained to do this. This dog will be Michael's constant companion.
>
> With the time and money going into this program it is important that in order for it to work the dog must attend school with Michael and although there won't be much for the dog to do other than pick up objects and carry books, opening closed doors he is still taking these commands from Michael. This dog will lose a lot of his training if left at home all these hours not doing his duties as he was trained to do.
>
> In closing I would like to add that Michael is a bright and wonderful person who is as independent as he can be at this time in his life and I am very proud of this. But as he gets older his needs will change and I feel as we have to change with him in continuing to help build his independence. Thank you for your time and consideration in this matter.

An official of the school replied:

> After consulting with Michael's teacher, therapists, and support personnel, we believe that an appropriate program of special education can be provided without the use of the service dog. Michael is able to open doors with the assistance of his motorized chair. He is sometimes assisted by staff in opening doors. His books are carried on the back of his chair. Michael's mobility needs are currently being met.
>
> It appears that the dog's greatest benefit to Michael would be in assisting him outside the educational program. We must recommend against the use of the dog in school because of the lack of any significant benefit to Michael's education.

At a subsequent meeting, school personnel continued to push for placing Michael in another school.

The parents brought suit under the Rehabilitation Act of 1973 but the court held that "the Education of the Handicapped Act[532] was the exclusive avenue through which a plaintiff may assert an equal protection claim to a publicly financed education." Since the parents did not pursue administrative remedies under the latter Act, the court granted summary judgment to the school officials. Subsequent to the case, the home school district where Michael lived allowed him to bring the dog into its classrooms, so further action was not pursued.[533] In a New York case, parents also could not require a school district to allow their child to bring a hearing dog to class because they had not followed proper administrative procedures.[534]

## DEPARTMENT OF EDUCATIONS RULES AND GUIDELINES

The Department of Education requires that individuals with disabilities have access to education, which includes access to transportation that brings children to schools. Regulations of the Department of education provides that children are to be able to obtain certain orientation and mobility services, including "To use the long cane or a service animal to supplement visual travel skills or as a tool for safely negotiating the environment for children with no available travel vision."[535]

## Postsecondary Education

Federal disability laws covering colleges and universities "are essentially silent on the treatment that covered entities must afford to individuals with disabilities in need of the use of an animal."[536] Administrative guidance from the Office of Civil Rights of the U.S. Department of Education has, in effect, adopted the Title III service animal framework of the Department of Justice for colleges and universities.[537]

Under 34 CFR 104.44, a school receiving federal funds directly or indirectly[538] must make such adjustments to its academic requirements as are necessary to ensure that the requirements do not discriminate or have the effect of discrimination against students with disabilities. This includes permitting students to bring dog guides to class.[539]

## STATE EDUCATIONAL STATUTES AND RULES

Educational institutions are sometimes part of the list of locations into which a person can bring a service animal.[540] Students, teachers, and trainers with service animals are entitled to use schoolbuses in California.[541] Animals are not permitted on school buses in Delaware but service animals are if a physician certifies that it is required.[542] Oregon administrative rules provide that assistance guide animals may be taken on school buses,[543] but such animals are to be distinctively identified, such as by wearing a green guide-dog jacket.[544] Some states follow federal guidelines in providing that children may be taught to use a service animal as a supplement to visual travel skills or for safety (for instance, Indiana and Ohio).

A Texas state employee with a disability is entitled to a leave of absence without a deduction in salary in order to attend a training program to acquaint the employee with an assistance dog he or she will use.[545]

## THERAPY DOGS IN SCHOOLS

The benefits to populations of children, including special needs classes, have been discussed in the chapter on therapy dogs. Many schools are anxious to have therapy dog visitations because they find it works wonders in the classroom, and children that have not been participating often begin to do so. Schools are, in my experience, generally only concerned that a therapy dog handler establish that his dog is registered with one of the major therapy dog organizations and thereby provided with insurance coverage.

# Chapter 13

# ANIMALS IN HEALTHCARE FACILITIES

*A physician in a Veterans Administration hospital suffered a spinal cord injury after falling off a horse. She permanently lost motion and sensation between her toes and her chest. For some years she relied on a wheelchair, but nine years after the accident she began to suffer overuse symptoms and acquired a service dog to help her with mobility. The VA hospital objected to the doctor bringing her dog to work, saying that the dog would take up too much space in elevators and would generally produce a "logistical nightmare." The hospital also said that the doctor would have access to areas where the dog should not be allowed. The hospital did permit patients to bring in seeing eye dogs and claimed that it was being reasonable. Was it?*

Healthcare facilities include hospitals, clinics, doctors' and dentists' offices, laboratories, imaging services, urgent care facilities, etc. Service animals may enter such facilities with employees, patients, visitors, instructors, volunteers, and students. Healthcare facilities have been quick to recognize the benefits of admitting service and therapy dogs, and have often been more open to giving them access to patients than any law would require. Hopefully, the VA case described below is the exception.

## DEPARTMENT OF JUSTICE GUIDANCE

A number of governmental and private organizations have considered the extent that service and therapy animals should be permitted to enter healthcare facilities. Although the basic rules on these issues rely on the Department of Justice Regulations regarding service animals,[546] the Centers for Disease Control, the Association for Professionals in Infection Control and Epidemiology, and Delta Society have attempted to consider how health and disease issues limit the scope of those regulations.

The preamble to rules proposed by the Department of Justice in 2008, states:

> As required by the ADA, a healthcare facility must permit a person with a disability to be accompanied by his or her service animal in all areas of the facility in which that person would otherwise be allowed, with some exceptions. Zoonotic diseases can be transmitted to humans through trauma (bites, scratches, direct contact, arthropod vectors, or aerosols). Although there is no evidence that most service animals pose a significant risk of transmitting infectious agents to humans, animals can serve as a reservoir for a significant number of diseases that could potentially be transmitted to humans in the healthcare setting. A service animal may accompany its owner to such areas as admissions and discharge offices, the emergency room,[547] inpatient and outpatient rooms, examining and diagnostic rooms, clinics,[548] rehabilitation therapy areas, the cafeteria and vending areas, the pharmacy, rest rooms, and all other areas of the facility where visitors are permitted, except those listed below.
>
> . . . Based on [Center for Disease Control and Prevention Guidance], it is generally appropriate to exclude a service animal from areas that require a protected environment, including operating rooms, holding and recovery areas, labor and delivery suites, newborn intensive care nurseries, and sterile processing departments.[549]

## ASSOCIATION FOR PROFESSIONALS IN CONTROL AND EPIDEMIOLOGY

In the "APIC State-of-the-Art Report: The Implications of Service Animals in Healthcare Settings,"[550] the Association for Professionals in Infection Control and Epidemiology, Inc., along with the National Service Dog Center of Delta Society, developed guidelines for service animals in healthcare settings. This report notes that healthcare facilities will often find it difficult to verify that an animal is performing functions that justify its being considered a service animal, given that the Department of Justice discourages inquiries into the nature of the owner's disability, and recognizes no particular registration or certification as definitively separating pets from service animals. "Minimal inquiry is best; this acknowledges the privacy needs of the person with a disability." A facility does not, however, have to allow a troublesome animal to remain inside.

> Subsequent observation of the behavior of the animal should help in assessing whether the animal constitutes a direct threat to health or safety or a fun-

damental alteration to the nature of the business. If the animal's presence or behavior creates such a direct threat or fundamental alteration, it does not have to be tolerated by the healthcare facility. Although "misbehavior" does not necessarily indicate that an animal does not meet the definition of service animal, the healthcare facility has recourse to protect itself by requiring the removal of the animal from the premises if its presence or behavior creates a direct threat to safety or a fundamental alteration.

Healthcare providers must differentiate between actual risks and mere inconvenience. Actual risks include:

- Zoonotic disease transmission
- Trauma
- Triggering allergic reactions
- Disruptive or destructive behavior.

Also, facilities "should not permit handlers with service animals to act as self-appointed animal-assisted therapy ("pet therapy") providers." Possible zoonotic risks from dogs include those listed in Figure 23.

| Disease[551] | Organism | Source | Prevention |
|---|---|---|---|
| Bacterial diarrhea | Variety of organisms, (campylobacter, etc.) | Feces | Handwashing |
| Dermatophytosis (ringworm) | Tinea (Microsporu, Tricho8phyton, etc.) | Contact | Handwashing |
| Giardia | Giardia protozoan | Feces | Handwashing |
| Leptospirosis | Leptospira interrogans | Urine | Handwashing |
| Lyme disease | Borellia burdorferi | Tick bite | Eradication of ticks |
| Rabies | Lyssavirus rhabdovirus | Saliva | Vaccination of animal |
| Rocky Mt. Spotted Fever | Rickettsia rickettsii | Tick bite | Eradication of ticks |
| Scabies | Sarcoptes cheyletiella | Feces | Handwashing |
| Toxocariasis (larval migrans) | Toxocara canis and T. cati | Feces | Handwashing |

Figure 23. Zoonotic diseases carried by dogs. Adapted from Duncan (2000).

The APIC report suggests that some areas, like an operating room, should always be off-limits to service animals, other areas may have to be considered on a case-by-case basis.

> Although it may be possible to identify certain areas where a service animal could not reasonably be permitted (e.g., an operating room where gowns and masks are required to reduce contamination), other areas may be subject to a case-by-case determination, based on the circumstances and the individual service animal. A birthing room is one example. If persons are allowed to be present without being required to observe special precautions (gowning, scrubbing, etc), it would be difficult to argue that a clean, healthy, well-behaved service animal should be denied entrance.

Other areas that might require a case-by-case determination include emergency departments, intensive care units, and recovery rooms.

The condition of the patient is also relevant. Although immunocompromised persons may have to be kept away from animals, this is not always the case since some studies indicated that such persons "may have some immunities that protect them from substantial risks through contact with their own animals." A patient recovering from severe burns may still have visitors accompanied by service dogs as long as direct contact with the dog is avoided.

The APIC report emphasizes that assumptions "about the service animal's health should not be made by non-veterinary health care providers." Thus, if a service dog is suspected of having introduced a disease to a human, a veterinarian should be consulted to confirm this. If a service animal causes an allergic reaction to other patients or employees, the facility is still obligated, under the Americans with Disabilities Act and its regulations, to provide services to an individual with a service dog. Where the facility requires that patients share rooms, roommate selection should take such conditions into account. If a service animal damages property, the APIC report follows general Department of Justice rules in providing that the handler is responsible for those damages.

## CENTERS FOR DISEASE CONTROL GUIDELINES

The Centers for Disease Control has issued guidelines for animals in healthcare facilities, looking at service and therapy animals, and research animals in such facilities.[552] The CDC is concerned that animals in healthcare environments "can serve as reservoirs for antibiotic-resistant microorganisms."

## Animal-Assisted Activities and Therapy, and Resident Animals

Therapy and companion animals may be brought into common areas of facilities, but also into patient rooms. The CDC argues that the "decision to allow this access to patients' rooms should be made on a case-by-case basis, with the consultation and consent of the attending physician and nursing staff." The CDC states that the evidence supporting animal-assisted therapy (AAT) is largely anecdotal.

The CDC discourages the use of non-human primates in AAT because of potential disease transmission and also because of their unpredictable behavior. All animals used in AAT or animal-assisted activities (AAA) should be up-to-date with recommended immunizations and prophylactic medications, such as heartworm prevention. "Regular re-evaluation of the animal's health and behavior status is essential." Animals less that a year old should not be used because of unpredictable behavior and elimination control. Also, young puppies can pick up diseases in healthcare settings because their immune systems are not fully developed.

Animals should be clean and well-groomed. Animal handlers should be trained in providing therapy dog service and should receive site-specific orientation to ensure that they work efficiently with the staff in the specific healthcare environment. Additionally, animal handlers should be in good health. "The most important infection-control measure to prevent potential disease transmission is strict enforcement of hand-hygiene measures (e.g., using either soap and water or an alcohol-based hand rub) for all patients, staff, and residents after handling the animals." Direct contact with animal urine or feces should be avoided, though such situations should be rare given the requirements of licensing agencies that certified animals should defecate and urinate on command.

Approximately 15 percent of the population is allergic to dogs and/or cats. CDC notes that some facilities do not allow animal visitations for patients with:

1. Asthma.
2. Known allergies to cats or dogs.
3. Respiratory allergies of unknown etiology.
4. Immunosuppressive disorders.

Animals should also be kept out of:

1. Food preparation kitchens.
2. Laundries.

3. Central sterile supply and storage areas for clean supplies.
4. Medication preparation areas.
5. Protective areas.
6. Areas where immunocompromised patients are housed.

A well-trained handler should be able to recognize stress in the therapy animal and terminate a session to minimize risk. Before I began therapy work with my dog, I was advised to watch the dog carefully for instances where the attentions of a patient may begin to irritate the dog. Sometimes it is the amount of time the animal has spent in the strange environment, with the smells of medicine and sickness. Sometimes a patient moves or behaves in a way that "spooks" the dog. The CDC states that when "an animal bites a person during AAA or AAT, the animal is to be permanently removed from the program."

Patients and staff that have been in contact with animals should wash their hands afterwards or use waterless, alcohol-based hand-hygiene products.

## Service Animals

Visitors, patients, and employees of healthcare facilities may use service animals.

> Although animals potentially carry zoonotic pathogens transmissible to man, the risk is minimal with a healthy, clean, vaccinated, well-behaved, and well-trained service animal, the most common of which are dogs and cats. No reports have been published regarding infectious disease that affects humans originating in service dogs. Standard cleaning procedures are sufficient following occupation of an area by a service animal.

The CDC accepts that, aside from certain protected areas of hospitals or other healthcare facilities, service animals should be permitted into other parts of facilities "unless an individual patient's situation or a particular animal poses greater risk that cannot be mitigated through reasonable measures." "No special bathing procedures are required prior to a service animal accompanying its handler into a health-care facility."

> The determination that a service animal poses a direct threat in any particular healthcare setting must be based on an individualized assessment of the service animal, the patient, and the health-care situation. When evaluating risk in such situations, health-care personnel should consider the nature of the risk (including duration and severity); the probability that injury will occur; and whether reasonable modifications of policies, practices, or pro-

cedures will mitigate the risk. . . . The person with a disability should con-tribute to the risk assessment process as part of a pre-procedure health-care provider/patient conference.

Service animals that become aggressive in attempting to protect their han-dlers may have to be excluded because of the danger this poses, but the CDC cautions that "exclusion of such an animal must be based on the actu-al behavior of the particular animal, not on speculation about how the ani-mal might behave."

As to whether a person using a service animal can remain with its handler during a hospital stay, the CDC says that the issues of each stage should be discussed with the patient.

> Healthcare personnel should discuss all aspects of anticipatory care with the patient who uses a service animal. Health-care personnel may not exclude a service animal because health-care staff may be able to perform the same services that the service animal does (e.g., retrieving dropped items and guiding an otherwise ambulatory person to the restroom). Similarly, health-care personnel cannot exclude service animals because the health-care staff perceive a lack of need for the service animal during the person's stay in the healthcare facility. A person with a disability is entitled to independent access (i.e., to be accompanied by a service animal unless the animal poses a direct threat or a fundamental alteration in the nature of services); "need" for the animal is not a valid factor in either analysis.

When someone has a hip or knee replacement, however, walking with a therapist is part of therapy, not just walking, and the dog cannot replace the function of the physical therapist.

For taking the animal out of the facility to relieve itself, this would be the obligation of the patient, who might have to rely on family members. Care of the service animal, according to the CDC, "remains the obligation of the person with the disability, not the healthcare staff."

**Verification of Service Animal Status**. As to how medical facility staff are to verify an animal's status as a service animal, the CDC follows Department of Justice procedures:

> Requiring documentation for access of a service animal to an area general-ly accessible to the public would impose a burden on a person with a dis-ability. When healthcare workers are not certain that an animal is a service animal, they may ask the person who has the animal if it is a service animal required because of a disability; however, no certification or other docu-mentation of service animal status can be required.

## THERAPY DOG CONTAMINATION RISKS

In 2005, researchers in the UK found that a Border Collie had acquired methicillin-resistant *Staphylococcus aureus* (MRSA) after visiting elderly-care wards of a hospital as a therapy dog. Swabs from the dog's nose, scalp, and paws were taken before and after visiting the wards and it was determined that only the swabs taken after the visit had MRSA.[553] MRSA is known to be increasing among companion animals and hospital contact is one possible reason. The researchers suggested six rules that should be implemented in hospitals because of their finding.

1. No dogs with open wounds or skin disease of any type should be allowed in the hospital environment.
2. Hand disinfection by patients and staff members before and after touching dogs.
3. Exclusion of pet therapy dogs from contact with patients known to be colonized or infected with MRSA; surgical, orthopedic and intensive care units; and contact with patients with indwelling catheters and wounds.
4. Pet bathing after each visit: paws should be kept clean of dirt, and bathed in chlorhexidene.
5. Terminally ill patients with MRSA or patients who fall in the above exclusion categories who specifically request pet visits should be seen at the end of the visit.
6. Banning cats from all clinical areas. Cats represent additional risks because of transmission of gastrointestinal tract diseases.

A Canadian group studied 26 therapy dog-handler teams, 12 of which visited acute care facilities and 14 of which visited long-term care facilities in Ontario. Each dog's forepaws and each handler's hands were sampled before and after each visit.[554] The dogs' coats were also tested. *Clostridium difficile* and MRSA were detected on some of the dogs after visits. The researchers concluded that the dogs could have been contaminated from handling or from contact with hospital floors or patient beds on which some of them were placed during the hospital visits. One investigator, who did not enter the hospital with a dog, had MRSA on his hands from petting the dog after a visit. This shows that contamination of a dog's body can be transferred to human hands. This means that therapy dogs can become a passive source of pathogen transmission. These researchers argued that routine screening for MRSA or *Clostridium difficile* would produce a false sense of security. Although they did not say it, they obviously believe that therapy dog hospital visitation programs should be severely curtailed, perhaps restricted to visiting rooms.

## HOSPITAL SERVICE ANIMAL ACCESS CASES

A physician, Chris Branson, working as an ambulatory care physician at the Lakeside Veterans Administration Health Care Center in Chicago since 1981, suffered a spinal cord injury during a horseback riding lesson in April 1985, breaking three vertebrae.[555] Her spinal cord was elongated and twisted and she permanently lost motion and sensation between her toes and her mid-chest. She spent four months at the Rehabilitation Institute of Chicago and learned to use a manual wheelchair. She returned to work in February 1986, and gradually returned to a full-time schedule. In 1992, she began to experience overuse symptoms in the upper body, resulting from the stress of using the manual wheelchair. Although she considered getting an electrical-powered wheelchair, she rejected the idea because it is not as maneuverable and would give her less cardiovascular exercise.

In the summer of 1994, she paid $7,000 to Paws With a Cause to train a service dog for her. She received the service dog, Nolan, in April of 1995. She worked with a trainer to learn to give Nolan commands to pick up and retrieve items, push her back to a sitting position if she got stuck with her hands on the floor, pull her wheelchair, brace when moving from the wheelchair to the bed, and brace her at other times. She could put her full weight on him, if necessary. Nolan accompanied her to stores, restaurants, and on planes. Paws With a Cause certified Nolan as Dr. Branson's service dog in November, 1995. Dr. Richard Penn, a neurological surgeon and professor of neurosurgery at Rush Presbyterian-St. Luke's Medical Center, supported Dr. Branson's decision to use a service dog because the manual wheelchair was producing overuse symptoms.

Lakeside VA objected to the idea that Dr. Branson bring her dog to work based in part on the opinions of the facility's engineer, who said that the elevators were too small. Dr. Branson filed a discrimination complaint with a Veterans Administration's Equal Employment Opportunity investigation committee, but the committee determined that Dr. Branson had not established that she was denied reasonable accommodation. She filed suit in federal court, and the case was assigned to Judge Nan Nolan of the Northern District of Illinois. The court determined, however, that Dr. Branson's being pulled by the dog took up no more space than a person walking beside her wheelchair. The court rejected the engineer's testimony as "unbelievable." The court continued with its criticism of the engineering argument:

[S]ince December of 1994 when Dr. Branson first raised the issue of a service dog accompanying her at work, Hughes [the engineer] has never spoken
to Dr. Branson about any logistical concerns he might have regarding her
use of a service dog in the hospital. . . . Hughes has not sought any assistance
from outside consulting services concerning any safety factors involved in a
service dog using Lakeside VA's elevators.

The hospital administration permitted seeing eye dogs into the hospital, but
said that allowing Dr. Branson to bring her service dog would produce a
"logistical nightmare." The court found no proof for this assertion, saying
only that the hospital would have a legitimate interest in restricting the dog's
access to specific areas of the hospital where his presence could pose a significant health risk, such as the operating room.

The court also noted that the VA hospital in San Diego has had a policy
of admitting service dogs with patients, visitors, and employees since June
25, 1997. That hospital's policy did allow keeping service animals from areas
in the hospital where patients are isolated, or from operating rooms, coronary care units, hemodialysis, and intensive care units. The VA hospital in
Puget Sound, Washington, has a similar policy dating from April 1998.

In deciding on injunctive relief (ordering the VA facility to allow Dr.
Branson to bring her dog to work), the court stated:

Only an injunction requiring the Secretary [Togo West, Secretary of the
Department of Veterans Affairs] to allow Dr. Branson to be accompanied by
her service dog in the workplace can prevent the continued harm to Dr.
Branson's physical well-being as well as the physical pain caused by her separation from Nolan during her working hours. Second, Dr. Branson's separation from her service dog during her working hours causes her emotional
and psychological harm because she is denied the ability to confront her disability in the manner of her choosing. Dr. Branson's separation from her
service dog during her working hours also impairs her ability to function as
an fully independent person with self-respect and dignity. Monetary damages are a seriously deficient remedy for the daily psychological harm
caused by Dr. Branson's separation from her service dog. Lastly, the skills
of Dr. Branson's service dog are eroded by their inability to work together
during the most active part of Dr. Branson's work day, and monetary damages cannot restore and improve Nolan's skills and his working relationship
with Dr. Branson.

The court also rejected the idea that Lakeside VA should supply Dr. Branson
with a full-time assistant who could perform the same tasks as a service dog,
noting that this would be "extremely humiliating and depressing." The court
noted that this would be an unnecessary budgetary burden on the hospital

and would not solve the engineer's space concerns.

The district court concluded that Lakeside VA had violated the Rehabilitation Act by failing to allow Dr. Branson to be accompanied by her service dog. The jury found that Lakeside VA had not made a good faith effort to identify and make a reasonable accommodation to her overuse symptoms. The facility was permanently enjoined from refusing to allow the doctor from bringing her service dog to work. Areas where she could not bring the dog would have to be specified, and the reason for the restriction would have to be given. Nor could the doctor and her dog be required to travel particular routes in the VA facilities, to travel at particular times, or to use service elevators. Nor could the facility attempt to minimize the presence of the dog "by, for example, relocating plaintiff's office to a first floor space near an exit."

The jury awarded Dr. Branson $400,000 and legal costs.

A hearing impaired veteran sought to keep his dog with him during a hospitalization at the Veterans Administration Medical Center in Chillicothe, Ohio. The Center paid for housing the dog during the hospitalization. The veteran, James Smith brought an action against the facility, but the district court granted summary judgment for the facility and dismissed the action. The Sixth Circuit affirmed, stating that Smith had failed to present evidence on which a jury could reasonably find in his favor. It is not clear if the dog was in fact functioning as a hearing dog.[556]

## ANIMALS TREATED IN HUMAN HEALTHCARE FACILITIES

Certain diagnostic technology can be used on both people and animals. As a result, health-care facilities "are increasingly faced with requests from the veterinary medical community for access to human healthcare facilities for reasons that are largely economical (e.g., costs of acquiring sophisticated diagnostic technology and complex medical instruments)." Because "an aesthetic and sociologic perception that animal care must remain separate from human care persists," and guidelines have not been developed. Therefore, the CDC recommends the following infection-control actions for such situations:

1. Whenever possible, the use of operating rooms or other rooms used for invasive procedures should be avoided (e.g., cardiac catheterization labs and invasive nuclear medicine areas).
2. When all other space options are exhausted and use of the aforementioned rooms is unavoidable, the procedure should be scheduled late in the day as the last procedure for that particular area such that

patients are not present in the department/unit/area.

3. Environmental surfaces should be thoroughly cleaned and disinfected using procedures discussed in the Environmental Services portion of [the CDC Guidelines] after the animal is removed from the care area.

4. Sufficient time should be allowed for ACH (air charges/hour) to help prevent allergic reactions by human patients.

5. Only disposable equipment or equipment that can be thoroughly and easily cleaned, disinfected, or sterilized should be used.

6. When medical or surgical instruments, especially those invasive instruments that are difficult to clean (e.g., endoscopes), are used on animals, these instruments should be reserved for future use only on animals.

7. Standard precautions should be followed.

The CDC guidelines also provide procedures regarding experimental animals in human healthcare facilities.

# Chapter 14

# FOOD SAFETY RESTRICTIONS

*A visitor to a brewery is blind and uses a guide dog. He wants to join his friends on a tour of the brewery. The brewery refuses, explaining that it has a policy against discrimination against individuals with disabilities, but that FDA regulations prohibit allowing an animal to go on the tour because the tour goes past several critical control points. Is the manufacturing facility correct?*

Rights of individuals with service dogs to enter restaurants and to take dogs to work, even in food establishments, are governed primarily by the Americans with Disabilities Act and the regulations implementing that Act issued by the Department of Justice. Restaurants are places of public accommodation under federal and state laws. Because of food safety requirements, however, there are some limits on where a service animal may go.

## FOOD MANUFACTURING FACILITIES

Regulations of the Food and Drug Administration state: "No pests shall be allowed in any area of a food plant. Guard or guide dogs may be allowed in some areas of a plant if the presence of the dogs is unlikely to result in contamination of food, food-contact surfaces, or food-packaging materials."[557] A sentence about guide and guard dogs seems odd in a provision concerning pest control, but it was added as the result of a comment to proposed food manufacturing regulations.[558] Guard dogs would include dogs that are maintained by a facility for security purposes, including dogs that are permitted to roam through parts of a facility at night.

In some facilities guide dogs might be working with blind individuals holding jobs, but one case that went to trial in Texas concerned a visitor to a brewery who wanted to bring his guide dog on a tour of the facility. In

*Johnson v. Gambrinus Company/Spoetzl Brewery,*[559] Franklin Johnson and his guide dog visited a brewery and joined a tour of the facility in the gift shop. The brewery had a blanket no animals policy based on its interpretation of Food and Drug Administration regulations, and Johnson and his dog were prevented from going beyond the gift shop. Johnson filed suit under the Americans with Disabilities Act and under Texas law. The district court determined that the brewery's no-animals policy was not compelled by any law and violated the ABA. The district court ordered the brewery to change its policy to permit service animals. The brewery owners appealed.

The brewery argued that the Food, Drug, and Cosmetic Act, regulations precluded allowing the guide dog to go on the tour, citing the regulation quoted at the beginning of this section The brewery claimed that the FDA regulation requires a blanket no animals policy because it has an open manufacturing system and the tour passes by places where the beer or the beer packaging is exposed to air, risking contamination from a dog, even a guide dog. A particular concern for a food manufacturer is a critical control point, defined in the FDA regulations "a point in a food process where there is a high probability that improper control may cause, allow, or contribute to a hazard or to filth in the final food or decomposition of the final food."[560] The brewery asserted that there were five such points on the tour, including an open trough flowing into the brew kettle, the lip and the lid of the brew kettle, the bottle and can filling stations, and the keg sealing area. The district court had held, however, that contamination was not likely at several of these points, noting that tourists were not required to wear hair or beard coverings and often put their faces directly into the opening of the brew kettle. The district court also noted that guide dogs are groomed daily and likely to shed less hair than other dogs.

A representative of the Texas Department of Public Health, which enforces FDA regulations in Texas, admitted under cross-examination that the agency had been aware of the tours for some years and had never issued a citation. From this testimony, the district court concluded:

> The Texas Department of Public Health will not issue a citation to the Spoetzl Brewery if, consistent with the Americans With Disabilities Act, the Spoetzl Brewery permits disabled persons to take their guide dogs on some parts of the brewery tour, subject to specific limitations that make contamination unlikely.

The district court concluded that contamination was virtually impossible if a guide dog were admitted to the hospitality room or the stairs leading to the brew house. The court had also found that any part of the production occurring before the boiling and filtering process could be exposed to a guide dog because the boiling and filtering would remove any contaminants. Thus, the early portion of the tour could also be open to a blind person accompanied by a guide dog. Contamination in the bottle filling station was, according to the district court, unlikely because presealed bottles are behind glass and tourists are only directly exposed to sealed, capped bottles. The circuit court found this a technical error on the part of the district court because the glass barrier was not in place at the time Johnson wanted to take the tour with his dog, but no reversal was required as the change had been made and indicated that precautions could reasonably be taken to prevent contamination.

The trial court awarded Johnson $100 under the Texas statute prohibiting discrimination against a blind person using an assistance dog.[561] The district court, as affirmed by the Fifth Circuit, mandated the revocation of the no-animals policy. The circuit court allowed for the possibility that some parts of the tour might still be closed to a person with a guide dog if the brewery could demonstrate a risk of contamination.

## FDA FOOD CODE

The Food and Drug Administration's Food Code defines a service animal as "an animal such as a guide dog, signal dog, or other animal individually trained to provide assistance to an individual with a disability."[562] As to this definition, Annex 3 to the Food Code states:

> The definition for "service animal" is adapted from 28 CFR 36.104 adopted pursuant to the Americans with Disabilities Act (ADA) of 1990 (42 U.S.C. 12101 et seq.). A service animal performs some of the functions that persons with a disability cannot perform for themselves, such as those provided by "seeing eye dogs"; alerting persons with hearing impairments to sounds; pulling wheelchairs or carrying and picking up things for persons with mobility impairments; and assisting persons with mobility impairments with balance. A service animal is not considered to be a pet.[563]

The Annex notes that Title III of the ADA prohibits privately owned businesses that serve the public from discriminating against individuals with disabilities, and that therefore people with disabilities can bring service animals onto businesses premises in whatever areas customers are generally allowed. As to employees, the Annex states: "Decisions regarding a food employee or applicant with a disability who needs to use a service animal should be made on a case-by-case basis. An employer must comply with health and safety requirements, but is obligated to consider whether there is a reasonable accommodation that can be made."

The FDA Food Code provides that service animals may be allowed on the premises of a food establishment into areas not used for food preparation that are usually open for customers, such as dining or sales areas, provided the service animal is "controlled by a disabled employee or person if a health or safety hazard will not result from the presence or activities of the service animal."[564] The term food establishment is "an operation that stores, prepares, packages, serves, vends, or otherwise provides food for human consumption," including restaurants, catering operations, markets, food banks, central preparation facilities that supply vending locations, and operations conducted in mobile facilities. It does not include food processing plants, produce stands, and kitchens in private homes.

Food employees are to wash their hands and exposed portions of their arms after caring for or handling service animals.[565] Food employees may handle or care for service animals if they wash their hands as required.[566]

## STATE LAWS ON FOOD SAFETY

A number of states, including Georgia, Pennsylvania, Rhode Island, Vermont, Virginia, and Wisconsin, specify that employees may use service animals in areas of a food establishment provided no health or safety hazard will result.[567] These rules generally conform to the Food and Drug Administration's Food Code, discussed above. Similarly, Indiana specifies that food employees may not care for or handle animals that may be allowed in restaurants, such as patrol dogs or service animals. They may handle their own service animals but must wash their hands before handling food.[568] California specifies that service and guard dogs may go into temporary non-profit charitable food facilities. Trainers of guide dogs may also enter such locations with dogs in training.[569]

# Chapter 15

# ACCESS RIGHTS OF TRAINERS
# AND TEMPORARY HANDLERS

Before highly trained guide dogs are given to blind or partially blind individuals, they must undergo rigorous training. Extensive training is also required for other types of service dogs including autism service dogs, dogs for the mobility impaired, and hearing dogs. Trainers must teach the dogs how to handle the environments in which they will live and work. Most states, therefore, provide access rights to trainers, though many states insist that trainers be employees of recognized training dog schools. Trainers must, under many codes, be prepared to produce documentation on their connection with a recognized training school, and that the dog is being trained to be a service animal.[570] The frequent references to recognized or accredited schools, centers, or organizations in the state codes indicate that many state legislatures anticipated that state governmental agencies (whether responsible for dog registration and licensing, agricultural regulation, or otherwise) would maintain lists of, or somehow know about, reputable service dog training facilities.[571] This is, unfortunately, not always, perhaps often, the case.

It must be noted that many service dog organizations now accomplish part of the training regimen using prison training programs. Here the access issue is sometimes inverted, as the organization must get authority for its supervisory staff to enter the prisons.

In *Clark County School District v. Buchanan,* a music teacher was a volunteer dog trainer at Canine Companions for Independence.[572] She asked her school district if she could bring a Golden Retriever named Maria into her classroom, but the district denied her request, saying that some children might fear dogs or be allergic to them. She filed a complaint under a Nevada statute that precludes places of public accommodation from refusing admittance to a person training a service animal.[573] A public accommodation in Nevada includes "any nursery, private school, university or other place of education."[574] The court described the case thus:

> In this appeal, [the School District] continues its dogged efforts by arguing that the district court did not properly apply NRS 651.075 or properly balance the hardships of the parties. Based on the reasoning in this opinion, there is an irresistible temptation to conclude that CCSD's appeal barks up the wrong tree. Accordingly, we affirm the district court's ruling, hopefully ending what might be viewed as another form of judicial dog fight.

One must sometimes forgive even judges the tendency to have fun with words.

The court held that the state's statutes were intended to protect persons with disabilities, such as teachers, but that the "policy and spirit" of the statute was to extend the same protection to trainers of assistance dogs. "Without such protection, helping dogs could not be properly trained to assist disabled individuals who work in public places." The court said, however, that "the right of a helping dog trainer to train a dog in a place of employment must be balanced against an employer's operational needs." Here, Buchanan had shown herself willing to be accommodating to those needs, in that she "was willing to place her dog under her desk or in another classroom to accommodate the needs of her students."

A dissent to the opinion voiced some valid concerns:

> One must wonder how the majority would deal with a newborn nursery in a hospital where one or more of the pediatric nurses insisted on having a service animal in training at her side. Today's ruling would not only permit it, but could subject the hospital to criminal sanctions if the nurse showed up training a helping dog on the job and was either terminated or forced to remove the dog. How about the bakery where the employee reaches down and pets or positions the service animal he or she is training, and then touches the bakery products destined for the consumer? Or how about the pharmacist who, while filling a prescription, is distracted by his training service animal to the fatal detriment of the customer? I am not comfortable with the anticipated response that people would not be that unreasonable, as we can expect otherwise based upon human experience.

This would presumably be answered by the majority with the argument that the operational needs of the facility could override the trainer's desire to train an animal in a specific environment.

The Department of Justice, in the preamble to the previously discussed proposed rules issued in June 2008, said that commenters had recommended training standards as a means of differentiating untrained pets and service animals. The preamble emphasizes the DOJ's insistence that "service animals be individually trained to do work or perform tasks for the benefit of an individual with a disability, but has never imposed any type of formal training requirements or certification process."[575]

> Because of the variety of individual training that a service animal can receive, from formal licensing at an academy to individual training on how to respond to the onset of medical conditions, such as seizures, the Department is not inclined to establish a standard that all service animals must meet. While the Department does not plan to change the current policy of no formal training or certification requirements, some of the behavioral standards that it has proposed actually relate to suitability for public access, such as being housebroken and under the control of its handler.[576]

This fails to take into consideration the increasing reliance of the industry on testing and certification, something commenters had brought up by noting that "without training standards the public has no way to differentiate between untrained pets and service animals." It also fails to take into consideration the fact that if no standard training or certification can be relied upon, businesses dealing with access issues, and courts dealing with disputes, are often left to make decisions that should more properly be left to those more familiar with industry standards. As noted in the above discussion regarding therapy dogs, the underlying tests of many organizations show considerable uniformity in what is required for an animal to be designated as qualified for service or therapy responsibilities.

# Chapter 16

# PROVING SERVICE ANIMAL STATUS
# AND FALSE ASSERTION OF SUCH STATUS

Another area of considerable confusion concerns how a trained animal's status may be verified by a place of public accommodation. Given the proliferation of functions that service animals, and particularly service dogs, perform, it is not surprising that business owners find it difficult to distinguish service animals from household pets. It is also not surprising that some pet owners take advantage of this confusion to assert that their pets are service animals. They may even think this, given what they see on news reports. Unfortunately, some training schools and internet sites that purport to train or certify service dogs also take advantage of the confusion. One website allows an individual to get a "personalized service dog certificate," a vest saying the dog is a service dog, and other paraphernalia, by doing no more than checking a box to indicate that the user's dog satisfies most of the items on a 10-point checklist. That is Step 1 on the website. Step 2 is to select a payment option to transfer $249 to the organization issuing the certificates.[577]

It should be emphasized again that any trained animal, even a guide dog, may be excluded from a place of public accommodation if it is out of control and the handler cannot get it under control, is not housebroken, is disruptive in a way that fundamentally alters the service the public accommodation provides (e.g., barking during a musical performance), or if the animal poses a threat to the health or safety of others.[578]

One agency that has not to date provided any verification procedures is the Internal Revenue Service. Since acquisition and maintenance expenses are deductible for service animals, this is unfortunate. Those who obtain bogus credentials to get their dogs into restaurants are likely to realize that the deductions related to a service dog may easily exceed that for a dependent child.

## VERIFICATION UNDER DEPARTMENT OF JUSTICE RULES

A public accommodation, according the proposed rules of the Department of Justice, may inquire about the qualifications of a service animal:

> A public accommodation shall not ask about the nature or extent of a person's disability, but can determine whether an animal qualifies as a service animal. For example, a public accommodation may ask if the animal is required because of a disability; and what work or task the animal has been trained to perform.[579] A public accommodation shall not require documentation, such as proof that the animal has been certified or licensed as a service animal.[580]

Verification involves a determination that the animal is qualified, but at least indirectly a determination that the individual served has a disability. The prohibition on requiring documentation deserves further consideration.[581] Since states register and license dogs and provide tags (often through political subdivisions), providing proof of certification could easily be part of the registration process. Animals that qualify as guide, hearing, or service status in many states receive identifiable tags or leashes. This could, at least at the state level, be a means of distinguishing service animals for the non-visibly disabled from house pets, arguably with less stress on the service dog user that an inquiry about what tasks a service animal can perform.

## VERIFICATION UNDER DEPARTMENT OF TRANSPORTATION RULES

Except for emotional support animals, the evidence of an animal's status as a service animal under Department of Transportation rules is very loose: "As evidence that an animal is a service animal, you *must* accept identification cards, other written documentation, presence of harnesses, tags, or the credible verbal assurances of a qualified individual with a disability using the animal."[582] In a guide published for the airline industry in 2005,[583] the Department of Transportation said the following concerning service animal status: "Under particular circumstances, you may see a need to verify whether an animal accompanying a passenger with a disability qualifies as a service animal under the law. You must accept the following as evidence that the animal is indeed a service animal:"

- The credible verbal assurances of a passenger with a disability using the animal,

- The presence of harnesses or markings on harnesses,
- Tags, or,
- Identification cards or other written documentation. . . .[584]

Keep in mind that passengers accompanied by service animals may not have identification or written documentation regarding their service animals.

Carriers may require that passengers traveling with emotional support animals present current documentation (i.e., dated within a year of the date of travel) from a mental-health professional stating that:

- The passenger has a mental health-related disability;
- The passenger needs the animal for the mental-health condition; and
- The provider of the letter is a licensed mental-health professional (or a medical doctor) and the passenger is under the individual's professional care.

Even if you receive sufficient verification that an animal accompanying a passenger is indeed a service animal, if the service animal's behavior in a public setting is inappropriate or disruptive to other passengers or carrier personnel, you may refuse to permit the animal on the flight and offer the passenger alternative accommodations in accordance with [14 CFR part 382] and your carrier's policy (e.g., accept the animal for carriage in the cargo hold).

**Example 1:** A passenger arrives at the gate accompanied by a pot-bellied pig. She claims that the pot-bellied pig is her service animal. What should you do?

While generally speaking, you must permit a passenger with a disability to be accompanied by a service animal, if you have a reasonable basis for questioning whether the animal is a service animal, you may ask for some verification. Usually no written verification is required.

You may begin by asking questions about the service animal, e.g., "What tasks or functions does your animal perform for you?" or "What has its training been?" If you are not satisfied with the credibility of the answers to these questions or if the service animal is an emotional support animal, you may request further verification.

You should also call a CRO [Compliance Resolution Official] if there is any further doubt in your mind as to whether the pot-bellied pig is the passenger's service animal.

Finally, if you determine that the pot-bellied pig is a service animal, you must permit the service animal to accompany the passenger to her seat as long as the animal doesn't obstruct the aisle or present any safety issues and the animal is behaving appropriately in a public setting.

This is not a ridiculous example. Pot-bellied pigs are sometimes considered service animals.[585] Variances from livestock zoning restrictions have sometimes been sought.[586] It has also been argued, successfully in one Alabama case, that pot-bellied pigs are pets, not livestock.[587]

**Example 2:** A deaf passenger is planning to board the plane with his service animal. The service animal is a hearing dog and is small enough to sit on the deaf passenger's lap. While waiting to board the flight, the hearing dog jumps off the passenger's lap and begins barking and nipping at other passengers in the waiting area. What should you do?

Since you have already made the determination that the hearing dog is a service animal and may accompany the deaf passenger on the flight, you may reconsider the decision if the dog is behaving in a manner that seems disruptive and infringes on the safety of other passengers. You should carefully observe the hearing dog's behavior and explain it in detail to a CRO (if the CRO is on the telephone). If, after careful consideration of all the facts presented, the CRO decides not to treat the dog as a service animal, you should explain your carrier's policy regarding traveling with animals that are not being allowed in the passenger cabin as service animals.

If an airline declines to accept an animal as a service animal, it "must explain the reason for your decision to the passenger and document it in writing. A copy of the explanation must be provided to the passenger either at the airport, or within 10 calendar days of the incident."[588]

The DOT precludes foreign carriers, absent a conflict of laws waiver, from imposing certification or documentation requirements for dogs beyond those permitted U.S. carriers.[589]

## FEDERAL FAIR HOUSING ACT DISPUTES ON SERVICE ANIMAL STATUS

A case, discussed above, arising in West Virginia under the Federal Fair Housing Act and state law demonstrates the difficulties that may arise without a certification system for establishing a dog's status as a service animal.[590] The court found that under the Federal Fair Housing Act and the West Virginia Fair Housing Act,[591] a landlord may require a tenant seeking to keep a service animal to establish a bona fide effort to locate a certifying authority.

If the tenant fails to locate a certifying authority, it is reasonable for the land-lord or person similarly situated to attempt to locate a certifying authority and, if one is located, to require certification of the service animal. If neither the tenant nor the landlord or person similarly situated can locate a certifying authority after reasonable attempts to do so, it is reasonable for the land-lord or person similarly situated to require that a recognized training facili-ty or person certify that the service animal has that degree of training and temperament which would enable the service animal to ameliorate the effects of its owners disability and to live in its owner's household without disturbing the peace of mind of a person of ordinary sensibilities regarding animals.

The housing project could require tenants to get additional verification of the skills of their dogs and their need to have them.

HUD has amended regulations governing requirements for pet ownership in HUD-assisted public housing and multifamily housing projects for the eld-erly and persons with disabilities. Prior to the October 2008 amendment to Part 5, a tenant had to certify that he or a member of his family was a per-son with a disability, the animal had been trained to assist persons with that specific disability, and the animal actually assisted with that disability. This requirement was eliminated, and HUD now requires "an identifiable rela-tionship, or nexus, between the requested accommodation and the person's disability."

Housing providers are entitled to verify the existence of the disability, and the need for the accommodation, if either is not readily apparent. Accordingly, persons who are seeking a reasonable accommodation for an emotional support animal may be required to provide documentation from a physician, psychiatrist, social worker, or other mental health professional that the animal provides support that alleviates at least one of the identified symptoms or effects of the existing disability.[592]

It is not clear if the documentation provided by the individuals in the lawsuit just discussed would be regarded as adequate by HUD.

## STATE VERIFICATION PROCEDURES

As with the federal government, many states have provisions regarding procedures that are appropriate for places of public accommodation that may question an animal's status as a service animal. States themselves and their political subdivisions may also verify service animal status for (1) waivers or reductions of license and registration fees, (2) special tagging or gear requirements, and (3) validation that trainers are working for qualified training schools.[593]

## Verification by Public Accommodations Under State Law

Only nine states statutorily specify that access is to be allowed if the dog is wearing specially colored gear or a distinctive tag, though given local administration of tagging this approach likely applies in more areas.[594] Some states provide that access is to be allowed if the handler presents a credential for inspection that has been issued by a training school.[595] Kansas allows training facilities to issue identification cards or letters with specified information to persons using dogs they have trained, but individuals who have trained their own dogs can obtain identification cards by applying to the state.[596] Utah encourages persons accompanied by service animals to display the animal's identification card, a service vest, or other form of identification.[597] Handlers of professional therapy dogs, as well as trainers of assistance dogs, are also to carry identification cards in Kansas.

Some states indicate the dog's status as a guide, signal, or service dog on its license, but do not specify whether such identification is to be used to assure access, though this can probably be assumed.[598] Some states specify that a charge of criminal interference with a service dog can only be lodged if the dog is wearing distinctive gear.[599] Some states allow a business to which a person with a disability is seeking access to ask what special tasks the dog can perform.[600]

More specific and sometimes stringent identification requirements are required in some states for trainers than for the persons who ultimately use the dogs.[601]

West Virginia does not permit demands for proof of an animal's service status.[602] In Arizona, discrimination includes "[r]equiring provision of identification for the service animal."[603] In Nevada, it is unlawful for a place of public accommodation to require proof that an animal is a service animal or service animal in training.[604] However, the place of public accommodation may:

A. Ask a person accompanied by an animal:
  1. If the animal is a service animal or service animal in training; and
  2. What tasks the animal is trained to perform or is being trained to perform.
B. Ask a person to remove a service animal or service animal in training if the animal:
  1. Is out of control and the person accompanying the animal fails to take effective action to control it; or
  2. Poses a direct threat to the health or safety of others.[605]

Thus, states vary considerably in how their registration and licensing systems provide evidence of a dog's special status.[606] To the extent the special status is indicated by gear and tagging, disputes as to the status of a service animal are reduced. This is particularly the case where a service dog is accompanying an individual with a non-visible condition.

## Verification by State and Local Governments

Many states do not charge owners of service dogs any licensing fee, and the owner will have to provide a document from a training school stating what the dog has been trained to be or do.[607] Some states indicate the dog's status as a service dog on tags issued to such animals, or mandate or recommend that owners of such dogs use specifically colored gear.[608] Ohio has a very complicated assistance dog registration law:

> When an application is made for registration of an assistance dog and the owner can show proof by certificate or other means that the dog is an assistance dog, the owner of the dog shall be exempt from any fee for the registration. Registration for an assistance dog shall be permanent and not subject to annual renewal so long as the dog is an assistance dog. Certificates and tags stamped "Ohio Assistance Dog-Permanent Registration," with registration number, shall be issued upon registration of such a dog. . . . Duplicate certificates and tags for a dog registered in accordance with this section, upon proper proof of loss, shall be issued and no fee required. Each duplicate certificate and tag that is issued shall be stamped "Ohio Assistance Dog-Permanent Registration."[609]

Tennessee law specifically conditions access to places of public accommodation on the person with the disability or the trainer first having "presented for inspection credentials issued by an accredited school for training dog guides."[610] As noted above, trainers of guide dogs must often be able to verify to places of public accommodation that they are training an animal at a recognized training school.

## FALSE AND QUESTIONABLE CLAIMS OF SERVICE ANIMAL STATUS

In the preamble to its recently proposed revisions to access provisions regarding service animals, the Department of Justice notes that it "continues to receive a large number of complaints from individuals with service animals." At the same time, some individuals with impairments, who would not be covered as individuals with disabilities, are claiming that their animals are legitimate service animals, whether fraudulently or sincerely (albeit mistakenly), to gain access to hotels, restaurants, and other places of public accommodation."[611] Some states have explicitly criminalized misrepresentation of a dog as a guide, signal, or service dog,[612] though other states may be able to bring a criminal action for such a misrepresentation under general fraud statutes.

# Part III

# CANINE CAREGIVERS, CRIMES, AND PRISONS

# Chapter 17

# REGISTRATION, LICENSING, TAGS, AND SPECIAL GEAR FOR SKILLED DOGS

M any states waive licensing fees for guide dogs and service animals, and some issue special tags or provide specially colored leashes for individuals to use with service animals. Some states criminalize counterfeiting service dog identification cards or fraudulently claiming to have a service dog. That some states do not statutorily waive license fees may not indicate that such fees are always charged as licensing and tagging are sometimes functions of municipality or county regulation.

## SPECIAL GEAR

Some states require that service dogs or dogs in training must be visibly identified as such for interference penalties to apply.[613] New Hampshire has very specific provisions, requiring:

1. A deaf or hearing impaired person using a hearing ear dog shall provide the dog with a leash and harness colored international orange.
2. A blind or visually impaired person using a guide dog shall provide the dog with a leash and harness designed specifically for this purpose.
3. A mobility impaired person using a service dog shall provide the dog with a leash colored blue and yellow.[614]

Virginia is even more complex:

Every totally or partially blind person shall have the right to be accompanied by a dog, in harness, trained as a guide dog, every deaf or hearing-impaired person shall have the right to be accompanied by a dog trained as a hearing dog on a blaze orange leash, and every mobility-impaired person

213

shall have the right to be accompanied by a dog, in a harness or backpack, trained as a service dog in [places of public accommodation]. . . . The provisions of this section shall apply to persons accompanied by a dog that is in training, at least six months of age, and is (i) in harness, provided such person is an experienced trainer of guide dogs; (ii) on a blaze orange leash, provided such person is an experienced trainer of hearing dogs; (iii) in a harness or backpack, provided such person is an experienced trainer of service dogs; or (iv) wearing a jacket identifying the recognized guide, hearing or service dog organization, provided such person is an experienced trainer of the organization identified on the jacket.[615]

Violation of the right-of-way of a blind or mobility impaired person sometimes requires that the dog be in harness or otherwise identified as a service dog.[616] Many states, however, specify in "white cane laws" that failure to use a cane or guide dog is not negligence on the part of the blind person.[617]

Unusual gear may sometimes raise suspicions that an animal is not really a service animal.[618] Most service animal training organizations will provide relatively well-designed vests that say something like MEDICAL ALERT SERVICE DOG/DO NOT PET," or the like.

## REGISTRATION, LICENSING, AND TAGS

Some states, such as New York, waive licensing fees for service dogs (and New York does for therapy dogs as well). Service animal status may be indicated on the registration form, or by issuance of a special tag. Although such indicia of service animal status have limited value in terms of access (see discussion in preceding chapters), it should be useful in verifying service animal status for federal and state deduction purposes.

## QUARANTINE LAWS

A number of states provide exceptions to quarantine rules for service dogs. In California a guide dog is not to be quarantined in the absence of evidence it has been exposed to rabies unless the master fails to confine the dog to his premises and make him available for inspection.[619] In Hawaii, if a guide, signal, or service dog has to be quarantined, the person with a disability who uses the dog "shall be permitted to reside on site for the duration of quarantine, if housing is available."[620]

# Chapter 18

# TRAFFIC PRECAUTIONS
# CONCERNING SKILLED DOGS

Failing to take necessary precautions as to blind persons using guide dogs is a crime in most states, at least under general laws. State statutes often cover persons with other disabilities using service dogs, but where only blind persons are covered it would appear that a mobility-impaired person would not have the same statutory protection. Given the number of veterans now using dogs because of mobility impairment, it is surprising that more states have not modified their statutes. Some states also give traffic protection to hearing dogs, which may have to wear special gear (e.g., in Minnesota).

Some states include trainers among those protected in traffic situations (Alabama, New Jersey). In a small number of states, the requirement to use necessary precautions applies not just to drivers but to other pedestrians who may encounter blind or mobility impaired persons on sidewalks (Colorado).

Some states specify criminal liability, usually at the misdemeanor level, in addition to civil liability. As noted in the section on special gear, criminal liability is in some states dependent on the person being visibly disabled or using a guide dog with a harness or other identifying gear.

"White cane laws" often specify that the failure of a blind person to use a cane or a guide dog is not per se evidence of negligence, specifically contributory negligence. This does not mean that a blind or disabled person cannot act with contributory negligence.[621] Some states leave liability in traffic situations to more general provisions in the penal or civil codes, so the absence of specific traffic provisions (or their treatment of infractions as minor), does not mean that more severe penalties or liability may not apply.

# Chapter 19

# CRUELTY AND CRIMINAL INTERFERENCE LAWS PROTECTING SERVICE ANIMALS

Animal cruelty laws are largely aimed at physical abuse of animals, which historically was often viewed as a minor crime, though an increasing number of states have felony level crimes for animal cruelty. Many states have general cruelty laws that will apply to specially trained dogs, but few differentiate trained dogs in defining the crimes relating to cruelty. Some increase criminal penalties where cruelty involves a service or police dog.

## SOCIOLOGY OF ANIMAL CRUELTY

Aggression by children and adolescents towards animals is often quite different from aggression committed by adults. Arrest rates are likely to be low because law enforcement agencies are often minimally trained or completely untrained in recognizing or responding to animal cruelty. Enforcement is often left to humane societies, though some states have begun to cross-train animal abuse and child abuse investigators.[622]

An analysis of animal abuse cases prosecuted by the Massachusetts Society for the Prevention of Cruelty to Animals between 1975 and 1996 found that dogs were the most common target, with suspects almost always being young males, who shot, beat, stabbed, or threw their victims. Adults were more likely to abuse dogs, while minors were more likely to abuse cats, often with peers present. "Less than half of the alleged abusers were found guilty in court, one-third were fined, less than one- quarter had to pay restitution, one- fifth were put on probation, one- tenth were sent to jail, and an even smaller percent were required to undergo counseling or perform community service."[623]

Battering of wives, and other partners, has sometimes been correlated with abuse of animals. Intake questionnaires used by shelters for battered women have found high proportions of the women reported maltreatment of pets in their households. It has been said that being viewed as a family member makes a pet vulnerable to violence from other family members.[624] Children witnessing abuse between their parents or of a parent abusing a family pet may "increase their propensity for interpersonal violence (via observational learning and/or identification with the aggressor), and make children's cruelty to animals more likely to emerge as a symptom of their distress."[625]

Not all animal abusers are male. A paper presented in 2005 looked at conviction data from a website, www.pet-abuse.com, and found that although 65.8 percent of case convictions involved only males and another 12.1 percent involved both male and female perpetrators, 22.1 percent involved only female perpetrators. Women, however, were generally guilty of either hoarding, or neglect and abandonment.[626]

Though not rising to the level of abuse, a related issue concerns whether owners of dogs with behavior problems tend themselves to have behavior problems, a question that a team of five scientists asked.[627] The study involved dogs that were brought to the Tufts University School of Veterinary Medicine for behavior problems. The owners of the dogs were tested on personality scales. The results indicated that owners of dogs with a behavior problem scored less favorably on 20 of the 23 personality scores measured. The researchers concluded that owner personality and the expression of canine behavior problems may be associated. The researchers believe that overcompliance (an unassuming, unforceful nature) on the part of the owner is associated with owner-directed dominance aggression, but may also facilitate fear aggression in dogs as well as producing separation anxiety.

## RESPONSIBILITIES OF VETERINARIANS

The American Veterinary Medical Association has issued the following statement regarding the responsibility of veterinarians to report animal cruelty:

> The AVMA recognizes that veterinarians may observe cases of animal abuse or neglect as defined by federal or state laws, or local ordinances. When these situations cannot be resolved through education, the AVMA considers it the responsibility of the veterinarian to report such cases to appropriate authorities. Disclosure may be necessary to protect the health and welfare of animals and people. Veterinarians should be aware that accurate record-keeping and documentation of these cases are invaluable.[628]

The requirement lacks teeth, given that resolving a situation through education might mean counseling the person responsible to do what he or she may continue to do anyway. Some states have laws on confidentiality that apply to veterinarians.[629] Injury or death of a service animal as a result of negligence of a veterinarian may result in substantial damages.[630]

Some service dog organizations require that individuals to whom they have leased dogs report to veterinarians who look for signs of stress or abuse.[631]

## CRIMINAL INTERFERENCE WITH SERVICE ANIMALS

Guide dogs and their handlers are vulnerable to attacks by other dogs. An attack can harm either the handler or the dog, or both, but the effect on the dog can be to make it so fearful that even if it recovers from the physical injuries it is no longer capable of performing its service.

Many states protect service dogs statutorily by making it a crime to harass, injure, or kill a service animal. Some states specify that the service animal must be performing its services, or must obviously be a service animal, for criminal liability to be imposed. Guide dogs usually wear special harnesses but hearing dogs may, in some states, have to wear an orange leash or collar to be sufficiently obvious for criminal liability to attach. The level of the offense usually depends on the degree to which the perpetrator was reckless or intended to harm the animal. Penalties range from the violation level and may in more aggravated cases be prosecuted as felonies, but the misdemeanor level is most common.[632] Fine ranges and imprisonment periods are usually specified by the class of misdemeanor or felony involved.

In addition to criminal penalties, persons convicted of criminal interference with a service dog are usually required to make restitution for the loss involved.[633] This can be the most serious aspect of the liability as restitution can involve veterinary care, costs or training a new dog or retraining a dog that has been temporarily disabled, and even replacement costs if the dog is killed or injured enough that it cannot return to service. With some dogs this may mean that the defendant will be liable for tens of thousands of dollars. This is appropriate even though some people with disabilities obtain substantial charitable assistance in acquiring their animals. Attacks by other dogs take a significant number of service dogs out of service every year, many of them permanently.[634] Replacement cost should not take into account the fact that for many service animals a portion or all of the cost of the training is actually paid for by charitable organizations.[635]

Although criminal interference may come from a group of teenagers harassing a person with a disability, the most common form of interference comes from other people with dogs they either cannot or will not control. Service dogs for the blind and mobility impaired are usually chosen from large breeds that may deter attacks from smaller dogs, but even smaller dogs can distract and harm a guide dog. Cruelty provisions specific to service dogs, as well as criminal interference statutes, sometimes apply to law enforcement dogs as well.

# Chapter 20

# BREAKING INTO PRISON

One of the most rapidly changing areas in the training of service and other dogs is where they are trained. The growth of prison training programs has been a phenomenon, both for prison administrations and for the press's and public's perceptions of prison possibilities. Arguably this development is taking work from the legitimate dog training industry, though often the programs involve the participation of skilled dog trainers. Prisoners who have been in such programs are now looking for work as dog trainers on their release. Dog training is for most dog trainers an economically marginal business and the influx of new dog trainers into this profession may ultimately present problems for the industry.

## HISTORY OF PRISON DOG TRAINING PROGRAMS

Dogs have been in human prisons for many reasons. Narcotics detection dogs are used by many states for random searches of cells.[636] Prisoners may be allowed to keep pets. Some therapists use animal-assisted therapy when working with inmates. The area of greatest growth, which is receiving attention for both prison psychologists and wardens, concerns programs in which prisoners become dog groomers or trainers. There are two basic models of prison dog training programs, often classified in prison management literature as a sort of vocational program.[637] The most common is the "second chance" model, where shelter dogs are socialized and trained by inmates to improve their chances of adoption as pets. The second most common type of program involves prisoners training assistance dogs.[638] In addition to the benefits the programs provide for the prisoners, comparisons of shelter dogs that go into the programs and those that do not show differences on both behavioral and physiological scales. One study found that dogs in a prison program showed less inclination to jump on unfamiliar humans, less vocalizing, and significantly more yawning.[639]

A recent doctoral thesis reports that prison dog training programs are found in at least 20 states.[640] A survey looking at all types of prison animal programs found that at least 36 states have some kind of program.[641] Historically, prisons often had farms, and programs involving the care of animals have not been uncommon in minimum security facilities, but dog training programs began to be developed mostly after 2000. There are now at least 150 such programs.[642] A survey of prison animal programs across the country found that some programs exclude certain prisoners based on the nature of their convictions, but others do not. Convictions that most often exclude prisoners are crimes against animals, sexual offenses, and crimes against children. Custody level is sometimes a factor for acceptance into a program. Prisoners may be removed from programs for disciplinary infractions. Most programs do not provide inmates with certificates for participation, but some programs qualify inmates for a state vocational certificate, a pet care technician certificate, and two programs allowed inmates to qualify as veterinarian assistants. One program provided a dog behavior modification certificate, and another a certificate in dog handling. Donations to such programs, either financial or in-kind in the form of feed or supplies have come from Walmart, PetCo, PetSmart, Iams, and Purina. Non-profit organizations, including humane societies, have been involved in many programs.[643]

An advantage of having prisoners train dogs is that they have more time to work with dogs than do trainers at private training facilities for specialized dogs. Eighty-seven percent of dogs trained by prisoners in New York, in a program called Puppies Behind Bars, were able to move on to more rigorous training, compared with only 50 percent of those trained by volunteers outside the prison walls.[644] In this program, puppies are usually rotated between correctional facilities to give inmates an opportunity to be apart from the dogs, which lessens the impact on them when the dog completes training and leaves. Dogs also leave the prison for weekends to expose them to cars, horns, riding in cars, moving in traffic, and other environmental experiences difficult to replicate in prisons.[645] Dog training programs in prisons have been shown to reduce the number of aggressive incidents in prison populations. In one prison, there were 68 aggressive incidents in the four months before a puppy program was instituted, 12 of which resulted in physical altercations. In the four months after the program began, there were only 39 aggressive incidents reported, six of which became physical.

## A VIRGINIA CORRECTIONAL FACILITY

A study at the Lorton Correctional Facility in Fairfax County, Virginia, found that 95 percent of inmates participating in a prison animal training program preferred to stay in the prison to work in the program rather than to go outside on a work release program. Nikki Currie, in a doctoral dissertation submitted to Kansas State University, described the service dog training program of the Ellsworth Correctional Facility in Ellsworth, Kansas.[646] Prisoners find that dogs give them a purpose for surviving the ordeal.

> *I love that dog. When she first came in here, I looked at her like, wow, that's a crazy looking dog. It was dirty and everything and I gave her a bath and overnight we bonded. All I did was hug her and love her and tell her it was going to be okay. I even sing to her and I talk to her.*

Prisoners learn about themselves in the process of training a dog.

> *If you're in the dog program you're gonna learn a whole bunch of stuff about yourself. I didn't realize how impatient I was, didn't realize how undisciplined I was. I'm not good at patience and she (the dog) helped me in that area.*

The prisoners appreciate the responsibility.

> *Having to take care of them 24 hours a day, 7 days a week makes you responsible for someone else's life so you make room in your life for a dog. A lot of time you've been selfish, you can't be. It makes you more responsible without the baggage because you don't want nothing to happen to them.*

Some inmates found giving up the dogs they had trained very stressful, but they were happy to focus on the next dog they would train. One inmate described the graduation of the dogs, when the end-users came in to meet the dogs and their inmate trainers:

> *[At graduation] we see all these different people come in with no contempt in their eyes and get to graduation with light in their eyes and they see us as individuals, not as inmates, and talk to us like we're human, like we're people and listen to what we have to say.*

The prisoners saw each other in a different light because of the dogs.

> *I have a friend in here who is a gang member, a big tough guy and this dude, when I bring my dog around to him, he looks to see where his homies are at and then*

*he's doing the whole baby talking, lay on the floor playing with the dog, throwing the ball, hugging the dog. In times like that you see that big tough guy fade away into the dude that you'd see next door playing with his dog and kids. It's an excellent feeling to see a gentleman who is so hard, so hard core that feels it's nice to be that way and he can break down because a dog's playing with him. The toughest guy in the joint turns into a baby with the dogs.*

One inmate said to the researcher regarding her study of the inmate training program:

*By people reading this research study and understanding what we do and understanding we have compassion and work ethic, I hope they will be more willing to sit down with other former inmates and give them a chance and view them as a person and what they can do and not by what they've done.*

Although the inmates are training the dogs, the dogs are training the inmates as well. Such programs have been found to improve the mental health of inmates, particularly of women. Professor Britton of Kansas State University has noted that this is particularly important because women in prison are three times more likely than men in prison to be prescribed psychotropic medications."[647]

The effectiveness of prison training programs is evidenced by the fact that six of the eight state prisons in Kansas operate dog training programs of one kind or another, but their work focused on the Ellsworth Correctional Facility and the Topeka Correctional Facility (for women). In these prisons, inmate trainers train dogs as their sole prison job assignment.[648] The most common impetus to become involved in the dog program was love for dogs, though few came to prison with any formal experience in training dogs, and none had worked with assistance dogs. At Ellsworth, a dog being trained lived with the inmate trainer, which some trainers said made them more visible to the guards but also to other inmates. The dogs were not to be fed table scraps, but other inmates sometimes did not respect the boundaries, though the researchers felt that this was generally not out of malice. Some inmates did not like being near the dogs but the inmates knew that dealing with such people was part of what they had to accept in training a dog. Dogs also mediate relationships between guards and inmates, creating "a sort of neutral ground between staff and inmates."[649]

Prisoners develop empathy with the individuals for whom they train assistance dogs.

*I know that sounds kind of weird, but we're locked up inside a fence, those people are locked up in their own bodies. I am glad that I can give them some freedom to live.*

Recipients of dogs also have interesting stories to tell about visiting the prisons to get a dog.

*[Before I went] my stomach was in knots, I was so scared. I had never been [to prison] and I just . . . all these things are going through my head, like what's going to happen, what if one of them gets upset, you know. [But now] I have a totally different outlook on it, just the opposite. When I got in there and they started introducing themselves and their dogs, it was just like everything just went away. I was relaxed. I was comfortable being around them. [This program] helps them to have a second chance at life, to get their stuff straight. I really believe that these dogs help them. I believe that whole-heartedly. It gives them a second chance, and it gives them a sense of responsibility, and it . . . if they're depressed or something, they can just sit there and love on the dog, and you know they're calm after that. It's like they take the stress out of you, and I just think that it's an amazing program.*

## AN INDIANA PROGRAM

The Indiana Canine Assistant and Adolescent Network (ICAAN) began in 2001 at a juvenile correctional facility but quickly spread to other facilities in the state. ICAAN trains dogs to work with children who have physical disabilities.[650] A study based on interviews of prisoners in the program described its benefits in the words of the prisoners. One prisoner said that patience was the most important thing he got from the program.

*Even though I am a father, patience is something that I think all of us lack to an extent. Having to deal with the dog, primarily when they were puppies, dealing with the dog from six in the morning until nine at night . . . just dealing with everything that comes along, with the training aspect. . . . Patience would probably be the biggest virtue.*

Many of the prisoners felt that working with the dogs gave them parenting skills and might help them re-establish their relationships with their children after release.

*[T]he responsibility and the compassion and the love and the caring obviously were probably some qualities that I lacked as a father, for me to make the mis-*

*takes that I did because I was thinking more of myself than of my family and my children. So being able to develop those type of parenting skills is definitely a plus.*

One prisoner had autistic children and made some observations oddly reminiscent of Temple Grandin's analogies of her own autism to the way animals think.[651]

*One way I looked at the dog training, and I hate to say this, the OC, operant conditioning, stuff how you train dogs to do things, and I was thinking maybe I might be able to apply that to teaching my children, you know, my two children how to do different things . . . they're autistic and one of the main things that it does, it just presents a major language barrier, you know and with the dog you realize that when you say sit to the dog, the dog doesn't know what "sit" means. They recognize the cue, they recognize the sound, but they don't know the definition of sit or stand . . . and I was thinking maybe I could train my children, my autistic children, to maybe further their communication, how to do different things.*

The program may have made him overly optimistic about his children: "It'd be therapeutic. It might bring 'em out of their autism, might bring out a different side of 'em." The prison trainers said that having the dogs they were training with them when their families visited made the children more willing to visit.

The prisoners were happy to be helping others though they found it difficult to lose the dogs once they were trained and placed with end-users, but one was happy to receive a video of the new master with the dog the prisoner had trained.

*Just to see the expression on that lady's face, how happy she was, has made it all worthwhile. That's probably the most selfless thing that I've ever done in my life. And to see how happy that lady was, ya' know, the icing on the cake for me.*

The presence of the dogs helped calm down other prisoners. One prisoner said:

*Go to a dorm that ain't, that don't, have dogs in it's got more tension in it. And if you go into a dorm that's got the dogs in it . . . it ain't got very much tension. It's very laid back. Everybody's thinkin' they're at home or something . . . it's a lot easier atmosphere to live in having the dogs around than not havin' the dogs. It takes a lot of the tension off.*

*It has changed this place a lot. A lot of people's, I'm not gonna say soft, but they're softer than what they was, ya' know. They let their feelings come out, lay down, play with the dogs, ya' know, talk real feminine to 'em and stuff like that. . . . It changed D dorm a lot, 'cause I was around D dorm before the dogs actually come in here and there was more fights and, 'ya know, a lot more aggressive stuff going on up there. Now you don't really see too much of that. It's like they just go over and pet the dog or something. Their whole attitude changes pretty much.*

When asked what he got from the program, another prisoner said:

*This kind of sounds kind of corny or whatever, but I think how to love again . . . when I came in here my family was stripped away, all my possessions, everything, I mean, you know, everything . . . this is the first time since I got arrested that I've been smiling and havin' a good time.*

Recidivism rates of prisoners who learn to be dog trainers may be lower than those of the average prison population, though more research is needed on this issue.[652] One prisoner in the Indiana program said:

*I don't expect any of us that are involved now to come back, partly due to the program. Because it has given us many opportunities and it's given us some marketable skills.*

Figure 24. Dog Training at the MacClaren Youth Correctional Facility. Photo by Joan Dalton, Executive Director, Project POOCH, Inc., Lake Oswego, Oregon.

One website reporting on the Indiana program states that 95 percent of inmate-trainers were certified as pet-care technicians by the American Boarding Kennel Association.[653]

## A YOUTH CORRECTIONAL PROGRAM

Dog training programs have also become popular in youth correctional facilities. (See Figure 24.) A program at the Youth Diagnostic and Development Center in Albuquerque, New Mexico, paired incarcerated adolescents with shelter dogs in some danger of being euthanized.[654] The idea of the program was to give a second chance to both the dogs and the animals, which were trained for three weeks by selected adolescents, to learn basic obedience skills, such as sit, stay, come, and heel. The young people also received a basic course in dog grooming and were required to keep kennel areas clean. At the end of three weeks, the dogs were returned to the shelter for adoption. The incarcerated trainers were asked to write a letter to potential adopters. Here are samples of what they wrote:

> Stuckers is a very loving dog. He will always sit by your side and is well trained. I think Stuckers once had a family, but they abandoned him and all he needs is some attention and love. . . . Whoever adopts Stuckers is very lucky to have such a well-behaved dog. I took very good care of Stuckers, and whoever adopts him, I hope will do the same.

> The first time I saw Tonka I immediately fell in love with her. I actually had to coax the others in the dog program to let me work with her. She has definitely been a challenge but her loving personality has made it all worth the while. When I first started working with Tonka, however, she did not know anything other than she wanted to be loved! At first she did not get along with the other dogs but that was just a matter of attention (You know how that is). Now she does not have any problems with other dogs. . . . I would recommend keeping Tonka inside while watering if your sprinkler heads mean anything to you.

The most touching letter was written by a boy who was paired with a Labrador-Pit Bull cross. The boy had trouble keeping his temper with the dog and several times other boys or a counselor intervened. Still, the boy seemed to learn things from the dog. This is what he wrote to prospective adopters.

> To who ever adopts my dog Sidnye
> Well just a few things about my dog to let you know what to expect of her.

My dog is six months old and she is still a puppy. She is a great dog and very loving and playful. I guess what I like about her is that she is beautiful and playful, but hard headed like me and that's what I like most about her. She will need a very caring owner to love and play with her. . . . I have worked with Sidnye for about three weeks and to let her go with someone new knowing I won't ever see her again makes me feel sad cause I've really got attached to her. Please don't tie or cage this dog up cause she does not need to be in a cage like a wild dog does. She will probably get you mad at her the first few days you have her cause she don't know you. I can only tell you that you will love her cause she will love you. She need lots of love and praise. Give her your hart and you will see what a great dog you have.

It is easy to see why more and more prison systems, and youth correctional systems, are adopting dog training programs.

Part IV

# CANINE CAREGIVERS
# AND SOCIAL BENEFITS

# Chapter 21

# KEEPING ANIMALS WITH HANDLERS IN EMERGENCIES AND DISASTERS

News coverage of Hurricane Katrina included dramatic footage of animals that had been ignored in rescue efforts.[655] In 2006, in the Pets Evacuation and Transportation Act of 2006,[656] added a provision to the U.S. Code on emergency preparedness operational plans, which states "In approving standards for State and local emergency preparedness operational plans . . . , the Director shall ensure that such plans take into account the needs of individuals with household pets and service animals prior to, during, and following a major disaster or emergency."[657] The Director of FEMA may make financial contributions to states and local authorities for animal emergency preparedness purposes.[658] The Department of Justice has also issued *An ADA Guide for Local Governments: Making Community Emergency Preparedness and Response Programs Accessible to People with Disabilities*, noting "Many shelters have a "no pets" policy and some mistakenly apply this policy to exclude service animals such as guide dogs for people who are blind, hearing dogs for people who are deaf, or dogs that pull wheelchairs or retrieve dropped objects."[659]

A number of states have provisions for rescuing service animals along with their users, including Louisiana,[660] Nevada,[661] New Hampshire,[662] New Jersey,[663] and New Mexico.[664] Oregon has a very specific statute:

> The assistance animal shall be allowed to accompany its owner in an ambulance or other mode of transportation in the event of a medical emergency. If the owner is unconscious, the assistance animal shall be placed in an emergency veterinary clinic until the person regains consciousness and can make arrangements for the animal, or a relative responsible for the injured person is contacted and can make arrangements for the animal, or until the injured person dies, in which case the authorities will attempt to contact the school, where the animal was trained, for further action.[665]

Maryland law states that training programs for first responders, emergency shelter operators, and 911 operators are to include "a segment concerning the rights of individuals with disabilities who are accompanied by service animals."[666]

Kentucky law provides that emergency medical treatment is not to be denied an assistance dog assigned to a person regardless of the person's ability to pay prior to treatment."[667]

The Department of Justice, in rules proposed in 2008, stated that service animals may accompany their owners into emergency rooms.[668]

# Chapter 22

# TAX BENEFITS AND SOCIAL
# SERVICE REIMBURSEMENT
# PROGRAMS FOR SERVICE ANIMALS

O wning service animals has economic benefits in lowering taxes and qualifying as a deductible expense in meeting the income threshold to qualify for various social services. Service animals, as medical expenses, will also not be attached in bankruptcy.

## TAX BENEFITS AND ISSUES

Tax issues include income tax (deduction) benefits, and other types of special taxes.

### Federal Income Tax

Tax regulations state that seeing-eye dog expenses are not to be disqualified just because they are capital. Thus, buying the seeing-eye dog is a capital expenditure.[669] As far back as mid-1950s, the IRS issued rulings about guide dogs.[670] Revenue Ruling 57-461 is worth quoting nearly in full:

> The Internal Revenue Service has been requested to state whether amounts paid by a blind individual for food, inoculations, and other expenses connected with the maintenance of a guide dog, which the individual uses daily in the conduct of his business, may be deducted as business expenses rather than as medical expense.

> The type of expenses involved in the instant case have however, been previously considered in Revenue Ruling 55-261, C.B. 1955-1, 307,[671] which specifically provides that the cost of a "seeing-eye" dog and its maintenance

were expenses paid primarily for the alleviation of the physical defect of blindness and are therefore, deductible as a medical expense, under and subject to the limitations prescribed in section 213 of the 1954 Code.

The Service noted that the costs of maintaining a seeing-eye dog were similar to the costs of maintaining a hearing aid.

In a 1968 ruling,[672] the question was the deductibility of costs for the acquisition, training, and maintenance of a dog purchased by the taxpayer for his daughter, who was deaf. The dog was described by the IRS as being able to warn the taxpayer's daughter "of conditions that might prove dangerous to her." The Service based this acceptance of hearing dogs on a broad reading of the regulations.

The IRS has expanded this to other service dogs for individuals with physical disabilities in publications. Publication 502, *Medical and Dental Expenses (Including the Health Coverage Tax Credit)*, states:

> Guide Dog or Other Service Animal
> You can include in medical expenses the costs of buying, training, and maintaining a guide dog or other service animal to assist a visually-impaired or hearing-impaired person, or a person with other physical disabilities.

Publication 907, *Tax Highlights for Persons with Disabilities*, lists, under "some of the medical expenses you can include in figuring your medical expense deduction," lists the cost "and care of a guide dog or other animal aiding a person with a physical disability."

Notice that the rather unofficial advice regarding service animals is limited to persons with physical disabilities. This would seem to preclude deductibility of expenses for psychiatric service dogs. The fact that no specific verification procedures are provided is to be noted. Given the increasing ease that the internet allows people to obtain bogus service animal certifications for their pets, the IRS should be concerned.[673]

## State Income Tax

Many states calculate income tax based in significant part on the federal return. In these states, the deductibility of the expenses of a service dog will effectively flow through to the state return. Some states specify such a deduction. In Pennsylvania, for instance, expenses for a guide dog and upkeep of a guide dog are deductible under state tax law.[674]

## Business Tax

An income tax credit of 50 percent is provided in Oklahoma for "qualified direct costs associated with the operation of a business enterprise whose principal purpose is the rearing of specially trained canines."[675]

## Sales Tax

Sales of guide, hearing, and service dogs are exempt from New York State sales tax if used by a person with a disability.[676] In Texas, a harness for a guide dog is exempt from state sales tax.[677]

## License Tax

A dog guide, hearing aid dog, or service dog is to be licensed in Nebraska, but no license tax is to be charged "upon a showing that the dog is a graduate of a recognized training school for dog guides, hearing aid dogs, or service dogs." If the dog retires from service, the owner becomes responsible for the license tax.[678] In Virginia, no license tax is to be levied on guide, hearing, and service dogs.[679] In Wisconsin, dogs "specially trained to lead blind or deaf persons or to provide support for mobility-impaired persons" are exempt from the dog license tax and the owner is to receive annually a free dog license from the local collecting officer upon application.[680]

## VETERANS ADMINISTRATION BENEFITS AND SERVICES

The Veterans Administration may provide blinded veterans with guide dogs, hearing impaired veterans with signal dogs, and veterans with spinal cord injury or dysfunction or other chronic impairments that limits mobility with service dogs.[681] Even if not enrolled in the VA healthcare system, a veteran may receive certain types of VA hospital and outpatient care, including guide dogs (other service dogs are not specified).[682] The Vocational Rehabilitation Independent Living Program of the VA has provided costs of purchasing and training psychiatric service dogs for a number of veterans of the Iraq wars. A number of programs provide service dogs to veterans. (See Figure 25 for a service dog in training at Fort Lewis, Washington.)

## SOCIAL SECURITY DISABILITY INSURANCE

In determining eligibility for Social Security Disability Insurance, impairment-related work expenses (IRWEs) are deducted in determining the recip-

Figure 25. Soldiers of the Warrior Transition Battalion, Fort Lewis, Washington, with Phoenix and Jessica Forman, a Puppy Raiser. Photo taken by Ingrid Barrentine, photo-journalist with the *Northwest Guardian;* thanks to Patty Dobbs Gross, North Star Foundation, Storrs, Connecticut.

ient's income level.[683] Expenses for guide dogs are recognized as such expenses.[684]

## FOOD STAMP ELIGIBILITY

Participation in the Food Stamp Program of the Department of Agriculture requires not exceeding income eligibility limits. The calculation of income for eligibility purposes is complex, but it will be noted here that one of the deduction items involves "[s]ecuring and maintaining a seeing eye or hearing dog include the cost of dog food and veterinarian bills."[685] This is something of an expansion of a legislative requirement under which "allowable medical expenses" are defined to include "the costs of securing and maintaining a seeing eye dog."[686] The Food and Nutrition Service of the Department of Agriculture has stated that guide dogs and hearing dogs are merely examples, and that the regulation "should be interpreted to include the costs associated with any animal specially trained to serve the needs of disabled Program participants."[687]

A number of states have modified the federal language to include other service animals than seeing eye and hearing dogs, including California ("service dog"),[688] Michigan ("other assistance animal"),[690] New Mexico (adding "service animal"),[689] and Virginia ("seeing eye or hearing dog or other attendant animal").[691] Oregon provides that medical deductions include expenses for "Prescribed, companion animals, and assistance animals (such as a Seeing Eye Dog, Hearing Dog, or Housekeeper Monkey).[692]

Washington provides that an "assistance unit" can deduct the cost "to obtain and care for a seeing eye, hearing, or other specially trained service animal," which includes the cost of food and veterinarian bills."[693] This deduction is not available if welfare assistance is being received by the food stamp applicant.[694] Thus, one can either get assistance aid for the service dog, or deduct its expenses in calculating the income of the "assistance unit" for eligibility purposes, not both.

## OTHER SOCIAL PROGRAMS AND INSURANCE ISSUES

Idaho's supplemental income rules for the aged, blind, and disabled specify that service animals and their food are in-kind medical items and are eligible for a "service animal food allowance." The animal must be trained by a "recognized school."[695] Illinois state assistance to the aged, blind and disabled includes an allowance of $13.07 for a trained service animal if "the animal is needed to assist with activities of daily living and to maintain independent functioning in the community."[696]

In Montana, personal care services may include maintenance of certified service animals specifically trained to meet the safety needs of the recipient.[697] Provision of medical equipment and supplies for the elderly and disabled may include providing supplies and care to maintain a service animal. Service animals do not include social therapy animals.[698] Supplies and care may also be provided for service animals for adults with severe disabling mental illness.[699] In Nebraska, an allowance for medical or maintenance expenses for a service animal is included provided a physician has provided a statement that the client requires a service animal.[700] In New Mexico, public assistance for long-term managed care includes service animals as a potential added service.[701]

In Texas, medical transportation service may include transportation for a service animal accompanying a recipient of services.[702] An assisted living or residential care facility may charge a pet deposit, but not for a service animal.[703]

The Washington Administrative Code provides that welfare assistance can extend to providing benefits for food for a service animal.

1. A "service animal" is an animal that is trained for the purpose of assisting or accommodating a person with a disability's sensory, mental, or physical disability.
2. We authorize benefits for food for a service animal if we decide the animal is necessary for your health and safety and supports your ability to continue to live independently.[704]

In determining whether an individual's income is high enough not to permit a claim for public assistance, the individual can deduct the cost "to obtain and care for a seeing eye, hearing, or other specially trained service animal. This includes the cost of food and veterinarian bills."

A Washington appellate court denied a woman's application for Medicaid coverage for the costs of her service animal, finding that the dog was not "durable medical equipment" under the state's administrative code.[705]

Special needs trusts sometimes provide for disbursements of funds for beneficiary's to acquire or pay for service animals.[706]

### Homeowners' Insurance

Homeowners' insurance will generally cover pets and service animals, though there have been reports of insurance companies refusing to insure certain breeds,[707] or otherwise making coverage unaffordable, even if a dog has been trained as a guide dog.[708] Modern DNA testing may is now capable of finding the breed origins of dogs. A dog may look like a pit bull but DNA testing may establish that the dog is actually comprised of a mix of other breeds.[709] DNA testing could be an evidentiary tool in such cases.

# AFTERWORD

There is no end to this story. Dogs have been with us and serving us for at least 15,000 years and will continue to do so as long as we both shall survive. Uses of dogs continue to evolve and be discovered. Some of these uses did not appear, or were not generally accepted, until we had the scientific tools to measure them. Verifying cancer sniffing abilities requires rigorous scientific procedures that could have preceded current technologies, but would have been much harder to demonstrate. The same may be said of many of the forensic uses of dogs, such as the use of scent lineups and the ability to extract odors for dogs to detect from tiny items, such as shell casings, with scent transfer units. Seizure alerting will probably remain controversial for some time, but I believe that some animals have this skill and that society's, and the law's, acceptance of this function, though perhaps premature, will in the end be justified.

There are many theories as to why the mere presence of dogs may be therapeutic for us. Some theories belong more to philosophy than to science, and some may even belong to religion if not the occult. It could be argued that we are trying to get back a closeness to our old friend that we have lost in a world of machines and obsessive cleanliness. Anyone who has traveled to France and many other countries will be familiar with dogs lying at their handlers' feet in cafes and bars (sometimes it seemed to me there were a few too many). Some of the chapters of this book would not need to be written in societies where separation from dogs has not been enforced without thought of whether this is beneficial for either us or the dogs.

The first laws on guide dogs were generally issued at a time when the presumption was that dogs should be excluded from as many human environments as possible. Social acceptance of dogs was minimal, and there was a strong belief that dogs were carriers of disease. Much has changed. Acceptance of service and therapy dogs is now much higher, and the changes in law often reflect changes that have already occurred in society without any need for enforcement. Dogs are no longer regarded as significant carriers of disease and when Chloe and I applied to volunteer at the Benedictine

Hospital in Kingston, I had to undergo more physical and other tests than she did for the simple reason that I am more likely to transmit a disease to a patient than she is.

Despite the fact that much of this book is devoted to legal issues, I have avoided one issue that is increasingly found on animal law websites and journals published by respected institutions, which is the question of whether animals themselves have legal rights. The English legal system, of which American law is, from an evolutionary perspective, but a branch, though a very heavy one, has relegated dogs to the status of chattels. People have rights over chattels. Chattels do not have rights. This fiction has been stretched almost beyond reason to deal with issues like animal cruelty and more recently in laws against docking tails and making other cosmetic modifications. In our anthropomorphic logic, we pretend to speak for our dogs, but our voices cannot be theirs in the end. I have avoided this issue because I'm not of one mind about it. I believe that when a professional football player hangs a dog, tortures it with electrodes, and kills it, he has murdered a sentient being. I do not believe that the punishment should be small because the crime involves his chattel. On the other hand, I do not think that a dog suffering from a progressive cancer must be kept alive because we cannot judge whether he might prefer to die. I can only hope that as we keep learning the value of our friend we will keep trying to give him a fair chance to live the life he was born and so very much wants to live.

This book has attempted to chronicle some aspects of the changes that are occurring in our social and legal perspectives on animals. Chloe, Joan, and I wish you well.

# Appendix

# SERVICE AND THERAPY DOG ORGANIZATIONS IN THE UNITED STATES

The following is a state-by-state list of service and therapy dog organizations. Some organizations are national in scope but have regional and local offices, such as Delta Society, Inc. Not all local offices are listed. We have attempted to verify basic web and physical location information, but must caution that changes of addresses, phone numbers, and even website addresses are quite common. Where we could not verify information about an organization, it was usually not listed, but will be listed on the website of the author, www.doglawreports.com. This directory is for information purposes only. The author and publisher do not endorse these organizations.

**Alabama**

Hand-In-Paw
Birmingham, AL
(205) 322-5144
www.handinpaw.org
Therapy dog visitation teams.

Therapy Partners, Inc.
Huntsville, AL
(256) 881-5700
www.therapypartners.org
Therapy dog visitation teams.

**Arizona**

Canine Co-Pilots
Flagstaff, AZ
(877) 596-6366
www.caninecopilots.org
Service, therapy and autism dogs.

Companion Animal Association of
    Arizona
Scottsdale, AZ
(602) 258-3306
www.caaainc.org
Therapy dog visitation teams.

Eye Dog Foundation for the Blind, Inc.
Phoenix, AZ
(602) 276-0051
www.eyedogfoundation.org
Guide dogs. Affiliate campus in
    Bakersfield, CA.

Happy Tails Service Dogs
Phoenix, AZ
(623) 580-0946
www.happytailsservicedogs.com
Teaches disabled individuals to train
    their own dogs for service.

Pets on Wheels of Scottsdale, Inc.
Scottsdale, AZ
(602) 735-6886
www.petsonwheelsscottsdale.com
Pet visitation teams for health care
    centers, homebound and schools for
    challenged children.

Power Paws Assistance Dogs
Scottsdale, AZ
(480) 945-0754
www.azpowerpaws.org
Service and hearing dogs.

Second Chance Canine Program
Tucson, AZ
(520) 742-0338
www.secondchancecanineprogram.org
Trains abandoned dogs to help individ-
    uals with disabilities; Prison-pet part-
    nership program.

Top Dog
Tucson, AZ
(520) 323-6677
www.topdogusa.org
Teaches disabled people to train their
    own dogs for service.

**Arkansas**

Pawsitive Connection
Fayetteville, AR
(501) 582-2064
www.geocities.com/
    pawsitiveconneciton/who.html
AAT and AAA services.

Southwest Service Dogs
Ft. Smith, AR
(479) 646-0886
www.southwestservicedogs.org
Service dogs.

**California**

Assistance Dog International, Inc.
Santa Rosa, CA
(707) 577-1700
www.adionline.org
Coalition of nonprofit organizations
    that train and place assistance dogs.

Bergin University of Canine Studies
Santa Rosa, CA
(707) 545-3647
www.berginu.org
Associate, Bachelor and Master degree
    programs in dog studies.

Canine Companions for Independence
Santa Rosa, CA (Headquarters)
(800) 572-BARK (2275)
www.cci.org
Hearing and service dogs. Training
    centers in California, Florida, New
    York and Ohio.

Canine Support Teams, Inc.
Temecula, CA
(951) 301-3625
www.caninesupportteams.org
Service and therapy dogs. Prison train-
    ing program.

Dogs for Diabetics
Concord, CA
(925) 246-5785
www.dogs4diabetics.com
Medical alert dogs for insulin-depend-
    ent diabetics.

Eye Dog Foundation for the Blind, Inc.
Bakersfield, CA
(661) 831-1333
www.eyedogfoundation.org
Guide dogs. Additional campus in
    Phoenix, AZ.

Foundation for Pet-Provided Therapy
Oceanside, CA
(760) 740-2326
www.loveonaleash.org
Pet therapy certification.

Furry Friends
San Jose, CA
(877) 433-7287
www.furryfriends.org
Pet assisted therapy.

Guide Dogs for the Blind, Inc.
San Rafael, CA
(800) 295-4050
www.guidedogs.com
Guide dogs. Second campus located
   near Portland, OR.

Guide Dogs of America
Sylmar, CA
(818) 362-5834
www.guidedogsofamerica.org
Guide dogs.

Guide Dogs of the Desert
Palm Springs, CA
Campus located in Whitewater, CA
(888) 883-0022
www.gddca.org
Guide dogs.

Latham Foundation for the
Promotion of Humane Education
Alameda, CA
(510) 521-0920
www.latham.org

Love on 4 Paws
Rancho Palos Verdes, CA
(818) 255-0806
www.loveon4paws.org
Animal Assisted Therapy.

Loving Paws Assistance Dogs
Santa Rosa, CA
(707) 569-7270
www.lovingpaws.org
Service dogs (majority placed with
   children with spinal cord injuries).

MS-Paws
www.mscare.org
Foster dog care for multiple sclerosis
   patients.

Paw Pals Assistance Dogs
Murrieta, CA
(951) 600-5852
www.paw-pals.org
Service dogs.

Paws'itive Teams
San Diego, CA
(858) 279-7297
www.pawsteams.org
Service dogs.

Paws 4 Healing, Inc.
Santa Ana, CA
(714) 542-9433
www.paws4healing.info
Therapy dog visitation teams. Ten
   chapters serving Southern California.

Paws for Healing
Napa, CA
(707) 258-3486
www.pawsforhealing.org
Canine-assisted therapy and listening
   dogs for young readers.

Prescription: Pets
Redding, CA
(530) 276-9164
www.prescriptionpets.org
Therapy dog visitation teams.

Therapy Pets
Oakland, CA
(510) 287-9042
www.therapypets.org
AAT services.

The San Francisco SPCA
(415) 554-3060
www.sfspca.org/aat.
AAT visitation teams for healthcare
    facilities, libraries and schools.
Children's Literacy program.

Tender Loving Canines Assistance
    Dogs, Inc.
Solana Beach, CA
(800) 385-1282
www.tenderlovingcanines.org.
Service, seizure alert, autism service
    dogs;
specialty assistance dogs.

**Colorado**

American Humane Animal-Assisted
    Therapy
Englewood, CO
(303) 948-6363
www.americanhumaneaat.org
Over 200 trained, skilled, and insured
    handler/animal teams.

Canine Partners of the Rockies, Inc.
Denver, CO
(303) 364-9040
www.caninepartnersoftherockies.org
Service dogs.

Colorado Therapy Animals
Lafayette, CO
(303) 287-9191
www.coloradotherapyanimals.org.
AAT and AAA services.

Freedom Service Dogs Inc
Englewood, CO
(303) 922-6231
www.freedomservicedogs.org
Service, companion and social dogs.

International Hearing Dog, Inc.
Henderson, CO
(303) 287-3277
www.ihdi.org.
Hearing dogs.

**Connecticut**

East Coast Assistance Dogs
Torrington, CT
(914) 693-0600
www.ecad1.org
Dog training to assist children, adults,
    and wounded veterans.

Fidelco Guide Dog Foundation, Inc.
Bloomfield, CT
(860) 243-5200
www.fidelco.org
Guide dogs. Nationwide service.

North Star Foundation
Storrs, CT
(860) 423-0664
www.NorthStarDogs.com
Service dogs for children with social,
    emotional or educational challenges.

Tails of Joy
Cromwell, CT
www.tailsofjoy.org
Therapy dogs.

**Delaware**

Paws for People, Pet-Assisted Volunteer
    Services, Inc.
Hockessin, DE
(302) 351-5622
www.pawsforpeople.org
Therapy dog visitations teams.

**District of Columbia**

People Animals Love
Washington, DC
(202-066-2171)
http://peopleanimalslove.org
Pet-assisted therapy.

National Capital Therapy Dogs, Inc.
Highland, MD
(301) 585-6283
Therapy dog visitation teams.

**Florida**

Florida Dog Guides for the Deaf, Inc.
Bradenton, FL
(941) 748-8245
www.floridadogguidesftd.org
Hearing and service dogs.

Kids and Canines
Tampa, FL
(813) 558-5406
www.kidsandcanines.org
Service, social and therapy dogs; autism
    dogs.

New Horizons Service Dogs
Orange City, FL
(386) 456-0408
www.newhorizonsservicedogs.org
Service dogs.

Paws for Friendship Inc.
Tampa, FL
(813) 961-2822
www.pawsforfriendshipinc.org
Volunteer animal assisted therapy
    services.

Pet Therapy, Inc.
Sarasota, FL
(941) 358-2225
www.pet-therapy.org
Therapy pet visitation teams.

Southeastern Guide Dogs Inc.
Palmetto, FL
(941) 729-5665
www.guidedogs.org
Guide dogs.

Star Bright Therapy Dogs
St. Lucie County, FL
(772) 342-5275
www.starbrightdogs.org
Therapy dog visitation teams.

Sunshine on a Leash
Jupiter/Stuart, FL
www.sunshineonaleash.org
Therapy dog visitation teams.

The Alpha Society, Inc.
Tampa, FL
(813-758-6106)
www.alphasociety.net
Therapy dog visitation teams.

Therapy Dogs of South Florida, Inc.
Boca Raton, FL
(561) 703-1614
www.therapydogsofsouthflorida.org
Therapy dog visitation teams.

**Georgia**

Canine Assistants
Alpharetta, GA
(770) 664-7178
www.canineassistants.org
Service dogs.

Happy Tails Pet Therapy
Roswell, GA
(770) 740-8211
www.happytailspets.org
Pet-assisted therapy.

**Hawaii**

Eye of the Pacific
Honolulu, HI
(808) 944-9368
www.eyeofthepacific.org
Guide Dogs and mobility services.

Hawaii Canines for Independence
Paia, HI
(808) 250-5799
www.hawaiicanines.com
Service and therapy dog teams.

Hawaii Fi-Do Service Dogs
Kahuku, HI
(808) 638-0200
www.hawaiifido.org
Service, social and therapy dogs.

**Idaho**

Pets with a Purpose
Pocatello, ID
www.petswithapurpose.org
Therapy dogs.

**Illinois**

Canine Therapy Corps
Chicago, IL
(773) 404-6467
www.caninetherapycorps.org
Goal-directed, interactive animal-
    assisted therapy in the Chicago area.

Paws 4 Patients
Chicago, IL
(312) 356-9888
www.paws4patients.org
Therapy dog visitation teams.

**Indiana**

Indiana Canine Assistant Network
Indianapolis, IN
(317) 250-6450
www.icandog.org
Service dogs.

Midwest Assistance Dogs
South Bend, IN
(574) 272-7677
www.midwestassistancedogs.org.

Northern Indiana Service Dogs
Plymouth, IN
(574) 952-1635
www.northernindianaservicedogs.com

**Kansas**

CARES, Inc.
Concordia, KS
(785) 243-1077
www.caresks.com
Service, hearing, seizure and therapy
    dogs.

Human-Animal Bond Program
Ft. Leavenworth, KS
(913) 684-6510
www.ftleavenworthhab.org
Therapy dog visitation teams.

KSDS, Inc.
Washington, KS
(785) 325-2256
www.ksds.org
Guide, service and social dogs.

MO-KAN Pet Partners
Overland Park, KS
(816) 942-6890
www.mo-kanpetpartners.org
Visiting animal-assisted therapy teams.

## Kentucky

AIM HI (Animals in the Military
   Helping Individuals)
Service Dog Training Center
Ft. Knox, KY
(502) 623-3945
Service dogs for wounded veterans.

Paws with Purpose, Inc.
Louisville, KY
(502) 689-0804
www.pawswithpurpose.org
Service dogs; prison training program.

Wags Pet Therapy of KY, Inc.
Louisville, KY
(502) 562-9247
www.kywags.org
Therapy dog visitation teams.

## Louisiana

Visiting Pet Program
New Orleans, LA
(504) 866-2532
www.visitingpetprogram.org
Animal assisted activity and therapy
   programs.

## Maryland

Dog Ears and Paws, Inc.
Sykesville, MD
(410) 655-2858
www.dogearsandpaws.com
Service dogs.

Fidos for Freedom
Laurel, MD
(301) 570-7570
www.fidosforfreedom.org
Service, hearing and therapy dogs.

Guide Dog Users, Inc.
Silver Spring, MD
(301) 598-7771
www.gdui.org
Guide dog advocacy and support.

Wags for Hope
Frederick, MD 21702
www.wagsforhope.org
Therapy dogs.

## Massachusetts

American Poodles At Work
Warren, MA
(413)436-0601
www.americanpoddlesatwork.org
Raises, trains and places standard poodles as assistance dogs.

Caring Canines Visiting Therapy
    Dogs, Inc.
(781) 729-8285
www.caringcanines.org
Therapy dog visitation teams serving
    Boston and area suburbs.

Dog B.O.N.E.S. Therapy Dogs of
    Massachusetts
Scituate, MA
(781) 378-1551)
www.therapydog.info.
Therapy dog visitation teams.
Flying High Farm, Inc.
Lunenburg, MA
(978) 582-7103
www.flyinghighfarm.com
Private therapy practice using AAT.

Massachusetts Pet Partners
www.masspetpartners.org
Animal-assisted activities and therapy.

NEADS (National Education for
    Assistance Dog Services)
Princeton, MA
(978) 422-9064
www.neads.org
Hearing and service dogs; prison dog
    training program.

Service Dog Project, Inc.
Ipswich, MA
(978) 356-0666
www.servicedogproject.org
Large breed service dogs to assist
    balance-impaired people.

**Michigan**

International Association of Assistance
    Dog Partners
Sterling Heights, MI
(586) 826-3938
www.iaadp.org
Advocacy group.

Leader Dogs for the Blind
Rochester Hills, MI
(248) 651-9011
www.leaderdog.org
Guide dogs for blind and deaf-blind
    individuals; accelerated O&M and
    GPS training.

Paws With A Cause
Wayland, MI
(800) 253-7297
www.pawswithacause.org
Guide and service dogs.

Sterling Service Dogs
Sterling Heights, MI
(586) 977-9716
www.sterlingservicedogs.org
Service and therapy dogs.

Therapaws of Michigan
Dexter, MI
(734) 332-9115
www.therapaws.org
Therapy dogs.

West Michigan Therapy Dogs, Inc.
Grand Rapids, MI
(616) 726-1256
www.wmtd.org
AAA and AAT services.

**Minnesota**

Hearing & Service Dogs of Minnesota
Minneapolis, MN
(612) 729-5986
www.hsdm.org
Hearing, service, autism, diabetes and
    seizure dogs. Emphasis on training
    shelter dogs for service.

Helping Paws Inc.
Hopkins, MN
(952) 988-9359
www.helpingpaws.org
Service dogs.

## Missouri

American Service Dog Association
Ellisville, MO
(314) 607-2361
www.americanservicedog.com
Service dogs.

CHAMP Assistance Dogs
St. Louis, MO
(314) 653-9466
www.champdogs.org
Service dogs for disabilities other than
    visual and hearing; therapy dogs;
    prison training program.

Support Dogs, Inc.
St. Louis, MO
(314) 997-2325
www.supportdogs.org/html/index.shtml
Service dogs.

## Montana

Service Canines of Montana
Laurel, MT
(406) 669-3149
Service dogs; prison training program.

## Nebraska

Lincoln Pet Partners, Inc.
Lincoln, NE
(402) 423-3596
www.geocities.com/lincolnpetpartners.
    com
Therapy dogs.

## Nevada

Paws for Love, Inc.
Reno, NV
(775) 826-5199
www.paws-for-love.org
Therapy dog teams, literacy work
    with dogs

## New Hampshire

New England Pet Partners
Pelham, NH
(603) 635-3647
www.newenglandpetpartners.org
Therapy dog visitation teams.

## New Jersey

The Bright & Beautiful Therapy
    Dogs, Inc.
Morris Plains, NJ
(888) 738-5770
www.golden-dogs.org
Full service nationwide therapy dog
    organization.

The Seeing Eye Inc.
Morristown, NJ
(973) 539-4425
www.seeingeye.org
Guide dogs.

TheraPet, Inc.
Clark, NJ
(732) 340-0728
www.therapet-inc.com
Therapy dog visitation teams.

Therapy Dogs International (TDI®)
Flanders, NJ
(973) 252-9800
www.tdi-dog.org
International regulating, testing and
    licensing organization for therapy
    dogs.

**New Mexico**

Assistance Dogs of the West
Santa Fe, NM
(505) 986-9748
www.assistancedogsofthewest.org
www.desertacademy.org
Service dogs.

Southwest Canine Corp of Volunteers
Albuquerque, NM
http://sccvtherapydogs.com
Therapy dog visitation teams for
   healthcare facilities.

**New York**

Angel on a Leash (The Westminster
   Kennel Club)
New York, NY
(877) 364-2643
www.angelonaleash.org
Therapy dog visitation teams for
   healthcare facilities.

Canine Companions for Independence
Miller Family Campus
Medford, NY
(631) 561-0200
www.cci.org
Service dogs.

Canine Helpers for the Handicapped
Lockport, NY
(716) 433-4035
www.caninehelpers.org
Guide dogs.

East Coast Assistance Dogs
Dobbs Ferry, NY
(914) 693-0600
www.ecad2.org
Service dogs.

Freedom Guide Dogs
Cassville, NY
(315) 822-5132
www.freedomguidedogs.org
Guide dogs.

The Good Dog Foundation
Brooklyn, NY
(718) 788-2988
www.thegooddogfoundation.org
Therapy dogs.

Guide Dog Foundation for the Blind
Smithtown, NY
(631) 930-9000
http://guidedog.org
Guide, service and therapy dogs.

Guiding Eyes for the Blind
Yorktown Heights, NY
(914) 245-4024
www.guidingeyes.org
Guide dogs and autism service dogs.

Hudson Valley Visiting Pet Program
Valley Cottage, NY
(845) 267-8795
www.hudsonvalleyvisitingpets.com
Therapy dog visitation teams.

Pet Partners of Syracuse
Syracuse, NY
(315) 446-8244
www.petpartnersofsyracuse.org
Therapy dog visitation teams.

Puppies Behind Bars
New York, NY
(212) 680-9562
www.puppiesbehindbars.com
Prison puppy training program.

## North Carolina

Canine Seizure Assist Society of North
   Carolina
Mooresville, NC
(704) 663-1427
www.seizureassistdogs.org
Seizure assist dog training.

Carolina Canines For Service, Inc.
Wilmington, NC
(910) 362-8181
www.carolinacanines.org
Service dogs. Prison-trained dogs for
   wounded veterans.

Lifeline Canines
Hubert, NC
(910) 326-1926
www.lifelinecanines.org
Service and therapy dogs.

Paws With A Purpose
Ashville, NC
(828) 301-5737
www.pawswithapurpose.org
Therapy dog visitation teams.

## North Dakota

Service Dogs for America
Jud, ND
(877) 737-8364
www.greatplainsdogs.com
Service dogs.

## Ohio

Assistance Dogs of America Inc.
Swanton, OH
(419) 825-3622
www.adai.org
Service, therapy and autism dogs.
   Prison training program.

Circle Tail Inc.
Pleasant Plain, OH
(513) 877-3325
www.circletail.org
Service and hearing dogs. Assist with
   owner trained teams.

Dogtors
Springfield, OH
(937) 323-0925
www.dogtors.com
Animal-assisted therapy.

4 Paws for Ability
Xenia, OH
(937) 374-0385
www.4pawsforability.org
Service dogs for children with any
   disability; autism and seizure
   specialty; wounded veterans.

K-9's for Compassion, Inc.
Hubbard, OH
(330) 534-2001
www.k9sforcompassion.org.
Therapy dog visitation teams.

Miami Valley Pet Therapy Association
Troy, OH
(937) 286-0028
www.mvpta.com
Therapy dog classes and visitation.

Pilot Dogs Inc.
Columbus, OH
(614) 221-6367
www.pilotdogs.org
Guide dogs.

Therapy Dogs of Greater Cincinnati
Mason, OH
(513) 754-0588
www.therapypetsofgreatercincinnati.org
Therapy dog visitation teams.

**Oklahoma**

Dog Ears
Oklahoma City, OK
(405) 478-2303
www.dogearscompanionhearing.com
Hearing dogs.

Therapetics, Inc.
Tulsa, OK
(918) 270-4226
www.therapetics.org
Service dogs.

**Oregon**

Autism Service Dogs of America
Lake Oswego, OR
http://autismservicedogsofamerica.com
Service dogs for autistic children.

Dogs for the Deaf Inc.
Central Point, OR
(541) 826-9220
www.dogsforthedeaf.org
Hearing and therapy dogs.

Guide Dogs for the Blind, Inc.
Boring, OR
(503) 668-2100
www.guidedogs.com
Second campus in San Rafael, CA.

Oregon Coast Therapy Animals
Waldport, OR
(541) 563-4946
www.oregoncoasttherapyanimals.org
Therapy dog visitation teams.

PAAWS (People and Animals Who
    Serve)
Eugene, OR
(541) 461-1188
www.peopleandanimalswhoserve.org.
Therapy dog visitation teams; crisis
    response teams.

Project Pooch
Woodburn, OR
www.pooch.org
Dog training program for troubled
    youth.

**Pennsylvania**

Amazing Tails, LLC.
Oxford, PA
(717) 529-6875
www.amazing-service-dogs.com
Service dogs.

Canine Partners For Life
Cochranville, PA
(610) 869-4902
www.k94life.org
Service, seizure and companion dogs.

Delaware Valley College Animal
    Therapy
Doylestown, PA
(215) 489-2305, (215) 345-1599
www.delval.edu/continuing/animal
    therapy.htm
Certificate program in AAA, Therapy
    and Education.

Susquehanna Service Dogs
Harrisburg, PA
(717) 599-5920
www.keystonehumanservices.org
Service, hearing and therapy dogs.

United Disabilities Services New Life
    Assistance Dogs
Lancaster, PA
(800) 995-9581
www.udservices.org
Service and companion dogs.

## South Carolina

PAALS Palmetto Animal Assisted Life
   Services
Columbia, SC
(803) 788-7063
www.paals.org
Service dogs.

## South Dakota

All Purpose Canines Inc.
Aberdeen, SD
(605) 225-1131
www.allpurposecanines.com
Autism Service Dogs.

## Tennessee

Canine Hope, Inc.
Johnson City, TN
www.caninehope.org
Service dogs; AAA, AAT, ACT
   services.

Human Animal Bond in Tennessee
University of Tennessee
Knoxville, TN
(865) 974-5633
www.vet.utk.edu/habit/index.ptp

Retrieving Independence
Linden, TN
(931)589-3838
www.retrievingindependence.org
Service dogs; veterans PTSD, TBI.

## Texas

College of Education, University of
   North Texas
Denton, TX
www.coe.unt.edu/counseling-and-
   higher-education/counseling
Counselor education program with animal assisted therapy.

Guide Dogs of Texas Inc.
San Antonio, TX
(800) 831-9231
www.guidedogsoftexas.org
Guide dogs for Texas residents.

Huntsville Pets Helping People
Huntsville, TX
(936) 291-8029
www.petshelpingpeople.com
Therapy dog visitation teams.

Patriot PAWS Service Dogs
Rockwall, TX
(972) 772-3282
www.patriotpawsservicedogs.com
Service dogs for disabled veterans.

PetShare
Houston, TX
(281) 772-0069
www.petshare.org
Pet therapy.

Texas Hearing and Service Dogs
Austin, TX
(512) 891-9090
www.servicedogs.org
Service and hearing dogs; fast track
   program for OEF/OIF injured
   combat veterans.

Therapet Foundation
Troup, TX
www.therapet.com
Training for animals working in therapy
   and advanced settings.

Therapy Pet Pals of Texas, Inc.
Austin, TX
(512) 347-1984
http://therapypetpals.org
Therapy dogs.

**Utah**

Intermountain Therapy Animals
Salt Lake City, UT
(801) 272-3439
www.therapyanimals.org
Volunteer therapy visitation teams
   (300+) serving Utah, Montana,
   Idaho and Nevada.

Reading Education Assistance Dogs
   (R.E.A.D.)
Salt Lake City, UT
(801) 272-3439
www.therapyanimals.org/read
Literacy support model utilizing 2,400+
   therapy dog teams nationwide and
   beyond.

Therapy Animals of Utah
(Utah Animal Assisted Therapy
   Foundation)
Salt Lake City, UT
www.uaata.org
Therapy dogs.

**Vermont**

Therapy Dogs of Vermont
Williston, VT
www.therapydogs.org
Therapy dog visitation teams.

**Virginia**

Animal Assisted Crisis Response
   Association
Chincoteague, VA
www.aacra.org
Therapy dog crisis response teams.

Blue Ridge Assistance Dogs
Manassas, VA
(703) 369-5878
www.blueridgeassistancedogs.org
Mobility impairment, autism, diabetes,
   veterans with PTSD, seizures, children and adults.

Center for Human-Animal Interaction
VCU School of Medicine
Richmond, VA
(804)827-7297
www.chaivcu.edu
AAT; research on health benefits of
   human-animal interaction.

Paws4people Foundation
Round Hill, VA
www.paws4people.org
Trains multiple types of assistance dogs.
Oversees the SlammerDogZ prison
   training program.

Psychiatric Service Dog Society
Arlington, VA
(571) 216-1589
www.psychdog.org
Education, advocacy, research, and
   training facilitation.

Saint Francis of Assisi Service Dogs
Roanoke, VA
(540) 342-3647
www.saintfrancisdogs.org
Service dogs. Prison dog training
   program.

Service Dogs of Virginia, Inc.
Charlottesville, VA
(434) 295-9503
www.servicedogsva.org
Service, autism and diabetic alert dogs.

The Shiloh Project
Fairfax, VA
(703) 273-4056
www.shilohproject.org
Teaches juvenile offenders respect for
  animals.

## Washington

Brigadoon Assistance Dogs, Inc.
Bellingham, WA
(360) 733-5388
www.brigadoondogs.com
Service, hearing and autism dogs.

Delta Society®
Bellevue, WA
(425) 679-5500
www.deltasociety.org
National therapy dog research and
  certification organization.

People Pet Partnership
Washington State University
Pullman, WA
(509) 335-7347
www.vetmed.wsu.edu.

Summit Assistance Dogs
Anacortes, WA
(360) 293-5609
www.summitdogs.org
Service, hearing and therapy dogs.

## Wisconson

Capable Canines of Wisconsin
Onalaska, WI
(608) 781-4419
www.capablecanineswi.com
Service dogs for physically disabled,
  autistic children and seizure alert.

Dogs on Call, Inc.
Baraboo, WI
www.dogsoncall.org
Therapy dog visitation teams.

Pets Helping People
Wauwatosa, WI
www.petshelpingpeople.org
Therapy dog training, accreditation,
  and placement in Southeast
  Wisconsin.

Therapy Dogs of Central Wisconsin
Wausau, WI
(715) 842-1453
www.wi-tdi-dogs.org
Therapy dog visitations in Marathon,
  Lincoln, and Portage counties.

Wisconsin Academy for Graduate
  Service Dogs
Madison, WI
(608) 250-9247
www.wags.net
Service dogs.

## Wyoming

Therapy Dogs, Inc.
Cheyenne, WY
(307) 432-0272
www.therapydogs.com
National testing and registry organization of therapy dog teams.

# NOTES

1. Maiuri (1953).
2. See Thurston (1996), suggesting that cancer sniffing dogs might be useful in poor countries.
3. Kirton, Winter, Wirrell & Snead (2008).
4. Melson (2004).
5. Currie (2008).
6. See Bronk v. Ineichen, 54 F.3d 425 (7th Cir. 1995), and other cases discussed in subsequent chapters.
7. New York State quantifies hearing impairment qualifying a dog that assists such an individual as a service animal, requiring "speech discrimination score of 40 percent or less in the better ear with appropriate correction as certified by a licensed audiologist or otorhinolaryngologist or a physician who has examined such person." New York Public Housing Code 11.223-b.
8. *The Diagnostic and Statistical Manual for Mental Disorders* (2007 and 2008), now in its fourth edition (generally referred to as "*DSM IV*"), is the standard classification of mental disorders used by mental health professionals in the United States and is published by the American Psychiatric Association.
9. Baron-Cohen (2009).
10. Connecticut, New Hampshire, and New Jersey. As discussed in a later chapter, deputized teams working under law enforcement and emergency work officials also have access to public accommodations to the extent of government canine teams in some states.
11. Nolan (2006). HOPE AACR (animal-assisted crisis response), formed in 1968, interfaces in crisis situations with FEMA, the American Red Cross, and NOVA, the National Organization for Victim Assistance; "they were even there on September 11." HOPE AACR's website indicates that there were five teams working with FEMA on that date (www.hopeaacr.org, under tab, "Service History").
12. Savolainen, Zhang, Luo, Lundeberg, & Leitner (2002); Pang, Kluetsch, Zou, Zhang, Luo, Angleby, Ardalan, Ekstrom, Skooermo, Lundebert, Matsumura, Leitner, Zhang, & Savolainen, (2009). For discussion in the popular press, see Wade (2002). Earlier genetic research, still cited and preferred by some, would put domestication as far back as 135,000 years ago. See Vila, Savolainen, Maldonado, Amorim, Rice, Honeycutt, Crandall, Lundeberg, & Wayne (1997).

Other dates have been suggested. Lindblad-Toh, Wade, Mikkelsen, & Karlsson E. K. (2005) suggest 27,000 years. It could also be argued that the wolf from which dogs descended separated from other wolf groups 135,000 years ago (Coppinger & Coppinger, 2001). Genetic research has concluded that domesticated dogs of American Indians came across the Baring Straits with their masters. Before the genetic research established the common ancestry of both Old World and New World dogs, many had believed that New World dogs had been domesticated from North American wolves, but studies confirm that New World dogs do not show genetic markers of New World wolves.

13. Clutton-Brock (1977). The Coppingers, however, make strong arguments that it is unlikely that cooperative hunting between wolves and men was a factor in domestication. It takes a long time to train a hunting dog. It is more probable that dogs were useful in eradicating pests, such as rabbits, from fields. Coppinger & Coppinger (2001.)

14. Miklosi, Topal, & Csanyi (1984).

15. Saetre, Lindberg, Leonard, Olsson, Pettersson, Ellegren, Befgstrom, Vila, & Jazin (2004).

16. Wayne (1986) found that small breeds are born smaller than normal and grow more slowly after birth, while large breeds are born larger and grow much faster after birth. The gestation period does not vary, remaining between 60 and 63 days.

17. Groves (1999).

18. Klinghammer & Goodmann (1987).

19. Frank & Frank (1982).

20. Gacsi, Gyori, Miklosi, Viranyi, Kubinyi, Topal, & Csanyi (2005).

21. Miklosi, Pongracz, Lakatos, Topal, & Csanyi (2005).

22. Feddersen-Petersen (1991) found wolves less aggressive in the first year of life than poodles in the same period.

23. Schliedt & Shalter (2003).

24. Wolfgang Schliedt quotes from a letter Jane Goodall wrote to him in 1997, saying that "even after hundreds of years of selective breeding, it would be hard if not impossible to produce a chimpanzee who could live with humans and have anything like such a good relationship as we have with our dogs. It is not related to intelligence, but the desire to help, to be obedient, to gain our approval."

25. Frank (1980).

26. Bradshaw (2006).

27. Lorenz (1954).

28. Raymond & Coppinger (2001).

29. Trut (1999). Much of the discussion of Dr. Belyaev's work here relies on this exceptional article by Dr. Trut.

30. Belyaev (1979).

31. Piebald spotting was a specific focus of Belyaev's research. See Belyaev, Ruvinsky, & Trut (1981).

32. There seems to be something about white hair and tameness. Albert (2008)

found that, when rats were bred in two different lines for tameness and ferocity, the tame line had measurably more white.

33. Some of the experimenters have raised tamed foxes at home. In an effort to raise money for the research, the Russian experimenters have begun selling some foxes to people who are raising them as pets.

34. Smith (1839), discussing the South American culpeo, *Dusicyon culpaeus,* noted that these animals were known to bark only if they had been domesticated.

35. Dogs, in contrast to socialized wolves, increase their gazing at the master when confronted with a problem they cannot solve. Humans interpret the gazing as a signal, and try to solve the problem. Miklosi, Polgardi, Topal, & Csanyi (2000.)

36. Miklosi, Kubinyi, Topal, Gacsi, Viranyi, & Csanyi (2003).

37. Gacsi, Miklosi, Varga, Topal, & Csanyi (2004).

38. Kubinyi, Viranyi, & Miklosi (2007).

39. Viranyi, Topal, Gacsi, Miklosi, & Csanyi (2004), stating: "Instead of the 'all or none' response relying upon whether the human is facing to the dog or not, dogs displayed different responsiveness when the Instructor oriented to a human partner versus to empty space."

40. Call, Brauer, Kaminski, & Tomasello (2003).

41. Miklosi, Polgardi, Topal, & Csanyi (1998) found that young dogs might not be able to use the gesture of glancing (without movement of the head) but older dogs were able to do so. Hare, Brown, Williamson, & Tomasello (2002) compared 11 dogs and 11 chimpanzees in their ability to use a cue to locate food hidden in one of two containers. An experimenter reached toward, gazed at, and marked the baited container with a wooden block. Nine of 11 dogs used the cue to find the hidden food, but only two of 11 chimpanzees did the same.

42. Miklosi et al. (2005) suggested the dog's ability to look at a human face was a key difference between dogs and wolves, and that this ability has led "to complex forms of dog-human communication that cannot be achieved in wolves even after extended socialization."

43. Lakatos, Soproni, Doka, & Miklosi (2007).

44. Soproni, Miklosi, Topal, & Csanyi (2002).

45. Szetei, Miklosi, Topal, & Csanyi (2003).

46. Fukuzawa, Uetake, & Tanaka, T. (2000). It is not clear that playing a tape of the trainer's command from a tape recorder behind the trainer while the trainer's face remains impassive proves very much. Most people, if talking to someone who did the same, would think that the person they were talking to was a ventriloquist or some kind of practical joker. I probably wouldn't respond either.

47. Kaminski, Brauer, Call, & Tomasello (2009).

48. Miklosi et al. (2000).

49. Wagging a longer tail seems to be more effective in one dog communicating to another. See Leaver & Reimchen (2008).

50. Miklosi et al. (2004), citing Price (1984).

51. Hare & Tomasello (2005).

52. Kubinyi, Viranyi, & Miklosi (2007).

53. Riedel, Schumann, Kaminski, Call, & Tomasello (2008).
54. Wynne, Udell, & Lord (2008) concluded that the performance of the dogs in following human cues did improve with age.
55. Reid (2009).
56. Horowitz & Bekoff (2007); Bauer & Smuts (2007).
57. The same researchers found that "whether a dog wins or loses tug-of-war games with a person does not affect dominance-related aspects of its relationship to that person." Rooney, Bradshaw, & Robinson (2000 and 2001); Rooney & Bradshaw (2006); Ward, Bauer, & Smuts (2008).
58. Toth, Gacsi, Topal, & Miklosi (2008).
59. Cools, Van Hout, & Nelissen (2008).
60. Mascheroni, Senju, & Shepherd (2008).
61. Moore (1942); Platek, Critton, Myers, & Gallup (2003); Provine (1986); Senju, Maeda, Kikuchi, Hasegawa, Tojo, & Osanai (2007).
62. Anderson, Myowa-Yamakoshi, & Matsuzawa (2006).
63. It can be argued that many situations are boring to both species. Heyes & Ray (2000).
64. Curless (2007) divided call classes of wolves into howls, duet howls, chorus howls, barks, growls, growl-barks, whines, and yarls. A duet howl is two overlapping howls. A chorus howl is three or more wolves howling at once. A growl-bark is a string of barks in rapid succession that are too close together in time to separate into individual barks. A whine is a repeated sound, relatively brief, and filling in pitch. A yarl is similar to a grown, but at higher frequencies.
65. Foxes also bark at the boundaries of their home range. See Darden & Dabelsteen (2008).
66. Nowak, Jedrzejewski, Schmidt, Theuerfauf, Myslajek, & Jedrzejewska (2007). Theuerkauf (2009) is particularly useful in understanding the daily activity patterns of wolves, and how those patterns are affected in locations where wolves live in proximity to humans.
67. MacDonald & Carr (1995).
68. For an analysis of the literature on barking, particularly on different ways to control it, see Hart (2006).
69. Belyaev (1979).
70. Vocalizations of cats have been found to vary based on the cat's desire for attention. Nicastro & Owren (2003).
71. Maros, Pongracz, Bardos, Molnar, Farago, & Miklosi (2008).
72. Yin, (2002); see also Yin & McCowan (2004).
73. Seyfarth & Cheney (1990); Shriner (1998).
74. Pongracz, Molnar, Miklosi, & Csanyi (2005).
75. Further research by some of the same researchers demonstrated the effectiveness of computer recognition of different types of barks and of the different dogs that emitted the barks. Molnar, Kaplan, Roy, Pachet, Pongracz, Doka, & Miklosi (2008).
76. Morris, Fiddler, & Costall (2000).

77. Mitchell & Edmunson (1997).
78. Mitchell & Edmonson (1999).
79. Rogers, Hart, & Boltz (1991).
80. Simonet, Versteeg, & Storie (2005). This team was not the first to suggest that dogs laugh. Fox (1998) suggested dogs have an "incipient laugh."
81. Milius (2001).
82. Recordings of the dog-laugh, a human imitation of the dog-laugh, and a dog pant are posted at www.laughing-dog.org.
83. Udell & Wynne (2008).
84. Some studies have attempted to correlate dog learning with learning patterns of children in the Piaget system. See Watson, Gergely, Csanyi, Topal, Gacsi, & Sarkozi (2001).
85. Pongracz, Miklosi, Kubinyi, Gurobi, Topal, & Csanyi (2001); Collier-Baker, Davis, & Suddendorf (2004).
86. Kaminski, Call, & Fisher (2004).
87. Overall (2000).
88. Stein, Dodman, Borchelt, & Hollander (1994).
89. Tuber, Hennessy, Sanders, & Miller (1996).
90. Cohen (2002).
91. Barker (1999).
92. Planchon, Templer, Stokes, & Keller (2002). Psychological and physical problems associated with grief over human deaths seem to occur in companion animal owners. Gerwolls & Labott (1994).
93. Serpell (2003).
94. Mithen (1996).
95. Kubinyi, Miklosi, Kaplan, Gacsi, Topal, & Csanyi (2004).
96. Bekoff (2004).
97. Caporael & Heyes (1997).
98. Miklosi (2007).
99. Goodwin, Bradshaw, & Wickens (1997). See also Dorey, Udell, & Wynne (2009); Kerswell, Bennett, Butler, & Hemsworth (2009).
100. Coppinger & Coppinger (2001) state: "No breed is more or less intelligent in any general sense."
101. Svartberg (2006).
102. 28 CFR 36.104. The same wording is used by the Department of Transportation in 49 CFR 37.3.
103. In Toyota Manufacturing, Kentucky, Inc. v. Williams, 534 U.S. 184 (2002), an employee with carpal tunnel syndrome was not disabled under ADA because condition did not prevent her from engaging in any major life activity even though it prevented her from doing her job at Toyota. This result might not have been reached after passage of the Americans with Disabilities Amendments Act of 2008, discussed below. See also Satterwhite v. City of Auburn, 2006 WL 510528 (Ala. Crim. App. 2006), which affirmed a conviction of criminal trespass because an individual failed to demonstrate she suffered from disability under ADA, meaning dog was not a service dog.

104. Briggs v. YMCA of Snohomish County, Docket C08-1326 RSM, 2009 WL 1360474 (WD Wa. May 14, 2009) reasoned that agoraphobia and panic or anxiety disorders did not qualify as disabilities under the Americans with Disabilities Act, granting summary judgment to a YMCA that had denied admission to a customer with a puppy he alleged was a service dog.
105. PL 110-325 (September 25, 2008).
106. See EEOC, "Regulations to Implement the Equal Employment Provisions of the Americans with Disabilities Act, as Amended," 74 Fed. Reg. 48431 (September 23, 2009) (proposing 29 CFR 1630.2(i)).
107. The preamble to recently proposed revisions to regulations under the Americans with Disabilities Act of 1990 indicates that commenters urged elimination of the phrase regarding minimal protection, but the Department of Justice believes it should be retained but understood to exclude attack dogs that pose a threat to others. Some commenters had noted that the mere presence of a dog may act as a crime deterrent and thus provide minimal protection, but the Department argues that this interpretation was not contemplated. The Department cites dogs that alert individuals of an oncoming seizure, or responding to the seizure, as the sort of situation contemplated. 73 Fed. Reg. 34508, 34516 (June 17, 2008).
108. The wording does not seem to cover seizure-alert dogs but the items specified are said not to be all inclusive.
109. Proposed 28 CFR 36.104.
110. Arkansas Public Health Code § 20-14-304(a); Colorado Government Code § 24-34-803(7); Delaware Commerce & Trade Code § 6-45-4502); Georgia Handicapped Persons Code § 30-4-2; Hawaii Blind and Visually Handicapped Persons Code § 7-347-13; Idaho Public Welfare Code § 56-701A(7); Illinois Civil Liabilities Code § 740.13/5; Louisiana Public Welfare Code § 46.1952; Maine Criminal Code § 17.1312.7, referring to personal care dogs; Massachusetts Criminal Code 1.272.98A; Michigan Penal Code § 750.50a; Mississippi Criminal Code § 97-41-21(5)(g), referring to a service dog for a "physically limited" individual; Missouri Public Health & Welfare Code § 12.209.150.4; New Jersey Civil Rights Code § 10:5-5.dd; Oklahoma Blind Persons Code § 7.19.1.D.2; Oregon Education & Culture Code § 346.680; South Dakota Personal Rights Code § 20-13-23.2; Tennessee Professions, Businesses and Trades Code § 62-7-112(a).
111. IRS Publication 502.
112. Connecticut Human Rights Code §§ 46a-44(a), (b); Maryland Disabilities Code §§ 7-704(c)(4), 7-705(d); New Hampshire Public Safety Code § 12.167-D:1.IX; Ohio Agriculture Code § 955.011(B), defining mobility impaired as including seizure disorders.
113. Some state statutory systems do not separately define any or all categories of service animals, but refer to guide, signal, and service dogs (by whatever terms) in provisions providing access rights to users, discrimination and criminal interference statutes, and otherwise.
114. A 1996 letter signed by Deval Patrick, Assistant Attorney General of the

Department of Justice Civil Rights Division, and the President of the National Association of Attorneys General provides basic guidelines regarding access rules. The letter indicated that 24 state attorney generals were simultaneously distributing a similar document along with state-specific requirements "to associations representing restaurants, hotels and motels, and retailers for dissemination to their members." Patrick & Harshbarger (1996).

115. Eustis (1927).
116. Frank & Clark (1957). There have been more books since. See Moor (996); Hall (2007). There was also a 1984 Disney TV movie, *Love Leads the Way*.
117. According to "Our Mission & History" on the organization's website (www.seeingeye.org).
118. Eames, Eames, & Diament (2001).
119. Fishman (2003).
120. International Guide Dog Foundation (2009).
121. Matsunaka & Koda (2008) noted that by 2006, there were only 958 dog guides working in Japan, though there were another 7,800 who wanted guide dogs. Despite laws, these authors note many refusals of access to hotels, restaurants, and public transportation. There are no penalties for refusing access and no agency has enforcement authority. A law effective in 2008 requires employers who employ more than 56 people to accept assistance dog users as employees. Stress levels were found to be high among guide dog users because of the rejections of access many encountered, particularly in restaurants, hotels, and taxis.
122. Lockett v. Catalina Channel Express, 496 F.3d 1061 (9th Cir. 2007).
123. The order against America West was posted on the Department of Transportation website. Retrieved from www.airlineinfo.com/ostdocket/ost995135.htm.
124. A survey of guide dog owners in the UK found that all had profound loss of visual acuity, contrast sensitivity, or visual fields, but only 43% were totally blind. Refson, Jackson, Dusoir, & Archer (2002).
125. EEOC v. AutoZone, Inc., 2008 WL 4418160 (D.C. Az. 2008).
126. See, e.g., 28 CFR Part 36, Appendix B (noting that 28 CFR 36.302 "acknowledges that in rare circumstances, accommodation of service animals may not be required because a fundamental alteration would result in the nature of the goods, services, facilities, privileges, or accommodations offered or provided, or the safe operation of the public accommodation would be jeopardized"); Nevada Business Code § 651.075.2 (place of public accommodation may ask a person with a service animal or service animal in training to remove it if it is out of control and the person accompanying the animal fails to take effective action to control it or it poses a direct threat to the health or safety of others).
127. Wisconsin Employment Code § 106.50(2r)(bm)2.
128. Arizona Counties Code § 11-1024.F.
129. California Civil Code § 54.7.
130. Alaska (7 AAC 43.755: school or shop); Delaware Welfare Code § 31-2117 (public conveyance); Kentucky Animal Control Code § 258.500(3); Mississippi Public Welfare Code § 43-6-155; Ohio Agriculture Code § 955.43(A);

Pennsylvania (52 P.S. § 29.102: dog to be properly leashed and may not occupy seat in a public conveyance); West Virginia General Powers Code § 5-15-4(c). The U.S. Department of Transportation, in issuing regulations seemed not to be against the idea of a service animal occupying a seat, but believed it would not often be necessary: "If a flight is totally filled, there would not be any seat available to buy. If the flight had even one middle seat unoccupied, someone with a service animal could be seated next to the vacant seat, and it is likely that even a large animal could use some of the floor space of the vacant seat, making any further purchase unnecessary. Of course, service animals generally sit on the floor, so it is unlikely that a service animal would ever actually occupy a separate seat." 73 Fed. Reg. 27635 (May 16, 2007).

131. Plonsky (1998).
132. Murphy, Zadnik, & Mannis (1992).
133. Naderi, Miklosi, Doka, & Csanyi (2001).
134. Id., citing Johnston (1990). John Moon of the NEADS organization in Princeton, Massachusetts, advises that many NEADS dogs are from guide dog training programs. Dogs assigned to veterans with mobility impairment are not supposed to be decision-makers the way guide dogs are.
135. Guiding Eyes for the Blind (2009).
136. Guide Dog Foundation (2009); The Seeing Eye (2009).
137. Schneider (2005).
138. A great many studies have been undertaken in an attempt to predict what character traits will be serve a guide dog. See Jones & Gosling (2005). Diederich & Giffroy (2006) found considerable variation in terms and purposes of dog behavior tests and recommending the development of consistent standards. Fearfulness has been a focus of a number of prediction studies. See Goddard & Beilharz (1984).
139. Serpell & Hsu (2001). This paper, and other research, is devoted to finding predictors of training success. It is not just the cost of the training that concerns guide dog owners and trainers, but the fact that the training is so extensive that a puppy is no longer a puppy by the time training is completed and it takes some effort to find a home for an older dog. Guide Dogs of America states on its website that it has a four to six year waiting list to adopt "Career Change Dogs" and retired guide dogs.
140. Murphy (1998) describes assessments of 20 categories of temperament by trainers at the Royal Guide Dogs Association of Australia.
141. Konrad (2009).
142. Franck (2007).
143. California Business and Professions Code § 7200(a).
144. Mezosi, Pallos, Komondi, & Topal (2008).
145. Taken from the website of International Hearing Dog, Inc. (www.ihdi.org). The organization has trained more than 950 dogs since its creation in 1979. See also Bergin (1984).
146. Eames & Eames (2001).
147. Information from "How the Charity Began," on the website of Hearing Dogs

for Deaf People (www.hearingdogs.org.uk). Bustad (1981) praised Washington State Governor Dixy Lee Ray for giving hearing dogs special legal status as soon as she heard of them.

148. Professional signal dog trainers have various devices for making the sounds a dog will alert to. For people home-training signal dogs, it is a good idea to check to see if the device can be set off on a trial basis, particularly with a remote control. Otherwise it may be difficult to teach the dog to recognize the sound.

149. Serpell, Coppinger, & Fine (2000).

150. Guest, Collis, & McNicholas (2006); Barker & Dawson (1998).

151. Hart, Zasloff, & Benfatto (1996).

152. Mowry, Carnahan, & Watson (1994).

153. Valentine, Kiddoo, & LeFleur (1993).

154. Mowry et al. (1999).

155. Serpell (1991).

156. Quotation from Valentine et al. (1993).

157. Mowry et al. (1994).

158. Assignment may involve transfer of title, but increasingly organizations that fund training and supply dogs for little or nothing to disabled individuals use leasing arrangements so that dogs can be removed from individuals who are abusive or unable to work with a dog. Lane, McNicholas, & Collis (1998).

159. International Hearing Dog, Inc., "General Information" (www.ihdi.org/). See also Dogs for the Deaf (www.dogsforthedeaf.org), NEADS (Dogs for Deaf and Disabled Americans) (www.neads.org).

160. 24 CFR 100.204.

161. Bronk v. Ineichen, 54 F.3d 425 (7th Cir. 1995).

162. Green v. Housing Authority of Clackamas County, 994 F.Supp. 1253 (D Or. 1998).

163. The International Association of Assistance Dog Partners estimated in 2006 that there are 9,000 service dogs in use in the U.S. by people who are neither blind nor deaf. Fields-Meyer & Mandel (2006).

164. See Froling (2003).

165. See Vaughn v. Rent-A-Center, 2009 WL 723166 (SD Oh. 2009).

166. Chairperson of the International Association of Assistance Dog Partners (www.iaadp.org).

167. Froling (2003).

168. Coppinger, Coppinger, & Skillings (1998)

169. Studies often find that retrieving dropped items is the most common service performed by dogs assisting the physically disabled. Camp (2001).

170. Fairman & Huebner (2000).

171. Allen & Blascovich (1996).

172. Assessed by the Rosenberg Self-esteem Scale. Rosenberg (1965).

173. Assessed by the Spheres of Control Scale. Paulhus (1983).

174. Assessed by the Affect Balance Scale. Bradburn (1969).

175. Assessed by the Community Integration Questionnaire. Willer, Ottenbacher,

& Coad (1994).

176. Collins, Fitzgerald, Sachs-Ericsson, Scherer, Cooper, & Boninger (2005).
177. Milan (2007).
178. Rintala, Matamoros, & Seitz (2008).
179. Camp (2001).
180. Lane et al. (1998).
181. Camp (2001).
182. Canine Assistants (2009).
183. Mader, Hart, & Bergin (1989). To the same effect, see Eddy, Hart, & Boltz (1988).
184. See 28 CFR. 36.104 (also in the revision to this regulation proposed in June 2008); Arizona Counties Code § 11-1024.J.5; California Civil Code § 54.1(6)(C)(iii); Delaware Commerce & Trade Code § 6-45-4502; Florida Social Welfare Code § 413.08(1)(d); Georgia Criminal Code § 16-11-107.1; Illinois Civil Liabilities Code § 740.13/5; Kansas Welfare Code § 39-1113(e); Missouri Public Health & Welfare Code § 12.209.150.4; New Jersey Civil Rights Code § 10:5-5.dd; North Dakota Disability Code § 25-13-01.1; 3 Pennsylvania Statutes § 459-102; Utah Human Services Code § 62A-5b-102(3).
185. Proposed 28 CFR 36.104.
186. Missouri Public Health & Welfare Code § 12.209.200.
187. New Hampshire Public Safety Code § 12.167-D:5. A deaf or hearing impaired person is to provide a "hearing ear dog" with a leash and harness colored international orange. No color is specified for guide dogs for the blind but they are to have "a leash and harness designed specifically for this purpose."
188. Counsel for Ms. Fulciniti, William Bishop, advised the author that the dog was also able to turn light switches on and off and turn the handles of the bathtub (personal communication, February 22, 2009).
189. Fulciniti v. Village of Shadyside Condominium Association, Civil Action 96-1825 (WD Pa. 1998).
190. Nason v. Stone Hill Realty Association, 1996 WL 1186942 (Mass. Super.Ct. 1996).
191. 42 U.S.C. 3604(f)(2)(A).
192. Massachusetts General Laws 151B, § 4(6)(b) (handicap discrimination). There were also allegations under landlord-tenant law not having to do with the animal.
193. Dalziel, Uthman, McGorray, & Reep (2003).
194. Rudy (1995).
195. 28 CFR 36.104.
196. *A Guide to the Air Carrier Access Act and Its Implementing Regulations,* 70 Fed. Reg. 41481, 41488 (July 19, 2005).
197. Florida Social Welfare Code § 413.08(1)(d). The National Conference of State Legislatures (2003) states that Florida was the first state to allow people with seizure disorders and epilepsy the right to be accompanied by a trained service dog in specific circumstances.
198. Illinois Criminal Code § 720.630/1 (emphasis added).

199. NJ Stat. Ann. 10-5-5dd.
200. Epilepsy Institute (2009).
201. Doherty & Haltiner (2007).
202. Ortiz & Liporace (2005).
203. Dalziel et al. (2003).
204. Strong & Brown (2000).
205. Edney (1993).
206. Brown & Strong (2001). Strong, Brown, & Walker (1999) used diaries of subjects to verify increasing ability of dogs to detect seizures.
207. Strong, Brown, Huyton, & Coyle (2002).
208. Kirton et al. (2004 and 2005).
209. Kirton, Winter, Wirrell, & Snead (2008).
210. Krauss, Choi, & Lesser (2007).
211. Karlsson & Lindblad-Toh (2008). Mutations have also been identified for "shaking puppy," cone degeneration, congenital night blindness, narcolepsy, and other diseases. Ellegren (2005) notes: "Several hundred genetic disorders between dogs and humans have been reported, many of which are found in just one or a few breeds."
212. Communications with researchers studying epilepsy in dogs did not produce any evidence that dogs alert to oncoming seizures in other dogs, but this appears not to have been studied with any rigor.
213. 73 Fed. Reg. 63834, 63836 (emphasis added). The "reasonable accommodation" concept is also found in Department of Labor requirements. See 29 CFR 1630.2(o), 1630.9. The Appendix to 29 C.F.R. Part 1630 states "it would be a reasonable accommodation for an employer to permit an individual who is blind to use a guide dog at work, even though the employer would not be required to provide a guide dog for the employee." See also Timberlane Mobile Home Park v. Human Rights Commission ex rel. Campbell, 122 Wn. App. 896 (2004) (dog that responded to migraines of tenant and alerted friends of the tenant of tenant's need for assistance was not a service animal because the animal's behavior was not the result of training).
214. Kansas Welfare Code § 39-1113(e) (emphasis added).
215. Personal communication, March 31, 2009, from Frances Rosemeyer, Volunteer Coordinator at Canine Assistants, a 501(c)(3) organization (www.canineassistants.org).
216. Duncan (2000). Descriptions of service dogs for Parkinson's victims can be found on blogs and web forums. See the forum on Mobility Dogs at http://servicedogcentral.org/forum (sign-in required).
217. States that restrict functions of service animals to the blind, deaf, and mobility impaired, might not include such animals, although Ohio defines mobility impairment as including seizures.
218. Duncan (2000) lists hypoglycemia alerting as a new function of service dogs.
219. Lim, Wilcox, Fisher, & Burns-Cox (1992).
220. Chen, Daly, Williams, Williams, Williams, & Williams (2000).
221. O'Connor, O'Connor, & Walsh (2008).

222. Timberlane Mobile Home Park v. Washington State Human Rights Commission ex rel. Campbell, 122 Wn. App. 896 (2004).
223. A study discussed in the section on epilepsy seizure-alert dogs noted that the presence of migraines was likely to increase a dog's ability to alert to a seizure. Dalziel et al. (2003).
224. Smith, Esnayra, & Love (2003).
225. The line between physical and mental disabilities is difficult to describe, and it has been legitimately questioned whether, at least from a legal perspective, it should exist at all. See Capp & Esnayra (2000).
226. The invisibility of mental health disabilities has been recognized as a reason why the rights of individuals with such disabilities are too often ignored. See Perlin (2000).
227. 73 Fed. Reg. 63835 (emphasis added).
228. Cornick-Kelly v. Fletcher Allen Health Care, Investigative Report, HRC Case PA05-0035 (August 17, 2005).
229. Corbeil v. The Music Club, Vt. Human Rights Commission Investigative Report PA04-0031 (August 17, 2005).
230. 73 Fed. Reg. 34508, 34521 (June 17, 2008).
231. Not all service dog organizations agreed that "do work" should be eliminated, since psychiatric service dogs can affect the mental health of a handler without performing a specific task.
232. Esnayra & Love (2008).
233. See Storms v. Fred Meyer Stores, Inc., 120 P.3d 126 (Wash. App. Div. 1, 2005).
234. Auburn Woods I Homeowners Association v. Fair Employment and Housing Commission, 121 Cal. App. 4th 1578, 18 Cal. Rptr. 3d 669, 2004 Cal. App. LEXIS 1476 (August 25, 2004).
235. Crossroads Apartments Associates v. LeBoo, 152 Misc.2d 830 (N.Y. 1991).
236. See also Whittier Terrace Associates v. Hampshire, 532 N.E.2d 712 (Mass. 1989) (tenant allowed to keep cat that provided psychological benefits).
237. See also Kleinschmidt v. Three Horizons North Condominiums, Inc., Fla. Div. of Administrative Hearings, Case 04-3873, 2005 WL 1255103 (May 22, 2005) (tenant failed to establish two untrained cats were necessary for him to have an equal opportunity to use and enjoy his dwelling).
238. DiLorenzo v. Costco Wholesale Corp., 515 F. Supp. 1187 (WD Ws. 2007).
239. See Gross (2006) for a discussion of the advantages dogs provide to families with autistic children.
240. Burrows, Adams, & Spiers (2008).
241. A $13,500 fee is charged for a trained dog, along with equipment and training placement. Autism Service Dogs of America has a website (http://autismservicedogsofamerica.com/about.cfm).
242. Wilderwood Service Dogs, a nonprofit organization, maintains a website with materials including an embedded video that demonstrates dogs working with autistic children (http://autism.wilderwood.org).
243. See Jewish Federation of Monmouth County (2003).
244. Batson, McCabe, Baun, & Wilson (1998); Churchill, Safaoui, McCabe, & Baun

(1999); Edwards & Beck (2002); Kongable, Buckwalter, & Stolley (1989); McCabe, Baun, Speich, & Agrawal (2002).

245. Studies of foster arrangements have focused on how puppy raisers can facilitate the ultimate purpose for which the dog will be trained in a guide dog school. See Koda (2001).
246. Coppinger & Coppinger (2001).
247. Fallani, Previde, & Valsecchi (2006).
248. Lane et al. (1998).
249. Hansen & Carson (2009).
250. Zamir (2006).
251. North Carolina Disabilities Code § 168-4.6.
252. Burrows et al. (2008).
253. Duncan (1996).
254. Bardill (1994), a nurse, observed Graham's interactions with adolescents in the ward over a two-month period as part of a master's thesis for the University of Florida.
255. The best-known book has been through a number of editions, most recently, Levinson & Mallon (1997). Levinson wrote many of the seminal and best articles on dogs in therapeutic settings. See Levinson (1962, 1965, 1970, 1978, 1984). See also Nimer & Lundahl (2007).
256. Kruger, Trachtenberg, & Serpell (2004).
257. Fredrickson & DePrekel (2004).
258. Information taken from the "Mission Statement and History" page of the TDI website (www.tdi-dog.org).
259. Other terms were common at first, particularly pet facilitated therapy and pet therapy. For a discussion of the terminology, see Samuels, Coultis, Meers, Odberg, & Normando (2006), noting that during the 1970s and 1980s there was no consistent terminology and that "pet" became inappropriate as farm and zoo animals were sometimes used.
260. Information from the Delta Society website (www.delatasociety.org).
261. I am a member of Therapy Dogs International, Inc., which provides coverage up to $1 million per occurrence under a Volunteer Accident policy issued by Hartford Insurance.
262. LaJoie (2003).
263. Samuels et al. (2006) argue for increased education and formal AAI programs.
264. Kruger & Serpell (2006).
265. Raupp (2002).
266. Meers, Coultis, Moons, & Normando (2006).
267. Vas, Topal, Gacsi, Miklosi, & Csanyi (2005).
268. Wilson, Netting, & New (1985).
269. For a good and balanced summary of the research (including research that has found negative effects from animal therapy), see Beck & Katcher (2003), who recommend that the U.S. Census should include questions on the number and types of animals in homes. See also Shiloh, Sorek, & Terkel (2003).
270. Stoffel & Braun (2006).

271. Charnetski, Riggers, & Brennan (2004).
272. McMahon (1995).
273. Wu, Niedra, Pendergast, & McCrindle (2002).
274. Caprilli & Messeri (2006) recommend asking parents to leave the room when children are meeting with dogs.
275. Friedmann, Katcher, Thomas, Lynch, & Messent (1983).
276. Anderson, Reid, & Jennings (1992).
277. Allen, Shykoff, & Izzo (2001).
278. Somervill, Kruglikova, Robertson, Hanson, & MacLin (2008) conclude that "long-term cardiovascular benefits associated with pet ownership affect survival and general cardiovascular health, but brief exposure to an animal may have only minimal or no long-term health benefits."
279. Friedmann, Katcher, Lynch, & Thomas (1980).
280. Macauley (2006); LaFrance, Garcia, & Labreche (2007).
281. Orlandi, Trangeled, Mambrini, Tagliani, Ferrarini, Zanetti, Tartarini, Pacetti, & Cantore (2007).
282. Barker & Dawson (1998).
283. Miller (2000).
284. Havener, Gentes, Thaler, Megel, Baun, Driscoll, Beiraghi, & Agrawal (2001).
285. Hansen, Messinger, Baun, & Mengel (1999). Nagengast, Baun, & Leibowitz (1997) found statistically significant differences when a companion animal was present during a routine physical exam, with greater reductions in children's systolic and mean arterial blood pressure, heart rate, and behavioral distress.
286. Allen, Blascovich, & Mendes (2002). Allen, Blascovich, Tomaka, & Kelsey (1991) found that women showed less physiological reactivity to a mental arithmetic task in the presence of a pet than in the presence of the experimenter alone or in the presence of their closest female friend.
287. Barker, Pandurangi, & Best 2003).
288. Tissen, Hergovich, & Spiel (2007); Poresky (1990); Ascione (1992); Ascione & Weber (1996).
289. Kotrschal & Ortbauer (2003).
290. See Behrend (2005).
291. Somervill et al. (2009).
292. Nagengast et al. (1997).
293. Lefkowitz, Paharia, Prout, Debiak, & Bleiberg (2005).
294. Barker, Barker, Dawson, & Knisely (1997).
295. Nebbe (1991).
296. Posted on CNN, May 4, 2009 at www.cnn.com/video/#/video/crime/2009/05/01/pkg.ca.court.dog.calms.kids.kusi.
297. Hart-Cohen (2009).
298. The Mississippi Children's Advocacy Center also has a cat named Pookie that is used in forensic interviews. See Phillips (2004).
299. See O'Neill-Stephens (2007).
300. Charnetski et al. (2004); see also Limond, Bradshaw, & Cormack (1997); Davis (2007); Martin & Farnum, (2002) exposed children to a toy ball, a stuffed dog,

and a live therapy dog. Children were more aware of their social environments in the presence of the therapy dog. This suggests that a therapy dog may be preferable to a stuffed animal as a testimony aid.

301. Stephens (2009).
302. Dellinger (2009).
303. See State v. Cliff, 116 Idaho 921, 782 P.2d 44 (Idaho App. 1989); State v. Marquez, 124 N.M. 409, 951 P.2d 1070 (New Mexico App. 1997) (child held teddy bear); State v. Hakimi, 124 Wash. App. 15, 98 P.3d 809 (Wash. App. 2004) (two children allowed to testify holding dolls); Smith v. State, 2005 Wyoming 113, 119 P.3d 411 (Wyo. 2005) (15-year-old girl allowed to hold teddy bear).
304. Leaser (2005).
305. Beyersdorfer & Birkenhauer (1990).
306. Hart (1995).
307. Siegel (1990).
308. Garrity, Stallones, Marx, & Johnson (1989).
309. Herbert & Greene (2001).
310. See Velde, Cipriani, & Fisher (2005).
311. Perelle & Granville (1993).
312. Velde et al. (2005).
313. Corson, Corson, Gwynne, & Arnold (1977).
314. Greenbaum (2006).
315. Gordon (2004).
316. John Moon of NEADS in Princeton, Massachusetts (www.neads.org), advises that basic service dog training involves 70 commands, after which additional commands are taught in the phase where a service dog is prepared for a specific handler. NEADS trains primarily hearing and mobility impairment dogs. See Zapf & Rough (2002).
317. Combined with "Assistance Dogs in Public" (www.assistancedogsinternational.org/Standards/AssistanceDogPublicStandards.php).
318. Test numbers refer to the test of Assistance Dogs International, Inc., which requires that dogs be Canine Good Citizens and pass additional testing requirements (testing requirements posted at http://www.tdi-dog.org/tditesting.html).
319. The author has experienced this himself in taking his dog to a nursing home, many of the patients in which are under hospice care, meaning that they are not expected to live longer than six months. Visits to the facility often put the dog to sleep for the rest of the day.
320. Heimlich (2001) states: "Although there in no conclusive evidence that Cody's illness was the result of the strain placed on him by the intense therapy regimen, one must question its impact."
321. 61 Fed. Reg. 56409, 56421.
322. Kansas Welfare Code § 39-1113(d).
323. Kansas Social Welfare Code § 39-1111(b).
324. Kansas Social Welfare Code § 39-1112.
325. New York Agriculture Code § 108.26. The author has been involved in draft-

ing legislation in New York state that would allow limited access for therapy dogs while going to or from or on assignments.

326. Oregon Criminal Code § 167.352(3)(b).
327. Search and rescue dogs, dogs that use their sense of smell to find escaped convicts, bodies, lost children, etc., are increasingly owned by private individuals and rented as necessary by law enforcement agencies. Like therapy dogs, privately owned search and rescue dogs are usually pets when they are not using the skills for which they have been trained. Because they are rented to law enforcement (along with the services of their masters), these dogs often have to travel significant distances to perform their functions. Two states, Connecticut and New Hampshire, have recognized the need that owners may have to obtain access to public accommodations and transportation facilities when they are going to and from assignments. Connecticut Crimes Code § 53-330a(a). Denial of rights to such a team member is a misdemeanor in Connecticut. Connecticut Crimes Code § 53-330a(b). New Hampshire defines a search and rescue dog is "any dog which has been trained to perform typical search and rescue operations and is certified by a competent authority or holds a title from a competent authority or organization recognized by the office of the governor, department of safety, department of fish and game, or the Federal Emergency Management Agency or its successor agency." New Hampshire Public Safety Code § 12.167-D:1.XI. Search and rescue dogs "involved in search and rescue missions at the request of a government agency" may be brought into the same places of public accommodation as guide, hearing, and service dogs "at the request of a government agency when such dogs are in the course of, or traveling to or from the scene of, their official duties." New Hampshire Public Safety Code § 12.167-D:4. In Pennsylvania: "It shall be unlawful for the proprietor, manager or employee of a theater, hotel, motel, restaurant or other place of entertainment, amusement or accommodation to refuse, withhold from, or deny to any person, due to the use of a working police dog used by any State or county or municipal police or sheriff's department or agency, either directly or indirectly, any of the accommodations, advantages, facilities or privileges of the theater, hotel, motel, restaurant or other place of public entertainment, amusement or accommodation. Any person who violates any of the provisions of this subsection commits a misdemeanor of the third degree."3 Pennsylvania Statutes § 459-602(c). Since the dog may be "used" in law enforcement, it presumably does not need to be owned by a law enforcement agency and could, therefore, be rented as contemplated in the New Hampshire and Connecticut statutes.
328. Brooks, Oi, & Koehler (2003).
329. Heaton, Cablk, Nussear, Medica, Sagebiel, & Francis (2008). Tortoises are identified for purposes of protecting an endangered species.
330. R.M. Engeman, Vice, Rodriquez, Bruver, Santos, & Pitzler (1998).
331. Wallner & Ellis (1976).
332. Welch (1990).
333. Konrad (2009).

334. Williams & Pembroke (1989). A dog tested by researchers in 2004 proved to be highly accurate at detecting melanomas. Pickel, Manucy, Walker, Hall, & Walker (2004).

335. Welsh, Barton, & Ahuja (2005).

336. Lesniak, Walczak, Jezierski, Sacharczuk, Gawkowski, & Jaszczak (2008).

337. Hearing Dogs for Deaf People is a UK nonprofit organization (www.hearing-dogs.org.uk).

338. Willis, Church, Guest, Cook, McCarthy, Bransbury, Church, & Church (2004).

339. McCulloch, Jezierski, Broffman, Hubbard, Turner, & Janecki (2006); Jezierski, Walczak, Gorecka (2008).

340. PL 109-308 (2006), amending the Robert T. Stafford Disaster Relief and Emergency Assistance Act, PL 93-288 (1974), § 613.

341. 49 U.S.C. 41705. The original language appeared in the Air Carrier Access Act of 1986, PL 99-435 (1986). See 14 CFR 382.3 defining Air Carrier Access Act and stating it is the principal authority for 14 CFR Part 382.

342. PL 101-336 (1990).

343. 42 U.S.C. 12182(a).

344. 42 U.S.C. 12181(7).

345. This language is repeated in the regulations at 28 CFR 36.302(a), where it is followed by specific examples having to do with service animals.

346. 42 U.S.C. 12187. By cross reference to 42 U.S.C. 2000a(e), the private club or establishment must generally not be open to the public.

347. 42 U.S.C. 12188.

348. PL 90-284 (1968).

349. PL 100-430 (1988).

350. 42 U.S.C. 3607.

351. 42 U.S.C. 3604.

352. 42 U.S.C. 3605.

353. 42 U.S.C. 3606

354. 42 U.S.C. 3604(f)(3)(B).

355. PL 93-112 (1973).

356. 29 U.S.C. 794(a).

357. See Southeastern Community College v. Davis, 99 S.Ct. 2361 (1979) (deaf applicant to nursing program was not otherwise qualified because she could not meet technical standards for admission to program).

358. 29 U.S.C. 794(b).

359. 29 U.S.C. 794(d), cross-referencing 42 U.S.C. 12111 et seq., 12201-12204, and 12210.

360. For example, Illinois Code § 720.630/1; New Jersey Civil Rights § 10:5-5.dd).

361. For a discussion of the inconsistencies in federal and state law regarding service and therapy dogs, see Ensminger & Breitkopf (2010).

362. See, e.g., Green v. Housing Authority of Clackamas County, 994 F.Supp. 1253 (D. Or. 1998); state law that signal dogs must use orange leashes could not preempt federal law on what qualifies as a service animal.

363. Cornick-Kelly v. Fletcher Allen Health Care, Vt. Human Rights Commission

Investigative Report, HRC Case PA05-0035 (August 17, 2005) (animal that performed tasks for woman suffering from post-traumatic stress disorder and panic attacks was given service animal status but labeled an emotional support animal by the Vermont Human Rights Commission).

364. 73 Fed. Reg. 34516.

365. Proposed 28 CFR 36.104.

366. 73 Fed. Reg. 34521.

367. Proposed 28 CFR 36.104.

368. The preamble notes that the Department of Housing and Urban Development uses the term "assistance animal," and that this usage denotes "a broader category of animals than is covered by the ADA." 73 Fed. Reg. 34521.

369. 73 Fed. Reg. 34516.

370. 73 Fed. Reg. 34521.

371. PL 110-325 (2008).

372. Department of Transportation rules regarding access to "vehicles and facilities" under 49 CFR 37.167, mention service animals in connection with sight, hearing, and mobility impairments, but do not mention individuals with mental handicaps. See Appendix D to 49 CFR Part 37, 61 Fed. Reg. 25416.

373. 73 Fed. Reg. 27636.

374. The Psychiatric Service Dog Society raised a number of issues regarding air carrier access rules, including questioning the Department of Transportation's acceptance of emotional support animals as a type of service animal. The Department of Transportation sought public comment on this and related issues in September 2009. Department of Transportation, "Nondiscrimination on the Basis of Disability in Air Travel: Request for comments on petition for rulemaking," Docket OST-2009-0093, 74 Fed. Reg. 47902 (September 18, 2009).

375. 73 Fed. Reg. 27659.

376. 73 Fed. Reg. 27655.

377. The final phrase before the end-parenthesis was added in technical corrections. 74 Fed. Reg. 11469, 11471 (March 18, 2009).

378. 14 CFR 382.117(e).

379. 73 Fed. Reg. 27636.

380. Department of Transportation, *Notice of Guidance Concerning the Carriage of Service Animals in Air Transportation from the United States to the United Kingdom,* 72 Fed. Reg. 8268 (February 26, 2007).

381. 72 Fed. Reg. 8271 (citing the UK's Civil Aviation Authority's Flight Operations Department Communication 3/2005 (March 11, 2005)).

382. Department of Housing and Urban Development, "Pet Ownership for the Elderly and Persons With Disabilities," RIN 2501-AD31, 73 Fed. Reg. 63834 (October 27, 2008). Proposed rules were issued for comment in October 2007. 72 Fed. Reg. 58448 (October 15, 2007).

383. 73 Fed. Reg. 63834.

384. Crossroads Apartments Associates v. LeBoo, 152 Misc.2d 830 (N.Y. 1981) (tenant permitted to demonstrate emotional and psychological dependence on

cat); Prindable v. Association of Apartment Owners of 2987 Kalakaua, 304 F. Supp.2d 1245 (D.C. Hi. 2003) (condominium complex could impose restrictions on access of emotional support animal to common areas); Whittier Terrace Associates v. Hampshire, 532 N.E.2d 712 (Mass. 1989) (tenant had emotional attachment to and perhaps psychological dependence on cat, so question for court was whether burdens on housing project were undue given benefits to tenant; absence of noises, odors, and fact tenant was ideal tenant indicate only reason for eviction was that she had a cat; "a narrow exception to the rigid application of the no-pet rule, involving no untoward collateral consequences, will enable a handicapped person to continue to function successfully on her own.")

385. Senate Bill 173 (signed into law, March 20, 2009).

386. Storms v. Fred Meyer Stores, Inc., 120 P.3d 126 (Wash. App. Div. 1, 2005).

387. This might sound extreme but the author was once stopped at a Costco exit because the checker noticed that one item had been rung up twice, meaning that there had been an overcharge. I had to wait for ten minutes for a store manager to arrive. During that time, a former law school professor passed by and pretended not to notice us. Both my wife and I worried that she might have thought we were being stopped for shoplifting. My wife had to convince me that I would only look more idiotic if I called her up and tried to explain. It was indeed embarrassing, though not malicious.

388. State officials will often cite Department of Justice regulations in state-level enforcement actions.

389. See Janush v. Charities Housing Development Corp., 169 F. Supp.2d 1133 (ND Cal. 2000) (denying defendant's motion to dismiss on grounds plaintiff's two birds and two cats could not be service dogs, noting that 28 CFR 36.104 defines a service animal as a guide dog, signal dog, "or other animal individually trained to do work or perform tasks for the benefit of an individual with a disability. . . .").

390. 28 CFR 36.104.

391. DiLorenzo v. Costco Wholesale Corp., 515 F. Supp. 1187 (WD Wa. 2007). See also Grill v. Costco Wholesale Corp., 312 F.Supp.2d 1349 (WD Wa. 2004) (Costco entitled to ask task or function in challenge of service animal status).

392. For another case that arose in the state of Washington, see Storms v. Fed Meyer Stores, Inc., 120 P.2d 126 (Wash. App. Div. 1 2005). That case cited ADA statutes and regulations, but was resolved primarily on state law.

393. See Stan v. Wal-Mart Stores, Inc., 111 F.Supp. 119 (ND N.Y. 2000).

394. 28 CFR 36.302(c)(1).

395. 28 CFR 36.104, incorporating the language of 42 U.S.C. 12181(7).

396. 28 CFR 36.104.

397. 28 CFR 36.302(c)(1). If a service animal must be separated from an individual with a disability to avoid a fundamental alteration or a threat to safety, it is the responsibility of handler to arrange for the care and supervision of the animal during the period of separation.

398. 28 CFR 36.302(a).

399. Lentini v. California Center for the Arts, Escondido, 370 F.3d 837 (9th Cir. 2004).

400. 28 CFR Part 36, Appendix B, which was the preamble to the 1991 regulations regarding nondiscrimination by public accommodations and in commercial facilities (July 26, 1991).

401. Department of Justice, "Nondiscrimination on the Basis of Disability by Public Accommodations and in Commercial Facilities," 73 Fed. Reg. 34508 (June 17, 2008) (proposed amendments to 28 CFR Part 36, concerning nondiscrimination in public accommodations and in commercial facilities). See also 73 Fed. Reg. 34465 (June 17, 2008) (proposed amendments particularly to 28 CFR Part 35, concerning nondiscrimination in provision of state and local governmental services).

402. 73 Fed. Reg. 34515-6.

403. Citing American Veterinary Medical Association (2005).

404. 73 Fed. Reg. 34524.

405. Citing Centers for Disease Control (2003).

406. Pool v. Riverside Health Services, Inc., 1995 WL 519129 (D Kan. 1995).

407. 42 U.S.C. 12182(b)(2)(B).

408. 49 U.S.C. 41705.

409. Department of Transportation (DOT), "Nondiscrimination on the Basis of Disability in Air Travel; Final Rule," RINs 2105-AC97, 2105-AC29, 2105-AD41, 73 Fed. Reg. 27613 (May 13, 2008). The Department had issued a notice of proposed rulemaking (NPRM) in November 2004 to apply the Air Carrier Access Act to foreign carriers. DOT, RIN 2105-AC97, 69 Fed. Reg. 64363 (November 4, 2004), among other things proposing to move the provisions of 14 CFR 382.55, regarding access with service animals, to 382.117. Another NPRM, which included proposals included in the final rules of 2008, concerned medical oxygen and portable respiration assistive devices, but did not mention service animals. DOT, RIN 2105-AC29, 70 Fed. Reg. 53108 (September 7, 2005). A third NPRM, issued in 2006, concerned accommodations for individuals who are deaf, hard of hearing, or deaf-blind, but also did not mention service animals. DOT, RIN 2105-AD41, 71 Fed. Reg. 9285 (February 23, 2006).

410. 14 CFR 382.27(c)(8).

411. 14 CFR 382.27(c)(9).

412. 73 Fed. Reg. 27659.

413. 14 CFR 382.117(b).

414. 14 CFR 382.81(c).

415. 73 Fed. Reg. 27634-5.

416. 14 CFR 382.117(c).

417. Miscellaneous Questions under "Guidance Concerning Service Animals," guidance response to question: Are there any situations in which an animal would not be permitted to accompany its user on a flight? 73 Fed. Reg. 27661.

418. 14 CFR 382.81(c).

419. The order against America West was posted (docket no. OST-99-5135) (empha-

sis added).

420. 14 CFR 382.117(g) (emphasis added).

421. 14 CFR 382.51.

422. 14 CFR 382.91.

423. 14 CFR 382.35.

424. 73 Fed. Reg. 27635.

425. 72 Fed. Reg. 8268 (February 26, 2007).

426. European Parliament and Council (2003).

427. European Parliament and Council (2006), stating: "Where use of a recognised assistance dog is required, this shall be accommodated provided that notification of the same is made to the air carrier or its agent or the tour operator in accordance with applicable national rules covering the carriage of assistance dogs on board aircraft, where such rules exist."

428. 72 Fed. Reg. 8271 (citing the UK's Civil Aviation Authority's Flight Operations Department Communication 3/2005 (March 11, 2005)).

429. 72 Fed. Reg. 8272.

430. Details are posted online by the Department for Environment, Food and Rural Affairs (www.defra.gov.uk/animalh/quarantine/index.htm).

431. 14 CFR 382.117.

432. Department of Transportation, *Transportation for Individuals with Disabilities: Passenger Vessels,* 72 Fed. Reg. 2833 (January 23, 2007). A service animal is defined for this purpose as "any guide dog, signal dog, or other animal individually trained to work or perform tasks for an individual with a disability, including, but not limited to, guiding individuals with impaired vision, alerting individuals with impaired hearing to intruders or sounds, alerting persons with seizure disorders to the onset of a seizure, providing minimal protection or rescue work, pulling a wheelchair, or fetching dropped items." 49 CFR 39.3. It is not clear if the Department intended the definition to be more restrictive than definitions now applied to airlines under the Air Carrier Access Act.

433. Proposed 49 CFR 39.91.

434. Proposed 49 CFR 37.91.

435. 49 CFR 37.21(b) and (c).

436. 49 CFR 37.167(d).

437. Settlement Agreement, Department of Justice and Budget Rent A Car Systems, Inc., DJ 202-79-16, 202-79-42, 202-79-50 (July 1997) (www.ada.gov/budget. htm); Settlement Agreement, Department of Justice and Skyway Group, Inc., d/b/a Arizona Shuttle Service, Tucson, AZ, DJ 202-8-36 (February 2001) (www.ada.gov/skywayse.htm).

438. See Stamm v. New York City Transit Authority, Docket 04-CV-2163, 2006 WL 1027142 (ED N.Y. 2006) (New York Transit Authority had issued cards to users of service dogs prior to 1999; change in policy was reasonable accommodation; TA employee intentionally incited other passengers against Stamm).

439. Settlement Agreement, Department of Justice and Yellow Cab Drivers Association, Inc., of Salt Lake city, Utah, DJ 202-77-34 (July 7, 2003) (www. ada.gov/yellocab.htm).

440. 49 CFR 37.3 (definitions).
441. 49 CFR Part 37, Appendix D.
442. 496 F.3d 1061 (9th Cir. 2007).
443. 42 U.S.C. 12182(b)(1)(A)(iii).
444. Looking specifically 28 CFR 36.208, 36.301(a), and 36.302(c). The use of the same definition of service animal for both Department of Justice regulations and Department of Transportation regulations means that the same result would be reached by a court applying either set of rules.
445. 28 CFR 36.208.
446. See Hawaii Blind and Visually Handicapped Persons Code § 7-347-15.
447. Carlisle-Frank, Frank, and & Nielson (2005).
448. For a review of the law that applies to no-pets policies, see Huss (2005).
449. Department of the Interior, *Housing Management Handbook* ¶ 3.1.6.C (April 2008) (providing "a field organization that does not allow residents to have pets must modify its policies and allow a tenant with a disability to have an assistive animal if the animal is needed as a reasonable accommodation').
450. 24 CFR Part 100: Discriminatory Conduct under the Fair Housing Act; Subpart D: Prohibition against Discrimination Because of a Handicap.
451. 24 CFR Part 5: General HUD Program Requirements; Waivers; Subpart C: Pet Ownership for the Elderly or Persons with Disabilities, 24 CFR 5.303. Subpart C "implements section 227 of the Housing and Urban-Rural Recovery Act of 1983 (12 U.S.C. 1701r-1) as it pertains to projects for the elderly or persons with disabilities. . . ." 24 CFR 5.100(a).
452. 24 CFR Part 960: Admission to, and Occupancy of, Public Housing; Subpart G: Pet Ownership in Public Housing. Under 24 CFR 960.101, "[t]his part [Part 960] is applicable to public housing." Public housing is defined, in 24 CFR 5.100, as housing assisted under the United States Housing Act of 1937 (42 U.S.C. 1437 et seq.) other than Section 8, 42 U.S.C. 1437f (low-income housing assistance, allowing persons eligible for public housing to rent from private owners, with the owners receiving a subsidy from the Government). Public housing includes dwelling units in a mixed finance project that are assisted by a public housing authority with capital or operating assistance. For a recent comparison of the regulatory regimes affecting service dogs in housing, see Ensminger & Breitkopf (2009).
453. The three sets of HUD regulations implement three different statutes, themselves created by three different Acts. 24 CFR Part 5, concerning projects for the elderly and disabled, implements 12 U.S.C. 1701r-1 (pet ownership in assisted rental housing for the elderly and disabled), itself a codification from the Housing and Urban-Rural Recovery Act of 1983. 24 CFR Part 960, regarding public housing, implements 42 U.S.C. 1437z-3 (pet ownership in public housing), codified from the Housing and Work Responsibility Act of 1988. Finally, the general reasonable accommodation rule of 24 CFR Part 100 implements 42 U.S.C. 3601 et seq., codified from the Fair Housing Amendments Act of 1988. All the regulatory provisions discuss "reasonable accommodation," yet the preamble to the 2000 rules under which 26 CFR 960.705 was issued

referred to that section as "exempting service animals for people with disabilities." However, in proposing the revisions to 24 CFR Part 5, HUD indicated that it was making the change "to conform the assistance animal provisions for housing serving the elderly or disabled families . . . to the public housing provisions. . . ." The question remains whether the same uniformity can apply substantively to the general housing provision. There should be such uniformity and the better reasoned case law supports such an argument. See particularly the discussion of Crossroads Associates v. LeBoo, 152 Misc.2d 830 (N.Y. 1991), Janush v. Charities Housing Development Corp., 169 F.Supp.2d 1133 (ND Cal. 2000), Majors v. Housing Authority of the County of DeKalb, Georgia, 652 F.2d 454 (5th Cir. 1981). Both Janush and Majors were cited by HUD in its 2008 rulemaking, noting that "the Department's position is consistent with federal case law that has recognized, in cases involving emotional support animals in the housing context, that whether a particular accommodation is reasonable is a fact-intensive, case-specific determination." 73 Fed. Reg. 63837.

454. See U.S. Department of Justice, Civil Rights Division (2006).

455. Notice PIH 2002-01 (HA) (January 31, 2003).

456. 42 U.S.C. 3601 et seq.

457. 42 U.S.C. 3604(f)(1).

458. 42 U.S.C. 3604(f)(3)(B). See also 24 CFR 100.204.

459. 42 U.S.C. 3603(b)(1).

460. 42 U.S.C. 3603(b)(2).

461. 24 CFR 100.204(b), Example (1).

462. *Joint Statement of the Department of Housing and Urban Development and the Department of Justice, Reasonable Accommodation Under the Fair Housing Act* (May 17, 2004) (posted at several government websites, including www.hud.gov/offices/fheo/library/huddojstatement.pdf). Curiously, in the 2008 update of the same guidance release, the example does not refer to a deaf person but only to a person with a vision disability seeking permission to live with her guide dog (posted at www.hud.gov/offices/fheo/disabilities/reasonable_modi fications_mar08.pdf). See also Bronk v. Ineichen, 54 F.3d 425 (7th Cir. 1995) ("Clearly, the situation of a deaf resident who wishes to keep a hearing dog is analogous [to the example of a seeing eye dog in 24 CFR 100.204(g)(1)].")

463. Posted in "Questions and Answers about Fair Housing" on HUD's website (www.hud.gov/local/shared/working/r10/fh/questions.cfm?state=wa).

464. See Housing Authority of the City of New London v. Tarrant, 1997 WL 30320 (CN 1997) (various problems caused by dog were sufficient to kill claim of violation by housing authority).

465. See Fulciniti v. Village of Shadyside Condominium, discussed above in the section on service dogs for the mobility impaired; Auburn Woods I Homeowners Association v. Fair Employment and Housing Commission, discussed above in the section on service dogs for the mentally disabled.

466. See Ridgewood Homeowners Assoc. v. Mignacca, Docket 01-PC 2615, 01-PC-2241, 2001 WL 873004 , Rhode Island Superior Court (July 13, 2001) (restrictive covenant applied arbitrarily to shed for miniature horse used by boy who

suffered from bacterial meningitis).

467. In re Kenna Homes Cooperative Corporation, West Virginia Court of Appeals, Civil Action 99-C-2745, No. 29644 (October 23, 2001).

468. West Virginia Legislative Rule (Human Rights Commission) 77-1-6.6, 77-1-7.5.

469. 28 CFR 36.104 (definition of service animal). The court also cited FAQs on Delta Society's website, the website of SD World (for scleroderma) (www.sdworld.org, under "service dogs"), and the University of Wisconsin Service Animal Policy (now at http://www.wisc.edu/adac/physical/service-dog.html).

470. Fulciniti v. Village of Shadyside Condominium Ass'n (Civil Action 96-1825, WD Penn., November 20, 1998) found that a condominium violated FHA in refusing to allow plaintiff to keep service animal that had received 1½ years of training, where doctors provided supporting letters, and the association presented no evidence dog created a disturbance or threat to any other residents in the association.

471. Requiring a disabled individual to obtain a letter from a health professional is much less intrusive than requiring that a tenant obtain the approval of a physician selected by an adverse party. See 73 Fed. Reg. 63835 (preamble to 2008 housing rules); 14 CFR 382.117(e) (Department of Transportation).

472. See Woodside Village v. Hertzmark, 1993 WL 268293 (CN 1993) finding that because "of the dog's toileting habits and the defendant's inability to adequately control him, the residents' health, safety and comfort is at risk."

473. Prindable v. Association of Apartment Owners of 2987 Kalakaua, 304 F.Supp.2d 1245 (D. Hi. 2003) aff'd sub nom. Dubois v. Association of Apartment Owners of Kalakaua, 453 F.3d 1175 (9th Cir. 2006).

474. Henderson v. Des Moines Municipal Housing Agency, 745 N.W.2d 95 (2007). Hawn v. Shoreline Towers Phase I Condominium Association, Inc., 2009 WL 691378 (N.D. Fla. 2009) concerned a condominium in Florida and a resident who obtained a dog in violation of the building's no-pets policy, tried but failed to change that policy, then claimed the dog was a service dog.

475. Oras v. Housing Authority of the City of Bayonne, 373 N.J. Super. 302, 861 A.2d 194 (2004).

476. Citing 24 CFR 966.7(a) and New Jersey Administrative Code 13:13-3.4(f)(2).

477. Zatopa v. Lowe, C 02-02543 WHA (N.D. Cal., August 7, 2002).

478. Companion animals have been found to reduce the stress of having AIDS. Siegel, Angulo, Detels, Wesch, & Mullen (1999).

479. At times it has seemed that there has almost been a national hysteria regarding pit bulls. See Cattafi (2008); Hanson (2005).

480. 1996 WL 1186942 (Mass. Super. Ct. 1996).

481. See Wikipedia, "Diane Whipple" (http://en.wikipedia.org/wiki/Diane_Whipple).

482. Szuchman (2009). Miklosi (2007) has stated: "It may be surprising, but one could make a 'Labrador retriever lookalike' in a few generations without using any of the hunting breeds."

483. Department of Housing and Urban Development, "Pet Ownership for the

Elderly and Persons With Disabilities," RIN 2501-AD31, 73 Fed. Reg. 63834 (October 27, 2008). Proposed rules were issued for comment in October 2007. 72 Fed. Reg. 58448 (October 15, 2007).

484. The preamble to the rules states that "HUD has taken the opportunity afforded by this final rule to conform the phrasing used in 24 CFR part 5, . . . to the phrasing in 24 CFR part 960, subpart G.

485. 24 CFR 5.303.

486. Under 29 U.S.C. 794(a), provides that no otherwise qualified individual with a disability in the U.S. may "be excluded from the participation in, be denied the benefits of, or be subjected to discrimination under any program or activity receiving Federal financial assistance."

487. 73 Fed. Reg. 63834 (emphasis added).

488. HUD Handbook 4350.3: *Occupancy Requirements of Subsidized Multifamily Housing Programs,* stating: "A housing provider may not refuse to allow a person with a disability to have an assistance animal merely because the animal does not have formal training. Some, but not all, animals that assist persons with disabilities are professionally trained. Other assistance animals are trained by the owners themselves and, in some cases, no special training is required. The question is whether or not the animal performs the disability-related assistance or provides the disability-related benefit needed by the person with the disability." Presumably "disability-related benefits" are to be distinguished from mere companionship.

489. See HUD Handbook 4350.3, states:
"[I]f a tenant or applicant seeks a reasonable accommodation for an assistance animal that provides emotional support, that individual may be required to provide documentation from a physician, psychiatrist, social worker, or other mental health professional that the animal provides support that alleviates one or more of the identified symptoms or effects of an existing disability. . . . However, a tenant or applicant should not be required to provide documentation of the disability or the disability-related need for the assistance animal if the disability is or the need is readily apparent or already known to the provider. For example, a blind tenant should not be required to provide documentation of his or her disability and the need for a guide dog."
Not all iterations of this language mention social workers.

490. 73 Fed. Reg. 63835 (emphasis added). The absence of the need for training with respect to a service animal could be a reference to seizure-alert dogs, as well as emotional support animals.

491. See Echeverria v. Krystie Mano, LP, Docket CV 07-1369, 2009 WL 857629 (March 30, 2009), where a plaintiff claimed that her disabilities prevented her from walking the dog far enough that it would not defecate on the premises of landlord's building and grounds. Partial summary judgment was granted on procedural grounds but there was considerable uncertainty as to what the landlord knew about the tenant's disabilities or whether the tenant's dog was a service dog or companion animal and the matter was to be scheduled for trial.

492. 73 Fed. Reg. 63836.

493. 28 CFR 36.104.

494. Kirton et al. (2008).

495. 28 CFR 36.302(c)(1).

496. 73 Fed. Reg. 34508.

497. See, e.g., Prindable v. Association of Apartment Owners of 2987 Kalakaua, 204 F.Supp.2d 1245 (D.C. Hi. 2003) (no evidence dog was an individually trained service animal so no accommodation was necessary).

498. Conflicts have often been resolved before reaching the courts. In Schultz v. Alticor/Amway Corp., 43 Fed.Appx. 797, 2002 WL 1787981 (6th Cir. 2002), a hearing impaired employee acknowledged his service dog was not essential for him to perform his functions and though the employer had approved his bringing the dog to work, the employee agreed not to do so after other employees complained.

499. 42 U.S.C. 12101.

500. 42 U.S.C. 12112(b)(5).

501. 42 U.S.C. 12111(9)(B).

502. 28 CFR 36.302(c).

503. See 29 CFR 1630.2(o), 1630.9.

504. 29 C.F.R. Part 1630, elaborating on 29 CFR 1630.2(o). The Appendix was included in the Federal Register in 1991. Equal Opportunity Commission, *Employment Opportunity for Individuals with Disabilities*, 56 Fed. Reg. 35726 (July 26, 1991). See also EEOC, A Technical Assistance Manual on the Employment Provisions (Title 1) of the Americans with Disabilities Act, EEOC-M-1A (January 1992).

505. EEOC Enforcement Guidance on Reasonable Accommodation and Undue Hardship under the Americans with Disabilities Act, Notice 915.002, Requesting Reasonable Accommodation, ¶ 16 (October 17, 2002).

506. For practical advice for employers, based partly on Department of Justice releases, see Batiste & Fuller (2009), who note that because there is no specific definition of service animal under Title I of the Americans with Disabilities Act, "employers may have to consider allowing an employee to bring in an animal that does not meet the title III definition of service animal, such as a therapy or emotional support animal. However, employers do not have to allow an employee to bring an animal into the workplace if it is not needed because of a disability or if it disrupts the workplace."

507. Christopherson v. John E. Potter, Docket 01-14478, 37 Fed.Appx. 978 (Table) (11th Circuit 2002), reversing 153 F.Supp.2d 1307 (M.D. Fla. 2001). The district court had negated a jury's award of $23,000 to a postal worker who was precluded from bringing her hearing dog to work. The services provided by the dog were not discussed by the district court or the circuit court.

508. The preamble notes that the Department of Housing and Urban Development uses the term "assistance animal," and that this usage denotes "a broader category of animals than is covered by the ADA." 73 Fed. Reg. 34521.

509. 73 Fed. Reg. 34508, 34516.

510. McDonald v. Department of Environmental Quality, 351 Mont. 243, 214 P.3d

749 (2009).

511. In the Matter of Human Rights Bureau Case No. 0051011370, 384-2006 (August 4, 2006). The decision was affirmed by the Montana Human Rights Commission in December 2006.
512. See, e.g., Administrative Rule 24.9.606.
513. Colorado Government Code § 24-34-803(3).
514. Colorado Government Code § 24-34-803(6).
515. Maryland Administrative Regulations § 15.03.02.05(9)
516. New Jersey Civil Rights Code § 10:5-29.1; see also New York Civil Rights Code § 47-a.
517. See, e.g., North Dakota Disability Code § 25-13-04.
518. Wisconsin Employment Code § 106.52(am)4.
519. Washington Labor Code §§ 49.60.180.
520. Washington Labor Code §§ 49.60.190.
521. Washington Labor Code §§ 49.60.200.
522. Washington Administrative Code § 162-22-060.
523. Georgia Department of Agriculture, Food Division Regulations § 40-7-1.67 (facility operation and maintenance)(12)(prohibiting animals)(b)3 (http://rules.sos.state.ga.us/docs/40/7/1/67.PDF); see also Georgia Department of Human Services, Public Health Regulations § 290-5-14-.07 (physical facilities).
524. Indiana Administrative Code, 410 IAC 7-24-435.
525. Rhode Island Administrative Rules, Food Code, 2-403.11 (handling prohibition).
526. Connecticut State Personnel Act § 5-247b.
527. New York Code of Rules and Regulations, Department of Civil Service, Title 4 § 21.3f (absence with pay).
528. Nelson v. Ryan, 860 F.Supp. 76 (WD N.Y. 1994).
529. DeFranco (1999).
530. B.C. v. Plumas Unified School District, 193 F.3d 1260 (9th Cir. 1999).
531. Gaudiello v. Delaware County Intermediate Unit, 796 F. Supp. 849, 77 Ed. Law Rep. 146, 3 NDLR 75 (ED Pa. 1992).
532. 20 U.S.C. § 1400 et seq.
533. Personal communication from Kyle Burch, counsel for the Gaudiellos (February 23, 2009). See also Clark County School District v. Buchanan, discussed in the chapter on access rights of trainers and handlers.
534. Cave v. East Meadow Union Free School District, 480 F.Supp.2d 610 (ED N.Y. 2007).
535. 34 CFR 300.34(c)(7)(ii)(B). The provision is contained under "orientation and mobility services," which are a subset of "related services" under 34 CFR 300.34(a).
536. Sidhu (2009) notes that rules allowing for emotional support animals are appropriate for educational environments.
537. Memorandum from the OCR Program Legal Group on Service Animal Guidance to OCR Office Directors and Chief Attorneys (October 25, 2006).
538. See 34 CFR 104.3(f).

539. 34 CFR 104.44(b). See also 34 CFR Part 104, Appendix A.

540. See Ohio Agriculture Code § 955.43(A).

541. California Education Code § 39839.

542. Delaware Administrative Code § 1105.6.15 (school transportation).

543. Oregon Administrative Rules 581-053-0010.

544. Oregon Administrative Rules 581-053-0015(j).

545. Texas Government Code § 661.910.

546. See letter of James Turner (1993, May 10), Acting Assistant Attorney, Civil Rights Division, Department of Justice to Senator John C. Danforth.

547. See Day v. Sumner Regional Health Systems, Inc., Docket 3:07-0595, 2007 WL 4570810 (M.D. Tenn. 2007) (facility's motion for summary judgment denied where facility had previously admitted Day's dog to emergency room, and only refused this time because dog was dirty; court interpreted pleadings in light most favorable to plaintiff, but did not suggest that evidence might not support facility at trial); Pool v. Riverside Health Services, Inc., Docket 94-1430-PFK, 1995 WL 519129 (D.C. Kan. 1995) (hospital could exclude dog that pulled wheelchair from entering with woman who was visiting her fiancé, a patient in the emergency room; hospital allowed service dogs in public areas of hospital but was not required to admit them to all areas if there was a reasonable basis for excluding them from a particular area).

548. See Sheely v. MRI Radiology Network, P.A., 505 F.3d 1173 (11th Cir. 2007) (appellant entitled to pursue action against radiology clinic for refusal to admit her guide dog when she was accompanying her minor son for a procedure despite subsequent change in policy of clinic to admit service dogs in such circumstances; longstanding and adamant opposition to allowing service dogs in the facility meant claim for injunctive relief was not moot; also damages might be available to appellant; cases remanded for further proceedings). See See Pannell (2008).

549. 73 Fed. Reg. 34508, 34524 (June 17, 2008) (citing CDC Guidelines).

550. See Duncan (2000).

551. See also Mayon-White (2005).

552. U.S. Department of Health and Human Services, Centers for Disease Control and Prevention (2003).

553. Enoch, Karas, Salter, Emery, Kearns, & Farrington (2005).

554. Lefebre & Weese (2009).

555. Branson v. West, Docket 97 C 3538, 1999 WL 1186420 (N.D. Ill. 1999), amended memorandum opinion and order (December 10, 1999). Additional background information can be found in Ed Eames (2008).

556. Smith v. Moorman, 2002 WL 31182451 (6th Cir. 2002).

557. 21 CFR 110.35(c).

558. Department of Health and Human Services, *Current Good Manufacturing Practice in Manufacturing, Packing, or Holding Human Food: Revised Current Good Manufacturing Practices,* 51 Fed. Reg. 22458, ¶ 69 (June 19, 1986). The proposed regulations had been published in 1979. 44 Fed. Reg. 33238 (June 8, 1979).

559. Johnson v. Gambrinus Company/Spoetzl Brewery, 116 F.3d 1052 (5th Circuit,

1997). See Harrington (1999).

560. 21 CFR 110.3(e). See also FDA Food Code, Annex 5: HACCP [Hazard Analysis and Critical Control Point] Guidelines.

561. Texas Human Resources Code § 121.003(c).

562. FDA Food Code 1-201.10(B)(74).

563. Annex 3, elaborating on Food Code 6-501.115.

564. FDA Food Code 6-501.115(B)(3).

565. FDA Food Code 2-301.14(C).

566. FDA Food Code 2-403.11(B).

567. Georgia State Rules § 40-7-1.67 (facility operation and maintenance)(12)(prohibiting animals)(b)3 (http://rules.sos.state.ga.us/docs/40/7/1/67.PDF); see also Georgia State Rules § 290-5-14-.07 (physical facilities); 7 Pennsylvania Statutes § 46.982(b)(iii); Vermont Health Law 5-214(E)(2); Rhode Island Administrative Rules, Food Code, 2-403.11; Virginia administrative code, 2VAC5-585-3310 (prohibiting animals); 12VAC5-421-3310; Wisconsin Administrative Code § 6-501.115.

568. Indiana administrative code, 410 IAC 7-24-435.

569. California Health & Safety Code § 114332.3.

570. See Alabama Handicapped Persons Code § 21-7-4 (trainers of guide dogs); Arizona Counties Code § 11-1024.E (anti-discrimination law includes trainer of service animal who is with an animal being trained); California Civil Code § 54.1(7)(C): trainers of guide, signal, and service dogs may take them into public places (but see Proffer v. Columbia Tower, 1999 WL 33798637 (S.D. Cal. 1999); Colorado Government Code §§ 24-34-803(2),-803(7)(g); Connecticut Human Rights Code §§ 46a-44(a), (b), 46a-44(d); Florida Social Welfare Code §§ 413.08(4), (8); Georgia Handicapped Persons Code § 30-4-2(b)(2); Idaho Criminal Code § 18-5812B; Illinois Human Rights Code § 775.30/3; Indiana Health Code § 16-32-3-2(d; Iowa Human Services Code § 216C.11; Kansas Social Welfare Code § 39-1109; Kentucky Animal Control Code § 258.500(7); Louisiana Public Welfare Code § 46.1955; Maine Criminal Code § 17.1312.4; Labor Code § 26.1420-A); Maryland Disabilities Code §§ 7-701(f), 7-705(a)(4), (c)); Massachusetts Agriculture & Conservation Code §§ 19.129.39D, F; Minnesota Public Welfare Code § 256C.02; Mississippi Public Welfare Code § 43-6-155; Missouri Public Health & Welfare Code § 12.209.152; Montana Human Rights Code §§ 49-4-214(3), (4); Nevada Business Code § 651.075; New Hampshire Public Safety Code § 12.167-D:4, D:1.VII; New Jersey Civil Rights Code §§ 10:5-29.3, 10:5-5.t; New Mexico Human Rights Code § 28-11-2; New York Civil Rights Code § 47-b.3, Agriculture Code § 121-b.1(d); North Carolina disabilities Code § 168-4.2(b); North Dakota Disability Code § 25-13-02.1; Ohio Agriculture Code § 955.43(A)(3); Oklahoma Blind Persons Code § 7.19.1.A, B; Oregon Education & Culture Code §§ 346.650, 346.685); South Carolina Social Services Code § 43-33-10(d); Tennessee Professions, Businesses and Trades Code § 62-7-112(a)(1)(B)(i); Texas Human Resources Code § 121.003(i); Utah Human Services Code § 62A-5b-104(2); Virginia Persons with Disabilities Code § 51.5-44; Wisconsin Employment Code § 106.52(am)2.

571. See the references to Connecticut, Georgia, Kansas, Minnesota, Missouri, New Hampshire, New Jersey, New Mexico, North Dakota, Ohio, Oklahoma, Tennessee, and Wisconsin in the preceding footnote.

572. Clark County School District v. Buchanan, 112 Nev. 1146, 924 P.2d 716 (1996). Canine Companions for Independence is headquartered in Santa Rosa, California (www.cci.org).

573. Nevada Business Code § 651.075.

574. Nevada Business Code § 651.050(2)(k).

575. 73 Fed. Reg. 34516.

576. 73 Fed. Reg. 34524.

577. A disclaimer on the website states that the "purchaser understands and agrees that the only involvement by servicedogsamerica.org is to supply the represented information and equipment. Also, "Servicedogsamerica.org is not responsible for any actions legal or otherwise caused by the use of the equipment or printed material supplied." The website does note that "You can train your Service Dog to meet the specific needs of your disability."

578. See, e.g., 28 CFR Part 36, Appendix B (noting that 28 CFR 36.302 "acknowledges that in rare circumstances, accommodation of service animals may not be required because a fundamental alteration would result in the nature of the goods, services, facilities, privileges, or accommodations offered or provided, or the safe operation of the public accommodation would be jeopardized"); proposed 28 CFR 36.302(c)(2). See also proposed 28 CFR 35.136(b), 73 Fed. Reg. 34504; Alaska Criminal Code § 11.76.133(c)(2); Florida Social Welfare Code § 413.08(3)(e); and Nevada Business Code § 651.075.2.

579. See DiLorenzo v. Costco Wholesale Corp., 515 F. Supp. 1187 (WD Wa. 2007).

580. Proposed 28 CFR 36.302(c)(6).

581. Patrick & Harshbarger (1996) concerned "Commonly Asked Questions About Service Animals in Places of Business." One such question was, "How can I tell if an animal is really a service animal and not just a pet?" To this the attachment replied: "Some, but not all, service animals wear special collars and harnesses. Some, but not all, are licensed or certified and have identification papers." Thus, it would appear that a state or local government-issued license specifying service animal status, or a certification, may be used, at least in the opinion of some Justice Department officials, to establish service animal status, though the document also cautions that "such documentation generally may not be required as a condition for providing service to an individual accompanied by a service animal."

582. 14 CFR 382.117(d) (emphasis added).

583. *A Guide to the Air Carrier Access Act and Its Implementing Regulations,* 70 Fed. Reg. 41481 (July 19, 2005).

584. Assistance Dogs International (2009) uses the same language in its Assistance Dog Model State Law.

585. Semmel (2002).

586. In another case, however, a variance was not granted. Barnes v. Board of Adjustment, 1999 Ok. Civ. App. 76, 987 P.2d 430 (1999).

587. Gebauer v. Lake Forest Property Owners Association, 723 So.2d 1289 (Ala. Civ. App. 1998). , A videotape of the pig was presented at trial showing the pig going up and down stairs, sitting on command, and performing tricks. See Herbster (2000).
588. 14 CFR 382.117(g).
589. 73 Fed. Reg. 27635-6.
590. In re Kenna Homes Cooperative Corporation, Civil Action 99-C-2745, No. 29644 (October 23, 2001).
591. See Fulciniti v. Village of Shadyside Condominium Ass'n (WD Pa., 1998) (condominium violated FHA in refusing to allow plaintiff to keep service animal that had received 11/2 years of training, where doctors provided supporting letters, and association had presented no evidence dog created a disturbance or threat to any other residents in the association).
592. 73 Fed. Reg. 63835.
593. Although most state statutes refer to the dog having been trained for its purpose (or "especially trained," "individually trained," etc.), some states specify, that the training must have been done at a certified or accredited school, particularly if a charge of discrimination or criminal interference is to be lodged. In Alabama, a penalty can be imposed for denial of access to a blind person being led by a guide dog wearing a harness when "the blind person presents for inspection credentials issued by an accredited school for training guide dogs. . . ." Alabama Animals Code § 3-1-7. See also Alaska Criminal Code § 11.76.130(c)(1); Iowa Human Services Code § 216C.11.1; Michigan Penal Code § 750.502c; Ohio Agriculture Code § 955.011(B); Tennessee Professions, Businesses and Trades Code § 62-7-112(a); Texas Human Resources Code § 121.002(1).
594. Connecticut Human Rights Code §§ 46a-44(a), (b), 46a-64(a) allows provided dog is wearing a harness or an orange-colored leash and collar. See also Mississippi Public Welfare Code § 43-6-7; New Hampshire Public Safety Code § 12.167-D:5; North Carolina Disabilities Code § 168-4.2(a), (b); Ohio Agriculture Code § 955.011(A); Oklahoma Blind Persons Code § 7.19.1.C; Rhode Island Public Utilities & Carriers Code § 39-2-13; Virginia Persons with Disabilities Code § 51.5-44; Wisconsin Employment Code § 106.52(am)2.
595. Hawaii Conservation & Resources Code § 3-143-4(6) provides that access is not to be denied if a guide, leader, seizure-alert, or seizure-response dog is wearing a harness and the handler presents credentials for inspection issued by a training school for the type of dog). See also Minnesota Human Rights Act § 363A.19; Tennessee Professions, Businesses and Trades Code § 62-7-112(a).
596. Kansas Social Welfare Code § 39-1111.
597. Utah Human Services Code § 62A-5b-104(4).
598. Hawaii Conservation & Resources Code § 3-143-4(6) (guide, signal, and service dogs to be designated as such on licenses); and New York Agriculture Code § 110.3 (licenses to be conspicuously marked with words "Guide Dog," "Hearing Dog," "Service Dog," "Working Search Dog," or "Therapy Dog"); Agriculture Code § 112.7 (special tags for guide, hearing, service, and detection

dogs).

599. Colorado Criminal Code § 18-13-107(3) provides that criminal interference applies if a dog is wearing harness normally used for dogs accompanying or leading persons with disabilities). See also Michigan Penal Code § 750.502c; South Dakota Animals & Livestock Code § 40-1-38.

600. Florida Social Welfare Code § 413.08(3)(a).

601. Georgia Handicapped Persons Code § 30-4-2(b)(1) provides that a guide or service dog must be identified as having been trained by a school for such dogs; dog with person raising or training to be a service dog must wear "appropriate apparel or device that identifies such dog with the accredited school. See also Kentucky Animal Control Code § 258.500(7); Maryland Licenses Code § 11-502; Montana Human Rights Code § 49-4-214(4); North Carolina Disability Code § 25-13-02.1.

602. West Virginia General Powers Code § 5-15-4(e) (service animal not required to be licensed or certified by a state or local government and no requirement for specific signage or labeling).

603. Arizona Counties Code § 11-1024.J.2(a)-(e).

604. Nevada Business Code § 651.075(f).

605. Nevada Business Code § 651.075.2.

606. Some traffic statutes indicate that a disabled person's use of special gear requires that drivers yield right of way.

607. Colorado Government Code § 24-34-803(5); Connecticut Dogs and Kennel Code § 22-345; Delaware Conservation Code § 7-1702(j) (license fee waived for "a seeing eye, lead or guide dog or as a dog which has previously served in a branch of the United States armed forces"); Hawaii Conservation & Resources Code § 3-143-4(6); Kentucky Animal Control Code § 258.500(9); Louisiana Welfare Code § 46.1958; Maine Animal Welfare Code § 9.3923-A; Maryland Licenses Code § 11-502; Massachusetts Public Safety Code § 20.140.139; Michigan Natural Resources Code § 287.291; Nebraska Livestock Code § 54-603; New Hampshire Animal Code § 45.466:8; New Jersey Agricultural Code § 4:19-15.3; New Mexico Livestock Code § 77-1-15.1.C; New York Agriculture Code § 110.3; North Carolina Disabilities Code § 168-4.3; North Dakota Municipal Government Code § 40-05-02(22); Ohio Agriculture Code § 955.011(A); Oregon Animal Control Code § 609.105; 3 Pennsylvania Statutes § 459-201(a); Virginia Agriculture Code § 3.2-6528; Washington Labor Code § 49.60.380; Wisconsin Dogs Code § 174.055. This list does not include waivers by political subdivisions within states.

608. See references in the preceding footnotes for California, Hawaii, Maryland (license to state "dog guide" in red ink), New Hampshire (individuals with signal dogs to fit dogs with leash and harness colored "international orange;" individuals with guide dogs to use leash and harnesses designed for such dogs; mobility impaired individuals to use blue and yellow leashes), New York (applicants for guide, service, hearing dogs may obtain special tag for the dog), Ohio (tabs to indicate assistance dog registration), Oklahoma (hearing dogs to be fitted with orange collars), Tennessee (Tennessee Council for the Deaf and

Hard of Hearing issues special credentials for signal dogs), and Utah (identifying gear recommended).

609. Ohio Agriculture Code § 955.011(A).

610. Tennessee Professions, Businesses and Trades Code § 62-7-112.

611. 73 Fed. Reg. 34515-6.

612. California Food & Agricultural Code § 30850 (person applying for assistance dog tag must sign affidavit that the dog is a guide, signal, or service dog); Penal Code § 365.7(a); Hawaii Conservation and Resources Code § 3-143-5; Kansas Social Welfare Code § 39-1112; Maine Criminal Code § 17.1314-A; Missouri Public Health & Welfare Code § 12.209.204; Nevada Public Welfare Code §§ 426.510.6(a), 426.805; New Hampshire Public Safety Code § 12.167-D:7.II; New Jersey Civil Rights Code § 10:5-29.5; North Carolina Disabilities Code § 168-4.5; Texas Human Resources Code § 121.006; Utah Human Services Code § 62A-5b-106; Washington Public Health Code § 70.84.060.

613. Alabama Animals Code § 3-1-7 (guide dog must be on harness); Alaska Criminal Code § 11.76.133(d)(4) provides that a service dog in training is to wear device or exhibit insignia of training facility. See also Colorado Criminal Code § 18-13-107(3); Michigan Penal Code § 750.502c; Montana Human Rights Code § 49-4-214(4); North Carolina Disabilities Code § 168-4.2(b); Oklahoma Blind Persons Code § 7.19.1.C; Oregon Education & Culture Code § 346.610(1), Vehicles Code § 814.110(1)(a), Education & Culture Code § 346.640(2); but see Green v. Housing Authority of Clackamas County, 884 F. Supp. 1253 (D Or. 1998), saying that state law could not limit definition of service dog for federal purposes); Tennessee Professions, Businesses and Trades Code §§ 62-7-112(a); Utah Human Services Code § 62A-5b-104(4).

614. New Hampshire Public Safety Code § 12.167-D:5. Not surprisingly, fitting a dog with such gear when the user is not disabled is a crime. New Hampshire Public Safety Code § 12.167-D:7.II.

615. Id.

616. Illinois Vehicles Code § 625. 5/11-1004 provides that a driver must yield to pedestrian with clearly visible disabilities, presumably including a service animal in harness. See also Iowa Transportation Code § 321.333; Michigan Administrative Rules 28.1715; Rhode Island Motor Vehicles Code § 31-18-14.

617. See, e.g., Connecticut Evidence Code § 52-175a; Hawaii Blind and Visually Handicapped Persons Code § 7-347-19.

618. See Thompson v. Dover Downs, Inc., 887 A.2d 458 (Del. Supr., 2005) (casino entitled to question patron as to training of dog due to dog's young age, uncommon method of affixing service vest, etc., which created genuine basis to doubt dog was a support animal).

619. California Health & Safety Code § 121680. See Florida Torts Code § 45.767.16; Utah Criminal Code § 76-9-307(6); .

620. Hawaii Conservation & Resources Code § 3-142-5.5. See Crowder v Nakatani, Docket 93-00213DAE (D.C. Hi. 1997) (rule to be adopted exempting guide dogs from quarantine requirements); See Crowder v. Kitagawa, 81 F.3d 1480 (9th Cir. 1996).

621. McCall v. Meyers, 94 P.3d 1271 (Col. App. 204).
622. Arluke & Lockwood (1997) note that aggression by children has been studied much more than that by adults.
623. Luke & Luke (1997).
624. Flynn (2000).
625. Ascione, Weber, & Wood (1997).
626. Gerbasi (2004); See Kuehn (2004) on animal hoarding.
627. Dodman, Patronek, Dodman, Zelin, & Cottam (2004).
628. American Veterinary Medical Association (2000).
629. Patronek (1997).
630. Nunalee & Weedon (2004).
631. Lane et al. (1998).
632. Kruse (2002).
633. For a survey of valuation issues regarding animal loss, see Roukas (2007).
634. Dawson (2004).
635. In McDonald v. Department of Environmental Quality, 2009 Mont. 209 (June 17, 2009), however, the Montana Department of Environmental Quality argued that it should not have to reimburse this portion of the replacement cost to an employee whose service dog was injured as a result of the agency's failure to install proper flooring. This issue, as part of the calculation of replacement costs, was not resolved on appeal but remanded to the trial court for further analysis. A partial dissent to the decision of the Montana Supreme Court argued that the charitable contribution that helped the plaintiff buy the dog should not reduce her award for damages.
636. Cell searches are to be done with another staff member besides the canine handler, "when possible." Visitors are less commonly subjected to dog sniffs, and prison staff members seldom are. Oregon Department of Correction (1989). Vehicles of visitors are sometimes subjected to dog sniffs in prison parking lots. See *U.S. v. Romo,* 46 F.3d 1013 (10th Cir. 1995); *U.S. v. Prevo,* 435 F.3d 1343 (11th Cir. 2006).
637. Furst (2006).
638. Britton & Button (2007).
639. Hennessy, Morris, & Linden (2006). The increase in yawning may indicate that this is a displacement behavior by which dogs avoid conflict.
640. Currie (2008).
641. Furst (2006). Some states, such as Kansas, Kentucky, Nevada, and Oklahoma have horse training programs. One program in Kansas involves cats. Kansas and Ohio have wildlife rehabilitation programs that involve caring for local wildlife found injured or abandoned. Some states have institutional agricultural programs where inmates care for domestic animals such as cattle, sheep, and pigs. Wisconsin has had such a program since 1885. Four programs with wild horses work with the Bureau of Land Management.
642. Pound Pup Legacy (2006).
643. Furst (2006).
644. The Oprah Winfrey Show (2009, June 19).

645. Harkrader, Burke, & Owen (2004).

646. Currie (2008). A similar program, begun in 1994, exists at the Norton Correctional Facility and is called "Second Chance Homeless Pet Society-Dogs for Adoption." Kansas Department of Corrections (2009).

647. Pound Pup Legacy (2006).

648. Britton & Button (2006).

649. Britton & Button (2007).

650. Turner (2007).

651. Grandin (2005).

652. Strinple (2003).

653. Assistance Dogs of America, Inc. (2009).

654. Harbolt & Ward (2001).

655. Pet custody disputes were also prevalent after Katrina. See McNabb (2007).

656. PL 109-308 (2006), amending the Robert T. Stafford Disaster Relief and Emergency Assistance Act, PL 93-288 (1974), § 613.

657. 42 U.S.C. 5196b(g),

658. 42 U.S.C. 5196(j)

659. Department of Justice (2008).

660. Louisiana Military, Naval and Veteran's Affairs Code § 29.726.B.(20)(a)(i).

661. Nevada Emergency Management Code § 414.095.

662. New Hampshire Government Code § 1.21-P.37-a.

663. New Jersey Statutes Appendix A: National Defense § A:9-43.2.

664. New Mexico Human Rights Code § 28-11-3B.

665. Oregon Education & Culture Code § 346.685(3).

666. Maryland Disabilities Code § 7-708.

667. Kentucky Animal Control Code § 258.500(11).

668. 73 Fed. Reg. 34524.

669. 26 CFR 1.213-1(e)(1)(iii). The section was amended by TD 7317, 39 Fed. Reg. 23995 (June 28, 1974).

670. Rev. Rul. 57-461, 1957-2 CB 116; see also Rev. Rul. 55-261, 1955-1 CB 307, Private Letter Rulings 5602244860A (February 24, 1956), 6806110470A, (June 11, 1968).

671. The 1955 ruling stated that the purchase and maintenance of a seeing-eye dog was deductible.

672. Rev. Rul. 68-295, 1968-1 CB 92.

673. For a comment letter to the Treasury Department regarding the need to update Treasury regulations regarding service animals, see Ensminger & Esnayra (2009).

674. 55 Pa. Code § 181.132(5)(i).

675. Oklahoma Administrative Rules 710:50-15-97.

676. New York Tax Code § 1115(s)(1).

677. Texas Sales, Excise, and Use Taxes Code § 151.313(10).

678. Nebraska Livestock Code § 54-603.

679. Virginia Agriculture Code § 3.2-6528.

680. Wisconsin Dogs Code § 174.055.

681. 38 U.S.C. 1714.
682. 38 CFR 17.37(i).
683. 20 CFR 404.976.
684. 20 CFR 404.1576(c)(6).
685. 7 CFR 273.9(d)(3)(vii). PL 96-58, Stat. 389-392 (August 14, 1979).
686. 7 U.S.C. 2012(c)(6).
687. Ohio Department of Job and Family Services, Administrative Appeal Section (1990, July 2).
688. California Administrative Code § 63-232.7.
689. Michigan BPB 2009-001, FAP Allowable Expenses (2009).
690. New Mexico Administrative Code 8.139.520.11(13) (General Deductions).
691. Virginia Food Stamp Manual, Part 10, Chapter A.5.7.
692. Oregon Administrative Rules 461-160-0055.5.c.C.
693. Washington Administrative Code § 388-450-0200.
694. Washington Administrative Code § 388-473-0040.
695. Idaho Administrative Rules 16.03.05 (rules governing eligibility for aid to the aged, blind, and disabled).
696. Illinois Administrative Code § 89.IVb.113.263.
697. Montana Administrative Rules 37.40.1101(7).
698. Montana Administrative Rules 37.40.1487(2)(b).
699. Montana Administrative Rules 37.90.449.
700. Nebraska Human Services Manual 3-004.03A6.
701. New Mexico Administrative Code 8.307.17.9.
702. Texas Administrative Code 1.15.380.203.
703. Texas Administrative Code 40.1.46.15(c)(15).
704. Washington Administrative Code § 388-473-0040.
705. Burnham v. Washington Department of Social and Health Services, 63 P.3d 816 (Wash. Ct. App. 2003) (interpreting Washington Administrative Code § 388-543-1000).
706. Denzinger (2003).
707. Cunningham (2004).
708. See proposed New Jersey legislation which would preclude an insurers from using underwriting guidelines that would terminate coverage of a guide dog or service dog if it were of a specific breed (presumably such as a Pit Bull or Rottweiler). Assembly Bill 1389, 2008-9 legislative session (sponsored by Fisher). This is a narrower approach than legislation proposed in some states that would preclude underwriting guidelines for homeowners insurance based on the breed of any pet, an issue that has been the focus of American Kennel Club attention. See American Kennel Club (2009), providing model legislation and proposals from California, Connecticut, and New Jersey.
709. Szuchman (2009).

# LEGAL SOURCES

## Court Opinions and Orders

**Federal**

Branson v. West, Docket 97 C 3538, 1999 WL 1186420 (ND IL 1999)

Briggs v. YMCA of Snohomish County, Docket C08-1326 RSM, 2009 WL 1360474 (WD WA, May 14, 2009)

Bronk v. Ineichen, 54 F.3d 425 (7th Cir. 1995)

Christopherson v. John E. Potter, Docket 01-14478, 37 Fed.Appx. 978 (Table) (11th Circuit 2002), reversing 153 F.Supp.2d 1307 (MD FL 2001)

Cornick-Kelly v. Fletcher Allen Health Care, Investigative Report, HRC Case PA05-0035 (August 17, 2005)

Crowder v. Kitagawa, 81 F.3d 1480 (9th Cir. 1996)

Day v. Sumner Regional Health Systems, Inc., Docket 3:07-0595, 2007 WL 4570810 (MD TN 2007)

DiLorenzo v. Costco Wholesale Corp., 515 F. Supp. 1187 (WD WA 2007)

EEOC v. AutoZone, Inc., 2008 WL 4418160 (DC Az. 2008)

Fulciniti v. Village of Shadyside Condominium Association, Civil Action 96-1825 (WD Pa. 1998)

Gaudiello v. Delaware County Intermediate Unit, 796 F. Supp. 849, 77 Ed. Law Rep. 146, 3 NDLR 75 (ED Pa. 1992)

Green v. Housing Authority of Clackamas County, 994 F.Supp. 1253 (D. Or. 1998)

Janush v. Charities Housing Development Corp., 169 F. Supp.2d 1133 (ND Ca. 2000)

Johnson v. Gambrinus Company/Spoetzl Brewery, 116 F.3d 1052 (5th Circuit, 1997)

Majors v. Housing Authority of the County of DeKalb, Georgia, 652 F.2d 454 (5th Cir. 1981)

Nelson v. Ryan, 860 F.Supp. 76 (WD N.Y. 1994)

Pool v. Riverside Health Services, Inc., 1995 WL 519129 (D Ks. 1995)

Prindable v. Association of Apartment Owners of 2987 Kalakaua, 304 F. Supp.2d 1245 (D Hi. 2003)

Proffer v. Columbia Tower, 1999 WL 33798637 (SD Cal. 1999)

Schultz v. Alticor/Amway Corp., 43 Fed.Appx. 797, 2002 WL 1787981 (6th Cir. 2002)

Sheely v. MRI Radiology Network, P.A., 505 F.3d 1173 (11th Cir. 2007)
Smith v. Moorman, 47 Fed.Appx. 755, 2002 WL 31182451 (6th Cir. 2002)
Southeastern Community College v. Davis, 99 S.Ct. 2361 (1979)
Stan v. Wal-Mart Stores, Inc., 111 F.Supp. 119 (ND N.Y. 2000)
Toyota Manufacturing, Kentucky, Inc. v. Williams, 534 U.S. 184 (2002)
Vaughn v. Rent-A-Center, 2009 WL 723166 (SD OH 2009)

**State**

*Alabama*
Gebauer v. Lake Forest Property Owners Association, 723 So. 2d 1289 (Ala. Civ. App. 1998)
Satterwhite v. City of Auburn, 2006 WL 510528 (Ala. Crim. App. 2006)

*Arizona*
Arizona v. America West , Docket OST-99-5135 (March 5, 1999) (retrieved from www.airlineinfo.com/ostdocket/ost995135.htm)

*California*
Auburn Woods I Homeowners Association v. Fair Employment and Housing Commission, 121 Cal. App. 4th 1578, 18 Cal. Rptr. 3d 669, 2004 Cal. App. LEXIS 1476 (August 25, 2004)
Zatopa v. Lowe, C 02-02543 WHA, order (August 7, 2002)

*Colorado*
McCall v. Meyers, 94 P.3d 1271 (Col. App. 204)

*Connecticut*
Housing Authority of the City of New London v. Tarrant, 1997 WL 30320 (Conn. 1997)
Woodside Village v. Hertzmark, 1993 WL 268293 (CN 1993)

*Delaware*
Thompson v. Dover Downs, Inc., 887 A.2d 458 (Del. Supr., 2005)

*Florida*
Kleinschmidt v. Three Horizons North Condominiums, Inc., Fla. Div. of Administrative Hearings, Case 04-3873, 2005 WL 1255103 (May 22, 2005)

*Idaho*
State v. Cliff, 116 Idaho 921, 782 P.2d 44 (Idaho App. 1989)

*Massachusetts*
Nason v. Stone Hill Realty Association, 1996 WL 1186942 (Mass. 1996)
Whittier Terrace Associates v. Hampshire, 532 N.E.2d 712 (Mass. 1989)

*Montana*
McDonald v. Department of Environmental Quality, 351 Mont. 243, 214 P.3d 749 (2009) (earlier history contained in Human Rights Bureau Case No. 0051011370, 384-2006 (August 4, 2006))

*Nevada*
Clark County School District v. Buchanan, 112 Nev. 1146, 924 P.2d 716 (1996)

*New Jersey*
Oras v. Housing Authority of the City of Bayonne, 373 N.J. Super. 302, 861 A.2d 194 (2004)

*New Mexico*
State v. Marquez, 124 N.M. 409, 951 P.2d 1070 (1997)

*New York*
Crossroads Apartments Associates v. LeBoo, 152 Misc.2d 830 (N.Y. 1981)

*Oklahoma*
Barnes v. Board of Adjustment, 1999 Ok. Civ. App. 76, 987 P.2d 430 (1999)

*Rhode Island*
Ridgewood Homeowners Assoc. v. Mignacca, Docket 01-PC 2615, 01-PC-2241, 2001 WL 873004, R.I. Superior Court (July 13, 2001)

*Vermont*
Corbeil v. The Music Club, Vt. Human Rights Commission Investigative Report PA04-0031 (August 17, 2005)
Cornick-Kelly v. Fletcher Allen Health Care, Vt. Human Rights Commission Investigative Report PA05-0035 (August 17, 2005)

*Washington*
Burnham v. Washington Department of Social and Health Services, 63 P.3d 816 (Wash. Ct. App. 2003)
State v. Hakimi, 124 Wash. App. 15, 98 P.3d 809 (Wash. App. 2004)
Storms v. Fred Meyer Stores, Inc., 120 P.3d 126 (Wash. App. Div. 1, 2005)
Timberlane Mobile Home Park v. Human Rights Commission ex rel. Campbell, 122 Wash. App. 896 (2004)

*West Virginia*
In re Kenna Homes Cooperative Corporation, W.V. Court of Appeals, Civil Action 99-C-2745, No. 29644 (October 23, 2001)

*Wyoming*
Smith v. State, 2005 Wyoming 113, 119 P.3d 411 (Wyo. 2005)

## Federal Legislation

Americans with Disabilities Amendments Act of 2008, PL 110-325 (2008)
Fair Housing Act, Title VIII of the Civil Rights Act of 1968, PL 90-284 (1968)
Rehabilitation Act of 1973, PL 93-112 (1973)
Robert T. Stafford Disaster Relief and Emergency Assistance Act, PL 93-288 (1974)
Fair Housing Amendments Act of 1988, PL 100-430 (1988)
Americans with Disabilities Act of 1990, PL 101-336 (1990)
Pets Evacuation and Transportation Act of 2006, PL 109-308 (2006)

## Statutes and Rules

*Federal Statutes*
29 U.S.C. 794
38 U.S.C. 1714
42 U.S.C. 2000, 3601-7, 12111-12112, 12181-12187, 12201-12210, 1437f, 5196, 5196b
49 U.S.C. 41705

## Federal Regulations and Rulings

14 CFR 382.28, 382.51, 382.55, 382.91, 382.117
24 CFR 5.100, 5.300, 5.303
24 CFR 100.204
24 CFR 960.101. 960.703 - 707
26 CFR 1.213-1
28 CFR 36.104
28 CFR 36.302
29 CFR 1630.2, 1630.9, Appendix
34 CFR 300.34, 104.3, 105.44
38 CFR 17.37
49 CFR 37.3, 37.21, 37.167

IRS Notice PIH 2002-01 (HA) (January 31, 2003)
IRS Revenue Ruling 55-261, 1955-1 CB 307
IRS Revenue Ruling 57-461, 1957-2 CB 11
IRS Revenue Ruling 68-295, 1968-1 CB 92
Private Letter Ruling 5602244860A (February 24, 1956)
Private Letter Ruling 6806110470A, (June 11, 1968)

## State Statutes and Regulations

*Alabama*
Animals Code § 3-1-7
Handicapped Persons Code § 21-7-4

*Alaska*
Criminal Code § 11.76.130 - 76.133
Administrative Code: 7 AAC 43.755

*Arizona*
Counties Code § 11-1024

*Arkansas*
Public Health Code § 20-14-304

*California*
Civil Code § 54.1, § 54.7
Penal Code § 365.7
Health & Safety Code § 121680
Education Code § 39839
Food & Agricultural Code § 30850
Administrative Code § 63-232.7

*Colorado*
Criminal Code § 18-13-107
Government Code § 24-34-803

*Connecticut*
Dogs and Kennel Code § 22-345
Human Rights Code §§ 46a-44
Evidence Code § 52-175a
Crimes Code § 53-330a
State Personnel Act § 5-247b

*Delaware*
Commerce & Trade Code § 6-45-4502
Conservation Code § 7-1702(j)
Welfare Code § 31-2117
Administrative Code § 1105.6.15

*Florida*
Torts Code § 45.767.16
Social Welfare Code § 413.08

*Georgia*
Criminal Code § 16-11-107.1
Handicapped Persons Code § 30-4-2
Department of Agriculture, Food Division Regulations § 40-7-1.02, 1.67
Department of Human Services, Public Health Regulations § 290-5-14-.07

*Hawaii*
Conservation & Resources Code §§ 3-142-5.5, 3-143-4, -5
Blind and Visually Handicapped Persons Code § 7-347-13, -15, -19

*Idaho*
Criminal Code § 18-5812B
Public Welfare Code § 56-701A
Administrative Rules 16.03.05

*Illinois*
Vehicles Code § 625.5/11-1004
Criminal Code § 720.630/1
Civil Liabilities Code § 740.13/5
Human Rights Code § 775.30/3
Administrative Code § 89.IVb.113.263

*Indiana*
Health Code § 16-32-3-2
Administrative Code, 410 IAC 7-24-435

*Iowa*
Human Services Code § 216C.11
Transportation Code § 321.333

*Indiana*
Criminal Code § 35-46-11.5

*Kansas*
Social Welfare Code §§ 39-1109, -1113

*Kentucky*
Animal Control Code § 258.500

*Louisiana*
Military, Naval and Veteran's Affairs Code § 29.726.B
Public Welfare Code §§ 46.1952, 46.1955, 46.1958

*Maine*
Animal Welfare Code § 9.3923-A
Criminal Code §§ 17.1312, 17.1314A
Labor Code § 26.1420-A

*Maryland*
Disabilities Code §§ 7-701 - 7-708
Licenses Code § 11-502

*Massachusetts*
Public Safety Code § 20.140.139
Criminal Code 1.272.98A
Agriculture & Conservation Code §§ 19.129.39D

*Michigan*
Natural Resources Code § 287.291
Penal Code § 750.502c
Administrative Rules 28.1715

*Minnesota*
Human Rights Act § 363A.19
Public Welfare Code § 256C.02

*Mississippi*
Public Welfare Code §§ 43-6-7, -155
Criminal Code § 97-41-21

*Missouri*
Public Health & Welfare Code §§ 12.209.150 - 12.209.204

*Montana*
Human Rights Code §§ 49-2-303, 49-4-214
Administrative Rule 24.9.606
Administrative Code §§ 37.40.1101, 40.1487, 90.449

*Nebraska*
Livestock Code § 54-603
Livestock Code § 54-603
Nebraska Human Services Manual 3-004.03A6

*Nevada*
Business Code § 651.075
Emergency Management Code § 414.095
Public Welfare Code § 426.510.6

*New Hampshire*
Government Code § 1.21-P.37-a
Public Safety Code § 12.167-D
Animal Code § 45.466:8

*New Jersey*
Agricultural Code § 4:19-15.3
Civil Rights Code §§ 10:5
Statutes Appendix A: National Defense § A:9-43.2
Administrative Code 13:13-3.4(f)(2)

*New Mexico*
Human Rights Code §§ 28-11-2, -3B
Livestock Code § 77-1-15.1.C
Administrative Code §§ 8.139.520.11, 8.307.17.9

*New York*
Civil Rights Code §§ 47-a, 47-b
Public Housing Code 11.223-b
Agriculture Code §§ 108.26, 121-b , 110.3
Tax Code § 1115

*Nevada*
Business Code §§ 651.050, 075

*North Carolina*
Disabilities Code § 168-4.2, -4.6

*North Dakota*
Disability Code § 25-13-01.1, -04
Municipal Government Code § 40-05-02(22)

*Ohio*
Agriculture Code §§ 955.011, 955.43

*Oklahoma*
Blind Persons Code § 7.19.1
Administrative Rules 710:50-15-97

*Oregon*
Criminal Code § 167.352
Education & Culture Code §§ 346.640 - 346.685
Animal Control Code § 609.105
Vehicles Code § 814.110
Administrative Rules 461-160-0055; 581-053-0010, - 0015

*Pennsylvania*
3 P.S. §§ 459-102, 459-201, 459-602
52 Pa. Code § 29.102
55 Pa. Code § 181.132

*Rhode Island*
Public Utilities & Carriers Code § 39-2-13
Motor Vehicles Code § 31-18-14
Administrative Rules, Food Code, 2-403.11

*South Carolina*
Social Services Code § 43-33-10

*South Dakota*
Personal Rights Code § 20-13-23.2
Animals & Livestock Code § 40-1-38

*Tennessee*
Professions, Businesses and Trades Code § 62-7-112

*Texas*
Human Resources Code § 121.002 - 121.006
Sales, Excise, and Use Taxes Code § 151.313
Government Code § 661.910
Administrative Code 1.15.380.203, 40.1.46.15

*Utah*
Human Services Code § 62A-5b-102 -106
Criminal Code § 76-9-307(2)

*Virginia*
Agriculture Code § 3.2-6528
Persons with Disabilities Code § 51.5-44

*Washington*
Labor Code §§ 49.60.180, 190, 200, 300
Public Health Code § 70.84.060
Administrative Code §§ 162-22-060, 388-450-0200, 388-473-0040

*West Virginia*
General Powers Code § 5-15-4
Legislative Rule (Human Rights Commission) 77-1-6.6, 77-1-7.5

*Wisconsin*
Employment Code § 106.50, 106.52
Dogs Code § 174.055
Madison Equal Opportunities Ordinance § 3.23(4)(h)

### Federal Register

Department of Health and Human Services, *Current Good Manufacturing Practice in Manufacturing, Packing, or Holding Human Food: Revised Current Good Manufacturing Practices,* 51 Fed. Reg. 22458 (June 19, 1986)

*Equal Opportunity Commission, Employment Opportunity for Individuals with Disabilities,* 56 Fed. Reg. 35726 (July 26, 1991)

Department of the Interior, *Housing Management Handbook* (April 2008)

Department of Transportation, *A Guide to the Air Carrier Access Act and Its Implementing Regulations,* 70 Fed. Reg. 41481, 41488 (July 19, 2005)

Department of Transportation, *Transportation for Individuals with Disabilities: Passenger Vessels,* 72 Fed. Reg. 2833 (January 23, 2007)

Department of Transportation, *Notice of Guidance Concerning the Carriage of Service Animals in Air Transportation from the United States to the United Kingdom,* 72 Fed. Reg. 8268 (February 26, 2007)

Department of Transportation, *Nondiscrimination on the Basis of Disability in Air Travel; Final Rule,* 73 Fed. Reg. 27613 (May 13, 2008)

Department of Justice, *Nondiscrimination on the Basis of Disability by Public Accommodations and in Commercial Facilities,* 73 Fed. Reg. 34508 (June 17, 2008)

Department of Housing and Urban Development, *Pet Ownership for the Elderly and Persons with Disabilities,* RIN 2501-AD31, 73 Fed. Reg. 63834 (October 27, 2008)

Department of Transportation, *Nondiscrimination on the Basis of Disability in Air Travel: Request for comments on petition for rulemaking,* Docket OST-2009-0093, 74 Fed. Reg. 47902 (September 18, 2009)

## Government Publications

H.R. Rep. No. 711, 100th Cong., 2d Sess, 18 U.S. Code Cong. & Admin. News 1988

HUD Handbook 4350.3: *Occupancy Requirements of Subsidized Multifamily Housing Programs*

IRS Publication 502, *Medical and Dental Expenses (Including the Health Coverage Tax Credit)*

IRS Publication 907, *Tax Highlights for Persons with Disabilities*

Joint Statement of the Department of Housing and Urban Development and the Department of Justice, Reasonable Accommodation Under the Fair Housing Act (May 17, 2004)

# BIBLIOGRAPHY

(Cases and citations from the Federal Register and U.S. Code Congressional & Administrative News are listed under Legal Sources following the bibliography.)

Albert, F. W. (2008). Uncovering the Genetic Basis for Tameness, A Research Strategy. *VOGiS Herald, 12*(1/2).

Allen, K., & Blascovich, J. (1996). The Value of Service Dogs for People with Severe Ambulatory Disabilities. *Journal of the American Medical Association, 275*(13), 1001–1006.

Allen, K., Blascovich, J., & Mendes, W. B. (2002). Cardiovascular Reactivity and the Presence of Pets, Friends and Spouses: The Truth About Cats and Dogs. *Psychosomatic Medicine, 64*(5), 727–739.

Allen, K. M., Blascovich, J., Tomaka, J., & Kelsey, R. M. (1991). Presence of Human Friends and Pet Dogs as Moderators of Autonomic Responses to Stress in Women. *Journal of Personality and Social Psychology, 61*(4), 582–9.

Allen, K., Shykoff, B. E., & Izzo, J. L. (2001). Pet Ownership, but not ACE Inhibitor Therapy, Blunts Home Blood Pressure Responses to Mental Stress. *Hypertension, 38*(4), 815–820.

Altschuler, E. L. (1999). Pet-Facilitated Therapy for Posttraumatic Stress Disorder. *Annals of Clinical Psychiatry, 11*(1), 29–30.

American Kennel Club. (2009). *Model Legislation to Protect Against Insurance Discrimination.* Retrieved from www.akc.org/insurance/model_legislation.cfm.

American Veterinary Medical Association. (2005). *Nonhuman Primates as Assistance Animals.* Retrieved from www.avma.org/issues/policy/nonhuman_primates.asp.

American Veterinary Medical Association. (2000). *Animal Abuse and Animal Neglect.* Retrieved from www.avma.org/issues/policy/animal_welfare/abuse.asp.

Anderson, J. R., Myowa-Yamakoshi, M., & Matsuzawa, T. (2004). Contagious Yawning in Chimpanzees. *Proceedings of the Royal Society, 271*(6), S468–S470.

Anderson, W. P., Reid, C. M., & Jennings, G. L. (1992). Pet Ownership and Risk Factors for Cardiovascular Disease. *Medical Journal of Australia, 157*(5), 298–301.

Arluke, A., & Lockwood, R. (1997). Guest Editors' Introduction: Understanding Cruelty to Animals. *Society and Animals, 5*(3), 183–193).

Ascione, F. R. (1992). Enhancing Children's Attitudes About the Humane Treatment of Animals and Empathy: Generalization to Human-Directed Empathy. *Anthrozoos, 5,* 176–191.

Ascione, F. R., & Weber, C. V. (1996). Children's Attitudes about the Humane Treatment of Animals and Empathy: One-Year Follow Up of a School-Based Intervention. *Anthrozoos, 9,* 188–195.

Ascione, F. R., Weber, C. V., & Wood, D. S. (1997). The Abuse of Animals and Domestic Violence: A National Survey of Shelters for Women who are Battered. *Society & Animals 5*(3), 205–218.

Assistance Dogs International. *Assistance Dog Model State Law.* Retrieved from www.assistance dogsinternational.org/modellaw.php.

Assistance Dogs of America, Inc. (2009). *Puppies in Prison.* Retrieved from www.adai.org/our dogs/puppyprison.html.

Baranyiova, E., Holub, A., & Tyrlik, M. (2007). Behavioural Traits of Four Dogs in Czech Households. *Acta Vet. Brno 76,* 627–634.

Bardill, N. (1994). *Animal Assisted Therapy With Hospitalized Adolescents.* (Master's Thesis, University of Florida). Retrieved from www.norinesnotes.thinkhost.com.

Barker, S. B. (1999). Therapeutic Aspects of the Human-Companion Animal Interaction. *Psychiatric Times, 16*(2), 45.

Barker, S. B., Barker, R. T., Dawson, K. S., & Knisely, J. S. (1997). The Use of the Family Life Space Diagram in Establishing Interconnectedness: A Preliminary Study of Sexual Abuse Survivors, Their Significant Others and Pets. *Individual Psychology, 53*(4), 435–450.

Barker, S. B., & Dawson, K. S. (1998). The Effects of Animal-Assisted Therapy on Anxiety Ratings of Hospitalized Psychiatric Patients. *Psychiatric Services, 49,* 797–801.

Barker, S. B., Pandurangi, A. K., & Best, A. M. (2003). Effects of Animal-Assisted Therapy on Patients' Anxiety, Fear, and Depression before ECT. *Journal of ECT, 19*(1), 38–44.

Baron-Cohen, S. (2009, November 10). The Short Life of a Diagnosis. *New York Times,* A35.

Batiste, L. C., & Fuller, C. (2009). *Service Animals as Workplace Accommodation. Department of Labor, Office of Disability Employment Policy, Accommodation and Compliance Series.* Retrieved from http://www.jan.wvu.edu/media/servanim.html.

Batson, K., McCabe, B. W., Baun, M. M., & Wilson, C. (1998). The Effect of a Therapy Dog on Socialization and Physiological Indicators of Stress in Persons Diagnosed with Alzheimer's Disease. In C. W. Wilson & D. C. Turner (Eds.), *Companion Animals in Human Health.* (pp. 203–215). Thousand Oaks, CA: Sage Publications.

Bauer, E. B., & Smuts, B. B. (2007). Cooperation and Competition During Dyadic Play in Domestic Dogs. *Canis familiaris. Animal Behaviour, 73*(3), 489–499.

Beck, A. M., & Katcher, A. H. (2003). Future Directions in Human-Animal Bond Research. *American Behavioral Scientist 47,* 79–93.

Behrend, C. (2005). *Breaking the Cycle of Violence: A Farmed Animal-Assisted Humane Education Program for At-Risk Children.* (master's thesis, Cambridge College, Cambridge, MA). Retrieved from www.humaneeducation.org/documents/view/59.

Bekoff, M. (2004). Wild Justice and Fair Play: Cooperation, Forgiveness, and Morality in Animals. *Biology & Philosophy 19,* 489–520.

Belyaev, D. K. (1979). Destabilizing Selection as a Factor in Domestication. *The Journal of Heredity, 70,* 301–308.

Belyaev, D. K., Ruvinsky, A. O., & Trut, L. N. (1981). Inherited Activation-Inactivation of the Star Gene in Foxes. *The Journal of Heredity, 72,* 267–274.

Bergin, B. M. (1981). Companion Animals for the Handicapped. In B. Fogle & A. Edney (Eds.), *Interrelations Between People and Pets* (pp. 191–236). Springfield, IL: Charles C Thomas.

Beyersdorfer, P. S., & Birkenhauer, D. M. (1990). The Therapeutic Use of Pets on an Alzheimer's Unit. *American Journal of Alzheimer's Care and Related Disorders and Research, 5,* 13–17.

Bjornerfeldt, S. (2007). *Consequences of the Domestication of Man's Best Friend, the Dog,* (doctoral dissertation, Uppsala University). Retrieved from http://uu.diva-portal.org/smash/record.jsf?pid=diva2:170023.

Bradburn, N. (1969). *The Structure of Psychological Well-Being.* Chicago, IL: Aldine Publishing, 1969).

Bradshaw, J. W. S. (2006). The Evolutionary Basis for the Feeding Behavior of Domestic Dogs (*Canis familiaris*) and Cats (*Felis catus*). *Journal of Nutrition, 136*(7), 1927S–1931S.

Britton, D. M., & Button, A. L. (2006). Prison Pups: Assessing the Effects of Dog Training Programs in Correctional Facilities. *Journal of Family Social Work, 9*(4), 79–95.

Britton, D. M., & Button, A. L. (2007). "This isn't about us:" Benefits of Dog Training Programs in Women's Prisons. In S. Miller (Ed.), *Criminal Justice and Diversity: Voices from the Field* (pp. 195–208). U. Lebanon, NH: U. Press of New England.

Brooks, S. E., Oi, F. M., & Koehler, P. G. (2003). Ability of Canine Termite Detectors to Locate Live Termites and Discriminate them From Non-Termite Material. *Journal of Economic Entomology, 96,* 1259–1266.

Brown, S. W., & Strong, V. (2001). The Use of Seizure-Alert Dogs. *Seizure, 10*(1), 39–41.

Burch, M. R. (1996). *Volunteering with your pet.* Indianapolis, IN: Howell Books.

Burrows, K. E., Adams, C. L., & Millman, S. T. (2008). Factors Affecting Behavior and Welfare of Service Dogs for Children with Autism Spectrum Disorder. *Journal of Applied Animal Welfare Science, 11*(1), 42–62.

Burrows, K. E., Adams, C. L., & Spiers, J. (2008). Sentinels of Safety: Service Dogs Ensure Safety and Enhance Freedom and Well-Being for Families with Autistic Children. *Qualitative Health Research, 18*(2), 1642–1649.

Bustad, L. K. (1981). *Animals, Aging, and the Aged: The Wesley W. Spink Lectures in Comparative Medicine.* Minneapolis: U. Minn. Press.

Call, J., Brauer, J., Kaminski, J., & Tomasello, M. (2003). Domestic Dogs (Canis familiaris) Are Sensitive to the Attentional State of Humans." *Journal of Comparative Psychology, 117,* 257–263.

Camp, M. M. (2001). The Use of Service Dogs as an Adaptive Strategy: A Qualitative Study. *American Journal of Occupational Therapy, 55*(5), 509–517.

Canine Assistants (2009). *Newsletter, Spring 2009.* Retrieved from www2.canineassistants.org/category/newsletter.

Caporael L., & Heyes, C. M. (1997). Why Anthropomorphize? Folk Psychology and Other Stories. In R. W. Mitchell, N. S. Thompson, and H. L. Miles (Eds.), *Anthropomorphism, Anecdotes, and Animals.* Albany, NY: State University of NY Press.

Capp, D., & Esnayra, J. (2000). Perspective: It's All in Your Head-Defining Psychiatric Disabilities and Physical Disabilities. *Thomas Jefferson Law Review, 23,* 97.

Caprilli, S., & Messeri, A. (2006). Animal-Assisted Activity at A. Meyer Children's Hospital: A Pilot Study. *Evidence-Based Complementary and Alternative Medicine, 3*(3), 379–383.

Carlisle-Frank, P., Frank, J. M., & Nielson, L. (2005). Companion Animal Renters and Pet-Friendly Housing in the U.S. *Anthrozoos, 18*(1), 59–77.

Cattafi, A. (2008). Breed Specific Legislation: The Gap in Emergency Preparedness Provisions for Household Pets. *Seton Hall Legislative Journal, 32,* 351.

Centers for Disease Control. (2003). *Guidelines for Environmental Infection Control in Healthcare Facilities: Recommendations of CDC and the Healthcare Infection Control Practices Advisory Committee.* Retrieved from www.cdc.gov/mmwr/preview/mmwrhtml/rr5210a1.htm.

Chandler, C. K. (2005). *Animal-Assisted Therapy in Counseling.* New York, NY: Routledge, Taylor & Francis Group.

Charnetski, C. J., Riggers, S., & Brennan, F. X. (2004). Effect of Petting a Dog on Immune System Function. *Psychological Reports, 95,* 1087–1091.

Chen, M., Daly, M., Williams, N., Williams, S., Williams, C., & Williams, G. (2000). Non-Invasive Detection of Hypoglycaemia Using a Novel, Fully Biocompatible and Patient Friendly Alarm System. *British Medical Journal, 321,* 1565.

Churchill, M., Safaoui, J., McCabe, B. W., & Baun, M. M. (1999). Using a Therapy Dog to

Alleviate the Agitation and Desocialization of People with Alzheimer's Disease. *Journal of Psychosocial Nursing, 37*(4), 16–22.

Clutton-Brock, J. (1977). Man-Made Dogs. *Science, 197,* 1340.

Cohen, S. P. (2002). Can Pets Function as Family Members? *Western Journal of Nursing Research, 24,* 621–638.

Collens, D. M., Fitzgerald, S. G., Sachs-Ericsson, N., Scherer, M., Cooper, R. A., & Boninger, M. L. (2005). Psychosocial Well-Being and Community Participation of Service Dog Partners. *Disability and Rehabilitation: Assistive Technology, 1*(1–2), 41–48.

Collier-Baker, E., Davis, J. M., & Suddendorf, T. Do Dogs (*Canis familiaris*) Understand Invisible Displacement?" *Journal of Comparative Psychology 118*(4), 421–433.

Collins, D. M., Fitzgerald, S. G., Sachs-Ericsson, N., Scherer, M., Cooper, R. A., & Boninger, M. L. (2005). Psychosocial Well-Being and Community Participation of Service Dog Partners. *Disability and Rehabilitation: Assistive Technology, 1*(1/2), 41–48.

Cools, A. K. A., Alain, J. M., Van Hout, A., & Nelissen, M. H. J. (2008). Canine Reconciliation and Third-Party Initiated Postconflict Affiliation: Do Peacemaking Social Mechanisms in Dogs Rival Those of Higher Primates? *Ethology, 114,* 53–63.

Coppinger, R., Coppinger, L., & Skillings, E. (1998). Observations on Assistance Dog Training and Use. *Journal of Applied Animal Welfare Science, 1*(2), 133–44.

Coppinger, R., & Coppinger, L. (2001). *Dogs: A Startling New Understanding of Canine Origin, Behavior, and Evolution.* New York, NY: Scribner.

Corson, S. A., Corson, E. O., Gwynne, P. H., & Arnold, L. E. (1977). Pet Dogs as Nonverbal Communication Links in Hospital Psychiatry. *Comprehensive Psychiatry, 18*(1), 61–72.

Cunningham, L. (2004). The Case Against Dog Breed Discrimination by Homeowners' Insurance Companies. *Connecticut Insurance Law Journal, 11*(1), 1–68.

Curless, D. (2007). *Classification of Wolf Call Types Using Remote Sensor Technology* (master's thesis, San Diego State University). Retrieved from http://hpwren.ucsd.edu/news/20070717.

Currie, N. S. (2008). *A Case Study of Incarcerated Males Participating in a Canine Training Program* (doctoral thesis, Kansas State University). Retrieved from http://krex.k-state.edu/dspace/bitstream/2097/1028/1/NikkiCurrie2008.pdf.

Dalziel, D. J., Uthman, B. M., McGorray, S. P., & Reep, R. L. (2003). Seizure-Alert Dogs: A Review and Preliminary Study. *Seizure, 12,* 115–120.

Darden, S. K., & Dabelsteen, T. (2008). Acoustic Territorial Signalling in a Small, Socially Monogamous Canid. *Animal Behaviour, 75,* 905–912.

Davis, J. B. (2007, July). At This Prosecutor's Office, a Furry Soft Spot for Kids. *ABA Journal, 93,* 18.

Davis, S. J. M., & Valla, F. R. (1978). Evidence for Domestication of the Dog 12,000 Years Ago in Natufian of Israel. *Nature, 276,* 608–610.

Dawson, S. D. (2004). Protecting a Special Class of Animal: An Examination of and Recommendations for Enacting Dog Guide Protection Statutes. *Connecticut Law Review, 37,* 569.

DeFranco, L. M. (1999). K-9 Partners: Who's Responsible for the Cost of Their Care? *Law Enforcement Technology, 26*(9), 78–81.

Dellinger, M. (2009). Using Dogs for Emotional Support of Testifying Victims of Crime. *Animal Law Review, 15*(2), 171.

Denzinger, K. L. (2003). Special Needs Trusts. *Probate & Property, 17,* 11.

Department of Housing and Urban Development. (2007). Handbook 4350.3: *Occupancy Requirements of Subsidized Multifamily Housing Programs.* Retrieved from www.hud.gov/offices/adm/hudclips/handbooks/hsgh/4350.3/43503HSGH.pdf.

Department of Justice. (2008). *An ADA Guide for Local Governments.* Retrieved from http://www.ada.gov/emergencyprepguide.htm.

Department of Justice, Civil Rights Division. (2006). DC Apartment Owner and Manager Will Cease Discriminating Against Guide-Dog Users. *Disability Rights Online News, 12,* 7. Retrieved from www.ada.gov/disabilitynews.htm.

*Diagnostic and Statistical Manual,* Fourth Edition (2007 and 2008). American Psychological Association. Retrieved from www.psychiatryonline.com/referral.aspx?gclid=CNDCsq WGzJ4CFSUsawodg32mrA.

Diederich, C., & Giffroy, J. M. (2006). Behavioural Testing in Dogs: A Review of Methodology in Search of Standardisation. *Applied Animal Behaviour Science, 97,* 51–72.

Dodman, N. H., Patronek, G. J., Dodman, V. J., Zelin, M. L., & Cottam, N. (2004). Comparison of Personality Inventories of Owners of Dogs With and Without Behavior Problems. *The International Journal of Applied Research, 2*(1), 55.

Doherty, M. J., & Haltiner, A. M. (2007). Wag the Dog: Skepticism on Seizure Alert Canines. *Neurology, 68,* 309.

Dorey, N. R., Udell, M. A. R., & Wynne, C. D. L. (2009). Breed Differences in Dogs Sensitivity to Human Points: A Meta-Analysis. *Behaviour, 81*(3), 409–415.

Duncan, S. L. (1996). Letter to the editor. *Journal of the American Medical Association, 12,* 953–4.

Duncan, S. L. (2000). APIC [Association for Professionals in Infection Control and Epidemiology] State-of the-Art Report: The Implications of Service Animals in Health Care Settings. *AJIC Am. J. Infect. Control, 28*(2), 170–180.

Eames, E. (2008, April). *Reasonable Accommodation and Assistance Dogs in the Workplace* (International Association of Assistance Dog Partners). Retrieved from www.iaadp.org.

Eames, E., & Eames, T. A. (2001). Bridging Differences Within the Disability Community: The Assistance Dog Movement. *Disability Studies Quarterly, 21*(3), 55–66.

Eames, E., Eames, T. A., & Diament, S. (2001). Guide Dog Teams in the United States: Annual Number Trained and Active, 1993–1999. *Journal of Visual Impairment and Blindness, 95,* 434–7.

Eddy, J. A., Hart, L. A., & Boltz, R. P. (1988). The Effects of Service Dogs on Social Acknowledgments of People in Wheelchairs. *The Journal of Psychology, 122*(1), 39–45.

Edney, A. T. B. (1993). Dogs and Human Epilepsy. *Veterinary Record, 132*(14), 337–338.

Edwards, N. E., & Beck, A. M. (2002). Animal-Assisted Therapy and Nutrition in Alzheimer's Disease. *Western Journal of Nursing Research, 24*(6), 697–712.

Ellegren, H. (2005). Genomics: The Dog Has Its Day. *Nature, 438*(8), 745–6.

Engeman, R. M., Vice, D. S., Rodriquez, D. V., Bruver, K. S., Santos, W.S., & Pitzler, M. E. (1998). Effectiveness of the Detectors Dogs Used for Deterring the Dispersal of Brown Tree Snakes. *Pacific Conservation Biology, 4,* 256–260.

Enoch, D. A., Karas, J. A., Slater, J. D., Emery, M. M, Kearns, A. M., & Farrington, M. (2005). MRSA Carriage in a Pet Therapy Dog. *Journal of Hospital Infection, 60,* 186–8.

Ensminger, J., & Breitkopf, F. (2010). Evolving Functions of Service and Therapy Animals and the Implications for Public Accommodation Access Rules. *Journal of Animal Law, 6.* Retrieved from www.animallaw.info/articles/arusensminger2009.htm.

Ensminger, J., & Breitkopf, F. (2009, July/August). Service and Support Animals in Housing Law. *ABA GP/Solo Magazine, 26*(5), 48–53.

Ensminger, J., & Esnayra, J. (2009). Service Dogs For the Mentally Handicapped Should Be Deductible Under Section 213." *Tax Notes, 124*(8), 815–826.

Ensminger, M. E. (1977). *The Complete Book of Dogs.* South Brunswick, NJ: A.S. Barnes & Co.

Epilepsy Institute. (2009). *Seizure Alert Dog Study.* Retrieved from www.epilepsyinstitute.org/ forms/index.htm.

Esnayra J., & Love, C. (2008). *A Survey of Mental Health Patients Utilizing Psychiatric Service Dogs.*

Retrieved from http://psychdog.org/tasks.html.

European Parliament and Council. (2003, May 26). *Regulation 998/2003 on the animal health requirements applicable to the non-commercial movement of pet animals and amending Council Directive 92/65/EEC*. Retrieved from http://eur-lex.europa.eu/LexUriServ/site/en/consleg/1992/L/01992L0065-20040703-en.pdf.

European Parliament and Council. (2006, July 5). Regulation 1107/2006 *Concerning the Rights of Disabled Persons and Persons with Reduced Mobility When Traveling by Air*. Retrieved from http://eur-lex.europa.eu/LexUriServ/LexUriServ.do?uri=OJ:L:2006:204:0001:0009:EN:PDF.

Eustis, D. H. (1927, November 5). The Seeing Eye. *Saturday Evening Post, 200,* 43–46.

Fairman, S. K., & Huebner, R. A. (2000). Service Dogs: A Compensatory Resource to Improve Function. *Occupational Therapy in Health Care, 13*(2), 41–52.

Fallani, G., Previde, E. P., & Valsecchi, P. (2006). Do Disrupted Early Attachments Affect the Relationship Between Guide Dogs and Blind Owners? *Applied Animal Behaviour Science, 100,* 241–257.

Feddersen-Petersen, D. (1991). The Ontogeny of Social Play and Antagonistic Behavior in Selected Canid Species. *Bonner Zoologische Beitraege, 42,* 97–114.

Fields-Meyer, T., & Mandel, S. (2006, July 17). Healing Hounds: Can Dogs Help People With Mental-Health Problems Get Better? *People Magazine, 66*(3), 101–102.

Fine, A. (2006). *Handbook on Animal-Assisted Therapy: Theoretical Foundations and Guidelines for Practice.* San Diego, CA: Academic Press.

Fishman, G. A. (2003). When Your Eyes Have a Wet Nose: The Evolution of the Use of Guide Dogs and Establishing the Seeing Eye. *Survey of Opthalmology, 48*(4), 452–458.

Flynn, C. P. (2000). Battered Women and Their Animal Companions: Symbolic Interaction Between Human and Nonhuman Animals. *Society & Animals, 8*(2), 99–127.

Fox, M. W. (1998). *Concepts in Ethology: Animal Behavior and Bioethics.* Malabar, FL: Krieger Publishing.

Franck, L. (2007). Guide Dogs Current Practice [review of Guide Dogs Current Practice]. *Journal of Visual Impairment and Blindness, 101*(11), 728.

Frank, H. (1980). Evolution of Canine Information Processing under Conditions of Natural and Artificial Selection. *Zeitschrift fur Tierpsychologie, 5,* 389–399.

Frank, H., & Frank, M. G. (1982). Comparison of Problem-Solving Performance in Six-Week-Old Wolves and Dogs. *Animal Behaviour, 30,* 95–98.

Frank, M., & Clark, B. (1957). *First Lady of the Seeing Eye.* New York, NY: Henry Holt & Co.

Fredrickson, M., & DePrekel, M. (2004, March 28). *Animal-Assisted Therapy for At-Risk Youth and Families* (University of Pennsylvania School of Veterinary Medicine, Center for the Interaction of Animals and Society, Conference, Can Animals Help Humans Heal? Animal-Assisted Interventions in Adolescent Mental Health). Retrieved from http://research.vet.upenn.edu/PastConferences/CanAnimalsHelpHumansHeal/Fredrickson/tabid/1957/Default.aspx.

Friedmann, E., Katcher, A. H., Lynch, J. J., & Thomas, S. A. (1980). Animal Companions and One-Year Survival of Patients after Discharge from a Coronary Care Unit. *Public Health Reports, 95*(4), 307.

Friedmann, E., Katcher, A. H., Thomas, S. A., Lynch, J. J., & Messent, P. R. (1983). Social Interaction and Blood Pressure: Influence of Animal Companions. *Journal of Nervous and Mental Disease 171*(8), 461–464.

Froling, J. (2003). *Assistance Dog Tasks.* Retrieved from www.iaadp.org.

Fukuzawa, M., Uetake, K., & Tanaka, T. (2000, March 25). The Analysis of Factors Influencing Auditory Cognition of Verbal Commands in Dogs (*Canis familiaris*). (abstracts of the Sixth

Annual Meeting Society for the Study of Human Animal Relations, Tokyo) p. 46.

Furst, G. (2006). Prison-Based Animal Programs: A National Survey. *The Prison Journal, 86,* 407.

Gacsi, M., Gyori, B., Miklosi, A., Viranyi, Z., Kubinyi, E., Topal, J., & and Csanyi, V. (2005). Species-Specific Differences and Similarities in the Behavior of Hand Raised Dog and Wolf Puppies in Social Situations with Humans. *Developmental Psychobiology, 47,* 111–122.

Gacsi, M., Miklosi, A., Varga, O., Topal, J., & Csanyi, V. (2004). Are Readers of Our Face Readers of Our Minds? Dog (Canis familiaris) Show Situation-Dependent Recognition of Human's Attention." *Animal Cognition, 7,* 144–153.

Garrity, T. F., Stallones, L., Marx, M. B., & Johnson, T. P. (1989). Pet Ownership and Attachment as Supportive Factors in the Health of the Elderly. *Anthrozoos, 3*(1), 35–54.

Gerbasi, K. C. (2005, July 11–12). *Gender and Animal Cruelty Cases: Conviction Data* from www. Pet-abuse.com (presented at ISAZ 14th Annual Conference). Retrieved from http://www. isaz.net/conferences/isaz2005.pdf.

Gerwolls, M. K., & Labott, S. M. (1994). Adjustment to the Death of a Companion Animal. *Anthrozoos, 7,* 172–187.

Goddard, M. E., & Beilharz, R. G. (1984). A Factor Analysis of Fearfulness in Potential Guide Dogs. *Applied Animal Behaviour Science, 12,* 253–265.

Goodwin, D., Bradshaw, J. W. S., & Wickens, S. M. (1997). Paedomorphosis Affects Agonistic Visual Signals of Domestic Dogs. *Animal Behaviour, 52*(2), 297–304.

Gordon, H. (2004). The Use of "Drug Dogs" in Psychiatry. *Psychiatric Bulletin, 28,* 196–198.

Grandin, T. (2005). *Animals in Translation: Using the Mysteries of Autism to Decode Animal Behavior.* New York: Simon & Schuster.

Greenbaum, S. D. (2006). Introduction to Working With Animal Assisted Crisis Response Animal Handler Teams. *International Journal of Emergency Mental Health, 8*(1), 49–63.

Gross, P. D. (2006). *The Golden Bridge. A Guide to Assistance Dogs for Children Challenged by Autism or Other Developmental Disabilities.* Ashland, OH: Purdue University Press.

Groves, C. P. (1999). The Advantages and Disadvantages of Being Domesticated. *Perspectives in Human Biology, 4*(1), 1–12.

Guest, C. M., Collis, G. M., & McNicholas, J. (2006). Hearing Dogs: A Longitudinal Study of Social and Psychological Effects on Deaf and Hard-of-Hearing Recipients. *The Journal of Deaf Studies and Deaf Education, 11,* 252–261.

Guide Dog Foundation. (2009). *FAQ: What is the Training Program Like?* Retrieved from www. guidedog.org/Progserv/getdog.htm#Anchor5.

Guide Dogs of America. (2009). *Adoption.* Retrieved from www.guidedogsofamerica.org/ adopt.html.

Guiding Eyes for the Blind. (2009). *Guide Dog Training.* Retrieved from www.guidingeyes.org/ volunteer/puppy-raising/next-steps/guide-dog-training.

Hall, B. (2007). *Morris & Buddy: The Story of the First Seeing Eye Dog.* Park Ridge, IL: Albert Whitman & Co.

Hansen, K. M., Messinger, C. J., Baun, M. M., & Mengel, M. (1999). Companion Animals Alleviating Distress in Children. *Anthrozoos, 12*(3), 142–8.

Hansen, V., & Carson, L. (2009). Rose of Assistance Dogs as Supportive Care Providers for Disabled Individuals. *Abstracts/Disability and Health Journal, 2,* e1–e15.

Hanson, B. (2005). Dog-Focused Law's Impact on Disability Rights: Ontario's Pit Bull Legislation as a Case in Point. *Animal Law Review, 12*(1), 217.

Harbolt, T., & Ward, T. H. (2001). Teaming Incarcerated Youth with Shelter Dogs for a Second Chance. *Society & Animals, 9*(2), 177–182.

Hare, B., Brown, M., Williamson, C., & Tomasello, M. (2002). The Domestication of Social

Cognition in Dogs. *Science, 298,* 1634–6.

Hare, B., & Tomasello, M. (2005). Human-Like Social Skills in Dogs? *Trends in Cognitive Sciences, 9,* 439–444.

Harkrader, T., Burke, T. W., & Owen, S. S. (2004). Pound Puppies: The Rehabilitative Uses of Dogs in Correctional Facilities. *Corrections Today, 65*(2), 74–80.

Harrington, J. C. (1999). Fifth Circuit Survey: Civil Rights. *Texas Tech Law Review, 30,* 507.

Hart-Cohen, D. S. (2009). Canines in the Courtroom. *GP/Solo Magazine, 26*(5), 54–57.

Hart, L. A. (1995). The Role of Pets in Enhancing Human Well-Being: Effects for Older People. In I. Robinson (Ed.), *The Waltham Book of Human-Animal Interactions: Benefits and Responsibilities.* Oxford, UK: Butterworth-Heinemann, Ltd.

Hart, L. A., Zasloff, R. L., & Benfatto, A. M. (1996). The Socializing Role of Hearing Dogs. *Applied Animal Behaviour Science, 47,* 7–15.

Hart, L. A. (2006). *A Bibliographic Search Grid, Review and Evaluation of Literature on Barking in Canids.* Retrieved from www.vetmed.ucdavis.edu/animal_alternatives/barkfinal.html.

Havener, L., Gentes, L., Thaler, B., Megel, M. E., Baun, M. M., Driscoll, F. A., Beiraghi, S., & Agrawal, N. (2001). The Effects of a Companion Animal on Distress in Children Undergoing Dental Procedures. *Issues in Comprehensive Pediatric Nursing, 24,* 137–152.

Heaton, J. S., Cablk, M. E., Nussear, K. E., Medica, P. A., Sagebiel, J. C., & Francis, S. S. (2008). Comparison of Effects of Humans Versus Wildlife-Detector Dogs. *The Southwestern Naturalist, 53*(4), 472–479.

Heimlich, K. (2001). Animal-Assisted Therapy and the Severely Disabled Child: A Quantitative Study. *Journal of Rehabilitation, 67*(4), 48–54.

Herbert, J. D., & Greene, D. (2001). Effect of Preference on Distance Walked by Assisted Living Residents. *Physical and Occupational Therapy in Geriatrics, 19,* 1–15.

Herbster, A. H. (2000). Note: More Than Pigs in a Parlor: An Exploration of the Relationship Between the Law and Keeping Pigs as Pets. *Iowa Law Review, 86,* 339.

Heyes, C. M., & Ray, E. D. (2000). What is the Significance of Imitation in Animals? *Advances in the Study of Behavior, 29,* 215–245.

HOPE. *Animal Assisted Crisis Response.* Retrieved from www.hopeaacr.org and www.animalassistedcrisisresponse.org.

Horowitz, A. C., & Bekoff, M. (2007). Naturalizing Anthropomorphism: Behavioral Prompts to Our Humanizing of Animals. *Anthrozoos, 20*(1), 23–35.

Huss, R. J. (2005). No Pets Allowed: Housing Issues and Companion Animals. *Animal Law Review, 11,* 69–129.

Internal Revenue Service Publication 502. (2009). *Medical and Dental Expenses (Including the Health Coverage Tax Credit).* Retrieved from www.irs.gov/publications/p502/index.html.

Internal Revenue Service Publication 907. (2008). *Tax Highlights for Persons with Disabilities.* Retrieved from www.irs.gov/pub/irs-pdf/p907.pdf.

International Guide Dog Foundation. (2009). *History.* Retrieved from www.ifgdsb.org.uk/page.asp?code=00010018.

Jewish Federation of Monmouth County. (2003, October 5). *Israel First in the World to Develop Alzheimer's Guide Dogs.* Retrieved from www.jewishmonmouth.org/page.aspx?id=50292.

Jezierski, T., Walczak, M., & Gorecka, A. (2008). Canine Olfactory Detection of Human Cancer Odor Markers. *Polish Academy of Sciences, 2008 Annual Report,* p. 64.

Johnston, B. (1990). *The Skillful Mind of the Guide Dog: Towards a Cognitive and Holistic Model of Training* (Guide Dogs for the Blind Association). Jacksonville, IL: Alexandra House.

Joint Statement of the Department of Housing and Urban Development and the Department of Justice. *Reasonable Accommodation Under the Fair Housing Act* (May 17, 2004). Retrieved from http://www.justice.gov/crt/housing/jointstatement_ra.php.

Joly-Mascheroni, R. M., Senju, A., & Shepherd, A. J. (2008). Dogs Catch Human Yawns. *Biology Letters, 4,* 446–448.

Jones, A. C., & Gosling, S. D. (2005). Temperament and Personality in Dogs (*Canis familiaris*): A Review and Evaluation of Past Research. *Applied Animal Behaviour Science, 95,* 1–53.

Kaminski, J., Call, J., & Fisher, J. (2004). Word Learning in a Domestic Dog: Evidence for "Fast Mapping." *Science, 304,* 1682–1683.

Kaminski, J., Brauer, J., Call, J., & Tomasello, M. (2009). Domestic Dogs Are Sensitive to a Human's Perspective. *Behaviour 146,* 978–998.

Kansas Department of Corrections. (2009). *Second Chance Homeless Pet Society.* Retrieved from (http://doc.ks.gov/facilities/ncf/dog-programs/?searchterm=dog).

Karlsson, E. K., & Lindblad-Toh, K. (2008). Leader of the Pack: Gene Mapping in Dogs and Other Model Organisms. *Nature Reviews: Genetics, 9,* 713.

Kerswell, K. J., Bennett, P., Butler, K. L., & Hemsworth, P. H. (2009). The Relationship of Adult Morphology and Early Social Signalling of the Domestic Dog (*Canis familiaris*). *Behavioural Processes, 81,* 376–382.

Kirton, A., Wirrell, E., Zhang, J. M, & Hamiwka, L. (2004). Seizure-Alerting and -Response Behaviors in Dogs Living with Epileptic Children. *Neurology, 62,* 2303–2305; 64(3), 581 (author reply).

Kirton, A.,Winter, A., Wirrell, E., & Snead, O. C. (2008), Seizure Response Dogs: Evaluation of a Formal Training Program. *Epilepsy Behavior, 13*(3), 499–504.

Klinghammer, E., & Goodmann, P. A. (1987). Socialization and Management of Wolves in Captivity. In H. Frank (Ed.), *Man and Wolf: Advances, Issues and Problems in Captive Wolf Research.* The Hague, Netherlands: W. Junk Publishers.

Koda, N. (2001). Inappropriate Behavior of Potential Guide Dogs for the Blind and Coping Behavior of Human Raisers. *Applied Animal Behaviour Science, 72,* 79–87.

Kongable, J. G., Buckwalter, K. C., & Stolley, J. M. (1989). The Effects of Pet Therapy on the Social Behavior of Institutionalized Alzheimer's Clients. *Archives of Psychiatric Nursing, 3,* 191–198.

Konrad, W. (2009, August 22). An Aide for the Disabled, a Companion, and Nice and Furry. *New York Times,* p. B5.

Kotrschal, K., & Ortbauer, B. (2003). Behavioral Effects of the Presence of a Dog in a Classroom. *Anthrozoos, 16,* 147–159.

Krauss, G. L., Choi, J. S., & Lesser, R. P. (2007). Pseudoseizure Dogs. *Neurology, 68*(4), 308–309.

Kruger, K. A., & Serpell, J. A. (2006). Animal-Assisted Interventions in Mental Health: Definitions and Theoretical Foundations. In A. Fine (Ed.), *Handbook on Animal-Assisted Therapy: Theoretical Foundations and Guidelines for Practice.* San Diego, CA: Academic Press.

Kruger, K. A, Trachtenberg, S. W., & Serpell, J. A. (2004). *Can Animals Help Humans Heal?* Animal-Assisted Interventions in Adolescent Mental Health (Center for the Interaction of Animals and Society, University of Pennsylvania School of Veterinary Medicine). Retrieved from www2.vet.upenn.edu/research/centers/cias/publications.html.

Kubinyi, E., Viranyi, Z., & Miklosi, A. (2007). Comparative social Cognition: From Wolf and Dog to Humans. *Comparative Social Cognition, 2,* 26–46.

Kuehn, B. M. (2004). Animal Hoarding: A Public Health Problem Veterinarians Can Take a Lead Role in Solving. *Journal of the American Veterinary Medical Association, 221*(8), 1087–1089.

Kruse, C. R. (2002). Baby Steps: Minnesota Raises Certain Forms of Animal Cruelty to Felony Status. *William Mitchell Law Review, 28,* 1649.

Kubinyi, E., Miklosi, A., Kaplan, F., Gacsi, M., Topal, J., & Csanyi, V. (2004). Social Behaviour of Dogs Encountering AIBO, an Animal-like Robot in a Neutral and in a Feeding Situation. *Behavioural Processes, 65,* 231–239.

Kubinyi, E., Viranyi, Z., & Miklosi, A. (2007). Comparative Social Cognition: From Wolf and Dog to Humans. *Comparative Social Cognition, 2,* 26–46.

LaFrance, C., Garcia, L. J., & Labreche, J. (2007). The Effect of a Therapy Dog on the Communication Skills of an Adult with Aphasia. *Journal of Communication Disorders, 40,* 215–224.

LaJoie, K. R. (2003). An Evaluation of the Effectiveness of Using Animals in Therapy (doctoral dissertation, Spalding University).

Lakatos, G., Soproni, K., Doka, A., & Miklosi, A. (2007). A Comparative Approach of How Dogs and Human Infants Are Able To Utilize Various Forms of Pointing Gestures. *International Journal of Comparative Psychology, 20,* 341–350.

Lane, D. R., McNicholas, J., & Collis, G. M. (1998). Dogs for the Disabled: Benefits to Recipients and Welfare of the Dog. *Applied Animal Behaviour Science, 59,* 49–60.

Leaser, A. (2005). See Spot Mediate: Utilizing the Emotional and Psychological Benefits of "Dog Therapy" in Victim-Offender Mediation. *Ohio State Journal on Disability Research, 20,* 943.

Leaver, S. D. A., & Reimchen, T. E. (2008). Behavioural Responses of Canis familiaris to Different Tail Lengths of a Remotely-Controlled Life-Size Dog Replica. *Behaviour, 145,* 377–390.

Lefebre, S. L., & Weese, J. S. (2009). Contamination of Pet Therapy Dogs with MRSA and Clostridium difficile. *Journal of Hospital Infection, 72,* 268.

Lefkowitz, C., Paharia, I., Prout, M., Debiak, D., & Bleiberg, J. (2005). Animal-Assisted Prolonged Explosure: A Treatment for Survivors of Sexual Assault Suffering Posttraumatic Stress Disorder. *Society & Animals, 13*(4), 274.

Lesniak, A., Walczak, M., Jezierski, T., Sacharczuk, M., Gawkowski, M., & Jaszczak, K. (2008). Canine Olfactory Receptor Gene Polymorphism and Its Relation to Odor Detection Performance by Sniffer Dogs. *Journal of Heredity, 99*(5), 518–527.

Levinson, B. M. (1962). The Dog as Co-Therapist. *Mental Hygiene, 46,* 59–65.

Levinson, B. M. (1965). Pet Psychotherapy: Use of Household Pets in the Treatment of Behavior Disorder in Childhood. *Psychological Reports, 17,* 695–698.

Levinson, B. M. (1970). Pets, Child Development, and Mental Illness. *Journal of the American Veterinary Medical Association, 157*(11), 1759–1766.

Levinson, B. M. (1978). Pets and Personality Development. *Psychological Reports, 42,* 1031–1038.

Levinson, B. M. (1984). Human/Companion Animal Therapy. *Journal of Contemporary Psychotherapy, 14,* 131–144.

Levinson, B. M., & Mallon, G. P (1997). *Pet-Oriented Child Psychotherapy.* Springfield, IL: Charles C Thomas.

Lim, K., Wilcox, A., Fisher, M., & Burns-Cox, C. I. (1992). Type 1 Diabetes and Their Pets. *Diabetic Medicine, 9* (suppl. 2), S3–S4.

Limond, J. A., Bradshaw, J. W. S., & Cormack, K. F. M. Behavior of Children with Learning Disabilities Interacting with a Therapy Dog. *Anthrozoos 10*(2/3), 84–89.

Lindblad-Toh, K., Wade C. M., Mikkelsen, T. S., & Karlsson E. K. (2005). Genome Sequence, Comparative Analysis and Haplotype Structure of the Domestic Dog. *Nature, 438,* 803–819.

Lorenz, K. (1954). *Man Meets Dog.* London, UK: Methuen & Co.

Luke, A., & Luke, C. (1997). Physical Cruelty Toward Animals in Massachusetts, 1975–1996. *Society & Animals, 5*(3), 195–204.

Macauley, B. L. (2006). Animal-Assisted Therapy for Persons with Aphasia: A Pilot Study. *Journal of Rehabilitation Research and Development, 41*, 357–366.

MacDonald, D. W., & Carr, G. M. (1995). Variation in Dog Society: Between Resource Dispersion and Social Flux. In J. Serpell (Ed.), *The Domestic Dog: Its Evolution, Behaviour, and Interactions with People.* Cambridge, UK: Cambridge University Press.

Mader, B., Hart, L. A., & Bergin, B. (1989). Social Acknowledgments for Children with Disabilities: Effects of Service Dogs. *Child Development, 60*, 1529–1534.

Maiuri, A. (1953). *Roman Painting.* Milan, Italy: Skira Publishing.

Maros, K., Pongracz, P., Bardos, G., Molnar, C., Farago, T., & Miklosi, A. (2008). Dogs Can Discriminate Barks from Different Situations. *Applied Animal Behaviour Science, 114*, 159–167.

Martin, F., & Farnum, J. (2002). Animal-Assisted Therapy for Children with Pervasive Development Disorders. *Western Journal of Nursing Research, 24*(6), 657–670.

Matsunaka, K., & Koda, N. (2008). Acceptance of Dog Guides and Daily Stress Levels of Guide Dog Users and Nonusers. *Journal of Visual Impairment and Blindness, 102*(5), 295–304.

Mayon-White, R. (2005). Pets-Pleasures and Problems. *British Medical Journal, 331*, 1254.

McCabe, B. W., Baun, M. M., Speich, D., & S. Agrawal, S. (2002). Resident Dog in the Alzheimer's Special Care Unit. *Western Journal of Nursing Research, 24*(6), 684–696.

McCulloch, M., Jezierski, T., Broffman, M., Hubbard, A., Turner, K., & Janecki, T. (2006). Diagnostic Accuracy of Canine Scent Detection in Early- and Late-Stage Lung and Breast Cancers. *Integrative Cancer Therapies, 5*(1), 30–9.

McMahon, S. M. (1995). Pets: A Source of Hope for Children with Life-Threatening Illness. In D. Addaris and E. Deveau (Eds.), *Beyond the Innocence of Childhood*, vol. 2 (pp. 83–100). Amityville, NY: Baywood Publications.

McNabb, M. (2007). Pets in the Eye of the Storm: Hurricane Katrina Floods the Courts with Pet Custody Disputes. *Animal Law, 14*, 71–108.

Meers, L., Coultis, D., Moons, C. P. H., & Normando, S. (2006). Assessing Animal-Assisted Interventions. *Latham Letter, 27*(2), 8–10.

Melson, G. F. (2004, March 28). *Animals in the Lives of Adolescents: A Biocentric Perspective in Development.* (University of Pennsylvania School of Veterinary Medicine, Center for the Interaction of Animals and Society, Conference: Can Animals Help Humans Heal? Animal-Assisted Interventions in Adolescent Mental Health). Retrieved from research.vet.upenn.edu/Portals/36/media/Melson.ppt.

Mezosi, T., Pallos, A., Komondi, P., & Topal, J. (2008). *Is It Reasonable to Forbid the Use of Dog Guides for the Blind as Predictors of Epileptic Seizures?* Hungarian Academy of Sciences, Institute for Psychology, case report. Retrieved from www.barathegyisegitokutya.hu.

Miklosi, A. (2007). *Dog Behavior, Evolution and Cognition.* Oxford, UK: Oxford University Press.

Miklosi, A., Kubinyi, E., Topal, J., Gacsi, M., Viranyi, Z., & Csanyi, V. (2003). A Simple Reason for a Big Difference: Wolves Do Not Look Back at Humans, but Dogs Do. *Current Biology, 13*, 763–766.

Miklosi, A., Polgardi, R., Topal, J., & Csanyi, V. (1998). Use of Experimenter-Given Cues in Dogs. *Animal Cognition, 1*, 113–121.

Miklosi, A., Polgardi, R., Topal, J., & Csanyi, V. (2000). Intentional Behaviour in Dog-Human Communication: An Experimental Analysis of 'Showing' Behavior in the Dog. *Animal Cognition, 3*, 159–166.

Miklosi, A., Pongracz, P., Lakatos, G., Topal, J., & Csanyi, V. (2005). A Comparative Study of the Use of Visual Communicative Signals in Interactions Between Dogs (Canis familiaris) and Humans and Cats (*Felis catus*) and Humans. *J. Comparative Psychology, 119*(2), 179–186.

Miklosi, A., Topal, J., & Csanyi, V. (2004). Comparative Social Cognition: What Can Dogs Teach Us? *Animal Behaviour, 67,* 995–1004.

Milan, R. W. (2007). *Quality of Life of Service Dog Partners* (master's thesis, University of Pittsburg). Retrieved from http://etd.library.pitt.edu/ETD/available/etd-03282007-161045/unrestricted/Milan_ETD2007final.pdf.

Milius, S. (2001, July 28). Don't Look Now, But Is That Dog Laughing? *Science News, 160*(4), 55.

Miller, J. (2000). Perioperative Nursing and Animal-Assisted Therapy. *AORN Journal, 72*(3), 477–483.

Mitchell, R. W., & Edmunson, E. (1997, July 24–5). What People Say to Dogs When They Are Playing With Them (paper presented at ISAZ 1997, International Society for Anthrozoology, Boston, Massachusetts. Retrieved from www.isaz.net/conferences/isaz 1997.pdf.

Mitchell, R. W., & Edmonson, E. (1999). Functions of Repetitive Talk to Dogs During Play: Control, Conversation, or Planning? *Society & Animals, 7*(1), 55–81.

Mithen, S. (1996). *The Prehistory of the Mind: A Search for the Origins of Art, Religion and Science.* London, UK: Thames & Hudson.

Molnar, C., Kaplan, F., Roy, P., Pachet, F., Pongracz, P., Doka, A., & Miklosi, A. (2008). Classification of Dog Barks: A Machine Learning Approach. *Animal Cognition, 11*(3), 389–400.

Moor, E. (1996). *Buddy: First Seeing Eye Dog.* New York, NY: Scholastic, Inc.

Moore, J. E. (1942). Some Psychological Aspects of Yawning. *J. Gen. Psychiatry, 27,* 289–471.

Morris, P., Fiddler, M., & Costall, A. (2000). Beyond Anecdotes: An Empirical Study of "Anthropomorphism." *Society & Animals, 8*(2), 151–165.

Mowry, R. L., Carnahan, S., & Watson, D. (1994). *Contributions of Hearing Assistance Dogs to Improving the Independent Living and Rehabilitation of Persons Who Are Hearing Impaired.* (Project Final Technical Report H133B10001, National Institute for Disability and Rehabilitation Research). Retrieved from http://naricspotlight.wordpress.com/2009/04.

Murphy, C., Zadnik, K., & Mannis, M. J. (1992). Myopia and Refractive Error in Dogs. *Investigative Ophtalmology & Visual Science, 33*(8), 2459–2463.

Murphy, J. A. (1998). Describing Categories of Temperament in Potential Guide Dogs for the Blind. *Applied Animal Behaviour Science, 55,* 163–178.

Naderi, S., Miklosi, A., Doka, A., & Csanyi, V. (2001). Cooperative Interactions Between Blind Persons and Their Dogs. *Animal Behaviour Science, 74,* 59–80.

Nagengast, S. L., Baun, M. M., & Leibowitz, J. M. (1997). The Effects of a Companion Animal on Physiological Arousal and Behavioral Distress in Children. *Journal of Pediatric Nursing, 12,* 323–330.

National Conference of State Legislatures. (2003). *Epilepsy-Related Legislation 2000–2002.* Retrieved from www.ncsl.org/programs/health/epilepsy3.htm.

Nebbe, L. (1991). The human-animal bond and the elementary school counselor. *The School Counselor, 38*(5), 362–371.

Nicastro, N., & Owren, M. J. (2003). Classification of Domestic Cat (Felis catus) Vocalizations by Naïve and Experienced Listerners. *Journal of Comparative Psychology, 117,* 44–52.

Nimer, J. & Lundahl, B. (2007). Animal-Assisted Therapy: A Meta-Analysis. *Anthrozoos, 20*(3), 225–238.

Nolan, F. (2006). Animal–Assisted Crisis Response Teams Bring Comfort and Joy to People Who Have Survived the Unexpected. *Latham Letter, 27*(2), 6–7.

Nowak, S., Jedrzejewski, W., Schmidt, K., Theuerfauf, J., Myslajek, R. W., & Jedrzejewska, B. (2007). Howling Activity of Free-Ranging Wolves (*Canis lupus*) in the Bialowieza Primeval

Forest and the Western Beskidy Mountains (Poland). *Journal of Ethology, 25,* 231–237.

Nunalee, M. E., & Weedon, G. Robert (2004). Modern Trends in Veterinary Malpractice: How Our Evolving Attitudes Toward Non-Human Animals Will Change Veterinary Medicine. *Animal Law Review, 10,* 125–161.

O'Connor, M. B., O'Connor, C. O., & Walsh, C. H. (2008). A Dog's Detection of Low Blood Sugar: A Case Report. *Irish Journal of Medical Science, 177*(2), 155–7.

Ohio Department of Job and Family Services, Administrative Appeal Section. (1990, July 2). Food Stamp Policy Memo 90–02. Retrieved from www.bsh.jfs.ohio.gov/03Mar2006/ Appeals/2006-AA-0246.pdf.

O'Neill-Stephens, E. (2009). Courthouse Dogs: A Case Study (2009, Summer). *ABA Animal Law Committee Newsletter, Summer 2009, 9,* 21–22.

The Oprah Winfrey Show. (2009, June 19). *Prison-Trained Puppies Help Wounded Troops.* Retrieved from www.cnn.com/2009/LIVING/wayoflife/06/19/o.puppies.behind.bars/ index.html.

Oregon Department of Corrections. (1989). *Controlling Drug Usage in Department of Corrections Institutions.* Retrieved from www.ncjrs.gov/App/Publications/abstract.aspx?ID=136463.

Orlandi, M., Trangeled, K., Mambrini, A., Tagliani, M., Ferrarini, Zanetti, A. L., Tartarini, R., Pacetti, P., & Cantore, M. (2007). Pet Therapy Effects on Oncological Day Hospital Patients Undergoing Chemotherapy Treatment. *Anticancer Research, 27*(6C), 4301–3.

Ortiz, R., & Liporace, J. (2005). Seizure-Alert Dogs: Observations from an Inpatient Video/EEG Unit. *Epilepsy & Behavior, 6*(4), 620–622.

Overall, K. L. (2000). Natural Human Models of Human Psychiatric Conditions: Assessment of Mechanism and Validity. *Progress in Neuro-Psychopharmacology and Biological Psychiatry, 24,* 727–776.

Pannell, S. J. (2008, January). Eleventh Circuit Allows Emotional Distress Award Under Rehabilitation Act. *TRIAL, 44,* 70.

Pang, J. F., Kluetsch, C., Zou, X. J. Zhang, A., Luo, L. Y., Angleby, H., Ardalan, A., Ekstrom, C., Skooermo, A., Lundebert, J., Matsumura, S., Leitner, T., Zhang, Y. P., & Savolainen, P. (2009). mtDNA Data Indicates a Single Origin for Dogs South of Yangtze River, Less than 16,300 Years Ago, from Numerous Wolves. *Molecular Biology and Evolution, 26,* 2849–2864.

Patrick, D., & Harshbarger, S. (1996). *Commonly Asked Questions About Service Animals in Places of Business.* Retrieved from www.ada.gov/archive/animal.htm.

Patronek, G. J. (1997). Issues for Veterinarians in Recognizing and Reporting Animal Neglect and Abuse. *Society & Animals, 5*(3), 195–204.

Paukner, A., & Anderson, J.R. (2006). Video-Induced Yawning in Stumptail Macaques (*Macaca arctoides*). *Biology. Letters, 2,* 36–38.

Paulhus, D. (1983). Sphere-Specific Measures of Perceived Control. *J. Pers. Soc. Psychol. 44,* 1253–1265.

Perelle, I. B., & Granville, D. A. (1993). Assessment of the Effectiveness of a Pet Facilitated Therapy Program in a Nursing Home Setting. *Society & Animals, 1*(1), 91–100.

Perlin, M. L. (2000). Lecture: A Law of Healing. *University of Cincinnati Law Review, 68,* 407–434.

Phillips, A. (2004). How the Dynamics Between Animal Abuse and Child Abuse Affect the Forensic Interview Process. *National Child Protection Center: Reasonable Efforts 1*(4). Retrieved from www.ndaa.org/publications/newsletters/reasonable_efforts_volume_1_ number_4_2004.html.

Pickel, D. P., Manucy, G. P., Walker, B. B., Hall S. B., & Walker, J. C. (2004). Evidence for Canine Olfactory Detection of Melanoma. *Applied Animal Behaviour Science, 89,* 107–116.

Planchon, L. A., Templer, D. I., Stokes, S., & Keller, J. (2002). Death of a Companion Cat or

Dog and Human Bereavement: Psychosocial Variables. *Society & Animals, 10*(1), 93–105.

Platek, S. M., Critton, S. R., Myers, T. E., & Gallup, G. G. (2003). The Rose of Self-Awareness and Mental State Attribution. *Cognitive Brain Research, 17,* 223–227.

Plonsky, M. (1998). *Dr. P's Dog Training: Canine Vision.* Retrieved from www.uwsp.edu/PSYCH/dog/LA/DrP4.htm.

Ponchillia, P. E., Rak, E. C., Freeland, A. L., & LaGrow, S .J. (2007). Accessible GPS: Reorientation and Target Location Among Users with Visual Impairments. *Journal of Visual Impairment and Blindness, 101*(7), 389–401.

Pongracz, P., Miklosi, A., Kubinyi, E., Gurobi, K., Topal, J., & Csanyi, V. (2001). Social Learning in Dogs: The Effect of a Human Demonstrator on the Performance of Dogs (*Canis familiaris*) in a Detour Task. *Animal Behavior, 62,* 1109–1117.

Pongracz, P., Molnar, C., Miklosi, A., & Csanyi, V. (2005). Human Listeners Are Able to Classify Dog (Canis familiarizes) Barks Recorded in Different Situations. *Journal of Comparative Psychology, 119*(2), 136–144.

Poresky, R. H. (1990). The Young Children's Empathy Measure: Reliability, Validity and Effects of Companion Animal Bonding. *Psychological Reports, 66,* 931–936.

Pound Pup Legacy (2006). *K-State Sociology Professor Finds Dog Training Programs in Kansas Prisons Are Beneficial to Both Inmates and Staff.* Retrieved from http://poundpuplegacy.org/node/14338.

Price, E. O. (1984). Behaviour Aspects of Animal Domestication. *Quarterly Review in Biology 59,* 1–32.

Price, S. (2006, September). *Service Animals Under the ADA: Equip for Equality.* ADA & IT Technical Assistance Centers Legal Briefings (Illinois). Retrieved from www.equipforequality.org/resourcecenter/ada_serviceanimals.pdf .

Provine, R. R. (1986). Yawning as a Stereotyped Action Pattern and Releasing Stimulus. *Ethology, 72,* 448–455.

Raupp, C. D. (2002). The "Furry Ceiling": Clinical Psychology and Animal Studies. *Society & Animals, 10*(4), 353–360.

Refson, K., Jackson, A. J., Dusoir, A. E., & Archer, D. B. (2002). Residual Visual Functions of Guide Dog Owners in the UK. *Ophthalmic and Physiological Optics, 21*(4), 277–185.

Reid, P. J. (2009). Adapting to the Human World: Dogs' Responsiveness to Our Social Cues. *Behavioural Processes, 80,* 325–333.

Riedel, J., Schumann, K., Kaminski, J., Call, J., & Tomasello, M. (2008). The Early Ontogeny of Human-Dog Communication. *Animal Behaviour, 75*(3), 1003–1014.

Rintala, D. H., Matamoros, R., & Seitz, L. L. (2008). Effects of Assistance Dogs on Persons . with Mobility or Hearing Impairments: A Pilot Study. *Journal of Rehabilitation Research & Development, 45*(4), 489–504.

Rogers, J., Hart, L., & Boltz, R. P. (1991). The Role of Pet Dogs in Casual Conversations with Elderly Adults. *Journal of Social Psychology, 133,* 265–277.

Rooney, N. J., Bradshaw, J. W. S., & Robinson, I. H. (1999, August 17–21). The Effects of Play on the Dog-Human Relationship: An Experimental Study (proceedings of the 33rd International Congress of the International Society for Applied Ethology. Lillehammer, Norway).

Rooney, N. J., Bradshaw, J. W. S., & Robinson, I. H. (2000). "A Comparison of Dog-Dog and Dog-Human Play Behaviour. *Applied Animal Behaviour Science, 66,* 235–248.

Rooney, N. J., Bradshaw, J. W. S., & Robinson, I. H. (2001). Do Dogs Respond to Play Signals Given by Humans? *Animal Behaviour, 61*(4), 715–722.

Rooney, N. J. & Bradshaw, J. W. S. (2006). Social Cognition in the Domestic Dog: Behaviour of Spectators Towards Participants in Interspecific Games. *Animal Behaviour, 72*(2), 343–352.

Rosenberg, M. (1965). *Society and the Adolescent Self-Image.* Princeton, NJ: Princeton U. Press.

Roukas, M. S. (2007). Determining the Value of Companion Animals in Wrongful Harm or Death Claims: A Survey of U.S. Decisions and Legislative Proposal in Florida to Authorize Recovery for Loss of Companionship. *Journal of Animal Law, 3,* 45–58.

Rudy, L. (1995). *Service Dogs for People with Seizure Disorders.* National Service Dog Center® Newsletter, 6(4). Retrieved from www.deltasociety.org/Document.Doc?id=227.

Saetre, P., Lindberg, J., Leonard, J. A., Olsson, K.,Pettersson, U., Ellegren, H., Befgstrom, T. F., Vila, C., & Jazin, E. (2004). From Wild Wolf to Domestic Dog: Gene Expression Changes in the Brain. *Molecular Brain Research, 126,* 198–206.

Samuels, W. E., Coultis, D., Meers, L., Odberg, F. O., & Normando, S. (2006). Can an AAI Educational Programme Improve Animal Welfare? 2006 Proceedings of the VDWE International Congress on Companion Animal Behaviour and Welfare, 119–128.

Savolainen, P., Zhang, Y., Luo, J., Lundeberg, J., & Leitner, T. (2002). Genetic Evidence for an East Asian Origin of Domestic Dogs. *Science, 298,* 1610–1613.

Schliedt, W. M., & Shalter, M. D. (2003). Co-Evolution of Humans and Canids: An Alternative View of Dog Domestication: Homo Homini Lupus? *Evolution and Cognition, 9*(1), 57–72.

Schneider, K. S. (2005). The Winding Valley of Grief: When a Dog Guide Retires or Dies. *Journal of Visual Impairment and Blindness, 99*(6), 368–370.

The Seeing Eye. (2009). *Instruction & Training.* Retrieved from www.seeingeye.org/aboutUs/default.aspx?M_ID=121.

Semmel, S. D. (2002). When Pigs Fly, They Go First Class: Service Animals in the Twenty-First Century. *Barry Law Review 3,* 39.

Senju, A., Maeda, M., Kikuchi, Y., Hasegawa, T., Tojo, Y., & Osanai, H. (2007). Absence of Contagious Yawning in Children with Autism Spectrum Disorder. *Biology Letters, 3,* 706–708.

Serpell, J. A. (1991). Beneficial Effects of Pet Ownership on Some Aspects of Human Health and Behavior. *Journal of the Royal Society of Medicine, 84*(12), 717–720.

Serpell, J. A. (2003). Anthropomorphism and Anthropomorphic Selection, Beyond the "Cute Response." *Society & Animals, 11*(1), 83–100.

Serpell, J. A., Coppinger, R., & Fine, A. (2000). The Welfare of Assistance Animals. In A. Fine (Ed.), *Handbook on Animal-Assisted Therapy: Theoretical Foundations and Guidelines for Practice.* San Diego, CA: Academic Press.

Serpell, J. A. & Hsu, Y. (2001). Development and Validation of a Novel Method for Evaluating Behavior and Temperament in Guide Dogs. *Applied Animal Behaviour Science, 72,* 347–364.

Seyfarth, R., & Cheney, D. (1990). The Assessment of Vervet Monkeys of Their Own and Another Species Alarm Calls. *Animal Behaviour, 40,* 754–764.

Shiloh, S., Sorek, G., & Terkel, J. (2003). Reduction of State-Anxiety by Petting Animals in a Controlled Laboratory Experiment. *Anxiety, Stress & Coping, 16*(4), 387–395.

Shriner, W. M. (1998). Yellow-Bellied Marmot and Golden-Mantled Ground Squirrel Responses to Heterospecific Alarm Calls. *Animal Behaviour, 55,* 529–536.

Sidhu, D. S. (2009). Cujo Goes to College: On the Use of Animals by Individuals with Disabilities in Postsecondary Institutions. *University of Baltimore Law Review, 38,* 267–303.

Siegel, J. M. (1990). Stressful Life Events and Use of Physician Services Among the Elderly: The Moderating Role of Pet Ownership. *Journal of Personality & Social Psychology, 58*(6), 1081–1086.

Siegel, J. M., Angulo, F. J., Detels, R., Wesch, J., & Mullen, A. (1999). AIDS Diagnosis and Dpresseion in the Multicenter Cohort Study: The Ameliorating Impact of Pet Ownership. *AIDS Care, 11*(2), 157–170.

Simonet, P., Versteeg, D., & Storie, D. (2005). *Dog-laughter: Recorded Playback Reduces Stress Related Behavior in Shelter Dogs*. (proceedings of the 7th International Conference on Environmental Enrichment). Retrieved from www.petalk.org/LaughingDog.pdf.

Smith, C. H. S. (1839). Dogs. In *Mammalia*, vol. xviii. Edinburgh, Scotland: William Jardine, Publisher.

Smith, M. J., Esnayra, J., & Love, C. (2003). Use of a Psychiatric Service Dog. *Psychiatric Services, 54*(1), 110–111.

Somervill, J. W., Kruglikova, Y. A., Robertson, R. L., Hanson, L. M., & MacLin, O. H. (2008). Physiological Responses by College Students to a Dog and a Cat: Implications for Pet Therapy. *North American Journal of Psychology, 10*(3), 519–528.

Somervill, J. W., Swanson, A. M., Robertson, R. L., Arnett, M. A., & MacLin, O. M. (2009). Handling a Dog by Children with Attention-Deficit/Hyperactivity Disorder: Calming or Exciting? *North American Journal of Psychology, 11*(1), 111–120.

Soproni, K., Miklosi, A., Topal, J., & Csanyi, V. (2002). Dogs' Responsiveness to Human Pointing Gestures. *Journal of Comparative Psychology, 116*, 27–34.

Stein, D. J., Dodman, N. H., Borchelt, P., & Hollander, E. (1994). Behavioral Disorders in Veterinary Practice: Relevance to Psychiatry. *Comprehensive Psychiatry, 35*, 275–285.

Stephens, E. O. (2009). *Use of a Courthouse Facility Dog in the Courtroom*. Retrieved from www.courthousedogs.com/courtroom.html.

Stoffel, J., & Braun, C. (2006). Animal-Assisted Therapy: Analysis of Patient Tesimonials. *Journal of Undergraduate Nursing Scholarship, 8*(1). Retrieved from www.juns.nursing.arizona.edu/articles/Fall%202006/stoffel.htm.

Strinple, E. O. (2003). A History of Prison Inmate-Animal Interaction Programs. *American Behavioral Scientist, 47*(1), 70–78.

Strong, V., & Brown, S. W. (2000). Should People with Epilepsy Have Untrained Dogs as Pets? *Seizure, 9*(6), 427–430.

Strong, V., Brown, S. W., Huyton, M., & Coyle, H. (2002). "Effect of Trained Seizure Alert Dogs on Frequency of Tonic-Clonic Seizures. *Seizure 11*(6), 402–405.

Strong, V., Brown, S. W., & Walker, R. (1999). Seizure-Alert Dogs-Fact or Fiction? *Seizure, 8*(1), 62–65.

Svartberg, K. (2006). Breed-Typical Behaviour in Dogs-Historical Remnants or Recent Constructs? *Applied Animal Behaviour Science, 96*, 293–313.

Szetei, V., Miklosi, A., Topal, J., & Csanyi, V. (2003). When Dogs Seem to Lose Their Nose: An Investigation on the Use of Visual and Olfactory Cues in Communicative Context Between Dog and Owner. *Applied Animal Behaviour Science, 83*(2), 141–152.

Szuchman, P. (2009, September 17). Beagle or Bichon: Can Dog Drool Provide Insight? *Wall Street Journal*, p. D1.

Theuerkauf, J. (2009). What Drives Wolves: Fear or Hunger? Humans, Diet, Climate and Wolf Activity Patterns. *Ethology, 115*, 649–657.

Thurston, M. E. (1996). *Lost History of the Canine Race: Our 15,000 Year Love Affair with Dogs*. Kansas City, MO: Andrews & McMeel.

Tissen, I., Hergovich, A., & Spiel, C. (2007). School-Based Social Training with and without Dogs: Evaluation of Their Effectiveness. *Anthrozoos, 20*(4), 365–373.

Toth, L., Gacsi, M., Topal, J., & Miklosi, A. (2008). Playing Styles and Possible Causative Factors in Dogs' Behaviour When Playing with Humans. *Applied Animal Behaviour Science, 114*, 473–484.

Trut, L. N. (1999). Early Canid Domestication: The Farm-Fox Experiment. *American Scientist, 87*, 160–169.

Tuber, D. S., Hennessy, M. B., Sanders, S., & Miller, J. A. (1996). Behavioral and Glucocorticoid Responses of Adult Domestic Dogs (Canis familiaris) to Companionship and Social Separation. *Journal of Comparative Psychology, 110*(1), 103–108.

Turner, J. (1993, May 10). *Letter to Senator John C. Danforth.* Retrieved from www.justice.gov/crt/foia/tal302.txt.

Turner, W. G. (2007). The Experiences of Offenders in a Prison Canine Program. *Federal Probation, 71*(1), 38–43.

Udell, M. A. R., & Wynne, C. D. L. (2008). A Review of Domestic Dogs' (Canis familiaris) Human-Like Behaviors: Or Why Behavior Analysts Should Stop Worrying and Love Their Dogs. *Journal of the Experimental Analysis of Behavior, 89*(2), 247–261.

U.S. Department of Health and Human Services, Centers for Disease Control and Prevention. (2003). *Guidelines for Environmental Infection Control in Healthcare Facilities,* Part I. H, Part II.H. Retrieved from www.cdc.gov/ncidod/hip/enviro/guide.htm.

U.S. Department of Justice, Civil Rights Division. (2006, April) DC Apartment Owner and Manager Will Cease Discriminating Against Guide-Dog Users. *Disability Rights Online News, 12,* 7.

Valentine, D., Kiddoo, M., & LaFleur, B. (1993). Psychosocial Implications of Service Dog Ownership for People Who Have Mobility and Hearing Impairments. *Social Work in Health Care, 19*(1), 109–124.

Vas, J., Topal, J., Gacsi, M., Miklosi, A., & Csanyi, V. (2005). A Friend or an Enemy: Dogs' Reation to an Unfamiliar Person Showing Behavioural Cues of Threat and Friendliness at Different Times. *Applied Animal Behaviour Science, 94,* 99–115.

Velde, B. P., Cipriani, J., & Fisher, G. (2005). Resident and Therapist Views of Animal-Assisted Therapy: Implications for Occupational Therapy Practice. *Australian Occupational Therapy Journal, 52,* 43–50.

Vila, C., Maldonado, J. E., & Wayne, R. K. (1990). Phylogenetic Relationships, Evolution, and Genetic Diversity of the Domestic Dog. *The Journal of Heredity, 90*(1), 71–77.

Vila, C., Savolainen, P., Maldonado, J. E., Amorim, I. R., Rice, J. E., Honeycutt, R. L., Crandall, K .A., Lundeberg, J., & Wayne, R. K. (1997). Multiple and Ancient Origins of the Domestic Dog. *Science, 276,* 1687–1689.

Viranyi, Z., Topal, J., Gacsi, M., Miklosi, A., & Csanyi, V. (2004). Dogs Respond Appropriately to Cues of Humans' Attentional Focus. *Behavioral Processes, 66,* 161–172.

Wade, N. (2002, November 22). From Wolf to Dog, Yes, but When? *New York Times,* p. C1.

Wallner, W. E., & Ellis, T. L. (1976). Olfactory Detection of Gypsy Moth Pheromone and Egg Masses by Domestic Canines. *Environmental Entomology, 5,* 183–186.

Ward, C., Bauer, E. B., & Smuts, B. B. (2008). Partner Preferences and Asymmetries in Social Play Among Domestic Dog, Canis lupus familiaris, Littermates. *Animal Behaviour, 76*(4), 1187–1199.

Watson, J. S., Gergely, G., Csanyi, V., Topal, J., Gacsi, M., & Sarkozi, Z. (2001). Distinguishing Logic From Association in the Solution of an Invisible Displacement Task by Children (Homo sapiens) and Dogs (Canis familiaris): Using Negation of Disjunction. *Journal of Comparative Psychology, 115,* 219–226.

Wayne, R. K. (1986). Limb Morphology of Domestic and Wild Canids: The Influence of Development on Morphological Change. *Journal of Morphology, 187,* 301–319.

Wayne, R. K., & Jenks, S. M. (1991). Mitochondrial DNA Analysis Implying Extensive Hybridization of the Endangered Red Wolf, Canis rufus. *Nature, 351,* 565–568.

Welch, J. B. (1990). A Detector Dog for Screw-Worms (*Diptera: Calliphoridae*). *Journal of Economic Entomology, 83,* 1932–4.

Welsh, J. S., Barton, D., & Ahuja, H. (2005). A Case of Breast Cancer Detected by a Pet Dog.

*Community Oncology, 2*(4), 324, 326.

Willer, B., Ottenbacher, K. J., & Coad, C. L. (1994). The Community Integration Questionnaire: A Comparative Examination. *Am. J. Phys. Med. Rehabil. 73*, 108–111.

Williams, H., & Pembroke, A. (1989, April 1). Sniffer Dogs in the Melanoma Clinic?" *Lancet 1*(8640), 734.

Willis, C. M., Church, S. M., Guest, C. M., Cook, W. A., McCarthy, N., Bransbury, A. J., Church, M. R. T., & Church, J. C. T. (2004). Olfactory Detection of Human Bladder Cancer by Dogs: Proof of Principle Study. *BMJ [British Medical Journal], 329*, 712–715.

Wilson, C. C., Netting, F. E., & New, J. C. (1985). Pet Ownership Characteristics of Community-Based Elderly Participants in a Pet Placement Program. *California Veterinarian 39*(3), 26-28.

Wu, A. S., Niedra, R., Pendergast, L., & McCrindle, B. W. (2002). Acceptability and Impact of Pet Visitation on a Pediatric Cardiology Inpatient Unit. *Journal of Pediatric Nursing, 17*(5), 354–362.

Wynne, C. D. L., Udell, M. A. R., & Lord, K. A. (2008). Ontogeny's Impacts on Human-Dog Communication. *Animal Behaviour, 76*, e1–e4.

Yin, S. (2002). A New Perspective on Barking in Dogs (*Canis familiaris*). *Journal of Comparative Psychology 116*(2), 189–193.

Yin, S., & McCowan, B. (2004). Barking in Domestic Dogs: Context Specificity and Individual Identification. *Animal Behaviour, 68*, 343–355.

Zamir, T. (2006). The Moral Basis of Animal-Assisted Therapy. *Animals & Society, 14*(2),180–199.

Zapf, S. A., & Rough, R. B. (2002). The Development of an Instrument to Match Individuals with Disabilities and Service Animals. *Disability & Rehabilitation, 24*, 47–58.

# INDEX

321

National Society for the Prevention of
    Blindness, 47
Natufian, 19
Neanderthals, 40
New York Lighthouse, 47
No-pets policies/rules), 6, 9, 12, 63, 78-79, 83,
    158, 160-2, 168, 172, 275
North Star Foundation, 236
Nursing homes, xii, 88, 91, 101-4, 111, 139,
    272

**O**

Obsessive-compulsive disorders, 39, 77
Ohio State University, 104
Olfactory receptor genes, 112
Oppositional defiant disorder (ODD), 98
Oxford University, 20

**P**

Panic attacks, xi, 39, 72, 75-76, 78-79, 119,
    145, 147, 262, 274
Paraplegia, 61, 165, 177
Parkinson's disease, 70, 267
Pedomorphosis, 16, 31
Perkins School for the Blind, 47
Pets Evacuation and Transportation Act, 120,
    148, 231-232
Philadelphia School for the Blind, 47
Piaget, Jean, 261
PICA (impulsive eating of nonfood items), 82
Piebalding, 16, 20-21, 270
Pit bulls, 91, 166-7, 227, 238, 292
Play (dog-dog, dog-human), 30, 33, 35-36,
    58, 75, 88, 105, 228
Portuguese water dogs, 114
Post-traumatic stress disorder (PTSD), 39, 100
Pot-bellied pigs (service animals), 126, 150,
    205-6
Primates (*see also* Monkeys), 31, 139-40, 188
Prison/prisoner (training programs), 9, 11,
    88, 167, 200, 220-228
Professional therapy dog, xii, 104, 110-1, 208
Psychiatric service animals (including dogs),
    xi, 9, 42, 44, 63, 74-84, 123-4, 128-
    133, 143-4, 146-7, 164, 234-5
Psychiatric Service Dog Society, Foreward
Psychogenic seizures (PNES), 68-9

Public accommodations, 10, 48-49, 73, 110-1,
    120, 132, 134-141, 157-9, 170-1, 174-
    5, 178, 196, 200, 203-4, 208-210, 214

**Q**

Quadriplegia, 61
Quarantine
    Foreign, 153

**R**

Rehabilitation Act 120-1, 154, 168, 180, 182,
    194
Retrieve, retrieving, 37-38, 41, 45, 57-58, 61-
    63, 82, 132, 166, 190, 192, 231
Rico (Border Collie skilled in word
    recognition), 37
Rosenberg Self-Esteem Scale, 59

**S**

Sales tax, 11, 235
San Francisco State University, 51-2
Saturday Evening Post, 46
Schliedt, Wolfgang, 17
School buses, 183
Schutzhund, 33-4
Search and rescue dogs, xii, 7, 44-45, 111, 272
Seeing Eye, The (organization), 7, 45, 47, 49,
    52
Seizure-alert dogs/seizure alerting, 8, 53, 64-
    70, 72-3, 122-3, 127, 132, 140, 143,
    170
Seizure-response dogs/seizure responding,
    42, 71, 170
Separation anxiety, 39, 94, 218
Serpell, James, 40-1, 277
Service animals/dogs (*see* types of service
    animals, e.g., Seizure-alert dogs)
Sexual abuse (*see* Abuse)
Shalter, Michael D., 17
Shepherd Dog Club of Germany, 46
Short-term lodging, 170-1
Signal dogs (*see* hearing dogs)
Social Security Disability Insurance, 235-6
South American culpeo (*Dusicyon clupaeus*),
    259
*Spina bifida*, 61
Spinal injuries, 192, 235

P.O. Box 19265
Springfield, IL 62794-9265

- Henderson, George & Willlie V. Bryan—**PSY-CHOSOCIAL ASPECTS OF DISABILITY. (4th Ed.)** '11, 254 pp. (7 x 10).

- Palmo, Artis J., William J. Weikel & David P. Borsos—**FOUNDATIONS OF MENTAL HEALTH COUNSELING. (4th Ed.).** '11, 486 pp. (7 x 10), 6 il., 3 tables.

- Storey, Keith & Craig Miner—**SYSTEMAT-IC INSTRUCTION OF FUNCTIONAL SKILLS FOR STUDENTS AND ADULTS WITH DISABILITIES.** '11, 272 pp. (7 x 10), 14 il., 31 tables.

- Bernet, William—**PARENTAL ALIENATION, DSM-5, AND ICD-11.** '10. 264 pp. (7 x 10), 15 il., 4 tables, $63.95, hard, $43.95, paper.

- Bryan, Willie V.—**SOCIOPOLITICAL ASPECTS OF DISABILITIES: The Social Perspectives and Political History of Disabilities and Rehabilitation in the United States. (2nd Ed.).** '10, 284 pp. (7 x 10), 12 il.. $61.95, hard, $41.95, paper.

- Ensminger, John J.—**SERVICE AND THERAPY DOGS IN AMERICAN SOCIETY: Science, Law and the Evolution of Canine Caregivers.** '10, 340 pp. (7 x 10), 25 il., 1 table, $69.95, hard, $47.95, paper.

- Jones, Carroll J.—**CURRICULUM DEVELOPMENT FOR STUDENTS WITH MILD DISABILITIES: Academic and Social Skills for RTI Planning and Inclusion IEPs. (2nd Ed.)** '09, 454 pp. (8 1/2 x 11), 50 tables, $63.95. (spiral).

- Rhoades, Ellen A. & Jill Duncan—**AUDITORY-VERBAL PRACTICE: Toward a Family-Centered Approach.** '10, 420 pp. (7 x 10), 19 il., 5 tables, $79.95, hard, $59.95, paper.

- Thyer. Bruce A.. John S. Wodarski. Laura L. Myers. & Dianne F. Harrison—**CULTURAL DIVERSITY AND SOCIAL WORK PRACTICE. (3rd Ed.)** '10, 370 pp. (7 x 10), 14 tables, $74.95, hard, $54.95, paper.

- Blomquist, Barbara Taylor—**INSIGHT INTO ADOPTION: Uncovering and Understanding the Heart of Adoption. (2nd Ed.)** '09, 212 pp. (6 x 9), $27.95, paper.

- Bryan, Willie V.—**THE PROFESSIONAL HELPER: The Fundamentals of Being a Helping Professional.** '09, 220 pp. (7 x 10), $51.95, hard, $31.95, paper.

- Emener, William G., Michael A. Richard & John J. Bosworth—**A GUIDEBOOK TO HUMAN SERVICE PROFESSIONS: Helping College Students Explore Opportunities in the Human Services Field. (2nd Ed.)** '09, 286 pp. (7 x 10), 2 il., 4 tables, $44.95, paper.

- Li, Yushi (Boni)—**EMIGRATING FROM CHINA TO THE UNITED STATES: A Comparison of Different Social Experiences.** '09, 250 pp. (7 x 10), $52.95, hard, $34.95, paper.

- Stepney, Stella A.—**ART THERAPY WITH STUDENTS AT RISK: Fostering Resilience and Growth Through Self-Expression. (2nd Ed.)** '09, 222 pp. (7 x 10), 16 il., (14 in color), 19 tables, $56.95, hard, $38.95, paper.

- Thompson, Richard H.—**THE HANDBOOK OF CHILD LIFE: A Guide for Pediatric Psychosocial Care.** '09, 378 pp. (7 x 10), 5 il., 15 tables, $79.95, hard, $55.95, paper.

- Wilkes, Jane K.—**THE ROLE OF COMPANION ANIMALS IN COUNSELING AND PSYCHOLOGY: Discovering Their Use in the Therapeutic Process.** '09, 168 pp. (7 x 10), 2 tables, $29.95, paper.

- Wodarski, John S. & Marvin D. Feit—**EVIDENCE-BASED INTERVENTIONS IN SOCIAL WORK: A Practitioner's Manual.** '09, 318 pp. (7 x 10), $62.95, hard, $42.95, paper.

- Geldard, Kathryn & David Geldard—**PERSONAL COUNSELING SKILLS: An Integrative Approach.** '08, 316 pp. (7 x 10), 20 il., 3 tables, $49.95, paper.

 easy ways to order!  PHONE: 1-800-258-8980 or (217) 789-8980  FAX: (217) 789-9130  EMAIL: books@ccthomas.com Web: www.ccthomas.com  MAIL: Charles C Thomas • Publisher, Ltd. P.O. Box 19265 Springfield, IL 62794-9265

**Complete catalog available at ccthomas.com • books@ccthomas.com**

Books sent on approval • Shipping charges: $7.75 min. U.S. / Outside U.S, actual shipping fees will be charged • Prices subject to change without notice